THE CLAIRMONT FAMILY LETTERS, 1839–1889

THE PICKERING MASTERS SERIES

THE CLAIRMONT FAMILY LETTERS, 1839–1889

Edited by
Sharon L. Joffe

Volume II

LONDON AND NEW YORK

First published 2017
by Routledge
2 Park Square, Milton Park, Abingdon, Oxon OX14 4RN

and by Routledge
711 Third Avenue, New York, NY 10017

Routledge is an imprint of the Taylor & Francis Group, an informa business

Editorial material and selection © 2017 Sharon L. Joffe; individual owners retain copyright in their own material

All rights reserved. No part of this book may be reprinted or reproduced or utilised in any form or by any electronic, mechanical, or other means, now known or hereafter invented, including photocopying and recording, or in any information storage or retrieval system, without permission in writing from the publishers.

Trademark notice: Product or corporate names may be trademarks or registered trademarks, and are used only for identification and explanation without intent to infringe.

British Library Cataloguing in Publication Data
A catalogue record for this book is available from the British Library

Library of Congress Cataloging-in-Publication Data
Names: Clairmont, Claire, 1798–1879 author. | Joffe, Sharon Lynne, editor.
Title: The Clairmont family letters, 1839–1889 / [edited by Sharon L. Joffe].
Description: Milton Park, Abingdon, Oxon; New York, NY: Routledge, 2016. | Series: The Pickering masters series | Includes bibliographical references and index.
Identifiers: LCCN 2016003434 (print) | LCCN 2016015149 (ebook) | ISBN 9781138758070 (volume 1) | ISBN 9781315543901 ()
Subjects: LCSH: Clairmont, Claire, 1798–1879—Family. | Clairmont, Claire, 1798–1879—Correspondence. | Shelley, Mary Wollstonecraft, 1797–1851—Family.
Classification: LCC CT788.C475 A4 2016 (print) | LCC CT788.C475 (ebook) | DDC 929.20973—dc23
LC record available at https://lccn.loc.gov/2016003434

ISBN: 978-1-8489-3553-2 (Set)
eISBN: 978-1-315-54386-4 (Set)
ISBN: 978-1-1387-5808-7 (Volume II)
eISBN: 978-1-315-54389-5 (Volume II)

Typeset in Times New Roman
by Apex CoVantage, LLC

Publisher's Note

References within each chapter are as they appear in the original complete work

CONTENTS

VOLUME II

List of Abbreviations and Identification Marks	vii
List of Illustrations	ix
Editorial Symbols	xi
Index of Letters	xiii
The Later Years	1
Letters from 28 March 1861–24 December 1889	7
Appendix	269
Genealogical Table	300
Index	303

LIST OF ABBREVIATIONS AND IDENTIFICATION MARKS

Abbreviations

CC	*The Clairmont Correspondence*
LMWS	*The Letters of Mary Wollstonecraft Shelley*
Novels	*The Collected Novels and Memoirs of William Godwin*

Identification

Following the precedent set by Marion Kingston Stocking in *The Clairmont Correspondence*, each letter in this collection is followed by the identifier: Unpublished. Text: M. S., Pf. Coll., CL'ANA number. Each letter is thereby designated as previously unpublished, and a manuscript within the Carl H. Pforzheimer Collection of Shelley and His Circle, The New York Public Library, Astor, Lenox and Tilden Foundations. The CL'ANA number follows the identifying information.

LIST OF ILLUSTRATIONS

Volume II

1 Autograph letter by Antonia Clairmont to Claire Clairmont, 21 December 1854. The Carl H. Pforzheimer Collection of Shelley and His Circle, The New York Public Library, Astor, Lenox and Tilden Foundations.   65
2 Autograph letter by Wilhelm Gaulis Clairmont to Claire Clairmont, 4 May 1860. The Carl H. Pforzheimer Collection of Shelley and His Circle, The New York Public Library, Astor, Lenox and Tilden Foundations.   66
3 Marriage Certificate of Wilhelm Gaulis Clairmont and Ottilia von Pichler, 8 August 1866. The Carl H. Pforzheimer Collection of Shelley and His Circle, The New York Public Library, Astor, Lenox and Tilden Foundations.   67
4 Photographic portrait of Wilhelm and Ottilia Clairmont, c. 1866. The Carl H. Pforzheimer Collection of Shelley and His Circle, The New York Public Library, Astor, Lenox and Tilden Foundations.   69
5 Photographic portrait of Pauline Clairmont, c. 1875. The Carl H. Pforzheimer Collection of Shelley and His Circle, The New York Public Library, Astor, Lenox and Tilden Foundations.   70
6 Photographic portrait of Wilhelm Clairmont, c. 1875. The Carl H. Pforzheimer Collection of Shelley and His Circle, The New York Public Library, Astor, Lenox and Tilden Foundations.   70
7 Autograph letter by Pauline Clairmont to Emma Taylor, 23 March 1879. The Carl H. Pforzheimer Collection of Shelley and His Circle, The New York Public Library, Astor, Lenox and Tilden Foundations.   71
8 Photographic portrait of Ottilia Clairmont by Josef Székely (photographer). Unknown date. The Carl H. Pforzheimer Collection of Shelley and His Circle, The New York Public Library, Astor, Lenox and Tilden Foundations.   72

LIST OF ILLUSTRATIONS

9 Photographic portrait of Alma, Paul, and Walter Clairmont, c. 1895. The Carl H. Pforzheimer Collection of Shelley and His Circle, The New York Public Library, Astor, Lenox and Tilden Foundations.   73

10 Clairmont family tomb, Evangelischer Friedhof Matzleinsdorf, Vienna, Austria. Heraldic-Genealogical Society Adler, Vienna, tng.adler-wien.eu   74

11 Mary Claire Bally-Clairmont, c. 2000. Mr. Peter Bally, Switzerland.   75

EDITORIAL SYMBOLS

~~word~~	Deleted legible word
[illeg.]	Illegible word
[~~illeg.~~]	An illegible word that has been deleted
c.	Editorial conjecture, typically used for a date
/	Line changes
{tear}	The manuscript is torn and is illegible
{ink}	An inkblot is visible, rendering the word(s) illegible
{section/line cut out of page}	Physical cut in the paper, made by an unknown person

INDEX OF LETTERS

Abbreviations for names of letter writers and recipients:

Claire Clairmont: ClC
Antonia Clairmont: AC
Charles Gaulis Clairmont: CGC
Pauline Clairmont: PC
Wilhelm Gaulis Clairmont: WC
Ottilia Clairmont: OC
Emily Clairmont: EC
Sidonia Clairmont: SC
Charles Gaulis Clairmont (Charley): ChC
Alma Clairmont: ACC
Clara Knox: CK
Alexander Knox: AK
Alma von Pichler: AP
Edward John Trelawny: EJT
Emma Taylor: ET

Volume II

	Date	CL'ANA Number	From	To	Page
153)	28 March 1861	CL'ANA 0245	WC	ClC	7
154)	25 April 1861	CL'ANA 0252	WC	ClC	8
155)	22 June 1861	CL'ANA 0255	WC	ClC	11
156)	12 July 1861	CL'ANA 0251	WC	ClC	13
157)	8 August 1861	CL'ANA 0246	WC	ClC	14
158)	2 September 1861	CL'ANA 0247	WC	ClC	17
159)	1 November 1861	CL'ANA 0248	WC	ClC	19
160)	17 November 1861	CL'ANA 0249	WC	ClC	21
161)	12 December 1861	CL'ANA 0250	WC	ClC	23
162)	10 September 1862	CL'ANA 0253	WC	ClC	24
163)	27 October 1862	CL'ANA 0254	WC	ClC	26
164)	29–30 December 1862	CL'ANA 0256	WC	ClC	29

INDEX OF LETTERS

165)	17 March c. 1863	CL'ANA 0208	PC	ClC	32
166)	9 April 1863	CL'ANA 0257	WC	ClC	34
167)	29 June 1863	CL'ANA 0258	WC	ClC	35
168)	11–12 July 1863	CL'ANA 0204	PC & WC	ClC	38
169)	17 July 1863	CL'ANA 0259	WC	ClC	40
170)	15 November 1863	CL'ANA 0205	PC & WC	ClC	41
171)	26 December 1863	CL'ANA 0421	AC	ClC	45

Box 1, bundle a, numbers 8–10

172)	17 March 1864	CL'ANA 0260	WC	ClC	46
173)	4 September 1864	CL'ANA 0261	WC	ClC	49
174)	26 October 1864	CL'ANA 0262	WC	ClC	51
175)	29 December 1864	CL'ANA 0263	WC	ClC	53
176)	23 February 1865	CL'ANA 0264	WC	ClC	55
177)	12 March 1865	CL'ANA 0265	WC	ClC	57
178)	19 April 1865	CL'ANA 0266	WC	ClC	59
179)	22 April 1865	CL'ANA 0184	OC	WC	62
180)	3 May 1865	CL'ANA 0267	WC	ClC	64
181)	18 May 1865	CL'ANA 0180	OC	PC	76
182)	21 May 1865	CL'ANA 0268	WC	ClC	77
183)	8 June c. 1865	CL'ANA 0219	PC	WC	79
184)	11 June 1865	CL'ANA 0269	WC	ClC	81
185)	10 October 1865	CL'ANA 0270	WC	ClC	84
186)	12 December 1865	CL'ANA 0271	WC	ClC	85
187)	6 February 1866	CL'ANA 0272	WC	ClC	88
188)	18 February 1866	CL'ANA 0273	WC	ClC	89
189)	23 April 1866	CL'ANA 0274	WC	ClC	91
190)	4 May 1866	CL'ANA 0275	WC	ClC	92
191)	22 May 1866	CL'ANA 0276	WC	ClC	94
192)	16 June 1866	CL'ANA 0277	WC	ClC	95
193)	22 December 1866	CL'ANA 0321	AC	ClC	97
194)	11 March 1867	CL'ANA 0278	WC	ClC	99
195)	22 June 1867	CL'ANA 0320	AC	ClC	100
196)	1 November 1867	CL'ANA 0279	WC & OC	ClC	102
197)	19 December 1867	CL'ANA 0280	WC	ClC	105
198)	25 February 1868	CL'ANA 0281	WC	ClC	106
199)	22 March 1868	CL'ANA 0282	WC	ClC	108
200)	24 July 1868	CL'ANA 0283	WC & OC	ClC	110
201)	3 August 1868	CL'ANA 0284	WC	ClC	113
202)	12 October 1868	CL'ANA 0286	WC	ClC	114
203)	17 December 1868	CL'ANA 0285	WC	ClC	117
204)	14 January 1869	CL'ANA 0287	WC	ClC	120
205)	26 January 1869	CL'ANA 0133	WC	OC	121
206)	2 February 1869	CL'ANA 0130	WC	OC	123
207)	5 March 1869	CL'ANA 0288	WC	ClC	129
208)	16–24 March c. 1869	CL'ANA 0203	OC & PC	ClC	132
209)	24 March 1869	CL'ANA 0289	WC	ClC	134
210)	7 April 1869	CL'ANA 0202	PC & WC	ClC	136
211)	12 May 1869	CL'ANA 0290	WC	ClC	138
212)	20 August 1869	CL'ANA 0291	WC & OC	ClC	141
213)	11 September 1869	CL'ANA 0292	WC	ClC	144
214)	29 October 1869	CL'ANA 0293	WC	ClC	146
215)	8 November 1869	CL'ANA 0294	WC	ClC	148

INDEX OF LETTERS

216)	11 January 1870	CL'ANA 0295	WC	ClC	150
217)	13 January 1870	CL'ANA 0296	WC	ClC	152
218)	24 January 1870	CL'ANA 0297	WC	ClC	155
219)	7 March c. 1870	CL'ANA 0228	PC	unknown recipients	156
220)	5 April 1870	CL'ANA 0421	AP	PC	159
	Box 2, bundle e, number 100				
221)	16 April c.1870	CL'ANA 0231	PC	AP	162
222)	30 April c. 1870	CL'ANA 0178	AP	PC	165
223)	19 July 1870	CL'ANA 0179	OC	ClC	167
224)	30 November 1870	CL'ANA 0298	WC	ClC	168
225)	10 January 1871	CL'ANA 0299	WC	PC	171
226)	25 January 1871	CL'ANA 0300	WC	PC	173
227)	9 February 1871	CL'ANA 0302	WC	ClC & PC	176
228)	23 February 1871	CL'ANA 0301	WC	ClC	178
229)	18 March 1871	CL'ANA 0303	WC	PC	179
230)	5 August 1871	CL'ANA 0304	WC	PC	182
231)	23 August 1871	CL'ANA 0306	WC	ClC	184
232)	14 September 1871	CL'ANA 0307	WC	ClC	185
233)	4 November c. 1871	CL'ANA 0225	PC	WC	187
234)	8 November 1871	CL'ANA 0305	WC	ClC	189
235)	19 June 1872	CL'ANA 0308	WC	ClC	190
236)	22 July 1872	CL'ANA 0309	WC	ClC	192
237)	29 December 1872	CL'ANA 0310	WC	ClC	194
238)	25 March 1873	CL'ANA 0311	WC	ClC	196
239)	29 May 1873	CL'ANA 0312	WC	ClC	197
240)	8 June 1873	CL'ANA 0317	WC	PC	199
241)	15 July 1873	CL'ANA 0421	WC	PC	201
	Box 1, bundle a, number 12				
242)	14 October c. 1873	CL'ANA 0421	PC	WC	203
	Box 3, bundle g, number 185				
243)	16 October c. 1873	CL'ANA 0421	PC	WC	205
	Box 3, bundle g, number 185				
244)	19 October c. 1873	CL'ANA 0421	PC	WC	208
	Box 3, bundle g, number 185				
245)	31 October c. 1873	CL'ANA 0421	PC	WC	210
	Box 3, bundle g, number 188				
246)	2 November c. 1873	CL'ANA 0421	PC	WC	212
	Box 3, bundle g, number 186				
247)	8 December c. 1873	CL'ANA 0224	PC	WC	214
248)	14 December c. 1873	CL'ANA 0223	PC	WC	215
249)	25 December 1873	CL'ANA 0313	WC	ClC	216
250)	20 January 1874	CL'ANA 0421	PC	WC	217
	Box 3, bundle g, number 201 bis				
251)	13 February c. 1874	CL'ANA 0229	PC	OC	221
252)	11 January 1875	CL'ANA 0316	WC	PC	222
253)	2 February c. 1875	CL'ANA 0217	PC	WC	224
254)	9 February 1875	CL'ANA 0200	AK	PC	225
255)	24 June c. 1875	CL'ANA 0431	PC	EJT	226
256)	27 February c. 1877	CL'ANA 0218	PC	WC	227
257)	30 June 1877	CL'ANA 0211	PC	ClC	230
258)	29.30 1877	CL'ANA 0315	WC	ClC	232

INDEX OF LETTERS

259)	9 June c. 1878	CL'ANA 0421	PC	WC	234
	Box 3, bundle g, number 207				
260)	1 July c. 1878	CL'ANA 0226	PC	WC	236
261)	5 September c. 1878	CL'ANA 0432	PC	ET	238
262)	22 December 1878	CL'ANA 0314	WC	ClC	240
263)	c. 1878	CL'ANA 0234	PC	WC	243
264)	23 March c. 1879	CL'ANA 0433	PC	ET	244
265)	25 April c. 1879	CL'ANA 0434	PC	ET	245
266)	18 March after 1885	CL'ANA 0222	PC	WC	246
267)	16 April after 1885	CL'ANA 0221	PC	WC	249
268)	20 July c. 1887	CL'ANA 0230	PC	ACC	251
269)	2 July c. 1888	CL'ANA 0220	PC	WC	253
270)	1 February c. 1889	CL'ANA 0216	PC	WC	256
271)	4 February c. 1889	CL'ANA 0215	PC	WC	259
272)	14 February c. 1889	CL'ANA 0214	PC	WC	261
273)	17 February c. 1889	CL'ANA 0213	PC	WC	263
274)	24 December c. 1889	CL'ANA 0227	PC	unknown recipients	265

Appendix

	Date	CL'ANA Number	From	To	Page
1)	7 February 1866	CL'ANA 0421	WC	OC	269
	Box 1, bundle a, number 85				
2)	10 February 1866	CL'ANA 0421	WC	OC	274
	Box 1, bundle a, number 16				
3)	17–18 February 1866	CL'ANA 0421	WC	OC	277
	Box 3, bundle f, number 160				
4)	14 March 1866	CL'ANA 0421	WC	OC	284
	Box 1, bundle a, number 64				
5)	17 March 1866	CL'ANA 0421	WC	OC	286
	Box 1, bundle a, number 13				
6)	24 March 1866	CL'ANA 0122	WC	OC	288
7)	26 March 1866	CL'ANA 0118	WC	OC	290
8)	6 April 1866	CL'ANA 0421	WC	OC	293
	Box 1, bundle a, number 1				
9)	8 April 1866	CL'ANA 0421	WC	OC	297
	Box 1, bundle a, number 2				

THE LATER YEARS

Seeking to improve his financial situation and perhaps to recoup the losses he had suffered in Australia, Wilhelm became a farmer in the Banat region of Europe after he returned from his Australian sojourn. He was joined for some years by Pauline. The Banat, which had been part of the Austrian Empire since 1718, was attractive to farmers, who were encouraged to move to the area. George Aberle defines the Banat's reach: "Three tributaries of the Blue Danube flow through these lands: the Theiss, the Maros and the Temes . . . In time the German settlers reached north to the river Karos. North and East of the Banat is Transylvania . . . The southern boundary was the Danube" (1981: 74). Nick Tullius records that the "old ('undivided') Banat comprises areas of present-day western Romania, north-eastern Serbia, and southern Hungary" (http://www.dvhh.org/banat/about.htm). The Ottoman Empire had dominated the Banat until 1718, but the Treaty of Passarovitz at the cessation of hostilities of the Austro-Turkish War of 1716–18 ceded it to Austria (Steigerwald 1985: 3). Wilhelm and many other aspiring farmers followed in a long tradition of migration to the region; as historian Nikolaus Engelmann records, some 15,000 colonists settled in the Banat between 1722 and 1726, attracted by a series of incentives the Austrian Habsburg rulers provided for relocation (Engelmann and Michels 1987: 8). Jacob Steigerwald describes these incentives as including "homestead, land, and livestock grants, [and] tax and statute labor (socage) exemptions" (1985: 3). These settlers of the "erste Schwabenzug" migration (first Schwaben/Swabian migration), created from the Banat "a productive breadbasket with thriving self-sufficient rural settlements" (Steigerwald 1985: 4). Engelmann records a subsequent settlement wave occurring after 1747, the Second Schwabenzug, when he estimates that between 1763 and 1770 an additional 4,000 Germans relocated to the Banat, while yet a third settlement transpired in 1780. Alternatively, G.C. Paikert divides the original migration, "Der grosse Schwabenzug" (the Great Swabian Migration), into three parts: the Karolinische Ansiedlung (or Caroline colonization) from 1718 to 1737 under Charles IV; the Maria Theresianische Ansiedlung from 1744 to 1772 under Maria Theresia; and the Josephinische Ansiedlung from 1782 to 1787 under Joseph II. He notes, of these settlers, "It is to their credit that they were fully aware of the extremely harsh conditions which were to face them in their new homeland"

(1967: 26). Yet, Paikert also observes that from the 1850s onwards, and particularly after the Dual Monarchy of 1867, conditions improved considerably in the region: "there was always a healthy domestic market for the various products of the multitude of nationalities that lived within its boundaries" (1967: 32). Thus, when Wilhelm relocated to the area in the 1860s, he fully expected to prosper. However, as his correspondence shows, and contrary to expectations, he found it extremely difficult to eke out a living and was ultimately forced to return to Vienna some years later.

Wilhelm's and Pauline's letters from the Banat reference some of the forty-six German villages established in the eighteenth-century erste Schwabenzug: Temesvár (Timişoara), Tschakowa (Ciakova), Grossbetschkerek (Zrenjanin), Lippa (Lipova) (Engelmann and Michels 1987: 9).[1] Paikert posits that the Habsburgs encouraged German as the local *lingua franca* in order to unify the disparate groups living in the Banat, saying it was "an expedient and efficient tool of rationality in the necessary process of amalgamating the different nationalities within the Habsburg realm" (1967: 15). When Wilhelm departed from the Banat for Vienna around 1874, the German settlers were likely well on their way to forming, as Paikert establishes they did thirty years later, "the most prosperous and best established agricultural communities in their environment" (1967: 26). At the same time, the German population in the Banat experienced some instability in this period. They had enjoyed a higher standard of living than most other regional minorities – particularly Slavs, Romanians, and Hungarians – until the Hungarian revolution in 1848–9. Broad social reforms that followed improved the living conditions for all Banat sub-groups, and the Banat Germans saw a rising tide of Hungarian nationalism as a threat to their preferred cultural and linguistic identity. The establishment in 1867 of the new empire of Austria–Hungary resulted in a dual monarchy which attempted to "magyarize" the area by promoting the Hungarian language and culture. As Steigerwald notes, only five million (38 percent) of a total Hungarian population of thirteen million were actual Magyars (1985: 17), but Hungarian officials instituted programs to convert the language of education to Hungarian in order to magyarize the Banat. Many Swabian Germans pledged allegiance to Hungary by magyarizing their names and supporting Hungarian nationalism in this period.

Wilhelm's, Pauline's and Ottilia's[2] letters reference the day-to-day difficulties of living under the Banat's harsh climate more than the political situation, from which they likely felt themselves apart. These letters confirm that Claire continued to send assistance whenever she was able. As the letters will show, Claire contributed financially to Wilhelm's enterprises in the Banat, putting herself at risk financially when she co-purchased Nikolaihof, an estate in Marburg (Maribor), with her nephew. In the wake of Wilhelm's failures in Australia, a country the family had hoped would inevitably provide prosperity to anyone who sought it, these acts suggest her devotion and loyalty to her brother's family.

Alas, Claire's investment would avail her nephew and his family little. Wilhelm's various farming enterprises in the Banat forced a permanent return to

Vienna in the 1870s. While it is unclear whether or not he actually sold Nikolaihof, the family relocated to Vienna in 1874, where Wilhelm served as a government employee. Neither he nor his family would ever return to the Banat, which was to know additional upheaval after World War I when it was partitioned between Romania, Hungary, and Yugoslavia after the dissolution of the Austro-Hungarian Empire. Place names were changed to reflect a change in territorial ownership, such that the names by which Wilhelm and Pauline refer to them within their letters were eventually altered: Temesvár became Timişoara in Romanian, Laybach became Ljubljana in Slovene, while Csakova became known as Ciacova in Romanian. By the twentieth century, after the partitioning of the Banat in 1918, new borders had changed the cultural and linguistic identity of many of the towns. Places like Bobda, where Wilhelm farmed, were eventually absorbed into Romania, and many Banat Germans immigrated to the United States, to Canada, or repatriated to Germany. Indeed, some German Banaters elected to repatriate to Germany after World War II because they feared the consequences of maintaining a German identity outside of Germany in post-World War II Europe.

Wilhelm's children would know a sunnier fate. He and Ottilia raised three children (Walter Claire, Alma Pauline, and Johann Paul), all of whom enjoyed a measure of success in their own lives (see photograph in the collection of the three children as adults). Paul's son, Christoph Clairmont, shared Walter Clairmont's story in "Eine Abendgesellschaft in Berlin im Jahre 1895" ("A Soirée in Berlin in the Year 1895"[3]). According to Christoph, Walter Clairmont trained as a chemist, earned a PhD in Chemistry, and worked for various chemical and textile enterprises. Marion Stocking recorded meeting Walter Clairmont in Munich in 1949 in order to peruse the Clairmont papers. Although Alma Crüwell-Clairmont was the "custodian of the family archive" (Stocking 1978: 372), she died in 1946, and the Clairmont family papers were passed to Walter by the American authorities, who had retrieved them on behalf of the family after the war (Stocking noted that Alma sent them "'to the country' for safekeeping" [Stocking 1978: 373]). Stocking confirmed that Walter had enjoyed a "distinguished career". She observed too that he had maintained his British citizenship and therefore had been "relatively unmolested" during World War II. Furthermore, according to Stocking, Walter "had opposed the Nazi regime, and profound political differences had caused him some years before to cease communication with his sister Alma" (1978: 373). She stated too that, while his knowledge of his family's involvement with the Shelley circle was a recent discovery, he found the connection "both fascinating and disturbing" (Stocking 1978: 373). Walter, it appears, had a vague recollection of his great-aunt Claire, but remembered "with great enthusiasm . . . his beloved Aunt Plin, a splendid linguist, who had taught him English and French" (Stocking 1978: 373). He did mock Pauline a little, however, when he told Stocking he preferred the food products she had sent him as a gift to Pauline's journals. Stocking's gift was "a lot more interesting than all the rubbish my good old Aunt wrote down so volubly in her journals" (1978: 374). Stocking records too that

Walter admitted that both Pauline and Claire were "pre-Victorians" and that their behaviors were to be considered through a different lens (1978: 383). Walter died in 1958 without issue.

Christoph Clairmont's account of the soirée in Berlin in 1895 also provided information about Alma's and Paul's later years, as did Michael Wladika's document in which he referenced Paul's life. Alma married Gottlieb Crüwell, director of the library at the University of Vienna. According to her nephew, "Alma Crüwell . . . beschäftigte sich vor allem mit dem Nachlaß Claire Clairmonts, der Freundin von Shelley und Byron, und den Beziehungen zu diesem Kreis" ("Alma Crüwell . . . was primarily focused on the legacy of Claire Clairmont, friend of Shelley and Byron, and relationships within this circle" [translation provided by Ann Sherwin]).[4] Paul Clairmont studied medicine in Vienna and trained as a surgeon at the University of Königsberg (Albertus-Universität zu Königsberg, formerly in East Prussia but since 1945 the Russian city of Kaliningrad) under Anton von Eiselsberg, the celebrated Austrian surgeon, who himself was a student of Theodor Billroth, considered the father of Austrian surgery. Later, Paul Clairmont joined von Eiselsberg at the University of Vienna (Universität Wien) when von Eiselsberg succeeded Billroth as head of surgery. In 1918, Paul moved to Switzerland to assume the chair of surgery in Zurich. He married twice. His first wife, Alexine, died without issue in 1920. His second wife, Emmy Koller (1893–1986) was the mother of his children.[5] Paul died in Switzerland in 1942. As the introduction to this collection documents, Pauline died in an accident while walking with Paul in Öblarn, Steiermark, in 1891. The Austrian writer Hugo von Hofmannsthal, a friend of Paul's, records that Paul grieved Pauline's death.[6] Von Hofmannsthal spent time with Paul in Salzburg shortly after the accident, and found him clearly affected by it. Ellen Ritter believes that, "Was Hofmannsthal wohl auch an Paul Clairmont interessiert haben mag, waren dessen verwandtschaftlichen Beziehungen zu den englischen Romantikern Shelley und Byron" ("What also interested Hofmannsthal about Paul Clairmont were his family connections to the English Romantics Shelley and Byron" [translation provided by Anja Reiner]).[7]

Stocking's relationship with Mary Claire Bally-Clairmont is well documented, both in "Miss Tina and Miss Plin" and in a copy of the unpublished correspondence from Bally-Clairmont, housed in the Pforzheimer Collection (see CL'ANA 0428, unpublished manuscript, Pforzheimer Collection). Stocking and Bally-Clairmont corresponded regularly about the Clairmont papers. Stocking notes that, in 1967, she was a guest of "the gracious namesake of both Mary Shelley and Claire Clairmont" (1978: 374), and a copy of a letter in the Pforzheimer Collection from 2005 attests to their continuing friendship. In that letter, Bally-Clairmont informed Stocking: "Dear Marion, whatever you will do with the family documents is alright, you have my agreement" (CL'ANA 0428, unpublished manuscript, Pforzheimer Collection). Bally-Clairmont died in 2009. Her husband, Hans Jörg Bally, survived her until February 2015. His ashes were interred next to Bally-Clairmont's in Basel, Switzerland. Christoph Clairmont died in 2004 after a successful career in archaeology. After his retirement from Rutgers, he moved to Switzerland. His wife, Victorine Clairmont-von Gonzenbach, died in February 2016. Her ashes were buried next to those of her husband in Ernen, Switzerland.

Notes

1 While many have assumed that these German Banat migrants came largely from south-western Germany, specifically from the region known as Swabia, Paikert claims that this perspective is, in fact, "erroneous" (1967: 1). See N. Tullius for Banat village names.
2 Wilhelm married Ottilia von Pichler in 1866, and she joined him in the Banat.
3 See http://www.navigare.de/hofmannsthal/abend.htm.
4 See http://www.navigare.de/hofmannsthal/abend.htm.
5 Stocking incorrectly identifies Alexine Clairmont as the mother of Paul's children. Alexine's death announcement, published in the *Neue Freie Presse*, of 30 March 1920, recorded her death on 27 March 1920. She was survived by her mother, Frau Adeline Payrhuber, and her husband, Professor Dr. Paul Clairmont (Austrian Newspapers Online, Österreichische Nationalbibliothek [Austrian National Library, http://anno.onb.ac.at/cgi-content/anno?apm=0&aid=nfp&datum=19200330&seite=13&zoom=2, p. 13]). Paul's children were born in 1922 and 1924.
6 See http://www.navigare.de/hofmannsthal/mozart.html.
7 http://www.navigare.de/hofmannsthal/mozart.html.

Bibliography

Aberle, G., *From the Steppes to the Prairies* (Bismarck, ND: Tumbleweed Press, 1981).
Austrian Newspapers Online, Österreichische Nationalbibliothek (Austrian National Library), http://anno.onb.ac.at/
Čerin, B. and F. Vogelnik, *Maribor* (Ljubljana: Cankarjeva zal., 1988).
Clairmont, C., "Eine Abendsgessellschaft in Berlin im Jahre 1895," *Navigare*, 1999, http://www.navigare.de/hofmannsthal/abend.htm#dulong2, 14 April 2015.
Clairmont, F., Receipt of Clairmont Correspondence. 22 September 1948. Records of the Reparations and Restitutions Branch of the U.S. Allied Commission for Austria (USACA) Section, 1945–1950, www.fold3.com/image/274319558/, 15 November 2014.
Clairmont, W. G., Letter to James Garrison. 15 July 1948. Records of the Reparations and Restitutions Branch of the U.S. Allied Commission for Austria (USACA) Section, 1945–1950, www.fold3.com/image/274319568, 28 October 2014.
Engelmann, N. and J. Michels, *The Banat Germans: Die banater Schwaben* (Bismarck, ND: University of Mary Press, 1987).
Frey, K. S., *The Danube Swabians: A People with Portable Roots* (Belleville, Ont.: Mika Pub. Co., 1982).
Garrison, J., Letter to Colonel Lorie. 27 July 1948. Records of the Reparations and Restitutions Branch of the U.S. Allied Commission for Austria (USACA) Section, 1945–1950, www.fold3.com/image/274319570/, 15 November 2014.
———, Letter about Clairmont Diaries. 30 March 1949. Records of the Reparations and Restitutions Branch of the U.S. Allied Commission for Austria (USACA) Section, 1945–1950, www.fold3.com/image/274319550, 15 November 2014.

———, Letter to Marion Kingston. 30 March 1949. Records of the Reparations and Restitutions Branch of the U.S. Allied Commission for Austria (USACA) Section, 1945–1950, www.fold3.com/image/274319555, 15 November 2014.

Google Maps, 2014–2015, Web, various dates, www.google.com/maps/

Great Britain Foreign Office, Historical Section, *Transylvania and the Banat* (Wilmington, DE: Scholarly Resources, 1973).

Hitchins, K., *Studies in East European Social History* (Leiden: Brill, 1977).

———, *A Concise History of Romania* (New York: Cambridge University Press, 2014).

Husband, R., Letter Confirming Receipt of Clairmont Materials. 13 August 1948. Records of the Reparations and Restitutions Branch of the U.S. Allied Commission for Austria (USACA) Section, 1945–1950, www.fold3.com/image/274319564/, 15 November 2014.

Kingston, M., Letter to Mr. Garrison. 21 March 1949. Records of the Reparations and Restitutions Branch of the U.S. Allied Commission for Austria (USACA) Section, 1945–1950, www.fold3.com/image/274319552, 28 October 2014.

Lee, R., Letter to Walter Clairmont. 7 September 1948. Records of the Reparations and Restitutions Branch of the U.S. Allied Commission for Austria (USACA) Section, 1945–1950, www.fold3.com/image/274319561/, 15 November 2014.

Luthar, O., *The Land Between: A History of Slovenia* (Frankfurt am Main: Peter Lang GmbH, 2013).

Paikert, G. C., *The Danube Swabians* (The Hague: Martinus Nijhoff, 1967).

Prunk, J., *A Brief History of Slovenia* (Ljubljana: Založba Grad, 2000).

Ritter, E., "Über Hofmannsthals Besuch der Mozart-Centenarfeier in Salzburg im Juli 1891," *Navigare*, 1999, http://www.navigare.de/hofmannsthal/mozart.html, 20 April 2015.

Steigerwald, J., *Tracing Romania's Heterogeneous German Minority from Its Origins to the Diaspora* (Winona, MN: Translation and Interpretation Service, 1985).

Stocking, M. K., "Miss Tina and Miss Plin: The Papers behind the Aspern Papers," in D. Reiman (ed.), *The Evidence of the Imagination* (New York: New York University Press, 1978), pp. 372–384.

——— (ed.), *The Clairmont Correspondence: Letters of Claire Clairmont, Charles Clairmont, and Fanny Imlay Godwin* (Baltimore, MD: Johns Hopkins University Press, 1995).

Tóth, I. G., *A Concise History of Hungary: The History of Hungary from the Early Middle Ages to the Present* (Budapest: Corvina, 2005).

Tötösy de Zepetnek, S., *The Records of the Tötösy de Zepetnek Family* (West Lafayette, IN: Purdue University, 1993).

———, (ed.), *Nobilitashungariae: List of Historical Surnames of the Hungarian Nobility* (West Lafayette, IN: Purdue University, 2010).

Tucker, E., Memo Confirming Delivery of Clairmont Materials to Frieda Clairmont. 27 September 1948. Records of the Reparations and Restitutions Branch of the U.S. Allied Commission for Austria (USACA) Section, 1945–1950, www.fold3.com/image/274319557/, 15 November 2014.

Tullius, N., A. Leeb, and J. Pharr, "Banat: Donauschwaben Villages Helping Hands," September 2015, http://www.dvhh.org/banat/.

Vrišer, S., *Maribor* (Motovun: Niro Motovun, 1984).

Wladika, M., "Egon Schiele, Mutter und Kind II, 1912," 2011, Leopold Museum, pp. 1–13, 14 April 2015.

LETTERS FROM
28 MARCH 1861–24 DECEMBER 1889

153 • Wilhelm Gaulis Clairmont to Claire Clairmont

[28 March 1861]

My dearest aunt.

Knowing the propensity of your nerves (if you knew of my coming) to treat you to an endless variety of the most lugubrious images terminating of course in nothing short of shipwreck with all the concomitant horrors of drifting in a small boat and casting lots who should be eaten next or being thrown on a lonely island unencumbered by the ordinary articles of dress – I wisely refrained from informing you of my intended migration; but as I cant subject you without warning to the shock my nepotic presence would inflict on you I beg you to be prepared for the awful calamity of seeing me walk into your apartment in ten minutes from this.[1]

Till then I remain
dearest aunt
yours affectionately
[illeg.] Clairmont [illeg.][2]

Florence
March 28th 1861.

Address: Miss Clairmont[3]

Unpublished. Text: M.S., Pf. Coll., CL'ANA 0245

---

1 In March 1861, Wilhelm finally returned to England from Australia. He paid a surprise visit to Claire but sent this note, apparently ten minutes before arriving at her home. Wilhelm recorded his travels from Australia to Europe and his first few weeks back in Austria in his Sands and Kenny's Diary, 1861 Number 2 (CL'ANA 0177, unpublished manuscript, Pforzheimer Collection). In this short and incomplete journal, Wilhelm also included a list of contact addresses, notably Claire's and the Tooth brothers' in London, as well as a list of all the boxes he sent to Baden. He quite thoroughly described his encounter with Claire in Florence. See Introduction for more details about Wilhelm's meeting with Claire.
2 Only Wilhelm's last name is legible. It is preceded and followed by scrawling letters.
3 This letter evidently was hand delivered, as the envelope has no address on it. Only Claire's name appears on the envelope.

154 • Wilhelm Gaulis Clairmont to Claire Clairmont

[25 April 1861]

My dearest aunt

I had a letter from Mamma today enclosing yours to her of the 9th March (but I suppose it is meant for 9th April)[1] – you seem to have quite forgotten your original proposal to give me £500 for stocking a farm! I was alarmed to read in some of the German papers that the manager of Her Majesty's theatre has failed.[2] Will this affect you? or will the theatre go on nevertheless? Pray reflect well before you allow me to <u>act</u> on your promise whether you will be both willing & able to keep it, for without your assistance I cannot for a moment dream of settling in this country as I have not money enough to undertake ~~some~~ anything – If you therefore cause me to give up Australia you are bound as the phrase goes to "stick to me" if you do not like the idea of binding yourself to such a course please tell me so at once. – Under any circumstances it would be difficult to manage with £1500 if the money is to be invested in a purchase, because it is not enough to buy a sufficiently large farm to maintain us. I have however lately heard of a speculation which might quite suit our circumstances I met on my travels a gentleman who was for many years Director of an Estate of [~~illeg.~~] Prince Windisch Grätz[3] in Illyria. I questioned him with reference to Trieste and Fiume,[4] but he quite bore out the account I had received of that country at Trieste which I reported to you already He told me however of a large moor situated at Laybach[5] 3 hours pr rail from Trieste which only wants draining to qualify it in a most eminent degree for farming purposes; the rail road goes right through it and the vicinity of Laibach and Trieste together with the commercially favourable position on the railway between Vienna and Trieste make it a very promising speculation.[6] All moors invariably turn out first class agricultural land but it must be borne in mind that besides buying them they must also be drained and worked which requires money the peat however obtained in draining from these places and which is readily bought by all the manufacturers defrays the expenses of drainage

A rich merchant of Trieste who failed some years ago commenced as an <u>amateur</u> to drain and reclaim some 400 acres of this farm he also erected farmbuildings on it cut drains and put it in all but working order when the matter was dropped in consequence of his failure – this estate I am told has been lying barren for the last 3 or 4 years and could be purchased for a mere song. The climate there is so lovely that the old Radetzky used latterly always to spend his winters there and the Emporer bought him for that very reason a handsome villa close by.[7] Laybach is a very thriving commercial and industrial city there are also several English families there. The "Laybach"[8] a navigable river flows right through the estate and the vicinity of two large cities offers great opportunities for dairy farming which is always most remunerative in cases when you have ready sale for the milk. Labour too is plentyful and cheap. As soon as I have completed my sheepbusiness[9] I shall have a look at it. I forgot to say that all the necessary buildings are erected and now stand empty This is worth a consideration especially as the climate is so fine.

28 MARCH 1861–24 DECEMBER 1889

Write to me to Baden; my whereabouts are uncertain but Mamma will forward my letters.

Yours truly
WGC

Troppau[10]
April 25th 1861.

Address: No envelope

Unpublished. Text: M.S., Pf. Coll., CL'ANA 0252

---

1 This letter does not survive.
2 Some twenty months later, in December 1862, Claire would tell Dina Williams Hunt that her opera box had brought in very little money. Given that London could maintain two opera companies, she could not comprehend why she received so little from her box rental. She also noted that, as she had no one in London to assist her with her box, she was forced to live on a "mere pittance of bread, cheese, and fire in the winter and sun in the summer" (*CC* II: 595). She rather comically observed that her income would be four times its value if she could live outdoors in a tub.
3 The royal Austrian house of Windisch-Grätz was created in 1804 ("Mediatized House of Windisch-Gratz". Web. 25 January 2015. http://www.almanachdegotha.org/id110.html) Alfred I (1787–1862) was Prince of Windisch-Grätz at the time Wilhelm wrote this letter. The term, Illyria, refers to the Illyrian Provinces which included the cities of Fiume, Laybach, and Trieste. Formerly land belonging to the Habsburgs, the Illyrian provinces were occupied by France in 1809 until 1816. The provinces were located on the Adriatic Sea and included the territories of Western Carinthia, Carniola, and Dalmatia (Luthar, p. 257). The capital city was Laybach (today's Ljubljana, the capital of Slovenia).
4 Trieste is an Italian city located on the Adriatic Sea in north-eastern Italy. Until 1918, the city was part of the Austro-Hungarian Empire. After a tumultuous history during the early part of the twentieth century, Trieste became an Italian city in 1954 (Požun, Brian. "Trieste's Burden of History". *Central European Review*. 12 February 2001. Web. 25 January 2015. http://www.ce-review. org/01/6/pozun6.html).

   Fiume, as the Italians and Hugarians called it, is the third largest city in Croatia and is known today as Rijeka. Situated on the Adriatic Sea, Rijeka is located 75 kilometers south-east of Trieste and 160 kilometers south-west of Zagreb, Croatia. See Pemac, Dajana. "Borderlands of Memory". Web. http://www.uni-regensburg.de/Fakultaeten/phil_Fak_III/Geschichte/istrien/route-rijeka.html 24 October 2015.
5 Laibach is the German name for Ljubljana, the capital of Slovenia. Wilhelm spelled it both as Laibach and Laybach. Ljubljana is located 94 kilometers east of Trieste.
6 In 1857, construction began on the Southern Railway which linked Trieste to Vienna. According to the Trieste Port Authority, the Port of Trieste was ranked the world's seventh busiest port in terms of cargo handling in the first decade of the nineteenth century (Trieste Port Authority. Web 21 January 2015. http://www.porto.trieste.it/eng/port/description). The original railway network went from Vienna, through Maribor (Slovenia) and Ljubljana (Slovenia) to Trieste. In 1857, construction also began on the link between Pragersko (Slovenia) and Nagykanizsa (Hungary) and then to Budapest (Bunijevac, Helena. "The First Rail-Line in Croatia". Web. 21 January 2015. http:// www.railfaneurope.net/ric/Medjimurje.htm). Ljubljana lies directly on the link from Trieste to Vienna.
7 Johann Joseph, Graf Radetzky von Radetz (1766–1858) was a Czech-born Austrian field marshal and veteran of many military campaigns. Emperor Franz Joseph I purchased Tivoli Castle (Grad

Tivolski) in Tivoli Park, Ljubljana, for Radetzky. In 1848, Johann Strauss the Elder wrote the *Radetzky March* in honor of Radetzky's victory in the Battle of Custoza (The Editors of Encyclopaedia Britannica. "Joseph, Graf Radetzky". *Encyclopaedia Britannica Online*. Encyclopaedia Britannica Inc., n.d. Web. 25 January 2015. http://www.britannica.com/EBchecked/topic/488394/Joseph-Graf-Radetzky).

8   The Ljubljanica River flows through Ljubljana and numerous bridges span it.
9   Wilhelm was traveling in search of a property on which to farm. In his journal entry of 9 April 1861, he recorded inspecting sheep (see CL'ANA 0177, unpublished manuscript, Pforzheimer Collection).
10 Troppau was the German name for the city of Opava, located in the Czech Republic. Wilhelm's travels after his Australian sojourn took him from Italy through Europe to England.

155 • Wilhelm Gaulis Clairmont to Claire Clairmont

[22 June 1861]

My dear Aunt.

On my arrival here yesterday I found your letter of the 13th June.[1] your commission with reference to Croydon[2] shall be attended to most punctually as soon as I have the sheep off my hands[3] – I have not yet seen the Pringles nor any one else. as I have already positively decided on not returning to Australia you are now quite at Liberty to speak about it to any whom my movements [illeg.] may interest. I have not yet seen Mr. Mort & Mr. Tooths (brother resident here) and hope they will make no difficulty about paying me my salary.[4]

I expect to return to Vienna in 4 or 5 weeks from this; one of my Vienna friends (who is now settled in Hungary) has taken this opportunity to come with me & see London – as he is a very old friend I do not feel my want of friends here – After our return we propose to go together to the Banat[5] (that is in Lower Hungary[6] where he lives) together and I shall then have a thorough opportunity of judging whether purchase I can settle there at all and whether purchase or renting a farm would be more advisable.[7] After that I proposed to visit you in florence say middle of October. – the Banater climate is mild as compared with Vienna – there is good society there and my friend who has also a tendency to be narrow chested finds the climate very suitable for his complaint. Mr. Smallbones[8] too an Hungarian Englishman who has been settled in Hungary for many years and is now the right hand of Prince Esterhazy[9] has told me that the prince contemplates great changes in the management of his estates and that if he could be of service to me he would – I am to meet him here in a few weeks when he will let me know further particulars. All things considered it is much better I should first look about me in Austria and then go to you and discuss and mature with you some definite plan than to have to do all that afterwards by letter. Goodbye now dearest aunt, see that Isabell does not marry some one else in the mean time I am quite anxious to see poor Violette. as soon as I have seen the Pringles I shall write again.

yours affectionately
WGC

London
June 22nd – 1861.

Direct:
Care of Mess. R. & F Tooth & Mort
155 Fenchurch street
London.[10]

Address: Signora Clairmont/ Palazzo Schneiderff/Ponte alla Carraja[11]/ Florence
Front postmark: LONDON – E.C./ 12/ JU 22/ 61
Rear postmark: FIRENZE/[illeg.]

Unpublished. Text: M.S., Pf. Coll., CL'ANA 0255

1 This letter does not survive.
2 By July 1858, Claire was writing to Antonia from Handcroft Road, Croydon, Surrey (see *CC*, volume 2). However, by the end of 1859, she had moved to Florence. The "commission" noted in Wilhelm's letter was the settling of Claire's affairs and the shipping of her furniture from England to Italy (see CL'ANA 0251).
3 Wilhelm referred to resolving his Australian affairs with Mort and Tooth.
4 The Tooth brothers, Robert Tooth (1821–1893), Edwin (1822–1858) and Frederick (1827–1893) were active in Australian business affairs. Both Robert and Frederick died in London.
5 See introduction to Volume II for a more detailed explanation of the Banat.
6 In 1814, Richard Bright wrote a record of his travels in Lower Hungary which he published in his book, *Travels From Vienna Through Lower Hungary* (Edinburgh: Archibald Constable and Company, 1818). Lower Hungary referred to the area that corresponds to today's western and central areas of Slovakia. Bright visited places Wilhelm and Pauline would mention in their letters to Claire: Pressburg, Lake Balaton, Keszthely, Ödenburg, and Varaždin. William Mahoney explains that the Hungarian Diet in the fifteenth century appointed "seven captains for different parts of the kingdom". Lower Hungary was one such captaincy (*The History of the Czech Republic and Slovakia* [Santa Barbara, CA: Greenwood Press, 2011], p. 83).
7 Hitschmann documented that Wilhelm was a"Gutspächter bei Temesvár in Ungarn" ("an estate tenant near Temesvár in Hungary") after leaving Altenburg (*Verzeichniss*, pp. 10–11).
8 See CL'ANA 0343 and CL'ANA 0421, Box 3, bundle g, number 185.
9 The Esterházy family had its origins in the Middle Ages and was considered the largest landowning family in Hungary. The family was active in the political and military life of the Empire ("Mediatized House of Esterházy". Web. 25 January 2015. http://www.almanachdegotha.org/id72.html). See CL'ANA 0343.
10 The London-based company, R. and F. Tooth and Mort, were agents for a variety of enterprises. Brothers Robert and Edwin Tooth started a brewing and merchant firm in Australia in 1843 which was known as R. and E. Tooth. In 1853, their brother, Frederick Tooth, worked for them and they changed the firm's name in 1860 to R. and F. Tooth & Company. Later Thomas Mort joined the company and it became R. & F. Tooth & Mort. Its London address was in Fenchurch Street (Walsh, G.P. "Tooth, Edwin (1822–1858)", *Australian Dictionary of Biography*. National Centre of Biography, Australian National University. 1976. Web. 21 January 2015. http://adb.anu.edu.au/biography/tooth-edwin-4944/text7851).
11 The Hotel Schneiderff was a fashionable location in the nineteenth century and was the chosen location for many foreigners who visited Florence (Paolini, Claudio. "Repertorio Delle Architetture Civili Di Firenze". Web. 24 October 2015. http://www.palazzospinelli.org/architetture/).

Antonia misspelled Ponte alla Carraia, a bridge with five arches that traverses the Arno River in Florence.

28 MARCH 1861–24 DECEMBER 1889

156 • Wilhelm Gaulis Clairmont to Claire Clairmont

London July 12th 1861

My dearest aunt

I duly recd. your second letter enclosing Miss Longs[1] to you – I was sorry to hear you suffered so much from headache but I hope it is over by this time I have been to Croydon to settle all your affairs – Hydes Bill for housing the chair was so enormous that it would have come to more than the value of the chair if sold – I therefore left it in his hands to pay himself as best he could – the Zannchair[2] and writing table I sold Mrs. Long she would not give more than 35/- for the lot and has her bill for warehousing amounted to £2.10.d I paid her the difference of 15/- and left her in possession of the chairs the Hamper only contained a teakettle coffeepot & fool bottle[3] which would have been sure to get smashed – I therefore left them behind – the writing desk I <u>opened</u> but there was <u>nothing</u> in any of the Drawers. the small trunk to be left in a bedroom Miss Long says you came back for and <u>removed</u> there are now only 3 large trunks or boxes and the portrait packed by Cataneo[4] carefully – these four articles Mr Long will get shipped by the very first vessel leaving for Leghorn[5] and he will send you an account of the expenses. I could not do it myself because Cataneo had not the portrait ready & I had to leave. the Custom house agent says that the contents of the boxes must be <u>declared</u> previous to their being entered for export – I told him I could not tell contents of boxes but that if the Law required it the Boxes should be opened and examined sooner than not sent at all – they have very trustworthy respectable customhouse agents who manage these things. Mr Long will see to all and it will be allright. I shall leave for Paris tomorrow where I shall stay only a week and then go on to Hungary to see what I can see. direct Baden – Violet is married – Captain Payton a very nice fellow.[6] the Pringles all desire to be remembered – Knox though in town never answered my note to him

yours affect nephew
WGC

Address: No envelope

Unpublished. Text: M.S., Pf. Coll., CL'ANA 0251

---

1 While in Croydon, Claire resided in the home of Mr. and Mrs. Long. Many of the letters in this collection were addressed to Claire, care of Mr. and Mrs. Long. Wilhelm was charged with settling Claire's affairs and with sending her boxes.
2 Wilhelm probably meant to write "sun chair". The German for sun is "Sonne," which would be pronounced with a "z" sound.
3 Probably a bottle to store a fool, a type of fruit and custard or cream dessert.
4 Unidentified.
5 Leghorn is the English name for Livorno, a port on the west coast of Italy. See also CL'ANA 0432.
6 Violet Pringle married Captain John Peyton in 1861. She died in 1866 at the age of 26 and was buried in India. See "Emily Georgina villet "Violet" Pringle Peyton". Web. 23 May 2015. http://www.findagrave.com/cgi-bin/fg.cgi?page=gr&GRid=89031580

157 • Wilhelm Gaulis Clairmont to Claire Clairmont

[8 August 1861]

My dearest aunt.

On my return to Baden from Vienna I found a letter from you which I then answered hastily and which I have no doubt you duly received this I write from Oroszlawje[1] the castle of my old schoolfriend Count Sermage[2] with whom I am now making a short stay this place is as I believe you are aware in Croatia. I traversed Hungary on my way here and saw a good many very tempting purchases, but the great difficulty is this that small ones such as I might buy for £1000 are all dear in as much as there are many competitors for these descriptions of estates, for all rich peasants who have saved a few hundred pounds want to buy land and thus became competitors; otherwise with larger estates it is quite a different thing for it is not every one that has 6 or eight thousand pounds and yet there are immense numbers of such estates for sale and consequently much cheaper for instance if a smaller estate with only a small cottage on it cost 200 florins per acre a larger estate with a mansion and all the necessary out houses will cost only 80 or 100 florins pr. acre. for instance I saw a splendid estate belonging to Count Alexander Festetics[3] of 1300 acres with a fine mansion with 20 rooms large cellar outhouses etz. everything furnished – for sale for 85.000 florins. this includes however the whole of this year's harvest in grain hay and fodder, 600 sheep all the working cattle and horses 80 in number 40 pigs poultry all the implements and tools etz. to be given in free of charge among the meadows there are 100 acres which if sold in small lots to the peasants would fetch a price of 300 ~~acres~~ florins pr. acre which is alone 30,000f then there is a forest of 424 acres of splendid beech wood In a few years the railroad between Oedenburg[4] and Pesth[5] will go close by this place when the <u>wood alone</u> will represent a value of 100,000f. Besides there is large brick-kiln a mill yielding a revenue of 500f and maybe revenue of of[6] 700f pr. ann. for vineyards but to the peasants the whole would yield a revenue of 8 or 9000 florins. If you could make up your mind to sell your operabox for an annuity and invest the rest of your capital in this purchase it would yield you better interest and be at once the means of uniting us all to a comfortable home there is a fine house ready for us to go into at once and if you wished to leave for the winter you could easily do so. the locality is very pretty and healthy in a few years the railroad will be completed where not only the forest will yield an immense amount but the value of the land itself will be doubled now the nearest railway station called Kanisa[7] is 22 Engl. miles off. to which there is a good road. with my present means I cannot undertake the matter, but if you would make up your mind to join me in the purchase I am sure you would find it turn out very well; the whole capital will be at least doubled in 5 or 6 years and and[8] we shall have an agreeable residence be united and I shall moreover have a much better chance & pretension of obtaining a rich wife. So think over it dear aunt and let me know what you think, but remember there is no time to be lost for I have no doubt that it will be taken up soon. 15.000f of the purchase money not on the ~~houses~~ estate to be paid off in

28 MARCH 1861–24 DECEMBER 1889

30 consecutive years like on Mama's houses this would reduce the debt to[9] 70000; if you could manage to make up £4000 from your shares or say £3,500 I could with Mammas assistance manage the rest. Now do think it well over and let me know what you think but if you do not contemplate entering on such a place pray let me know have the £500 you promised me for a farm enterprise at once for now is the time to rent cheap it does not therefore follow that I shall not be able to get away to see you for there is not much to do in the winter time.

Pray write soon what you think of doing I shall in the mean time see other estates and farms I expect to leave count Sermages in a week. direct as stated on the paper enclosed and believe me dear aunt[10]

yours affectionately
WGC

Oroszlawje
August 8th 1861

WCG (signature)
pr. Addresse Graf Roggendorf[11]
Gross Becskereck, Banat
Hongrie.[12]

Address: No envelope

Unpublished. Text: M.S., Pf. Coll., CL'ANA 0246

---

1 Oroslavje is located in Croatia, about 44 kilometers north of the capital city of Zagreb.
2 Richard von Sermage attended the k.k. höheren landwirthschaftlichen Lehranstalt in Ungarisch-Altenburg (Altenburg, Hungary) with Wilhelm in 1850–1. According to Professor Hitschmann's records, Sermage was born on 27 August 1831 in "Oroszlavje, Kroatien" (*Verzeichniss*, pp. 68–9). Hitschmann recorded that he was a count ("Graf") and that he was a "Gutsbesitzer" after graduation in Oroszlavje (German for "estate owner").
3 Originally from Croatia, the Festetics family took up residence in Hungary in the eighteenth century. Their family palace, the Festetics Palace, is located in Keszthely, on the western shore of Lake Balaton. The German name for Lake Balaton is Plattensee (see CL'ANA 0254). See also "Helikon Kastélymuzeum" Web. 21 January 2015. http://helikonkastely.hu/en/festetics-palace/). Steven Tötösy de Zepetnek includes the Festetics de Tolna surname in his *List of Historical Surnames of the Hungarian Nobility*. Count Alexander Festetics de Tolna was born in 1805.
4 Known as Ödenburg in German, Wilhelm referred to the Hungarian town of Sopron which was located 127 kilometers from Keszthely. The railway line between Sopron and Nagykanizsa was constructed in the 1850s ("History of Sopron". Web. 21 January 2015. http://www.budapest.com/hungary/cities/sopron/history.en.html).
5 Buda-Pesth, Buda (German, Ofen) and Pesth, twin cities that later would form Budapest, the capital of Hungary.
6 Correct as stated in the letter.
7 Wilhelm meant Kanizsa, another name for Nagykanizsa. The town is near Lake Balaton (see note 3) and was an important station on the railway line from Trieste to Budapest. See CL'ANA 0254.

8 Correct in the original letter.
9 Wilhelm cross-wrote the following sentences (from "70000 . . . winter time") on the first page of the letter.
10 Wilhelm cross-wrote these two sentences on page 2 of the letter.
11 Wilhelm included the following address on an insert in the letter. Of Austrian origin, the Rogendorf family had owned property in Hungary since the eighteenth century and were active in government and local administration (*Magyar Nemzetségi Zsebkönyv*. Ed. József Szinnyei and László Fejérpataky. Budapest: Magyar Heraldikai és Genealógiai Társaság, 1888–1905. Vol. 1, 522–23. Translation by S. Tötösy de Zepetnek). József von Rogendorf (1784–1842) owned Rogendorf Castle, an estate which was located near to Großbetschkerek ("The Rogendorf Castle". Web. 22 January 2014. http://serbia.superodmor.rs/culturalhistorical-heritage/castles/1302/the-rogendorf-castle). The castle is situated in Banatski Dvor which is some 24 kilometers from Großbetschkerek (today's Zrenjanin, Serbia).
12 The city of Zrenjanin, located in the autonomous province of Vojvodina in Serbia, was known as Großbetschkerek in German and Nagybecskerek in Hungarian. It was the largest town of the Serbian Banat and was part of the Austro-Hungarian Empire in the nineteenth century. Wilhelm would have traveled a distance of over 511 kilometers to reach Großbetschkerek from Oroslavje. "Hongrie" is the French for Hungary.

158 • Wilhelm Gaulis Clairmont to Claire Clairmont

[2 September 1861]

My dear Aunt

On my arrival here[1] which took place only yesterday I found two letters from you one dated the 16th August the other without date both written from Borgo alla Collina.[2] In the one you write me to send my signature saying that I should get the money in question £500 at once but in the other you state that you are in difficulties ~~and that~~ through the failure of the theatre and that it will cause you great difficulties to keep your promise I am quite wretched at the receipt of this letter I cannot of course expect you to keep your promise of the £500 at the expense of your own most essential comforts but I cannot believe that your position is really so bad I think you must have written the second letter in a gloomy moment when everything appeared worse to you than it really is, for on the writing of your first letter and on a previous occasion where I wrote to you on hearing of the failure of her Majesty's theatre you still said that you would be able to let me have the £500. – I must leave the matter entirely in your hands but pray remember that without the £500 my prospects are entirely ruined. what I have now is not sufficient to commence operations with so what am I to do. the news came on me like a clap of thunder I have now traversed part of Hungary and the whole of Croatia and Slavonia[3] – through Sermage who is a Hungarian Magnat[4] and who traveled with me we had the best introductions everywhere and were in direct communications with some of the richest landowners with a little capital immense advantages may be gained, but without nothing can be done in order to increase our means I was about entering a partnership with Zoepf[5] we were in communication with a rich landowner in Slavonia regarding a farm near Essegg[6] where there is splendid land and famous opportunities for money making but now all my plans are in jeopardy I cannot however think that you will be so cruel as to crush all my prospects and therefore enclose my signature as you directed in your first letter – As to my settling in Italy dearest aunt it is impossible having no means of my own I must live in a country where I can earn money. In Italy this is impossible because the soil is all cut up among small proprietors and in consequence of the dense population the rent of land is immensely high In Italy I must starve but here I cannot only live but make money. these are circumstances which one must be ruled by one entering on such an enterprise – do not therefore think that it is my obstinacy – the climate in the southern parts of Hungary is very mild in the summer the heat is great. I trust you have recovered from the effects of the intense heat – here it is quite mild now

Believe me dear aunt yours
very affectionately
WGC

Direct
Rogendorf
Becskereck

Banat
September 2ⁿᵈ 1861
pray write soon

Address: La signora Clairmont/ Borgo alla Collina/ da my Lady Lennox[7]/ Poppi La Toscana[8] Italia
Rear postmark: WIEN/ ⁵/₉/5. E.; FIRENZE/9/SET/3; [illeg.]

Unpublished. Text: M.S., Pf. Coll., CL'ANA 0247

---

1 See CL'ANA 0246. After he left Oroslavje and the home of Richard von Sermage, Wilhelm went to stay at the home of Count Rogendorf.
2 See CL'ANA 0092. Borgo alla Collina was the name of the villa of Lady Sussex Lennox with whom Claire had renewed her friendship. See CL'ANA 0327, CL'ANA 0378 and *CC* II: 473.
3 Slavonia is located in eastern Croatia and is one of the four historical regions of the country. Osijek, Slavonia's largest city (see note 6 below), was also known by the German name, Esseg. Slavonia was originally part of the Austro-Hungarian Empire. After the Second World War, Slavonia was included in the country of Yugoslavia and then, after the conflicts in the 1990s, it became a Croatian region.
4 Hungarian magnates, comprising some two hundred families, controlled most of the economic resources of nineteenth-century Hungary. In her study of estate management in eighteenth-century Hungary, Rebecca Gates-Coon explains how the Esterházy house belonged to the magnate class which owned one-third of all Hungarian land. Gates-Coon records that Hungarian magnates used peasant labour to work their estates and to make possible their opulent lifestyles (Keith Hitchins, (ed.), *Studies in Eastern European Social History* [Leiden: Brill, 1977], p. 157). Historically, the upper chamber in the Hungarian parliament was made up of magnates.
5 See CL'ANA 0354.
6 The city of Osijek in Croatia was known in German as Esseg or Essegg. Osijek is located on the Drava River in eastern Croatia. It is one of the principal cities in the region of Slavonia, and the fourth largest city in Croatia. Osijek lies some 282 kilometers east of Zagreb.
7 Italian for "from my Lady Lennox".
8 The municipality of Poppi is located about 40 kilometers from Florence in Tuscany. Poppi Castle (Castello di Poppi) is located in the Casentino Valley in Tuscany.

159 • Wilhelm Gaulis Clairmont to Claire Clairmont

[1 November 1861]

My dearest aunt.[1]

Yesterday I received through Mamma your letter to her of the 24th Octob. in which you state having written to me on the 11th Septb – and by some strange chance I got only <u>today</u> this very letter it has been lying at the postoffice of Becskerek[2] ever since the 22nd September and was only by chance discovered in a pigeon hole; for all the other letters which I received in the mean time were duly delivered – It ~~was~~ is very unfortunate that this good news was withheld from me so long for I was in the mean time very wretched partly because I fancied you could not give me the money and, that all my plans were upset and partly because I latterly began to fear that you must be ill for I felt positive~~l~~ that you would not remain silent simply to save yourself the unpleasant task of informing me that you could not give me the money – Now all these doubts are dispelled and I thank you very much dearest aunt for the great sacrifice you have made to set me up– I shall immediately revive my negotiations concerning the farm near Esseg;[3] without your assistance I could not have undertaken it. I think you would like to live there in the Summer months for the winter it would be rather cold though much milder than Vienna, but I am told they are about to establish a railroad to Fiume[4] so that Italy is within easy reach of us – the winter is however very short I shall write to you again as soon as something is decided, but I think it would be better that you should not calculate on joining me till next spring for on the first commencement there is always a deal of uphill work and arriving in the dead of winter the journey would be unpleasant and I should have no chance of preparing things for you – As to my trip to Florence it is now impossible to say anything till I see how my business turns out I should like very well to go; but I frankly confess that I should dread the ~~idea~~ expense of the journey unless the chances of success were pretty certain for every £50 is of imense value to me at the first out let I shall write again as soon as something is decided yours truly

WGC

Rogendorf Novb. 1st 1861[5]

   WG. Clairmont Esq
name in full William Gaulis
Clairmont ~~present~~ direction
care of Count Rogendorf Becskerek[6]
   Hungary Austria.

I enclose signature in case it should be wanted – [7]
Did your picture arrive yet and was it well packed? I am anxious to hear about it.[8]

Address: A la Signora Clairmont/ 799³ Lung Arno delle Grazie/⁹ <u>Italie</u>. Florence
Rear postmark: Four illegible postmarks

Unpublished. Text: M.S., Pf. Coll., CL'ANA 0248.

---

1 The initials "WGC" are imprinted on the top of the page.
2 See CL'ANA 0246.
3 See note 6, CL'ANA 0247.
4 Fiume is the Italian name for Rijeka, a port city in Croatia today. It is located on the Adriatic Sea. See note 4, CL'ANA 0252.
5 Wilhelm enclosed two inserts in this letter. He wrote what follows on the front of the first insert.
6 See CL'ANA 0246.
7 Wilhelm wrote this sentence on the back of the first insert.
8 Wilhelm wrote this sentence on the second insert.
9 The river Arno flows through Florence, dividing the city in two. The paths alongside the Arno are known as lungarni (singular: lungarno). The number is correctly written with the superscript.

160 • Wilhelm Gaulis Clairmont to Claire Clairmont

[17 November 1861]

My dearest aunt[1]

I duly received your letter of the 10th Novb. I since also had a letter from the Chief Cashier of the Bank of England informing me that the money is at my disposal (£500) so this matter is all right and I thank you a thousand times for your selfsacrificing generosity – I sincerely wish to give you a call at Florence – not only on account of the marriage scheme but also to see you & thank you more effectively than I can by letter – the only question is about my being able to get away but this difficulty must solve itself in a very short time – So write me in the mean time your address where I can find you and also where the Beauclercs[2] are and whether you deem the present time a fitting one to try the experiment. I must call your attention once more to this most important point whether you are quite certain that the girls have the fortune you say viz £1000 down and an income of £200 a year each I dont ask this from mercenary motives for all the riches in the world shall not persuade me to marry her unless she is pleasing at the same time, but without such pecuniary assistance from her part I could not, as you well know, afford to maintain a wife – and consequently it would turn out a great sell both for them and myself to find at the 11th hour that their expectations were not what I was lead to believe they were. direct to Baden as I expect to be there before your letter answer can return – I believe I have already told you that your letter of the 11th Septb thought lost was not really lost – It lay at the post office of Besckerek ever since the 22nd Septemb ! dont therefore take any steps against your servants or the postoffice officials in Italy for it was not their fault – Goodbye now dearest aunt, as soon as something is decided concerning my affairs I shall write again – I hope to hear from you soon

yours very affectionately
WGC

Rogendorf
Novemb. 17th 1861

Address: No envelope

Unpublished. Text: M.S., Pf. Coll., CL'ANA 0249

---

1 The imprint, "WCG," is at the top of the letter.
2 Stocking notes that Claire had hoped to conclude a matrimonial match between a Miss Beauclerk and Wilhelm (*CC* II: 592–3, note 1). See also CL'ANA 0250. Stocking does not identify Miss Beauclerk. However, the Beauclerk family were friends of the Shelleys. Sunstein records how Mary Shelley made the acquaintance of Mrs. Charles (Emily) Beauclerk and her children when the Shelleys were living in Pisa (p. 207). Miranda Seymour suggests that the proximity of the Beauclerk family home to Sir Timothy Shelley's Field Place made the Beauclerks and the Shelleys

both "near neighbours and friends," which perhaps encouraged Mary Shelley to "hope to reach Sir Timothy without having always to approach him through his fiercly protective lawyer" (p. 415). Indeed, of all the Beauclerk children, Mary Shelley was particularly close to Georgiana Beauclerk (1805–47, later Gee Paul). Sunstein also explains that Mary Shelley "was seriously attracted" to Aubrey Beauclerk (1801–54), who "began to fall in love with her" after Mary Shelley had assisted his sister, Gee, during Gee's separation from her husband (p. 316). Aubrey Beauclerk later married Ida Goring, thereby dashing Mary Shelley's hopes. While the Miss Beauclerk of Wilhelm's letter is unidentified, it is probable that she was connected to the family of Aubrey Beauclerk. See *CC* for a genealogical table of the Beauclerk family.

161 • Wilhelm Gaulis Clairmont to Claire Clairmont

[12 December 1861]

My dear aunt.[1]

I was much relieved to learn from your last letter to Pauline that you did not expect me for positive for although I had gone so far in my preparations as to exchange my English into french money still it was next to impossible for me to have left for matters with reference to my farm have not been settled as speedily as I hoped & it would have been difficult for me to leave here [illeg.] till these negotiations are settled moreover it would have greatly embarrassed my position vis à vis Miss Beauclerk not to be able to state that I had some settled prospect of revenue[2] – I have been here at Baden for the last 10 days with a view of urging these matters but wherever lawyers are concerned there is a deal of delay and worry – I found Mamma very well which is a great consolation to me Pauline too looks well & seems very cheerful ; she came to spend a day with me last week. I hope sincerely that you feel yourself well and that your head ache is gone. With me the winter agrees very well ; I am getting alarmingly stout – For the present until something is decided concerning my farming enterprise I shall remain in Baden so please direct to this place.

Believe me my dearest aunt yours most affectionately

        WGC

Baden
Decemb. 12th 1861

Address: No envelope

Unpublished. Text: M.S., Pf. Coll., CL'ANA 0250

---

1 "WCG" initials imprinted on the paper.
2 See CL'ANA 0249.

162 • Wilhelm Gaulis Clairmont to Claire Clairmont

[10 September 1862]

My dearest aunt.

I got your letter of the 1st September a few days ago on my return to Rogendorf.[1] I am sorry to say that my prospects with reference to my intended farm have since then undergone a (most unpleasant change. It has turned out not only that there is no water there near the dwellinghouse (this I knew before) but also that owing to the high position of the house for it does lie on a hill and the peculiarity of the subsoil it is next to impossible to procure water by ordinary pumps or wells – This circumstance together with others, such as the notorious evil and lazy disposition of the inhabitants of the surrounding village and the consequent difficulty in procuring labour than the poorness of the soil decided me to petition government to undo the lease for my intended farm was part of a crown property. I have not as yet obtained the formal assent of government, but as in the absence of water it becomes a matter of dire impossibility for me to settle there I have no doubt that the matter will be arranged. It is bad enough for me as it is for my hopes have been destroyed and I have had a clean loss of £50 in travelling expenses and other preliminary disbursements. You seem to upbraid me for having said nothing about your joining me to live with me – but how could I think you would be inclined to do so – when in a previous letter I alluded to the probability of your joining me you said: you could not afford to come on a mere <u>visit</u> and to stop altogether would not suit you on account of the climate. But I hope yet dearest aunt that your intention of living with me will be realized to be sure there is little hope for this winter because the season is too far advanced but I sincerely hope something will turn up next spring. As to the details you demand concerning the house I now do not write any because the affair is given up – but I may state for your relief that my farm was but <u>too</u> far removed from the fertile plains which have succeeded in place of the previous marshes – you must not trust to any books which have been written on this subject unless quite lately, for this country has undergone a complete change in course of the last 10 years in consequence of most extensive works of regulation of the rivers and drainage of the swamps intervening between them – Count Rogendorf with whom I am now living is only <u>29</u> years of age[2] he is[3] an estate of 3000 acres of which in his fathers time only 500 acres were arable land and even that exposed to inundation – [illeg.] the rest was a vast extent of swamp and morass overgrown with reeds and inhabited only by wild ducks and geese – which my friend as a boy of 17 or 18 years used to shoot in scores close to his house – Now there is not a square rod[4] of the whole 3000 acres but what is ploughed and sown every year and in a like proportion the whole country has been drained and improved – I would not advise your young friend to come here and try his luck in an agricultural enterprise; there is always a hitch to every farm either the soil is an excellent one as {ink blot} the whole of Lower Hungary[5] where good crops will grow even without manuring the land – but then you can get no people to work the land – or in the more mountainous districts where there are lots of people the land is bad. where you have good land and plenty people there is no rain or the distance from market too great. the average [illeg.] rent of land but to which in most cases there are no farmbuildings attached is from 24/s to 12/s. in English money per Austr. acre – the English acre is equal to $^7/_{10}$ of an Austrian acre – consequently an Austr. acre a little short of one and a half Engl. acre – As to Pauline I am sorry you were vexed about her trip to London I assure you it was not a premeditated one she went as far as Berlin with and at the expense of her ladyfriend – her going on to London from there was a mere matter of impulse produced I suppose by the propinquity and attraction of the Exhibition[6] – I quite agree with you that as regards her reputation such solitary trips are not desirable, but you would really wrong her were you to imagine that[7] it was a want of affection for you which caused her to go to London rather than Florence.

Goodbye now my dear aunt. I hope your health is quite restored you write of having had some blood spitting[8] I trust this is {ink blot}

I am perfectly well your most affectionate nephew

WGC

Rogendorf
Gross Becskerek
10th Septemb. 1862

Address: No envelope

Unpublished. Text: M.S., Pf. Coll., CL'ANA 0253

---

1 See CL'ANA 0246.
2 Wilhelm was residing with Count Robert von Rogendorf (1833–1887), son of József von Rogendorf (see CL'ANA 0246).
3 Probably "he has".
4 Archaic. Unit of square measure, 30.25 square yards or 25.29 square meters to a rod.
5 See CL'ANA 0255.
6 The International Exhibition of 1862 was London's second exhibition. The first International Exhibition of 1851, remembered primarily for its Crystal Palace setting, was an enormous financial success. The 1862 Exhibition, housed in South Kensington, was deemed a complete failure.
7 Wilhelm cross-wrote the words that follow.
8 In her letter to Dina Williams Hunt of 31 December 1862, Claire stated that she was not in such good health. She identified her "so many cares for my relations which prey upon my mind and prevent the repose I ought to have" (*CC* II: 595).

163 • Wilhelm Gaulis Clairmont to Claire Clairmont

[27 October 1862]

My dearest aunt. Being absent from Rogendorf at my new farm[1] I got yours of the 17th only today – I was rather vexed to find that Pauline had forestalled me for I had written to her not to tell you about my new prospects – and I myself did not intend to write you of it until the lease were actually signed – This I regret to say is not yet accomplished because they think I got too good a bargain and will not agree to the terms on which I insist and which I knew they must come to because they want money immediately and it is now too late in the season for some one else to think of taking the farm – Today I at last got the intimation so long expected that they would agree to my terms and that the lease would be sent down to me for signature in a few days – so you see that the thing though not quite settled may be looked upon as all but arranged – and now I will proceed to give you all the details concerning the farm it is the property of one Countess Smetov a Hungarian lady by birth who married a Prussian count – she is young tolerably pretty goodhearted but rather giddy and a great flirt – the farm has 385 Austrian acres, which is equal to exactly 550 English acres – the soil is of the very best imaginable and the position favourable as it is [illeg.] 3 Engl. miles distant both from the railway and a navigable Canal leading into the Danube. there are also comparatively speaking plenty hands to be got. Rent is £400 pr.annum lease for 12 years – I have been residing here now for a fortnight and have poked about the farm a great deal and spoke with many of the labourers and peasants and my good opinion has been rather confirmed than otherwise. Of the House, I enclose you a plan which will save me a long description[2] – I think, unless you expect to find a fine mansion that we shall have plenty of room; Dwellingroom No II might consigned to your use – No I as being on the outside and next to the doorway would be more suited for me and No III might be used as Parlour – Of the storeroom we should have to make a spareroom for occasional guests. I am delighted at the idea of your coming dearest aunt I am sure we shall get on famously – the £80 pr. ann. would be quite sufficient only I [illeg.] two things I am doubtful about how you will get on with the servants and what you will do for society? I would not advise your coming before May so that I may have time to get everything ready – You have no occasion to come by Vienna there is a nearer route branching off at Pragerhof[3] going by the beautiful "Platten See"[4] direct to Pest leaving Vienna altogether to the left. By this route you reach Pest almost sooner than you would Vienna by the other way thus saving the whole of the distance from Vienna to Pest. I have no time now to refer to my book about expense of journey but will do so in my next letter – Your plan of buying land here you will find to turn out very good – we shall also have the most splendid opportunities for purchasing for adjoining my farm there is a settlement of Croatian Noblemen, a whole village of them who have all lived so far above their income that they are head over ears in debt and obliged to sell off land year by year to keep themselves afloat – They have also very fine farmhouses with orchards gardens and all the necessary outbuildings which are often sold at a mere trifle because the Jews and moneylenders who are their only recourse dont like to take buildings as a security because they are not so readily sublet as land. I had made up my mind long before the arrival of your letter to invest in this manner the £1000 I have in the houses as soon as these are sold. – and as I firmly hope to save another £1000 during the course of my 12 years lease I should have a nice little property to start on at the expiration of it – But if you join we shall buy the more the cheaper and readier there is such a scarcity of ready money in this part of the world that people will do almost anything for a few hundred Pounds cash – I have not yet had any application from any of your friends concerning land – if I do I shall attend to it – I shall not go to Meclenburgh.[5] I had a letter from old Mr. Tooth[6] to whom I wrote that the travelling Expenses from here to Meclenburgh and back would be something considerable in consequence of which he said he would not trouble me – the winters here are uncertain some are severe and some mild – but they are much milder than Austrian winter which may be gathered from the fact that rough ploughing is carried on all through the winter here and the commoner kinds of cattle and sheep remain day and night in the open air all through the winter. Goodbye dearest aunt – remember all is not settled yet – but as soon as ever I have the lease in my hands I shall write again

      yours affectionately
        WC

Bobda
Octob. 27th 1862.
Direct[7]
W.G.C. Bobda Gyertyámos/in Banat.
Bobda is the name of the farm. the dwelling house is in the village of Bobda –

Address: No envelope

Unpublished. Text: M.S., Pf. Coll., CL'ANA 0254

---

1 Wilhelm's farm was in Bobda, a town in western Romania some 90 kilometers north-east of Großbetschkerek. Today, Bobda is part of the commune of Cenei which is located in Timiș County, Romania. Bobda and Cenei are both villages in the commune ("Cenei". Web. 10 May 2016. http://www.cenei.ro/). The village of Cenei was known as Csene in Hungarian.
2 Wilhelm enclosed a hand-drawn sketch of his home in Bobda. It shows the dimensions of the three "dwelling" rooms (the larger of the two each measured 29 feet by 25 feet and contained "stoves"), the kitchen with the hearth, the servant's room which had a stove, a "storeroom," and the water closet. Wilhelm added the following words next to the storeroom: "may be converted into a stable or dwellingroom". Wilhelm recorded on the plan: "the dimensions of each room are given in English feet. Where the lines are interrupted it signifies a door where this is: __ a window. 0 Well". He drew a small rectangular shape for each window and a double zero for the well. He also showed the entrance to the cellar, the doorways, the village streets, and the courtyard. He described a verandah which was "covered on top open on sides".

3 Known today as Pragersko, the town is located in Slovenia. The 1857 Vienna-Trieste mainline included Pragersko as a stop. A connecting line to Budapest via Lake Balaton (Plattensee) was built in 1860 (Bunijevac, Helena. "The First Rail-Line in Croatia". Web. 21 January 2015. http://www.railfaneurope.net/ric/Medjimurje.htm).
4 German term (Plattensee) for Lake Balaton in Hungary. Major towns around Lake Balaton include Keszthely (location of the Festetics Palace, see note 3, CL'ANA 0246) and Siófok. Lake Balaton is Europe's "largest thermal lake" ("Lake Balaton". Web. 23 May 2015. http://www.budapest.com/hungary/lake_balaton.en.html).
5 Region in Northern Germany.
6 Either Robert or Frederick Tooth. See CL'ANA 0089 and CL'ANA 0255.
7 Wilhelm wrote these words on the rear of the sketch.

164 • Wilhelm Gaulis Clairmont to Claire Clairmont

[29–30 December 1862]

My dearest Aunt.[1] I received 2 letters from you since my last to you. the latter of the two was dated the 20 Oct. and was directed to Baden where I got it soon after my arrival which took place about a week ago. Mamma and Pauline I found in tolerable health and spirits – the first even in very good spirits as the houses are now prospering very well and even promising to do better the Xmas days Plin[2] came out to Baden and so we formed a very happy contented trio – Mis[illeg.][3] thanks you very much for your kind mention of her and your new years wishes all of which she entertains for you in like manner you may think that we talked a great deal of you in connection with our plans for the future – If but your health will mend – I am very uneasy about it and hope you will give more favorable reports in you next – Pauline has made up her mind to join us at Bobda and so I am sure that all will go well there if we can but make the money question meet satisfactorily – the principal thing now is to arrange about your boxes and also about your journey – I was in Vienna yesterday and made enquiries – the price of goods from Trieste to Gyertyamos[4] by rail I cannot ascertain here but have written to Trieste about to ascertain and the price of loading from the Danube to Temesvar I could not ascertain because the office of the Steamboat agency was closed but will ascertain tomorrow and enclose you a postscript before I post this letter – As to your boxes I would give you the advice to bring nothing but what is either essential to your comfort or what is easily packed for we have now experienced so often that the cases are opened and robbed at the customs[5] a happy new year.[6] houses that I would strongly urge you to send ~~nothing~~ as few things as possible – the looking glass for instance; I would most decidedly not send, for there is the expence of its carriage and getting packed and the risk of its being stolen or broken besides it would be much more economical to buy one here.

I[7] must also tell you that owing to the increasing stability of the Austrian Government the funds and exchange have risen so much that we now only gain 17 percent in English money instead of as before 25% that is to say £10 which before made 125f now is[8] worth only 117f and very likely the rate of exchange will sink even lower. – I have thought about the Brougham you want me to buy – It will be much better to take a Calesch[9] because a Brougham is more dangerous with regards to upsetting when the roads are bad – it would cost at least 400f which is £35 that is of course[10] an old one not a new one. this is a heavy expense which I cannot bear myself more especially as I already have a gig for my own use – About bedding furniture and all the rest I have already talked and consulted largely with Pauline and Mamma and I hope we shall manage to do it pretty cheaply – Goodbye for the present

Yours affectionate
WGC

Baden 29th Decemb.

P.S. I have now been to the office of the Steamboat agency the Austrian hundred weight will cost from Galaz to Temesvar 5 shillings Engl money freight and shipping Expenses will be about 9d pr. [illeg.] or 1/- say 6f altogether; the goods must be directed to the Agency of the [illeg.] First Priviledged Austrian Danube Steamboat Company at Galaz[11] to whom I will give all further directions – the Goods can be forwarded on to me at Temesvár without being opened any where for douane[12] purposes but at Temesvár where I can be present myself – nor will there be anything to pay but at Temesvar on receipt of the goods – but the steamboats to do not commence plying on the Lowerdanube[13] till the 1st of March – As soon as I get my answer from Triest[14] I shall let you know – and we shall then judge which is best I shall know the freight from Triest or from Galaz to Temesvar and you must ascertain the freight from Florence to Triest and to Galaz and by putting the two together we shall find which is cheapest. Nevertheless I cant warn you sufficiently to send as little as possible for one is robbed dreadfully and the expense is heavy. I write this from Paulines home in Vienna who sends you her best love she would add a few lines but there is no time

your affectionate
nephew WGC

Vienna
Decemb. 30th 1862

Address: La Signora [illeg.]/ Casa Lombardi No. {tear} /
Via Santa Caterina/ Florence
Rear postmark: FIRENZE; [illeg.]

Unpublished. Text: M.S., Pf. Coll., CL'ANA 0256

---

1 The initials "AC" are imprinted at the top center of the page.
2 Pauline was also known as Plin. In "Miss Tina and Miss Plin," Stocking explains that Herbert Huscher recorded in a letter that "in the family she was usually referred to as 'die Ampel' (i.e. a hanging lamp), a further contraction of 'Aunt Plin'" (p. 383, note 4).
3 See CL'ANA 0258. The word appears to be "Missel," and was probably a term of affection for Antonia.
4 For Trieste, see note 4, CL'ANA 0252. Gyertyámos was the Hungarian name for Cărpiniș, a Banat village in Timiș County, Romania, situated 28 kilometers from Timișoara. Bobda is located 12 kilometers from Cărpiniș.
5 Continued cross-writing on the first page of the letter.
6 Written above the remainder of the paragraph.
7 Cross-writing beginning on page 2.
8 Cross-writing beginning on page 3.
9 "Calèche," French for a two-wheeled or four-wheeled horse-drawn cart. A brougham was a four-wheeled carriage with an enclosed body.

10 Cross-writing beginning on page 4.
11 In 1829, John Andrews and Joseph Pritchard started the "First Austrian Danube Steam-Navigation Company" (Henry Hajnal, *The Danube* [The Hague: Martinus Nijhoff, 1920], pp. 123–5). Following the initial trip from Vienna to Pest in 1830, steamboats regularly plied the waters of the Danube. The German name, Galatz, refers to the city of Galați in Eastern Romania, a port city on the Danube. Galați is located 1,504 kilometers east of Trieste and 692 kilometers from Timișoara/Temesvár.
12 French for "custom".
13 Today, the Lower Danube Euroregion consists of areas in eastern Romania, Moldavia, and the Ukraine. Galați (Galatz) plays an important role in the Lower Danube Euroregion.
14 German spelling for Trieste.

165 • Pauline Clairmont to Claire Clairmont

[17 March c. 1863]
Bobda March 17.[1]

Dearest Aunt

I had hoped that the reasons I gave you for my reluctance in writing on the subject mentioned in my last would have proved satisfactory be assured that I only wished to avoid giving you pain, & foreseeing that we could not discuss our (Willy & my) present circumstances without afflicting you I tried to evade it, feeling it to be quite useless, as it was out of your power to do any thing for us. Your letter dated 10th inst is before me, & Willy is writing to you now to answer the important question concerning his own money – about mine I have already told you. I have also a piece of good news to tell you id. I received my dividend of 11£5. this month quite unexpectedly copper having much risen in price & the company having consequently an overplus on 8000£. there was a meeting to choose a new directors & I was asked to attend or send a proxy, but I of course declined & wrote to the Head manager or chairman Sir H. Schneider[2] & am now in possession of my cheque which is really a blessing as I can amply provide for my personal wants & get many little things wanted in the house without troubling poor W. for every farthing. I asked him if he wished me to sell those shares – but he said no because if we had a bad year again that sum would not save us & I should be deprived of every thing & if we had a good year he would not want it.

If you receive my letters unstamped somebody must have taken the stamps off. Ever since my return from Australia & when you first went to Florence I put the same amount in value of stamps on your my letters as you put on yours which was 15xr[3] that was before the italian war – I had to pay up your letters the same as you paid up mine then you wrote to me to put 25xr on my letters as in consequence of a new postal arrangement the letters going out or or coming to Austria could be paid the whole way – Since that time I have always put 25xr on my letters not wishing to put you to any expense. I cannot remember if I stamped my letters to you before going to Australia or before coming to England but as postage stamps have not been in use very long in Austria it is just possible that the letters were thrown into the box by the servant & the money pocketed.

I hope you are better now, & am very sorry my letter agitated you I should never say one word about our misfortune to you as I know it must grieve you, & am was only against my will forced to speak about it. I am a sinful & wicked creature in the eyes of the Lord[4] – & he has seen fit to punish me – but Willy is so noble minded so pure & good that it grieves me more than my own death to see him suffer.

Spring must be advancing now & that will give you new strength & health please remember me to Lady S.[5] & dear Mme Paparoni & believe me your very affte

Pauline

Address: La Signora Clairmont/ 14 Lung'arno delle/Grazie Florenz.[6]
Front postmark: [illeg.]. AUS. S<u>m</u>
Rear postmark: FIRENZE; [illeg.]

Unpublished. Text: M.S., Pf. Coll., CL'ANA 0208

---

1 Pauline probably wrote this letter in 1863, the year she came to live on Wilhelm's farm. She remained at Bobda when she found herself pregnant, as her Viennese community would have disdained her condition. Pauline never named the father of her child in her letters but Gittings and Manton speculate that he was American (p. 230). Stocking explains that Pauline had been involved in a relationship in Vienna with someone called "Adolphe L" and that Pauline later in her journal called her daughter "a child of 'free America'" (*CC* II: 621). According to Stocking (who in 1949 read Pauline's now-lost journal from 1864), after Georgina's birth in 1864, Pauline sent the child to live with Countess Károlyi in Rakičan, Hungary (see "Miss Tina and Miss Plin," p. 377). Pauline would visit her daughter a few times a year until 1871 when she removed the child from the Countess's care and took her to live in Florence with Claire. The journals that cover this period in Pauline's life are missing. In "Miss Tina and Miss Plin," Stocking informs her readers that she had seen Pauline's journals during a visit to Walter Clairmont in 1949. However, by 1967 when Stocking visited Mary Claire Bally-Clairmont, some of the journals (volumes xi to xv) were missing: "It may be that Dr. Clairmont expressed his distaste at the 'rubbish' by destroying them" ("Miss Tina and Miss Plin," p. 374). Among the lost volumes was Volume xi, from 1859 to 1866, in which Pauline records the birth of Georgina. Similarly, Volume xv, with its description of Georgina as a "child of 'free America'" is also missing. Thus, Stocking's account from notes she made when she viewed the journals in 1949 is the strongest indication of Georgina's parentage that survives.
2 Henry Schneider (1839–1887) was the son of John Schneider who owned the London house of John Schneider and Company, which had mining interests in Britain and South America. In 1838, Henry Schneider became a director of the Anglo-Mexican Mining Association and later its chairman in 1851. In 1851, Schneider also became a director of the English and Australian Copper Company. In 1852, he became a director of the Port Phillip and Colonial Gold Mining Company (John Woodland, *Money Pits: British Mining Companies and the Californian and Australian Gold Rushes of the 1850s* [Burlington: Ashgate, 2014], pp. 25–8).
3 Abbreviation for Kreuzer.
4 Pauline was unmarried and her journal records her sexual affairs; doubtless she refers to those here.
5 Lady Sussex Lennox. See 0247. Mrs. Paparoni was probably Antonia's landlady. See CL'ANA 0321.
6 German for the city of Florence.

166 • Wilhelm Gaulis Clairmont to Claire Clairmont

[9 April 1863]

My dearest aunt

This minute I got your letter of the 2nd April which I answer now without a minutes delay – The name of the station near which I live is <u>Gyertyámos</u>.[1] If you will let me know before hand I shall await you at Gyertyamos with a conveyance – the distance is not above 3 or 3 ½ <u>English</u> miles – By going 10 hours a day pr. rail it will take you about 5 days to come from Florence to Bobda – I think if you take with you £25 you will have plenty but to make sure and as Paulines journey also is to be paid for I would advise you to take with you £<u>35</u>. Do start as soon as you can and do not allow anything to unsettle your mind I have written to Pauline to bully Mrs. M. and on no account to yield – there is also a telegraphic wire to Gyertyámos so that when Pauline is with you you can send me a telegraphic message from <u>Pest</u> to say ~~when~~ by what train I am to expect you I have no time to write more

your affectionate nephew
WGC

Bobda
9th April 1863.

Address: No envelope

Unpublished. Text: M.S., Pf. Coll., CL'ANA 0257

---

1 Wilhelm underestimated the distance when he noted that the station was some 3.5 miles from his farm. Bobda is located 12 kilometers from Gyertyámos.

28 MARCH 1861–24 DECEMBER 1889

167 • Wilhelm Gaulis Clairmont to Claire Clairmont

[29 June 1863]

My dear aunt.[1]

Although I have until this moment been prevented from ~~send~~ writing to you having been absent from home ever since my arrival here, I did not fail to claim your boxes immediately on my return and got them Keys and all safely locked up in my ~~box~~. store. the amount I paid for their freight & carriage was

	46 fl. 78 kr.
postage	30 "
total.	47f 8 kr.

which sum please to send me per[2] post. I have not even had time to open the case with pictures so cant say whether they are safe. there are 3 boxes besides the pictures – the heat here is intense and of course not a drop of rain lately – the few showers we had during my absence sufficed to yield me some 6 loads of hay so that my own horses at least are now safe from starvation through the winter – but the peasants horses are so weak and reduced from starvation that one of them died while fetching in the hay today – the distress in the whole county is so great that a general meeting of the magnates[3] and large landed proprietors was convoked and held yesterday to consult as to means for averting this dreadful famine many peasants have even now nothing to eat and how they can live through the winter is a mystery to me. I shall endeavour to get away so as not to be a witness to all this misery – Goodbye now dearest aunt

yours affectionately
WGC

Bobda
June 29th 1863.

As there are no Postoffice orders in Austria money letters must be taken to the postoffice unsealed. so that the post official can see the money put in – ~~the~~ for which you get a receipt the letter is then sealed both with the official and your own seal which you must for that purpose take with you to the postoffice[4]

Meine liebste Mutter Ich hätte dir schon geschrie ben, doch war ich seit meiner Ankunft hier immer abwesend. Ich habe auch nichts neues zu melden, als daß die während meiner Abwesenheit gefalle nen Regen, trotz der in den letzten Wochen wieder eingetretenen Dürre doch meine Situation soweit gebessert haben, daß ich 8 Fuhren Heu bekommen habe – die Weitzen ernte fängt morgen an geht alles enorm gut so kann ich doch vielleicht 50 oder 60 Sach sechsaen, Haver wird sich besser gestalten und Kukrautz kann, wenn es noch Regen giebt sogar noch ziemlich gut warden Gestern war ich auf den 3 Stunden von hier entfernten Markt um meine Pferde zu verkaufen ~~aber die~~ weil eines davon manch mahl krum wird – allein die Geldnoth ist so groß daß kein einzigen Käufer dagegen ab

3000 Pferde zum Verkaufe da waren. Die [illeg.] ist sehr brav und fleißig – hat inzwischen schöne Vorhänge an die fenster und alles sehr nett gemacht. Heute macht sie Weichsel Eingesottenes von unseren Weichseln aus den [illeg.]itras. sie steht alle Tage um 6 Uhr und auch früher auf ohne zu Murren sie hat mir auch einver standen, daß ihr das Rauchen jetzt auf einmahl nicht mehr schmeckt. Gräfin Schenatton und Frau von [illeg.] sind nun beide in Bobda außerdem haben wir in Cseney einige netten Bekantschaften gemacht welches nur ¼ Stunde von hier zu fahren ist, allein es ist so heiß daß man sich wirklich nicht aus dem Hause heraus wagt. Nun adiß süßes Missel
dein aufrichtiger Sohn
WGC

Bobda
Juni 29th 1863

Translation (German transcription and English translation provided by Ann Sherwin):

My dearest Mother

I would have written you already, but since my arrival here, I was always absent. I also don't have anything new to report, except that the rains that fell during my absence, despite the drought that returned in the last few weeks, improved my situation to the extent that I got 8 loads of hay. The wheat harvest starts tomorrow, and if all goes tremendously well, I can perhaps sow 50 or 60 sacks [illeg.]. Oats will grow better, and if there's more rain, even the cowherb could turn out fairly good. Yesterday I was at the market, three hours from here, to sell my horses ~~but the~~ because one of them gets buckled sometimes, but the money shortage is so bad that not a single buyer was there, though there were over 3000 horses for sale. [illeg.] is very dutiful and diligent. In the meantime, she has hung beautiful curtains at the windows and made everything very nice. Today she is making sour cherry preserves from our cherries in the [illeg.]. She gets up every day at 6 o'clock or even earlier without complaining. She also admitted to me that smoking has suddenly lost its appeal for her. Countess Schenatton[5] and Mrs. von [illeg.] are both in Bobda now. In addition, we got to know some nice people in Cseney, which is only a fifteen-minute drive from here. But it is so hot that we really don't venture outside the house. Now goodbye, sweet Missel.[6]
Your faithful son,
WGC

Bobda
June 29th 1863

Address: M[rs] Clairmont/ 492 ~~Baden/Wien.~~/partita per[7]/Venezia[8] poste rest
Rear postmark: GYERTYAMOS/[illeg.]; 9–11 Fr./ WIEN/ [illeg.]

28 MARCH 1861–24 DECEMBER 1889

Unpublished. Text: M.S., Pf. Coll., CL'ANA 0258

---

1 Wilhelm's initials, "WGC," are imprinted on the first page.
2 There is a blank space in the letter corresponding to the imprint from the first page.
3 See CL'ANA 0247.
4 The word "post office" is written on the first page of the letter and is surrounded by the second half of a bracket.
5 Unidentified.
6 See CL'ANA 0256.
7 Italian for "departed for".
8 Gittings and Manton believe that Claire traveled to Venice with Lady Sussex Lennox in 1863 (p. 224).

168 • Pauline Clairmont and Wilhelm Clairmont to Claire Clairmont

Bobda July 11. [1863]

My dear Aunt

This morning I received Mama's letter saying you had gone to Venice & wished to know if I was willing to come & stay with you, giving a few lessons at the same time. But all that she says seems very vague – you do not seem decided as to your future movements & so it is difficult for me to give a decided answer. For the present I have no money to pay my journey & will not have any till the month of October when my coupons come due – but those 30 fl will not pay my journey from here to Venice which is 70 fl (or nearly) however I could sell one of my trinkets if I was certain of then finding a home with you that is board & lodging leaving me to provide for my dress, washing & other personal expenses – I have 70 fl per annum from my savings which is quite sufficient for my dress at present as I have plenty of clothes to last me the winter. If I was certain of staying with you the whole winter without expense of board & lodging I should be very glad to come & I think it would be a <u>mutual advantage</u> as I am very fond of Venice & have some kind friends there who would be sure to help me

Of course you cannot stay all by yourself without Friends or relations at Venice if therefore you will be good enough to let me know your intentions, I shall be able to give you an answer.

Willy is very well & so am I & hope you are better than you were at Baden.

With kind love to Lady Sussex[1]

believe me your aff^{te} niece

Pauline.

My dear aunt.[2] Immediately on my return here I wrote to you and Mamma under <u>one</u> cover from Mamma's last letter I perceive this letter never reached her nor you – I shall therefore repeat what I said in it – the boxes are safely stored here. I had to pay 46 florins 78 xr. which together with 30 xr. for postage makes in a round sum 47 florins /:fortyseven florins:/ which amount please send me as soon as possible – as there are particular regulations at the austrian postoffice for transmission of money too long to detail here you had better enquire after them and send the money in accordance with them – the keys of course arrived together with the boxes sealed up in a parcel – the boxes have not been opened by me and seem to all outward appearance all right – the package with pictures I opened – the pictures were packed very badly the screws were not long enough and the frame of the smaller picture /:that yourself :/ kept knocking against that of the large portrait so that the latter's frame was damaged considerably – Lady Sussex's portrait is uninjured glass and all – I am very busy now with our wretched harvest therefore cannot write more – I hope the journey in July did not disagree with you

yours affectionately
W. Clairmont[3][illeg.]

Bobda
[illeg.] Cseney Banat.⁴
July 12ᵗʰ 1863.

Address: Mrs. Clairmont/ Poste restant/ Venedig.⁵
Rear postmark: Illegible

Unpublished. Text: M.S., Pf. Coll., CL'ANA 0204

---

1 See CL'ANA 0247 and CL'ANA 0258.
2 Both these letters were written on the same piece of paper. Pauline's was written on the first two pages, followed by Wilhelm's on the last two.
3 Wilhelm ended his signature with an illegible word which might read "Esquire".
4 Cseney is the Hungarian name for Cenei in Romania. Cenei commune contains the villages of Bobda and Cenei. Bobda is located 4.3 kilometers north-west of Cenei.
5 German for Venice.

169 • Wilhelm Gaulis Clairmont to Claire Clairmont

[17 July 1863]

My dear aunt.

I have time only to scratch off a very few lines to you to inform you of the safe arrival of your letter enclosing the [illeg.] 48f. for which many thanks – the pictures are unpacked & hung up in my room the boxes are in my store – as we have not had any rain yet you need entertain no apprehensions of anything being spoilt by the damp – Goodbye dear aunt compts to Lady Lennox[1] – yours affectly.

WGC

Bobda
July 17th 1863.[2]

Pauline sends her love. she wrote you on the 26th June did you get her letter?[3]

Address: Mrs. Clairmont/Poste restante/Venedig.
Rear postmark: GYERTYAMOS/23/7

Unpublished. Text: M.S., Pf. Coll., CL'ANA 0259

---

1 Lady Sussex Lennox.
2 The back of the envelope has a seal with the initials "WC" imprinted.
3 This last line was written on the back of the final page of this letter.

170 • Pauline Clairmont and Wilhelm Clairmont to Claire Clairmont

Bobda Nov. 15.[1] [1863]

My dearest Aunt – Two letters of yours lie unanswered before me – one Octb 19th & the last Nov. 9th & should have answered the first long ago only you said I need not write directly in a month's time would do. I now hasten to tell you that all the desired inquiries were made concerning the letters at the Post office of Cseney, Gyertyamos & Temesvar [2]– one black edged letter came after much delay being very vaguely & awkwardly directed which Willy enclosed in one of his directed to you the moment we knew you were at Florence – the other one we desired the Postmaster to return – those were all the letters that came for you.

The next important subject is about Willy that is his food. You must know that I have become a tolerable cook & my dinners are eatable c'est beaucoup dire – when you come to think that I do it all by intuition a regular self-taught genius. We have a substantial breakfast – he takes coffee a good plate of meat either cold fowl or goose or cold pie or beafsteak or hash with a sufficient quantity of bread & butter – we like our own bread now – so we are sure of having sound good flower & the best yeast used – at one we dine 3 courses very good soup I take care to make – meat with vegetables & sauce & a sweet pudding at 7 we have tea or supper as you may call it if he has been out on the fields all day long exercise and air give him an extra appetite he takes meat again but generally only one dish either macaroni or tea cakes or fried fish if we can get it At dinner we have very good Hungarian wine & now that the weather is cooler he will get some beer. He is looking very well & has got neither unduly stout nor the contrary – only his hair is getting very silvery owing to the endless troubles this unblessed country gives him – he says if next year is like this he will shoot himself – what else can he do? As it is we are reduced to the meanest work already – he trudges on foot all day long not the lowest of his servants in Australia walked so much – & I do all the common housework I cook sweep the rooms I iron all the linen mend all the clothes – last week I had 18 dozen to iron – we could not get any water & could consequently not wash – but saddest of all is that I have no Piano & shall not be able to get one for a very long time[3] – indeed everything that is beautiful & above everyday labour have we been obliged to give up – not only every elegance but many comforts of life. I consider my residence in this place & under these circumstances a punishment for not having more energetically opposed Willy's remaining in Europe. I foresaw it all as plain as the reality now lies before me and even said so, but in a timid cowardly manner & now I consider it my duty to do whatever lies in my power to lessen his misery – I must say for myself that there is no selfishness in me – if I dont care for a person I would never accept a sacrifice from them, but if I love a person there is no sacrifice that I would not joyfully perform for them – I do not say all this dear Aunt to reproach either you or Mama for having brought us into such misery & want – I sincerely believe that you both meant well, so also Willy's other friends – but you were made the unhappy instruments in the hands of

Providence. I am a thoro' fatalist which I consider a purely Christian Doctrine – & forgive all those who trust us into suffering & there is no ill will in my heart against any of you – I shall only be glad when poor Willy & I can lay our heads in the cool grave – pray for us that we may not be buried in this desolate place – but perhaps we shall share our poor Father's fate & be buried where we suffered most.

the Island of New Zealand I must tell you where the revolution took place is not the one Willy was going to – there are as you know two islands one inhabited by blacks with the capital Auckland the other one inhabited by Europeans who when they took possession of the island drove all the natives over to the other island. So you see that W. would be out of all danger & most likely a rich man by this time.[4] Poor fellow here – in Europe he will never be able to marry he will never know the joys of a wife & a home & children to cheer his old days.

Forgive me dear Aunt for this dwelling upon our own troubles – but it is very painful to see such a generous & stout heart dropping – you & Mama are far away – you have had your way in keeping him here – but you do not witness the daily anxiety that lies like a heavy cloud upon his forehead & turned his black locks to grey that has driven the cheerful smile & merry laugh from his lips –

Miss Chapman[5] was no doubt sorry to die & so I am sorry for her – what you say about the pulse I will attend to – as W. is really not so strong as he looks & I am afraid overworks himself – having no horse to ride & being obliged to be on the fields before daybreak & then comes home so tired & can scarcely muster strength to lift his head up to drink a cup of tea. I have begged of him to buy a common cart horse for 20£ only to ride out on the Puszta[6] but he wont and says I will deny myself everything & slave on as long as I can – if the smash[7] comes next year nobody shall say I spent my money on myself instead of on the farm.

His erruption is nearly quite gone Gastein[8] did him much good but of course he could not dream of going again next year.

One thing I should like to ask of you – to let me sell the copper shares – I have had no dividend for 18 month it is as good as lost to me – & if I had the capital it would pay Willy's rent for one year & he would give me the same interest as they did in former times.

Good night dear Aunt – give my love to dear Marianna[9] & Lady Sussex & believe me your very affte

      Pauline.

My dearest aunt[10] I was quite glad to see your handwriting again for although your letter is directed to Pauline this is all the same as far as my anxiety went to hear from you again – first of all about the letters – I was at Cseney[11] – it is a small country office not dispatching more than from 15 to 20 letters pr. diem as for unclaimed letters or any of the other complications of a large town post office they never occur here On the contrary the postmaster being naturally of an inquisitive disposition and having next to nothing to do is of an remembers for a week to come every letter especially foreign ones passing through his hands – I myself have looked through the ½ dozen pigeonholes there are in his office and am prepared to state there are none of your letters here – so whatever became of them I know not – as to NewZealand I am very sorry that things look so bad there – Having lived in the bush so long I can fancy what it is to have to contend with such an enemy in addition to all the difficulties natural to the position – I really am very glad that I escaped this fate although I believe that this horrid war is carried on in another Island than the one I was going to I was going to the Southern Island where there are hardly any natives at all[12] – It is very unpleasant for us to be cut off from all English news, but Plin and I have determined to subscribe to an English weekly paper as soon as our finances prosper a little more. On this subject viz. finances I have not much good news to give you – the year has been so bad that I was obliged not only to beg for the ensuing year ~~not only~~ what we consume ourselves but also what I want to issue to the men the hay and corn wanted for the horses and oxen for next winter and the whole of wheat barley oats maize etz. required for seed – Under these circumstances you may well conceive that I have all expenses and no income, and it is all I shall be able to manage with the greatest prudence to weather the storm till next harvest – if this too turns out bad I am of course lost, but if it turns out well I may be yet recompensed for all the serious expense I have had – I am glad to hear that Ada[13] has at length come into her property but I do not think it was very sensible of her to change her name I am very sorry to hear of Mr. Wright's death but I do not know whether this is the one I knew as young Denny Wright – or his father who I believe was Captain Wright? As to Mama we have little news to give you of her she writes us very rarely once every 6 or 7 weeks, but she is well in health and enjoys the prospect of a nice cool winter – I connection with the chapter on finances[14]

I[15] forgot to mention to you that scarcity of the circulating medium[16] has determined me to decide on giving up my idea of going to Vienna or Baden for the winter but Plin and I shall spend all the winter here Goodbye dearest aunt give my compts to Lady Sussex and believe me yours affectly
WGClairmont

Bobda Cseney
Novbr: 15th 1863.

Address: La Signora Clairmont/ 14 Lungo' Arno delle Grazie/ Florence.
Front postmark: BOLLO INSUFFICIENT{tear}[17]; DEB.AUS.S^M
Rear postmark: GYERTYA[illeg.]/ [illeg.]

Unpublished. Text: M.S., Pf. Coll., CL'ANA 0205

---

[1] This letter, and the one that followed from Wilhelm, were both enclosed in the same envelope and have the same record number, CL'ANA 0205.

2 Temesvár is the Hungarian name for Timișoara, a city in Romania today. The German name was Temeswar.
3 See the introduction to The Australian Sojourn on the piano at Brucedale. See also CL'ANA 0209 and CL'ANA 0210.
4 South Island and North Island are the two largest of the over 600 islands that make up New Zealand. The cities of Auckland and Wellington are located on the North Island while Christchurch is the largest city on the South Island. The original inhabitants of New Zealand are known as Māori. (*The Encyclopedia of New Zealand*. Web. 23 May 2015. http://www.teara.govt.nz).
5 Unidentified.
6 Hungarian for "plain".
7 "Financial ruin".
8 Gastein, also known as Bad Gastein, is a spa town in Austria famous for its thermal springs. See CL'ANA 0401.
9 Possibly Marianna Hammond (see CL'ANA 0041).
10 The date of this letter follows after Wilhelm's signature line.
11 See CL'ANA 0204.
12 Neville Ritchie explains that British and colonial forces fought land wars against Māori tribesmen in New Zealand between 1845 and 1872. In the Waikato War of 1863–4, for example, over 12,000 British troops took action against no more than "about 2000 men at any one time" in what was "a well orchestrated and deliberate land grab" ("The Waikato War of 1863–64". Department of Conservation, pp. 5, 38. 2007. Web. 1 November 2015. http://www.doc.govt.nz/documents/conservation/historic/by-region/waikato/waikato-war-of-1863-64.pdf).
13 Ramsbottom. See CL'ANA 0191.
14 Wilhelm cross-wrote the remainder of this letter.
15 Wilhelm cross-wrote this last paragraph on the first page of the letter.
16 A medium of payment, such as bank notes.
17 Italian for "insufficient stamp".

171 • Antonia Clairmont to Claire Clairmont

Baden 26th dec.
492. 1863

My dear Claire.[1]

I put off answering yours of the 31ᵗ of August where you tell me of your safe arrival at Florence, at which I felt very glad – with occassionall[2] twists of conscience till we are suddenly arrived at the conclusion of the year; take my best wishes for the coming one, I hope you will spend it in good health in the fine climate you love so much and that the winter is kind to you – we have a very one[3], no trace as yet of snow nor hardly of frost – but are by no means glad of it. if it goes on so like last year poor W. will be ruined this is the only grief we have the children could not come up to see me [illeg.] for economy's sake, and also to watch his property; which would be exposed by his absence – it is a great trial such a grand loss the first year! at Baden every thing goes as usual. Colonel Becker lives now at my house and his poor Sister having died – she was ten years older than he – so his niece will come and keep his house for him – Mr Carl and my other friends came for a little chat, but never in the evening for I must keep very quiet and never go out– so my health is pretty well, only the care for dear W. hurts me! all my friends, chiefly Mrs Fallenböck – Becker and Carl[4] send their best compliments and wishes for the season – and I take the liberty to add my likeness – and beg you will also send yours. at the receipt of your last I went directly to the post office to inquire for letters but they said you had already given your direction; where to sent the letters that might arrive but there were none. Have you seen the niece of I. F. Smith?[5] tell her his works are so much read in translation – you can never get one at the library if I only knew the English titles. I have so little opportunity now to get English books I must be glad to get translations – good bye dear Claire and write to me soon – What a blessing you did not go to Bobda, what a time of misery and care you would have had of it! ever

yours affect. A.C.

Address: Mrs Clairmont/ <u>Florence.</u>/3 Via Santa Catarina/ Piazza del' Indipendenza.[6]
Rear postmark: [illeg.]

Unpublished. Text: M.S., Pf. Coll., CL'ANA 0421, Box 1, bundle a, numbers 8–10

---

1 Imprint of raised initials "AC" at the top center of the first page.
2 Spelled as such.
3 Correct in original.
4 All unidentified.
5 Possibly the poet, Horace Smith (1779–1849). Smith also wrote a number of novels, such as *The Tor Hill*, *Brambletye House*, and *Zillah*.
6 Antonia wrote the actual street address on the left side of the envelope.

172 • Wilhelm Gaulis Clairmont to Claire Clairmont

[17 March 1864]

My dear aunt. I perceive from your last to Pauline that you are desirous of learning something respecting the state of my finances. I gathered from sundry remarks in your last few letters that you are under entirely erroneous impressions with refference to two points 1st the amount of capital required to stock a farm either here or in England or any where else – secondly some suspicion that has beset you that I did not go to work with sufficient economy – It is needless to say that I have no sort of secret from you in this matter; on the contrary were you a stranger and not my aunt I should still consider that the generous assistance which you gave me towards commencing my farm enterprise would entitle you to an enquiry as to how I had spent my tin[1] so as to enable you to judge how far your gift had been well or ill deserved and applied by its recipient – This I mean would be my sentiment towards any stranger who had given me £500 in the way you did – towards you of course both my inclination and obligation to give you any information you desire is infinitely stronger – As it is next to impossible to be clear in any matter of accounts without going actually into figures I must trouble you to follow me through the subjoined columns – A careful perusal of the same will enlighten you not only as to what was my original capital and how it was spent, but also what is the present state of my cashbox and by what means I covered my hitherto deficiencies – first of all you must go through the detached account giving you the expenditure of my 1st farming year – it is an extract of my balance sheet and perfectly correct – most of the items contained in this act. you will not be able to judge of; but those which do come within the scope of your experience – I feel confi such as household expenses – my personal expenses inclus. trip to Gastein[2] which alone cost 300f – then the furnishing of our house and kitchen I feel confident you will allow to be as moderate and economical as possible – I will now give you a resumé of my whole finances commencing with the Receipts–:

Original stock at starting	15.000f
Interest derived from same	1.500
proceeds of my farm 1st year /:330:/	330.44
Borrowed from Pauline 1600f Oblig.	1.070.
Dto. Mama 200f.	130
Total	18.030f44

I now come to the Disbursements showing how this money was spent:

Expenses from my first arrival in Europe till 1st of Octob. 1862 on settling at Bobda	1000f.
Expenses of my first farming year as pr. account [illeg.]	10.665.81
rent of farm for second year[3] 1863 to 1864	4000.

Expenses of second year from 1st Octob. 1863 till this moment expenses not yet drafted under separate heads because accounts not yet balanced	2.304.63
Cash in hand	60.
Total	18.030f44xr[4]

From this account you will see that my original stock together with the interest thereon was all consumed and that I have been hitherto obliged to borrow the sums stated from Mama and Pauline – you will also see that I have now not more than 60f cash in hand – Mama has however promised to send me another obligation of 500f. which is equal to about 300f ready money with which assistance I must struggle on the best way I can till the first receipts come in from my farm – I am glad to say that this fearful drought is at least at an end – we have had very copious rains – the winter crops are looking very promising and everybody is looking forward with hope and expectation to the next year – the only drawback is that it will be such a long time yet till the produce can be harvested and sold – I shall also have more farming expenses this than last year because the poor peasants cattle which I hired last year are now nearly all dead and I shall have to buy my own [illeg.] in order to get the work done at all – I hope dearest aunt that this explicit exposé of my finances will satisfy you – it is hard for a farmer to subsist when a farm on which he spent in the first year 10.665f returns him only 330f. had I not been extremely saving I could not have survived this financial shock and as it is I should have been lost without Mamma and Pauline's assistance. the reason of this disaster is solely the uncommonly bad past season, one so unparalleled in the annals of agricultural history that the oldest men do not remember the like of it.[5] death and famine are raging about here in the most dire shape and parliament has voted an extra credit of 20 million to relieve the misery of this part of the empire – so you may fancy it was not what is commonly called a "bad year" – Good bye now dearest aunt, I do hope you are well, yours most affectionately

WGC

17th March 1864.

Expenditure of my 1st farming year from 1st of Octob. 1862 to 1st of Octob. 1863.

Rent	4000f.
Law Expenses	184.65
Wages	351.85
Tradesmens accounts	37.50
Expens. in new buildings and repairs	480.50
Stocking of farm /:<u>inclus of calesh</u>[6]:/	1605.27
Stocking of house	782.88
Building Materials	811.47
Seed and forage	831.48

Freight and carriage	163.23
travelling expenses	223.4
household expenses	361.34
personal expenses inclus trip to Gastein:/	639.43
diverse farm expenses	159.30
Deficit in act. unacct. for	33.87
Total	10.665f81.

the above account is in Austrian florins & Kreutzers[7] 10 Austrian florins equal to 1 £ Engl. money –

Address: No envelope.

Unpublished. Text: M.S., Pf. Coll., CL'ANA 0260

---

1 A slang term for "money" (British).
2 See CL'ANA 0205. In that letter, Pauline wrote to Claire about Wilhelm's trip to Gastein, noting that his visit to the thermal springs there might be the reason that his "erruption is nearly quite gone" She stated too that Wilhelm "could not dream of going again next year," probably a result of the expense involved.
3 As Hitschmann confirmed, Wilhelm was a "Gutspächter bei Temesvár in Ungarn" ("estate tenant near Temesvár in Hungary"). See *Verzeichniss*, p. 11.
4 Kreuzer.
5 *The South Australian Advertiser* of 10 March 1864 referenced the bleak conditions in Hungary in an article from the *Express* entitled "The Hungarian Famine": "Hungary, a large wheat-growing and grain-exporting country, long accustomed to provide bread for no small portion of Europe, is now literally starving, and begging bread for herself . . . It began with excessive rain and was followed by excessive drought . . . The grass was burnt up on plains formerly covered with sheep and cattle, which have been either killed or driven away . . . Extraordinary efforts have been made to relieve it; but it is difficult to support a whole nation by charity" (National Library of Australia, http://nla.gov.au/nla.news-article31834140, p. 2). As Zoltán Fónagy explains, "In the 1860s and 1870s the occasional bad harvest would have resulted in whole districts suffering from hunger" (István Tóth, ed., *The Concise History of Hungary* [Budapest: Corvina, 2005] p. 455). And even though, as G. C. Paikert has asserted, the "German settlers (more precisely those who lived in the exceptionally fertile Banat and Bačka region), within a century of their arrival, made up the most prosperous and best established agricultural communities in their environment" (*The Danube Swabians*, p. 26), drought and famine certainly impeded Wilhelm's prosperity.
6 See CL'ANA 0256.
7 English spelling (with faulty capitalization) for "Kreuzers".

173 • Wilhelm Gaulis Clairmont to Claire Clairmont

[4 September 1864]

My dear aunt. I cannot tell you what a relief it was to us both to hear from you again for since Miss Hammond's[1] letter we were both of us in the greatest anxiety concerning you – You wish for full explanations concerning our circumstances – you shall have them and you will see in the course of my narration how I came to be silent so long. – What you read in the Times is perfectly true this has been as reacher[2] harvest than has been for many years and our hopes and exaltations were very high in consequence. I only waited till we had done thrashing the sheaves taken from each field as a sample of the yield so as to enable the farmer to form an idea as to the approximate crop he is likely to harvest – the result of this which turned out most satisfactory I only awaited in order to communicate it to you where a fresh unforeseen calamity rose to blight all our hopes that is the prices of wheat barley oats hay in fact of every sort of agricultural produce fell so low that they are <u>below the half</u> of ordinary average prices – indeed they are in fact for the present at least unsaleable – but if one could sell at such prices it would be ruinous to do so as one would not even net the costs of production[3] – To add to our difficulties labour, which is of course much in request in consequence of the extensive harvest, is so dear that the howing and thrashing of the crops costs twice the usual sum – whereas the crop itself when got ready for market is barely saleable, and if so commands not one half of its usual value. first we all hoped that this would be only a passing fluctuation in the market, but since then prices have been going on steadily sinking so that I am now afraid this state of things will last all the winter – these pleasant tidings I could not of course communicate to you considering what account Miss Hamd[4] gave of your health; nor would I now if you had not most directly requested it. Our difficulty now is to obtain tin[5] to get through the thrashing and pay our next installment of rent due the end of Octob – by the spring I have no doubt prices will look up again – Pauline wrote for this reason to Hagg. & Hale[6] to borrow some money on her shares but we have no answer from him – We are therefore greatly depressed just now but give yourself no concern on our account I dare say we shall weather through it somehow or other – Do not be angry with Pauline she cannot help being eccentric; I assure you if you could see what a sister she is to me you would be quite generous enough to forgive her not being quite as excellent a niece to you – I always tell her that she has the best heart but very little brain – her affections once sincerely given quite run away with her poor little understanding and cause her to be so extreme in her excess either of de[illeg.]votedness for the object of her affections or animosity against its real or supposed antagonists. Common justice towards the latter is of course quite out of the question with her. for she is under such circumstances quite incapable of quite deliberation – I must however say in her deffence that in <u>my</u> opinion the letter which caused Miss Hammond to favour us with her unamiable letter contained nothing whatsoever to warrant the acrid tone of her note – As you yourself repeatedly and most energetically desired Pauline to give you a full account of our circumstances she could not avoid complying any longer and cannot be held responsible for the consequences of having done so – You no doubt thought that we were now quite set up and comparatively rolling in wealth /: mislead by the accounts in the papers :/ and no doubt it would have been a most ungenerous return of your love and the anxious interest with which you followed us through our last years troubles had we now withheld such good news from you – but as you will perceive that this supposed prosperous state of things never existed, there was also no culpable omission on Pauline's part. – Now goodbye dearest ~~Pauline~~ aunt I have written you a long letter and hope you will not be bored by it

I hope my next will contain better news.

yours most affectionately
WGC

Bobda Cseney
Septemb. 4th 1864.

P.S. I am very glad you directed me to direct this letter to the post office for I confess I do not appreciate Miss Hammond's kind offices in providing a person to open my letters to you to decide whether you may be allowed to read them. but I trust that with your restored health all pretense for such tender tutelage may be removed –

Address: Mrs Clairmont/ Signora Inglese/Poste restante/Via [illeg.] Caterina/ Florence./1623.
Written on rear of letter: Lungi arno dalle grazzie/ N° 14.
Front postmark: Czeney/ $^5/_9$; BOLLO INSUFFICIENTE
Rear postmark: Gyertyamos/5/9; FERRARA/9/SET/ARRIVO

Unpublished. Text: M.S., Pf. Coll., CL'ANA 0261

---

1 See CL'ANA 0041.
2 Wilhelm's misspelling for "richer".
3 G.C. Paikert observes that wheat was Hungary's "chief export" after 1848 and that the "steadily rising prices of the agricultural products, primarily wheat" improved the economic conditions of the people living in the Banat (p. 32).
4 Hammond.
5 Slang for "money".
6 The London broker firm of Messrs. Haggard, Hale, and Pixley. The firm was located at 26 Austin Friars, London.

174 • Wilhelm Gaulis Clairmont to Claire Clairmont

[26 October 1864]

My dear aunt. I got your letter of the 27th Septbr.[1] but was until now prevented from answering it and even now I am so busy that I have time for only a few lines – just to let you know that we carry on here much in our usual slow way without any either very pleasant or unpleasant incidents – prices have risen a trifle but just enough to mark the fact that they do not continue to fall any lower – still the price of wheat is 50 percent below the average price[2] – My rent was due yesterday I have not as yet paid it, but am in treaty with my proprieteress[3] for the attainment of easier terms – In the mean time a few weeks pass on and I gain time to get the money ready – I have also succeeded since writing to you last, in selling my hay for the supply of some cavalry which has been stationed in the vicinity as horse provender of any kind is so plenty̶iful this years I had fully made up my mind not to find a purchaser for it not would I but for this chance. I shall have to permit them about 3 tons a week in all it will return me about 1200 florins and will as it comes in in monthly installments just serve to cover my current expenses. besides the carting of the hay will occupy my horses just at that season of the year when they have nothing else to do. so you see dear aunt although the disappointment has been very great still things are taking a turn for the better and you need give yourself no further uneasiness because you could not send me any help – I hope to hear soon that your health is quite restored although now the season of the year is approaching which you bear the worst – I suppose all your Florentine friends will carry their heads rather high at the prospect of having their native city promoted to the capital of Italy, but I fear their triumph will be but of a transitory nature[4] – As for myself I have quite given up politics and am quite farmer I am selfish enough to wish for a jolly good war /: anywhere but in this vicinity :/ as then prices would rise – Pauline desires me to send you her best love and will with pleasure [illeg.] write to you again provided her letters be acceptable to you. Now Goodbye dearest aunt please write to me soon – I shall also be more diligent now in writing as the slack season is approaching fast. yours most affectionately

WGC

Bobda
Octob. 26th 1864.

Address: La Signora Clairmont/4 Piazza dell' Indipendenza/Florence.
Front postmark: BOLLO INSUFFICIENTE

Unpublished. Text: M.S., Pf. Coll., CL'ANA 0262

---

1 This letter has been lost.
2 See CL'ANA 0261.

3 See CL'ANA 0254.
4 Florence was the capital city of Italy from 1865 to 1870. Rome became the capital city after Victor Emmanuel II acquired the Papal States, realizing what had always been part of the Risorgimento's plan for a united Italy. See also Charles Killinger, *The History of Italy* (Westport: Greenwood Press, 2002).

175 • Wilhelm Gaulis Clairmont to Claire Clairmont

[29 December 1864]

My dearest aunt.

A few days ago we got your nice letter full of your kind wishes for Christmas by this time you will also have got Pauline's letter which is now fully 3 weeks since it was sent off. I need hardly say that we both return all your kind wishes – I only regret that fate decrees that we should live so far apart, how nice if could have found some suitable farm nearer to you[1] – ! as to our moneyaffairs give yourself no concern – I think that is I hope we shall rub through it somehow. we conquered the drought last year – so I dare say we shall likewise brave the present ruinous forces; at any rate if we do not succeed we shall not have to make any reproaches to ourselves for I assure you we have reduced our expenses to a minimum of and made all the retrenchments it was possible to make and Pauline is the best little housekeeper in the world and helps me more than I could by myself to carry out all our economical plans – the weather hitherto has been very mild; there were two or three degrees of Reaumure[2] in the night – the thermometer has once gone down as low as 7 below zero of course Reaumure but you may judge that it is not very cold from this circumstance that the field works still progress. Of Mama [illeg.] after whom you enquire so kindly I have the best news to give – we had a letter from her only yesterday – she says her health is better than ever; she has no more difficulty in breathing and hardly any palpitations of the heart but she has an occasional rheumatic pain in the hip which renders her even more helpless in point of locomotion than she was before. still she writes in very good spirits and she says that her she has let her principal lodging again for 2 years to a very good tenant a Baron Reisner a pensioned colonel in the Austrian army. the remaining minor lodgings she says she will let readily furnished in the spring – I am sorry that the transfer of the Italian capital to Florence threatens to affect your private interests so unpleasantly; but I am strongly inclined to think that with the exception of houserent nothing will become so much dearer for in our age of railroads it is as easy to concentrate all the commercial requirements of a large city about Florence as about Turin.[3] It will be as well for you not to talk any politics in your letters for they are again very much on the alert. Punch[4] was recently forbidden to be brought to Austria on account of an article against the emperor –

Goodbye dearest auntie – I wish I had a few hundred florins to spend I would make you and Mama a visit

Goodbye
WGC

Decbr 29th 1864.

Address: No envelope

Unpublished. Text: M.S., Pf. Coll., CL'ANA 0263

1 Claire was in Florence, some 1,208 kilometers from her nephew.
2 See CL'ANA 0377.
3 Harry Hearder suggests that Florence "lacked the scale and dignity" to be an appropriate capital city. He records a "housing shortage" at the time and explains that architectural projects had commenced to improve the city's infrastructure (*Italy in the Age of the Risorgimento: 1790–1870*, London: Routledge, 1983), p. 280. Wilhelm seemed unaware of the city's ability to support an influx of inhabitants although he recognized a possible increase in rental fees.
4 *Punch* was a satiric magazine, published between 1841 and 2002. Named for the French paper, *Le Charivari*, *Punch* was subtitled "The London Charivari" ("History of Punch". Web. 31 January 2015. http://www.punch.co.uk/about/). Richard Scully recognizes that the writers and cartoonists of *Punch* had shifted tone to a more conservative one by 1861 ("The Other Kaiser: Wilhelm I and British Cartoonists, 1861–1914", *Victorian Periodicals Review*, 44: 1 [2011], p. 70). In spite of this shift, *Punch* was still considered radical enough for Franz Joseph I to censor.

176 • Wilhelm Gaulis Clairmont to Claire Clairmont

[23 February 1865]

My dear aunt. I just now received yours of the 15th inst. and hurry to answer the principal question in your last letter as to whether we are likely to remain in Bobda or not – only a few days ago I should have thought I could have answered this question with perfect certainty at least so far that we were at any rate sure to stop here till autumn to give us time to get in the harvest we sowed last autumn – that much seemed mathematically certain to me and as to whether we then stopped on any longer must of course depend on the issue of the year; that is to say what crops we got and at what prices they could be sold – Since the last week however we have had such a continuation of snowstorms that the snow is now lying nearly 2 feet deep in the fields and everybody tells me that this unheard of quantity of snow is very likely to cause an inundation in this low country – I hope of course that such may not be the case, but if it should, it may lead to my having to quit Bobda at once – that is as soon as the certainty becomes apparent that all is lost – the reason why Paulines accounts of our misfortunes differ so much from mine – is this that she is essentially a creature of impulses and feelings accordingly when she talks of a subject on which she feels strongly she is apt to use also stronger language whereas I rather avoid this topic altogether partly because I am quite sick of it and partly, seeing that you cannot help me I see no purpose in worrying you by a recital of it – My last letter to you and its invitation to you to come here for the summer had however [illeg.] nothing to do with all this – you wrote that rents in Florence had risen so much that you could not stop there[1] – so I and Pauline in return did thus (and do now still) ask you to come if it suits you and take up your sojourn with us for the summer. you will then see how it pleases you and you will also have time to determine as to where to go for the winter – and I repeat what I also said in my last letter that we consider you under no sort of obligation to determine and to announce to us beforehand whether you intend to come or not, for as we are now too poor to make any extra preparations for your reception we can dispense with any fixed engagement on your part whether you intend to come or not and this freedom of action will I have no doubt but prove a great relief to you – should the dreaded inundation come I will of course loose not a minutes time in advising you of it. Major Becker I have not paid because he prolonged the terms I pay him his interest as a matter of course I will not even if I could get more money borrow it to carry on my business for if that also failed I should not be able to pay the debts back and that would be double misery – My health is now well before I was rather poorly but the cold does me good it has quite restored my appetite – Goodbye now dearest aunt Plin[2] and I should be much pleased to see you – if there is anything more you would like to know write to yours affectly

WGC

Bobda
Febr. 23rd 1865.

Plin intended to add a postscript but as an opportunity offers just now of sending to the post I dont want to delay the letter – she sends her best love[3]

Address: No envelope

Unpublished. Text: M.S., Pf. Coll., CL'ANA 0264

---

1 See CL'ANA 0263.
2 See CL'ANA 0256.
3 Wilhelm cross-wrote the final sentence on the last page of the letter.

177 • Wilhelm Gaulis Clairmont to Claire Clairmont

[12 March 1865]

My dearest aunt. I received your kind good letter today having been absent from home for several days and I need not tell you how much touched I was by your kind offer and even more by the tender concern you express for my wellbeing – I assure you I had considered that you had done already infinitely more than enough in giving me the £500 on my arrival in Europe so this new offer quite overwhelms me, for although you are considerate enough, by claiming interest on it, to give it the face of a loan – still considering the sinking state of my projects it looks more like alms than an investment – Nevertheless dearest aunt it is not false shame that prevents me from accepting indiscriminately your kind offer it is also a motive of prudence [illeg.] which renders me disinclined to sink more capital in an enterprise which has hitherto promised so poorly – It is true what you say that the utmost pains should be taken to maintain my position till things take another turn for the better but on the other hand a certain limit must be recognized so as not to go too far in ones sacrifices and be left destitute in the event of a final failure – If prices were too rise even now I might [illeg.] get out of it tolerably well for I have still some produce to sell; but if the present unprecedently low prices keep up for another year I am must give up. Therefore dearest aunt I would like you, if possible to leave it open to me for 6 or 8 weeks whether to take the £200 or not I should by that time be in a position to tell whether I can apply them advantageously or not for the present I have still a little money left to go on with – that is not exactly money but produce – I have still 900 bushels of wheat which will pay my rent till 1st Novemb then I have left 600 bush. maize and 300 bushels rye representing together at present prices a value of say 1000f. with these I must rub on till the harvest comes. Of course it will not be enough, but I shall see by that time how things go – Therefore I send you the signature all the same and I need not say I thank you all the same but I will not draw just immediately the loss of interest which you sustain I must of course make up – Becker I have not yet paid but of course I pay him his interest regularly – his year will be up on the 1st of June I will if you desire it pay him by that time, but the amount is 700fl. that is seventy pounds – but I would of course have to pay it out of your £200 – the danger of water is still very great – the water is rising steadily it is not yet on any of my fields but already on those of my neighbours – it comes from a dry water course which forms one of my boundaries – in ordinary times it has no water at all, but when the neighbouring large rivers are flooded it also becomes filled and floods the country surrounding it. they told me it was an occurrence that hardly took place once in twenty years. even now the water may subside without doing any injury but I am afraid it will swamp us.[1] – Your letters arrive all paid – I fo[illeg.]repay mine till the Austr. frontier as you have repeatedly requested me not to pay them – Plin is not at home just now I packed her off for a week on a visit to Párdány[2] a place about 20 Engl. miles from here; she is getting very morose and irritable; the constant solitude and sameness coupled with fretting for the future tells on her nervous system – she bears up bravely against it, but becomes irritable in spite of herself, so I thought the change would do her good – she goes to the house of a Mr. Isekutz³ an old retired manager of estates – his wife is dead long ago, but his daughter who is also married and has already grown up girls is the lady of the house and to her Pauline went they are nice hospitable people –

Now goodbye dearest aunt; many thanks for your good excellent heart, I hope I may find an opportunity of requitting it. yours most affectionately

WGC

Bobda March 12th 1865.

Address: No envelope

Unpublished. Text: M.S., Pf. Coll., CL'ANA 0265

---

1 George Aberle explains that, while the fertile land of the Banat was "exceedingly productive" due to its excellent soil, the area was "swampy". In the eighteenth century, when Empress Maria Theresia assisted with the settlement of Germans in the Banat, one of her main aims was to have the land prepared for agricultural production. Aberle records that a "system of canals" was therefore devised to drain the swampy land (*From the Steppes to the Prairies*, pp. 75–6). Wilhelm observed that flooding was not prevalent in Bobda.

2 Párdány (in Hungarian) was known as Pardan in German. The Treaty of Versailles (1919) made the town a Romanian possession, but today it is part of an independent Serbia. After the Second World War, the town was renamed Međa. Párdány/Međa is located about 43.5 kilometers (27 miles) south of Bobda. Wilhelm has slightly underestimated the number of miles between the two towns (Nick Tullius and Alex Leeb. "Banat Villages". Donauschwaben Villages. Web. 15 April 2015. http://www.dvhh.org/banat_villages/Vojvodina/Central_Banat_District/Pardan.htm).

3 Unidentified.

178 • Wilhelm Gaulis Clairmont to Claire Clairmont

[19 April 1865]

My dearest aunt. I have been somewhat remiss in writing to you of late as I was some weeks from home. yesterday I got yours of the 12th inst. answering your intended change of habitation, and as I think that a letter may be going about 4 days, I hope this will be just in time to find you in your new lodging. – About the state of my affairs I can give you as yet little satisfactory that is to say – definite news – I was absent from home in Croatia and Baden and Pest with a view of effecting a change between Mama's houses in Baden and a landed estate situated in this vicinity, the proprietor of which a certain Baron Hussard lives in Pest.[1] However I find that he asks more than would under the present circumstances be prudent to give and so the thing has dropped to the ground – The innundation was happily averted from us – but the prices, although they had risen a very little as compared with what they were in winter, are still so low as to make farming an unpaying speculation excepting at such low rents as are in accordance with the present low prices of produce. I was [illeg.] that now at Pest on that account and represented to the lawyer of Countess Schenetton[2] that having battled against the unpropitious terms for 3 years and paid my rent punctually notwithstanding, my honour would not be blemished if I could no longer carry on the farm especially as already hundreds of farmers have either failed or given up their contracts – but that I would get myself passed through the insolvent court unless she of her own free will consented to make a reduction in my rent of 3f. pr. acre – I now pay 10 ½ florins – A few days ago ago[3] I received her answer saying that she would not consent. so I suppose I must unless prices should rise quite unexpectedly quietly prepare to look [illeg.] for something else – for rents farms are now to be had very cheap. You ask me whether I still think you should buy land in Hungary – I still think so, indeed I think now more than ever – that is to say I would counsel to wait till next autumn if the prices do not take a sudden rise, land will be then very cheap – but of course one must not buy land at any price but await one's chance with the cash in hand ready to seize the opportunity when ever it offers – the value of landed property has depreciated immensely within the last few years, but of course all this will find its level again as soon as prices rise again and you will then have the cheap land and good prices – one thing I must caution you though that the exchange has now sunk so much that there is only a trifle of some 5 percent in favour of Austria and this is swallowed by the commission one has to pay the bankers –

The £200 I do not want just now, although I may want some more money in the autumn when I perhaps take a new cheap farm – However as you wish it I shall pay off Beker his debt of 700f. for the £10 which you want to give to me and the £20 to Pauline I thank you very much dearest aunt; it is very kind of you always to think of us especially when you do not have so very much yourself. to Pauline your present is particularly welcome for she again got no dividend and is very poorly off. her wardrobe is already very shabby; the little money she had she buys things for the house with instead of looking to her own little wants. I assure you she never got your letter with Naudino's[4] photograph – why surely you give us credit for sufficient common decency not to have left such an attention on your part unnoticed – I shall therefore draw on the Bank for £100. for 70 of which I am to pay you 3 percent interest as agreed – I enclose you a blank formula of how I intend to draw, so that if it be not correct you can tell me of it. Becker's term is up by the 1st of June; so I ought to have the tin[5] by the last week in May – Appropos of photographs. I got some made of myself and if you wish it I will send you one; I do not enclose it now because the people find that many letters containing photographs are stolen In Vienna they discovered and cashiered a post-office official who purloined all letters containing photographs. because I made a collection of them I suppose Naudino figures in some such illicit collection – Of poor dear Ma I have had very sorry news to give you – I spent 3 days with her; but I I[6] have found her very much shaken and aged – her mind is as vigorous as ever, but her body has become very infirm – she has not been out of her room for 6 months; the palpitations of her heart are not so very bad; but she suffers from a kind of stiffness in all her limbs and joints like rheumatic but not so painful which prevents her from taking any kind of exercise – she limps about[7] in her room only with great difficulty and not without the assistance of a stick. It made me very sad to see poor Mama more especially is she still persists in insisting to live by her self – I am very sorry to hear too that your eyes are so bad and that the consequent ennui is so trying to you – in Vienna there are very excellent oculists;[8] poor Becker was all but blind and now he is getting better rapidly and the doctor says if he had not neglected the evil so long he would have quite cured him – Goodbye now dearest aunt many thanks for your kindness write soon and give some better news of your health

       yours affect
       WGC

Bobda April 19th 1865.

Address: No envelope

Unpublished. Text: M.S., Pf. Coll., CL'ANA 0266

---

1 Probably of the Huszár de Mezőkövesd family who were Hungarian barons (Steven Tötösy de Zepetnek, *nobilitashungariae: List of Historical Surnames of the Hungarian Nobility*, p. 97). The town of Mezőkövesd is situated 131 kilometers north-east of Budapest. Bobda is 283 kilometers south-east of Budapest.
2 See CL'ANA 0258.
3 As written in the letter.
4 Unidentified.
5 See CL'ANA 0260.

6 As written in the letter.
7 Wilhelm cross-wrote the following lines.
8 In describing "prominent oculists" of the eighteenth and nineteenth centuries, Johann Hermann Baas recorded that the work of the "famous oculist" Georg Beer (1763–1821) contributed to the excellent reputation of the University of Vienna in the field of ophthalmology. Among Beer's students were von Walther, von Graefe, Jaeger, and Mackenzie (*Outlines of the History of Medicine and the Medical Profession*, New York: Vail and Co., 1889), p. 672.

179 • Ottilia von Pichler (later Clairmont) to Wilhelm Gaulis Clairmont

Saturday 22th April [1865]

²²/₄ 65.
N°. 3¹

Dear Mr. Clairmont;

Though I was sure you would truly keep your promise you gave me by sending your phothograph – I was still more rejoiced by the nice little letter you joined
I am sure you are convinced that without the necessity to affirm you that I duly received both, I could not have done otherwise as to thank you myself and to express you my pleasure about it.
Your letter was so very kind and your phothograph – I think it perfectly well and quite like you thought there is something of a too severe expression in it but it's rather better than to look so sad or melancolic as mine to let people think still more I feel unhappy! What an idea! I am very glad you did not mind asking myself about it because I fear Alma² could not convince you so perfectly as I that I neither felt unhappy the evening you spent at our house, and at present, or that there is a grief I have alone or have no heart sympathising with
I think I am a very blessed girl because many people are so very kind towards me and I do not merit it at all – But it gives me strength to grow better and let's me feel happy even in every hour of grief and sorrow.
I fear you will think me a very foolish girl, writing you in that way, but do not laugh about it – I do not – I would have felt sorry not to answer you sincerely –.

Sunday morning

It was so very late last night I could not finish my letter but I am rather glad I did not – as I received to day at last a very long and pleasant letter from Csakova³ – with many news about your staying there
It was a charming idea you undertook this little voyage during the holydays – and I am quite astonished myself I feel not offended in considering how impossible it was last year to see both of you during my stay at Csakova – and how lucky Alma was. I was exceedingly rejoiced by the way of your judging Alma the other day – I assure you she is quite a capital girl and I think I never could feel sad or lonely as long as she is with me.
Indeed it is very hard to be separated from her – but I am exceedingly happy she is at Csakova because it will do her very good –

Unsere genaue Adresse ist Beatrixgasse Nr. 19⁴

The other day I received too a very ~~kind~~ nice letter from my cousin Nadler,⁵ don't think it is my merit – when people are speaking so kind from me. I only believe it is a proof for her own excellent character.

Daß ich Ihnen einen ganzen Brief englisch schreiben sollte ohne einen einzigen <u>deutschen</u> Gruß daß ist nicht möglich – es ware überhaupt doch vielleicht etwas Vernünftigeres zu Stande gekommen wenn ich nicht gerade Ihnen gegenüber

immer so eine besondere Lust fühlte mich englisch auszudrücken ich habe Ihnen nicht nur einen recht unzusamenhängenden aber auch so unleserlichen Brief geschrieben daß ich garnicht denken kann er wird Ihnen eine kleine Freude machen oder ~~beweisen können wie~~ ein starkes Beweis für den Ihrigen sein – die ~~lange~~ Zeit zum Briefschreiben ist mir aber jetzt so knapp zugemessen daß ich jeden freien Augenblick dazu benützen muß ob er gerade gemütlich ist oder nicht. Give my best love to your sister – I hope to receive soon some news from the Bobda and very good ones. and[6] that if you have time and pleasure you will not fail to add some lines at your sister's letter –
Good-bye your friend Ottilie

Translation (German transcription and English translation provided by Ann Sherwin):

For me to write you an entire letter in English without a single <u>German</u> greeting – that is not possible. Perhaps something altogether more sensible would have materialized if I didn't always have such a strong desire to express myself in English to you of all people. I have written you a not only very disjointed but also illegible letter, so that I can't imagine that it will please you even a little or ~~be able to prove to you how~~ be strong evidence for your family – but the ~~long~~ time I had for letter-writing has gotten to be so scarce that I have to use every free minute for it, whether it's convenient just then or not.

Address: No envelope

Unpublished. Text: M.S., Pf. Coll., CL'ANA 0184

---

1 Written in red ink at the top of the letter and in a different handwriting. We know from Wilhelm's letters that he numbered the letters he received from Ottilia von Pichler (1843–1913), an Austrian from Vienna who would become his wife. Ottilia was twelve years younger than Wilhelm; see CL'ANA 0079 for Wilhelm's comments about marrying someone younger. The daughter of a lawyer, Johann Franz Hofrath von Pichler, and his wife Fanny, Ottilia wrote Wilhelm about her sisters, Emily and Alma, and brother Moritz. According to a genealogical table her granddaughter Mary Claire Bally-Clairmont drew, Ottilia was one of five children. Her sister, Emily, married Wilhelm's friend, Rudolf von Hauer. Wilhelm and Ottilia married in 1866. They had three children, Walter Claire (1868–1958), Alma Pauline (1869–1946), and Johann Paul (1875–1942). The Pforzheimer Collection has a color photograph of a painting of Emily and Ottilia as children. Mary Claire Bally-Clairmont wrote on the back of the snapshot: "links in weiss/Emily von Pichler/rechts in Blau mit Katze unsere Grossmutter/ Ottilie v. Pichler/ verh. Clairmont/ Bild aus Velden im Besitz von Marianne Fieber, Wien. (Photo von Henna Fieber erhalten)" Translation from the German: "Left in white/ Emily von Pichler/ right in blue with cat our grandmother Ottilie v. Pichler/ married Clairmont/ Picture from Velden owned by Marianne Fieber, Vienna (Photo obtained from Henna Fieber)".
2 Ottilia's younger sister, Alma von Pichler.
3 Known as Tschakowa in German, Csák in Hungarian, and Ciacova in Romanian, the town is located 34 kilometers south-west of Timişoara and 50 kilometers south-east of Bobda. Ottilia and Alma's sister, Emily, lived there with her husband, Rudolf von Hauer, Wilhelm's school friend from Altenburg. See CL'ANA 0267.
4 Ottilia wrote these words upside down at the top of the page. The German translation is: "Our exact address is Beatrixgasse No. 19".
5 See CL'ANA 0421, Box 3, bundle g, number 185.
6 Ottilia wrote these final words on the side of the page.

180 • Wilhelm Gaulis Clairmont to Claire Clairmont

[3 May 1865]

My dear aunt.

I was absent from home for a few days at Csakova where my friend Hauer[1] lives, we were together at Altenburg; and so I come to answer this with a delay of a few days – first about business – thank you much dearest aunt for your explanations as to how to write to the Bank. I will draw out the order in accordance with your instructions I will write it on the same paper and with the stamp impression of my initials on it like the signature I now enclose for the guidance of the cashier of the Bank.[2] About the use to ~~not~~ which the money shall be turned you can make yourself easy, it is perfectly [~~illeg.~~] easy to spend money on purposes tending only to ones pleasure – and Plin and I thank you most heartily for being so minute and precise in your directions as to how the money is to be spent – Pauline for her part is quite of one mind with you as to the way in which her share is to be spent, but she laughs much at me for saying that I thought I should feel very awkward with a ring on my finger as I had never had one in my life –[3] Dont be angry with poor Mama; she enquired very much after you when I was at Baden we have had more bad news from her; the doctors seem to fear that the sore on her breast is a kind of cancer.[4] she has become very infirm; it is not unlikely Pauline will go to join her.[5] for a time at least. you may imagine how this clouds what little pleasure we have. Our harvest prospects are so far tolerably prosperous; but there is again much want of rain and prices notwithstanding make no appearance of a rise –[6] Now Goodbye dearest aunt I write this letter so short to get it off by todays post – I sent you my photograph; did you get it. Plin told me yesterday to send her best love, she is still asleep.

                    yours most affectly
                    WGC

Bobda Cseney
May 3rd 1865.

Address: La Signora Clairmont/ Casa Recanati/665 Piazza della Frontina/Pisa/Italia.

Unpublished. Text: M.S., Pf. Coll., CL'ANA 0267

---

1 Professor Hitschmann lists "Rudolf von Ritter Hauer" as one of the students who entered Altenburg in 1850–1. According to Hitschmann, von Hauer was born in Vienna in 1830, he resided in Csakova after graduation, and he was listed as a "Gutsbesitzer" (German for "landowner") (*Verzeichniss*, pp. 24–25). Hitschmann's book was published in 1865, the year Wilhelm visited von Hauer. Von Hauer was a witness to Wilhelm's marriage (see Marriage Certificate, photograph in this collection) in 1866. His title was that of "Ritter," German for Baronet.
2 This signature is lost.
3 See CL'ANA 0219.
4 See CL'ANA 0268, for a description of Antonia's surgical procedure.
5 See CL'ANA 0268 and CL'ANA 0219 for Wilhelm's account of Pauline's stay in Baden.
6 See CL'ANA 0260 for a description of the adverse conditions in Hungary.

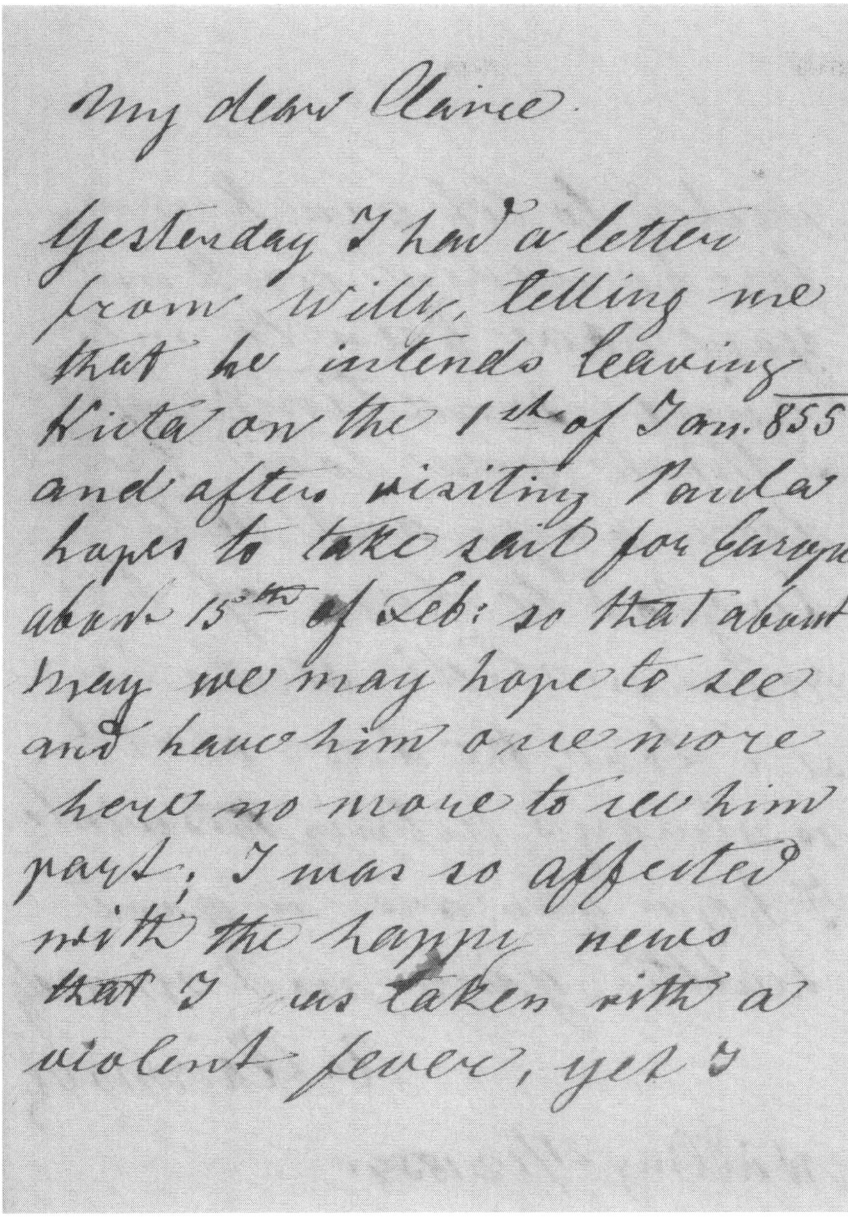
My dear Claire.

Yesterday I had a letter from Willy, telling me that he intends leaving Victa on the 1st of Jan. 855 and after visiting Paula hopes to take sail for Europe about 15th of Feb: so that about May we may hope to see and have him once more here no more to see him part, I was so affected with the happy news that I was taken with a violent fever, yet I

Image 1 Autograph letter by Antonia Clairmont to Claire Clairmont, 21 December 1854.

Source: Dec. 21, 1854. 1 Manuscript.

Credit Line: The Carl H. Pforzheimer Collection of Shelley and His Circle, The New York Public Library, Astor, Lenox and Tilden Foundations.

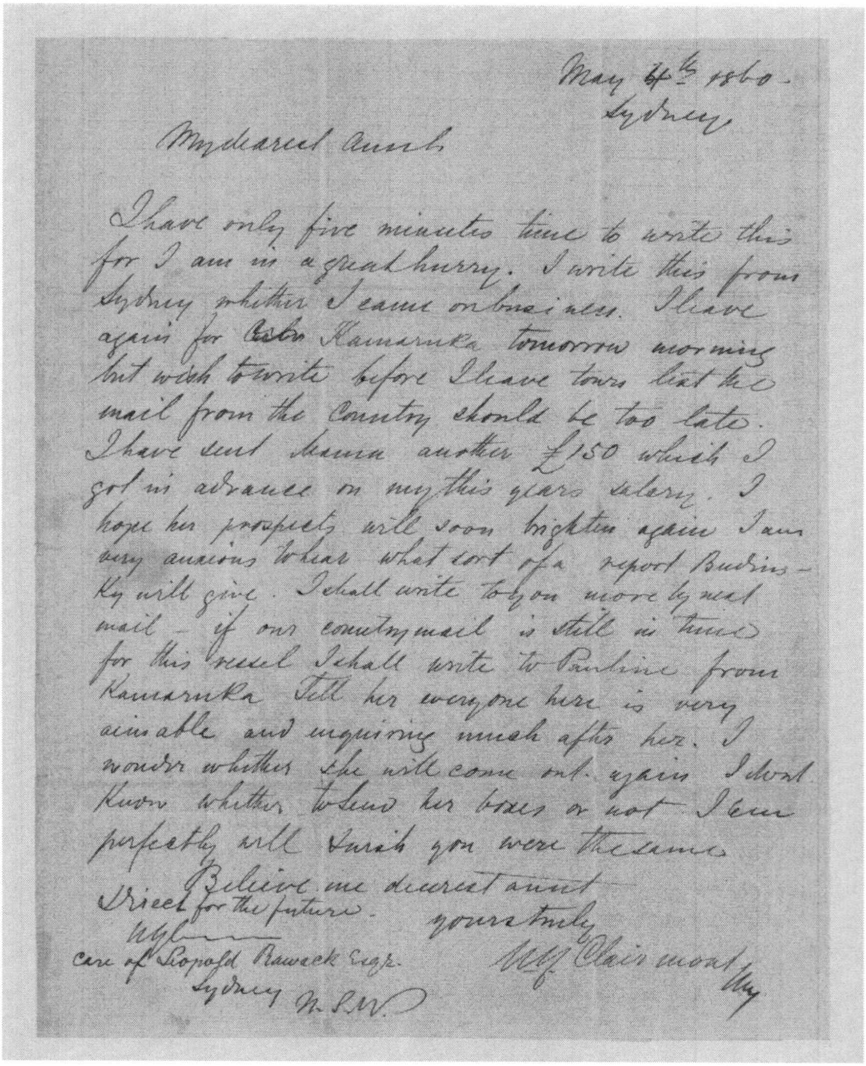

Image 2 Autograph letter by Wilhelm Gaulis Clairmont to Claire Clairmont, 4 May 1860.
Source: May 4, 1860. Manuscript.
Credit Line: The Carl H. Pforzheimer Collection of Shelley and His Circle, The New York Public Library, Astor, Lenox and Tilden Foundations.

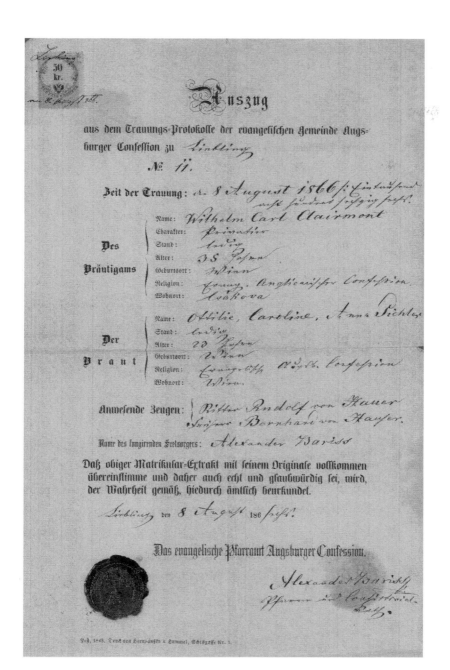

Image 3 Marriage Certificate of Wilhelm Clairmont and Ottilia von Pichler, 8 August 1866.

Source: Clairmont family papers. Aug. 8, 1866. recto Manuscript.

Credit Line: The Carl H. Pforzheimer Collection of Shelley and His Circle, The New York Public Library, Astor, Lenox and Tilden Foundations.

English translation: [stamp]50 kr. on August 8, 1866

Extract

from the marriage records of the Protestant Church, Augsburg Confession, in Liebling No. 11. Date of marriage: August 8, 1866 (one thousand eight hundred sixty-six)

The groom's	name:	Wilhelm Carl Clairmont
	character:	man of independent means
	marital status:	single
	age:	35 years
	birthplace:	Vienna
	religion:	Protestant, Anglican Confession
	place of residence:	Csákova
The bride's	name:	Ottilie Caroline Anna Pichler
	marital status:	single
	age	23 years
	birthplace:	Vienna
	religion:	Protestant, Augsburg Confession
	place of residence:	Wien
Witnesses present:		Baronet Rudolf von Hauer
		Baron Bernhard von Hauser
Name of officiating clergyman:		Alexander Bariss

It is hereby officially attested as true that the above register extract agrees completely with its original and therefore is also genuine and reliable. Liebling, August 8, 1866. [wax seal] The Protestant Parish Office, Augsburg Confession. Alexander Bariss Pastor and Member of the Consistory
(Translation provided by Ann Sherwin)

Image 4 Photographic portrait of Wilhelm and Ottilia Clairmont, c. 1866.
Source: Visual materials from the Carl H. Pforzheimer Collection. c. 1866. Photograph.
Credit Line: The Carl H. Pforzheimer Collection of Shelley and His Circle, The New York Public Library, Astor, Lenox and Tilden Foundations.

Image 5 Photographic portrait of Pauline Clairmont, c. 1875.

Source: Visual materials from the Carl H. Pforzheimer Collection. c. 1875. Photograph.

Credit Line: The Carl H. Pforzheimer Collection of Shelley and His Circle, The New York Public Library, Astor, Lenox and Tilden Foundations.

Image 6 Photographic portrait of Wilhelm Clairmont, c. 1875.

Source: Visual materials from the Carl H. Pforzheimer Collection. c. 1875. Photograph.

Credit Line: The Carl H. Pforzheimer Collection of Shelley and His Circle, The New York Public Library, Astor, Lenox and Tilden Foundations.

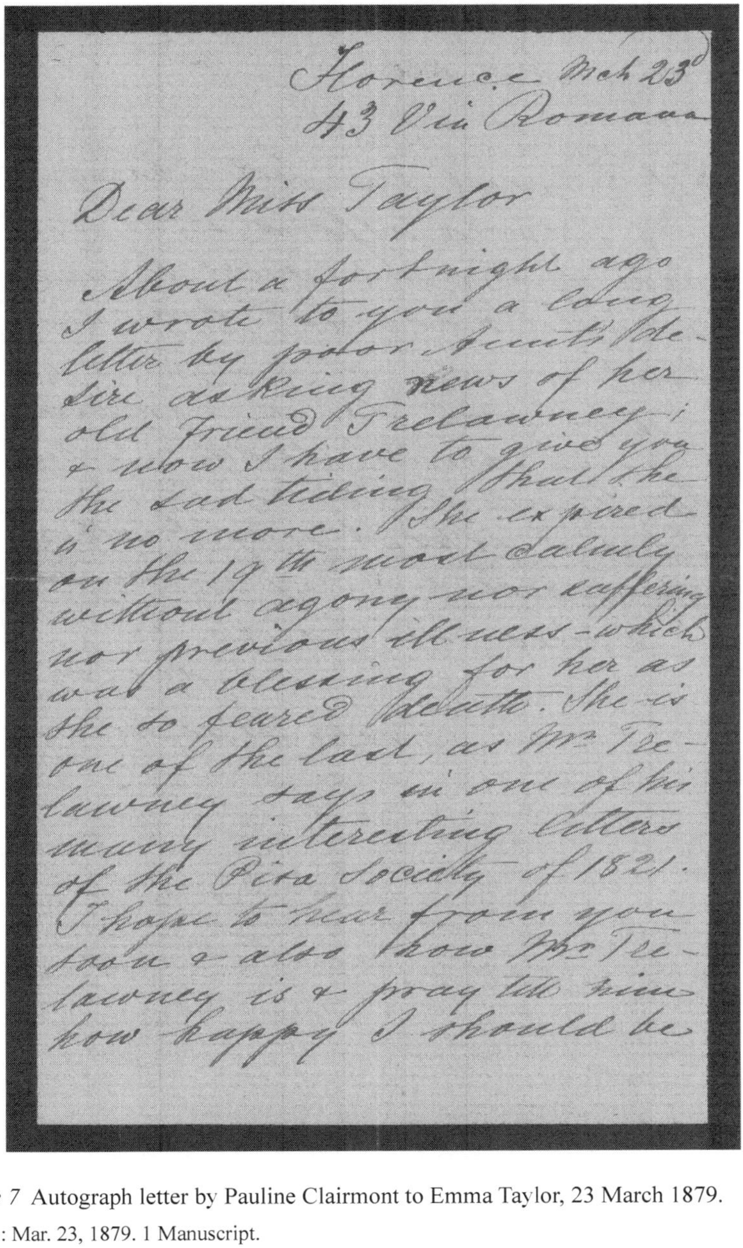

> Florence, Mch 23d
> 43 Via Romana
>
> Dear Miss Taylor
>
> About a fortnight ago I wrote to you a long letter by poor Aunt's desire asking news of her old friend Trelawney — & now I have to give you the sad tiding that she is no more. She expired on the 19th most calmly without agony nor suffering nor previous illness — which was a blessing for her as she so feared Death. She is one of the last, as Mr Trelawney says in one of his many interesting letters of the Pisa Society — of 1821. I hope to hear from you soon & also how Mr Trelawney is & pray tell him how happy I should be

Image 7 Autograph letter by Pauline Clairmont to Emma Taylor, 23 March 1879.

Source: Mar. 23, 1879. 1 Manuscript.

Credit Line: The Carl H. Pforzheimer Collection of Shelley and His Circle, The New York Public Library, Astor, Lenox and Tilden Foundations.

Image 8 Photographic portrait of Ottilia Clairmont by Josef Székely (photographer). Unknown date.

Source: Visual materials from the Carl H. Pforzheimer Collection. Photograph.

Credit Line: The Carl H. Pforzheimer Collection of Shelley and His Circle, The New York Public Library, Astor, Lenox and Tilden Foundations.

Image 9 Photographic portrait of Alma, Paul, and Walter Clairmont, c. 1895.

Source: Visual materials from the Carl H. Pforzheimer Collection. c. 1895. Photograph.

Credit Line: The Carl H. Pforzheimer Collection of Shelley and His Circle, The New York Public Library, Astor, Lenox and Tilden Foundations.

Image 10 Clairmont family tomb, Evangelischer Friedhof Matzleinsdorf, Vienna, Austria.
Source: Heraldic-Genealogical Society Adler, Vienna, tng.adler-wien.eu
Credit Line: Heraldic-Genealogical Society Adler, Vienna, tng.adler-wien.eu

Image 11 Mary Claire Bally-Clairmont, c. 2000.
Source: Mr. Peter Bally, Switzerland.
Credit Line: Mr. Peter Bally, Switzerland.

181 • Ottilia von Pichler (later Clairmont) to Pauline Clairmont

Thursday 18th of May [1865]

My dear Miss Pauline!

I was exceedingly surprised to hear by your brother's letter the other day of the very sudden resolution you took to come here –

Though I believe the reason, you undertook this travel is a very sad one as your poor mama did not feel well lately – I hope all is better now and I may rejoice from all my heart at our next meeting.

It is the very reason I write you my dear Miss Pauline that you may be so kind to give me more than only such a very little time to stay with you –

It is unnecessary to assure you whenever you come to Vienna that we will feel very glad to see you at our house Though we have nothing to offer you neither amusements nor pleasure I can at least convinse you that we will all feel rejoiced to have such a dear and seldom guest –

If it is in any way possible do let me know the day you intend to arrive here – as I am very often not at home and would feel very sorry not to be the first to expect and see you my dear – I could also manage all my business in that way that I have time then to stay with you – and to help you perhaps as you will have certainly some business in town

Mama[1] will not return but the next week – but I hope it is no reason at all you are to delay your coming –

Our adress is Landstrasse, Beatrix Gasse N°.19 in the first floor

You must only be so kind to expect nothing at all, because our household is very small and simple – but [illeg.] you may be assured that you will make feel very glad your

ever affectionate
Ottilia.

P.S. Pray be so kind to give my best compliment to your Mama though I have not the honour of knowing her –.

Address: No envelope

Unpublished. Text: M.S. Pf. Coll., CL'ANA 0180

---

1 Fanny von Pichler. In Mary Claire Bally-Clairmont's genealogical table (CL'ANA 0428, unpublished manuscript, Pforzheimer Collection), she recorded that Fanny von Pichler was born in 1805 and that she died in 1874. The table documents that she married "Johann Franz Hofrath von Pichler (1799–1892)" in 1835. They had five children.

182 • Wilhelm Gaulis Clairmont to Claire Clairmont

[21 May 1865]

Dearest aunt.

Your letter to Pauline I duly forwarded to Baden – and she has no doubt ere now acknowledged it as I thought she would write to you sooner than I, I forwarded her a photograph of mine to enclose you in her next letter to you – In case her letter should have miscarried or she should not yet have had written to you /: which I do not for a moment suppose :/ I will at the risk of repeating what you already know inform you of the changes that have taken place here – It turned out that the sore on poor Mamma's breast was of a cancerous nature and required an immediate operation – this really took place, and that quite successfully with the aid of Chloroform on the 13th inst.[1] there were 4 physicians present. Dr Landesmann[2] Dr Milleitner,[3] one Dr Wildner[4] a friend of the Daningers[5] and the operator a Dr Guma one of the first doctors in Vienna who accompanied the Empress to Madeira[6] so it came to pass that Pauline had to go to Baden quite suddenly – to assist M. through her trials – happily she now writes me very satisfactory letters; she says the doctors express no doubt as to the satisfactory result of the operation – the Court Journal[7] for Pauline duly arrived but I have not as yet forwarded it; this will explain to you why she does not acknowledge the receipt of it. And now about the Cashier – I sent you the second signature [illeg.] not for an other £100. but because you returned me [illeg.] the first signature with certain corrections made thereon – so I am afraid you have not sent any signature to the Chief Cashier and my cheque will not be honoured – I have sent it through a Temesvarer banker more than 10 days ago, but hitherto received no answer – If you have not sent any signature please forward the one you have at once – for I want a little money just now very much – I wanted to sell a little produce to cover my immediate expenses in weeding all the crops etz etz – but wheat and everything else has after a momentary rise fallen so much again that I cannot make up my mind to sell just now. for the second £100 which you wanted to send me I thank you dearest aunt but I wont take it so long as I can shift without – but please send the signature to the Cashier immediately so that I may have no delay in getting the first £100 out of which Becker is to be paid. the chapter about land in Hungary is too long and difficult for me to enter on now – I am in a great hurry & fidget but I will write again shortly when I acknowledge receipt of money.

yours affectly
WGC

21 May 1865.

I enclose you the first signature I sent you that you may remember having returned it me[8]

Address: No envelope.

Unpublished. Text: M.S., Pf. Coll., CL'ANA 0268

1 See note 8, CL'ANA 0059.
2 According to Dr. Ruth Koblizek of the Medizinische Universität Wien, Dr. Max Landesmann (1805–1881) had an interest in "bath-therapy". From 1860 onwards, he worked as head of a clinic in the Marien Hospital in Weikersdorf (Dr. Ruth Koblizek, Medizinische Universität Wien, personal correspondence: 9 February 2015). Founded in 1813 by Princess Maria Karoline Schwarzenberg, the hospital does not exist anymore. Today, Weikersdorf is part of the city of Baden.
3 Franz Mülleitner. A physician, he died in 1868.
4 Franz Wildner (1833/4–1900) was a physician and surgeon. He worked from 1860 onwards in Innsbruck as a doctor and as a veterinarian. According to Dr. Ruth Koblizek, comparisons between human and animal anatomical systems were very important at the time, so Wildner worked in both arenas. The medical and veterinary faculties of the university were separated at a later date (Dr. Ruth Koblizek, Medizinische Universität Wien, personal correspondence: 11 February 2015). *The Naturalists' Universal Directory (International)*, compiled in 1905, listed Wildner in Part II, Austro-Hungary. He was referenced as "Dr. med., a. o. Prof der Tierheilkunde" ("medical doctor and also Professor of Veterinary Medicine"). He worked at Leopold-Franzens University, Innsbruck. His interest was noted as "anim. domest" (domestic animals) (Salem, MA: Samuel Edson Cassino, 1905), p. 31. Today, Leopold-Franzens University is part of the University of Innsbruck.
5 Unidentified.
6 Dr Albin Kumar (born 1830 in Styria – 1918) is listed in *Schmidt's Jahrbücher* of 1892 under the heading "Bauch, Brust und Becken" ("Belly, Breast/Chest and Pelvis"). He published two academic papers that year (Leipzig: Otto Wigand, 1892), p. 321. He was the personal physician and surgeon to the Empress Elisabeth of Austria (1837–1898), the wife of Emperor Franz Joseph I. Dr. Kumar worked as the head of Rudolfstiftung Hospital (Krankenanstalt Rudolfstiftung der Stadt Wien) which still exists today. From 1876, he worked at Wiedner Hospital. In 1945, during the Second World War, Wiedner Hospital was bombed and then demolished in the 1950s. Dr. Kumar accompanied the Empress, who had tuberculosis, on her travels to Madeira, where doctors had advised her to seek benefit from the warmer weather. A newspaper article in the *Innsbrucker Nachrichten* from 24 November 1860 records that Dr. Kumar wrote to his teacher, Dr. Škoda, during the journey, for advice on her case (Dr. Ruth Koblizek, Medizinische Universität Wien, personal correspondence: 11 February 2015).

As Alex Sakula documents, Dr. Josef Škoda (1805–1881) was a Czech physician whose primary interest lay in cardiopulmonary disease. He became Chair of Internal Medicine at the prestigious Vienna Medical School in 1846 and three years later was Vice-Dean of the medical faculty (Alex Sakula, "Joseph Skoda 1805–81: a centenary tribute to a pioneer of thoracic medicine", *Thorax*, 36 [1981], pp. 404–11).
7 *The Court Journal* was a weekly journal published in London by Alabaster, Passmore and Sons from 1829 until 1919. See CL'ANA 0298 and CL'ANA 0320.
8 Wilhelm wrote this sentence on the back of the last page of this letter.

183 • Pauline Clairmont to Wilhelm Gaulis Clairmont

Baden June 8.[1] [c. 1865]

Dear Bill – Got yours yesterday with the enclosed – I am glad you write in tolerable good sp.[2] & that things dont look too bad – I do wish you had gone to Pesth[3] & let the rape[4] do the best it could – if I had been there I would have made you go – you were very foolish not to go – what is the good of living without pleasure & sunshine – night & old age come soon enough – Ma is always getting stronger and more energetic – for 2 years she had not been able to get up before 9 now she is up at 5 & has barely patience to wait till 6 till I get up to wash & dress her as she must not use her right arm – the wound is now healed up to half the size it is now about the size of this page the Doctors say she will now be in better health than for years previously. – the pain in the joints has quite disappeared she has only some difficulty in walking owing to weakness & want of exercise the doctor says that now half her strength goes towards healing the wound – as soon as that is accomplished she will feel strength return into her nerves & limbs – she also takes a little wine every day at dinner & at 10 o clock.

Of course I must stop till the wound is healed, – I think that will be by the end of June she thinks it will last longer if Birra[5] was not to be confined I would not insist so much on coming back but I dont see how you can leave the house to an entire stranger & you live out on the Puszta – [6]

My plan is to come in the first days of July stay with you till all the work is done & then pop off – therefore I am sorry to hear you talk of <u>hay making</u> I wish you could have sold the fields at whatever price About the winter I do not know how we shall manage time will show – if you can only give me those 1000 fl so that some of the installments could be paid off then M. at least would be at ease for at least 3 years – & that would be one care off our shoulders. About the money from Claire please send me 50 for me & if you want me to buy a ring you must add some more the rest please keep till I come – – [7]

I am going to send you some white piqué[8] for a waistcoat as soon as can go to town but till now M. will not let me stir out of the house –

Dear Bill I am going to be very troublesome again – it is awfully cold here & I would very much like to have my grey paletot.[9] if you have time & would be so very good as to send it me It is in one of the drawers of that press[10] where you found the brown dress but in which drawer I cannot precisely determine but believe bottom. It is a long wide concern very small chequered white & black English tweed bound with black & black buttons to it – dont prepay it – who would have thought it would turn to cold – clouds of dust raving up & down the street. Dear B. my greatest pleasure would be to see you get rid of Bob[11] not because I dont like the place – for in spite of difficulties we have managed to make ourselves comfortable & happy but because it is so far away & I can do nothing for you

your ever aff[te]
Palo.

I want to put off selling my shares but it is a satisfaction to M to have the papers here. I will apply to the Anglo Aust BK.[12] if the sale must be
How are all the fowls & is the S[illeg.]mutz[13] no worse? What does Birra say is the event to
come off in Septb?[14]

Address: No envelope

Unpublished. Text: M.S., Pf. Coll., CL'ANA 0219

---

1 This letter has neither envelope nor date for the year. However, factual information within it dates it to 1865 as Pauline mentioned the ring Wilhelm thought of buying (see CL'ANA 0267) and her desire for Wilhelm to leave Bobda, an event which occurred in October 1865.
2 Possibly "spirits".
3 Budapest. See CL'ANA 0269 in which Wilhelm wrote to Claire about his longing to visit Budapest.
4 Rapeseed plants belong to the mustard family. Its seeds can be used to make rapeseed oil. The plant's Latin name is *Brassica napus Linnaeus* (The Editors of Encyclopaedia Britannica. "Rape". *Encyclopaedia Britannica Online*. Encyclopaedia Britannica Inc., n.d. Web. 10 January 2015. http://www.britannica.com/plant/rape-plant).
5 Possibly Wilhelm and Pauline's housekeeper.
6 Hungarian for "plain".
7 See CL'ANA 0267.
8 Piqué refers to fabric made of either cotton or silk with raised cords.
9 A fitted jacket worn by women in the nineteenth century.
10 Cupboard.
11 Bobda.
12 These two sentences were written inside a square shape at the bottom of the final page of the letter. The Anglo-Austrian Bank was established in 1863. In 1926, the bank joined with the British Trade Corporation to form the Anglo-International Bank ("Anglo-International Bank Ltd". Web. 14 February 2015. http://heritagearchives.rbs.com/companies/list/anglo-international-bank-ltd.html). Alice Teichova records that in 1926, the Viennese branch of the Anglo-Austrian Bank was taken over and that the Bank of England had a "controlling interest" in that branch (*Handbook on the History of European Banks* [Manfred Pohl and Sabine Freitag (eds.), Hants, England: Elgar Publishing, 1994], p. 29).
13 Possibly "Schmutz" (German for dirt or mud).
14 These last two sentences were cross-written.

184 • Wilhelm Gaulis Clairmont to Claire Clairmont

[11 June 1865]

My dear aunt.

I am afraid you will have thought me very neglectful for not having written to you so long. but I can assure you it was utterly impossible I had so much to do I was engaged from morning till 10 or 11 at night and then I am tired for I get up at 3 or 4 in the morning – from now till harvest time, there is a little comparative peace so I seize the first chance I have of writing to you. –

first about the <u>draft</u>. I have now got the money all right, but it seems the Banker has not yet got the money from London unless within the last few days. You are much mistaken if you fancy that one can get a cheque cashed here at sight. Credit here is at such an utter discount that no one would dream of doing it – and if I had to wait search till I got a Temesvár banker who would cash a cheque at once I might search in vain for ever so long. Many thanks dearest aunt for the money which came to me like a true godsend – Paulas £20 are still in my hands – she being away at Baden – but she knows this money is here at her service. Becker I did not pay either because the fresh month was infringed on & I would have to pay him interest all the same for that month, but I will manage to pay him off by the end of the month; so you see I have stuck to all the tin. for the £10. you layed out for my pleasure I have also not yet bought anything for I have never been off the farm for the last 3 or 4 weeks. I was much tempted though to lay it out in a visit to Pesth for there left a cheap excursion train went by Gyertyamos the other day to Pest[1] to see all the festivies at the emperors arrival – however I did not go because I could not just then afford to leave the farm there was also an exhibition of agricultural machinery which would have interested me very much –

You asked me the other day about purchasing land in Hungary & I told you I had then no time to answer the question in full – I can only say now the same as I did before; I consider it now even a better speculation than before because the price of land has become so much depreciated through the bad times and the low prices – but the moment things go up again, land must regain its previous standard of value – It is the same thing when speculating in shares – buy them when high and you are almost sure to lose. buy them when low and you have at least a fair chance of gain provided of course the concern be a sound one and this of course agricultural land always is – there is for instance my friend Hauer at Csakova – he has an estate of about 1000 Austrian acres near Csakova – this he bought in straggling bits from the peasants but it is now being collected into one fine square block of land whereby it of course becomes increased in value at least by treble.[2] This property cost him inclusive of a house in Csakova /: separate from the property of 1000 acres :/ and several other expenses about £5000. If you were to give him now £3000 ready money I am sure he would give it up at once, for he has been now 3 years without revenue and always had to expend instead of receiving from the property – and he is utterly heartsick in consequence –/: this is not Rudolph Hauer my friend residing in Csakova but his older brother residing at Vienna who is the real proprietor of the property³ :/ Now supposing you were to buy this property; you would pay him down £3000 [illeg.] suppose even you paid him £4000. you would then want £1000 more for the construction of the necessary farmbuildings for there are none now, so that your entire investment would amount to £5000. for which you would be the proprietress of 1000 acres of land and nice house in Chakova which alone formerly cost £500.

Now if you were to let me this farm I could pay you with perfect ease 4/s an acre rent for it the government taxes amount to also 4/- so that I would pay in all 8/- an acre which would secure to you 4 percent for a capital invested in landed property and to me a very good living – for only think that here I pay 21/- an acre so that it would be to me a clean saving of 13/- an acre – allow 3/- an acre difference for the inferior quality of the soil and situation leaves me still a gainer of 10/- an acre. this on 1000 acres would be £500; for me a splendid income – last year notwithstanding the very low prices I managed to escape without almost any loss – this year owing to the awful drought we had it will be the same. so I have had no revenue this year, although also no loss – but you must remember that I have been paying a rent at the rate of 21/- per acre; if on your farm I pay only 8/- rent and taxes there is a clean balance in my favour of 13/- an acre this makes on 400 acres £260 which for me would be a very nice revenue. I do not say all this with a view of convincing you, that <u>I</u> personally would fare well by such a transaction but I wish to convince you that as <u>your tenant</u> I would even in unprosperous years such as these last have been, make quite a tidy income and that there is therefore no danger of my not being in a position to pay the rent properly and punctually – and of course I would be perfectly willing to enter into any arrangement with you to pay you more than the stipulated rent in case of the times and circumstances minding. for you it would be a very good speculation; for the money would be perfectly safe and the interest good – I do not however wish to urge you – this is my opinion and if I had any money I would invest it so and no otherwise but I feel that you have a right to regard my opinion with diffidence seeing that I have been so unsuccessful in my own enterprise. I am glad you liked my photograph – it was done at Pest. the name of my banker in Temesvár is "Gotthilf Söhne"[4] there agent in Vienna is Ribaz[5] but his correspondent in London they do not know – Of Mamma there is excellent news – she is recovering her appetite spirits and <u>combativeness</u> fast – how are you dear aunt – I hope you are well – Goodbye now dearest aunty yours most

                affectionately
                WGC

Bobda
June 11th 1865–

P.S. there is no B. in Hauer's estate it is called "Gilad".[6]

this minute I am in receipt of yours of the 4th inst. enclosing note from the Chief Cashier – the money I have got; but I am glad you sent me the Chief Cashier's note as I will show it to the Temesvarer Banker and make him a row and make him pay interest on the money for the whole time it was unlawfully held back – in return to your inquiries about Mamma I send you Plin's note which I received this minute and which gives you all the information required.

Address: No envelope

Unpublished. Text: M.S., Pf. Coll., CL'ANA 0269

---

1 Budapest is 273 kilometers north-west of Cărpiniș, Romania (Gyertyámos in Hungarian). From 6–9 June 1865, Kaiser Franz Joseph I visited Ofen (German for Buda) for "political conferences" (Glenn Jewison and Jörg Steiner. "Austro-Hungarian Land Forces". Web. 2 February 2015. http://www.austro-hungarian-army.co.uk/index.htm).
2 Gilad is 6.4 kilometers south of Ciacova.
3 Rudolf's brother, Francis von Hauer. See CL'ANA 0271.
4 The *Handels-und Gewerbe-Addressenbuch* ("Trade and Industry Address Book") lists Eduard Gotthilf as head of the trading house Franz Gotthilf Söhne (Franz Gotthilf's Sons) in Temesvár. He is listed as a "Chef des Handlungshauses" (head of the trading house), (Vienna: Förster & Bartelmus, 1863), p. 274.
5 John Murray's *A Handbook for Travellers in Southern Germany* suggests Ribarz as a "money changer" in Vienna. Ribarz was located on "Kärnthner Strasse" (London: William Clowes, 1873), p. 204.
6 Known as Gilad in both German and Hungarian, and Ghilad in Romanian, the estate to which Wilhelm refers is in the Timiș region of Romania. The commune consists of the towns of Gad and Ghilad. Ghilad is situated 51 kilometers south of Bobda. Wilhelm drew a short line under half of the word "Gilad" to separate his final paragraph from the rest of the letter.

185 • Wilhelm Gaulis Clairmont to Claire Clairmont

[10 October 1865]

My dearest aunt.

This so long since I had any news from you that I do not even know your present direction & must send this to Pauline who is now staying with Mamma to have it forwarded to you. the most important news I have to give you is that I leave Bobda this week and settle on a new farm about 25 engl miles S.E. from here[1] – the fatal B.[2] occurs not in its name – you may imagine what a trudge of packing and moving I had to do and that all by myself. by the by what do you wish me to do with your boxes? as it seems now pretty well determined that you will never join us in the Banat, would you perhaps wish them to be returned to you? and if so by what rout? the money to Becker I need not tell you has been paid ages ago. but he was so good natured he would insist on my still keeping it – pray write me again to let me know something about you, fore now that I am separated from Plin I hear nothing of you unless you write to me directly – I will give you my full direction below – do not be angry if at times I am not as regular a correspondent as I should be – at the times I have so much to do I cannot get through it all goodbye dearest aunt

yours affectly
WGC

Octob 10th 1865. Bobda
W.G. Clairmont
Offszeniza Bánlok[3]
In Bánat

Address: No envelope

Unpublished. Text: M.S., Pf. Coll., CL'ANA 0270

---

1 The actual distance is 34 miles.
2 See CL'ANA 0269.
3 Known as Banloc in Romanian, Wilhelm combined both the German spelling (Banlok) and the Hungarian spelling (Bánlak). The commune of Banloc is in Timiş County, Romania. Ofseniţa is one of the four towns in the commune which includes the town of Banloc itself. Timişoara is located 52 kilometers north of Banloc, which is 3 kilometers south of Ofseniţa. Ghilad is 6 kilometers north of Ofseniţa. As Wilhelm explained in CL'ANA 0271, his house was located in the village of Ofseniţa.

28 MARCH 1861–24 DECEMBER 1889

186 • Wilhelm Gaulis Clairmont to Claire Clairmont

[12 December 1865]

My dearest aunt

I was much delighted to get some news from you at last although it was none of the very best – as far as your health is concerned. however you must only make the best of it dearest aunt when summer comes round again no doubt you will again feel better – You must not blame Plin for having delayed the dispatch of my letter to you – for she wrote to me at the time that she could not forward it immediately as you were either then moving or about to move – I forget which – About my new farm I have as yet of course no positive account to give; as the one cannot tell till next harvest comes round – but as far as I have improved my knowledge of the soil and other local circumstances while sowing my winter crops I have every reason to be satisfied. I believe I have told you that I have taken this farm together that is in partnership with an old schoolfriend of mine Hauer[1] whoses Brother is the proprietor of the estate we rented – we do not pay our rent in ready money but in wheat so that if the present low prices of breadstuffs continue we are the loosers only <u>in part</u> because our chief payment is we viz the rent is made in kind, so that its price does not effect us – Rudolf Hauer hitherto managed the estate for his brother Francis – he is clever, thoughtful, cautious painstaking and has very sound technical information – he is also extremely honest just and generous – the only fault I discover in him as a partner in business is that he is not firm & energetic enough in important matters but on the other hand sometimes a little entêté[2] in trifles. I am however sure that we will agree very well together – You ask me a number of questions about my new abode which I will answer – My house is situated in the village of Offszenitza[3] and is only ten minutes walk from our farm we intend however to build a house for me there next spring if circumstances will permit. you need give yourself no concern about my new abode it is in every respect very healthy – wind and water tight; the stoves do <u>not</u> smoke. the house is placed with its frontage towards the South which is pleasant enough in winter but I do not know how it will be in summer. About your boxes and pictures you need not give yourself any concern; they are all safe. I agree with you that Banat would be an unsuitable place for you to live in nevertheless we have had very fine weather until within a few days ago when the frost commenced – It would be very nice if you could settle some where at or near Fiume;[4] there is no doubt you would find it very cheap and Pauline could come at times & be with you; they also talk of establishing a line of rail between the Banat and Fiume; but Heaven knows when that will come to pass. they have been talking about it ever since I am here in this part of the world – the unfavorable account you give of Italy also holds good in a great measure of in this country they all complain here too of the bad times many tradesmen are ruined because there is a general tendency to avoid spending money –[5] the farmers as a matter of course are all ruined in consequence of the low prices of breadstuffs that have been obtaining most pertinaceously for the last two or three years; and in a country like this, that has neither commerce nor manufacturers but only agriculture a flagging ~~of~~ in that interest immediately causes a depression in the whole business world –

Paula – the noughty girl did not write me anything of the misfortunes poor Australia met with; she is very prejudiced in favour of it – What a horrid fate the poor Duncan Dunbar met with I knew both the vessel and its captain – she was a fine large ship of more than a 1000 tons – and belonged to Messrs. Green of Blackwell – there was the <u>Dunbar</u> and the <u>Duncan Dunbar</u>.[6] how strange that both these vessels should have met such a horrid fate – the Dunbar was smashed to pieces on the rocks at the foot of Sydney lighthouse after a most successful passage from England all hands on board were lost including passengers and all excepting one sailor a blackman who was wafted from the vessel by a strong wave into a crevice between the rocks where he stuck high and dry – he was the only one left to relate the history of the illfated vessel. The captain, an old and experienced sailor who was then making his twentyfirst trip to Australia was ambitious to shorten the passage by one day and stood in for the harbour although the sea was very high and the night pitchdark. When close in he mistook a low gap some hundred yards distant from the lighthouse for the entrance between the Sydney heads and the vessel was accordingly run against the rocks and swallowed in an instant by the waves which ran uncommonly high – This happened the last year that I spent in Australia and now the Dun[~~illeg.~~]bar must meet a similar fate – I know all the Morts; but there are so many of them I do not know which Mrs Mort that must have been on board the Duncan Dunbar –[7]

Plin has given up Colonel B.[8] I believe – I was not against it as soon as I saw she was serious, only I deprecated against his being trifled with – Mamma & Uncle George[9] are so desperately against it and I really must say I think unjustly so. Uncle George says that he is so unpresentable and that he has uncleanly habits – but I never heard the details about that the only plausible reason I know against the union is that he is given to the idea that everybody wants to poison him, which makes him wander about from inn to inn and take his food every day at another place – now he might take this spleen also against his wife and then what a pleasant state of things that would be!

Thank you dearest aunt for your kind wishes for Xmas & new year I am sure I return them to you most cordially with a wish for many more happy returns of them – Now the postage has been reduced in Austria from 15 to 5 kr. which is something near one penny English money – this is very jolly because it will enable one to write and get so many more letters. Goodbye dearest best aunt many, many thanks for your solicitude for my welfare, I wish we could meet again then one can put up with another bit of separation

yours most affectionately
WGC

Decemb. 12<u>th</u> 1865.
Please direct instead of formerly

only Clairmont Csákova Banat
Hungary.

Address: La Signora Clairmont/665. Piazza della Fontina/Pisa.
Front postmark: BOLLO INSUFFICIENTE

Unpublished. Text: M.S., Pf. Coll., CL'ANA 0271

---

1 See CL'ANA 0267 and CL'ANA 0269.
2 French for stubborn or obstinate.
3 See note 3, CL'ANA 0270.
4 See CL'ANA 0252.
5 Wilhelm continued this letter on a new set of pages and he marked them with a "2)".
6 The *Dunbar* and the *Duncan Dunbar* were two ships the firm of James Laing and Sons, in Sunderland, England built. During inclement weather and at night on 20 August 1857, the *Dunbar* with Captain Green at the helm attempted to approach Port Jackson by passing through the Sydney Heads, a series of rocks. The ship ran into the rocks and almost all of the 121 crew members and passengers drowned. The only survivor was James Johnson, a sailor ("Objects Through Time". Migration Heritage Center. Web. 25 April 2015. http://www.migrationheritage.nsw.gov.au/exhibition/objectsthroughtime/dunbar/). In 1865, the *Dunbar*'s sister ship, the *Duncan Dunbar*, was wrecked on the reef of Las Rocas, Brazil. According to a report published on 22 January 1866 in *The Sydney Morning Herald*, all 117 passengers were saved (National Library of Australia, http://nla.gov.au/nla.news-article13125117, p. 5).
7 In a letter to passenger George Thornton, Esquire, which was included in *The Sydney Morning Herald* report of 22 January 1866, twenty-eight passengers expressed their thanks and gratitude for the way in which Thornton "in this emergency . . . came forward, and, . . . introduced system, and changed confusion into order" (National Library of Australia, http://nla.gov.au/nla.news-article13125117, p. 5). Twenty-eight passengers signed the letter, including Maria Mort, Eliza S. Mort, and Katie Mort. Maria Mort was the wife of Henry Mort, pastoralist, politician, and younger brother of Thomas Sutcliffe Mort (see CL'ANA 0075). Eliza Mort and Katie Mort were presumably their daughters, as the passenger list included "Mrs. Mort and family" (Barnard, Alan. "Mort, Thomas Sutcliffe (1816–1878)", *Australian Dictionary of Biography*. National Centre of Biography, Australian National University. 1974. Web. 25 October 2015. http://adb.anu.edu.au/biography/mort-thomas-sutcliffe-4258/text6777).
8 Unidentified. However, in 1869, Pauline would have a relationship with Major Adams. See CL'ANA 0294.
9 Antonia's brother.

187 • Wilhelm Gaulis Clairmont to Claire Clairmont

[6 February 1866]

My dearest aunt.

You will be pleased to hear that I am at last engaged to be married. my betrothed is called Ottilia[1] she is the sister in law of my friend Hauer[2] and the daughter of a Hofrath[3] Pichler in Vienna – she is an extremely nice and although I say it handsome girl – she has it is true no fortune but every quality of heart and head one could desire she is extremely well educated still very simple and free from any pretensions our wedding is not to be till [illeg.] autumn because I want to await the result of this years' harvest. I am sure you will like Ottilie very much if you could come to see her; if we had once a good harvest I would willingly take her to Florence or Pisa for you to see her; but for the present we have bad times. Ottilia was stopping here until shortly when she went to Vienna to join her family; she is the best girl and loves me most ardently which makes me very happy – the affair is already of 3 years standing I wanted to put off coming to a declaration until my circumstances should be improved but I could not any longer.

Goodbye dearest aunt; I hope you will sympathise with me and give me your blessing believe me dearest aunt yours

most affectionately
WGC

Csakova
February 6th 1866.
my present direction is:
Csakova. Banat.

No envelope.

Unpublished. Text: M.S., Pf. Coll., CL'ANA 0272

---

1 Ottilia was known as Ottilie. Wilhelm also referred to her as Tilly, Tits, and Titsy.
2 Rudolf von Hauer married Emily von Pichler, Ottilia's sister.
3 The term "Hofrath" in Austria referred to a Privy Councillor (Michael Clyne, *Language and Human Relations* [New York: Cambridge University Press, 2009], p. 145).

188 • Wilhelm Gaulis Clairmont to Claire Clairmont

[18 February 1866]

My dearest aunt

I got yesterday your nice warmhearted letter acknowledging the receipt of mine announcing my engagement. I cannot tell you what pleasure it gave me. you are the best dearest aunt I have and I love you now even much more than I did before because you are so kind and affectionate towards my Ottilia. she is not here now – she returned to her parents' in Vienna but I have sent her your direction and she will forestall your intentions of writing to her. she speaks English tolerably well, but her writing is not very good however I dare say you will be able to make it out. she also writes me a great deal in English. I read your letter to her sister Mrs Hauer who was exceedingly rejoiced at it the more as I must own to you in confidence that Mamma has not behaved well towards me on this occasion at all – Tilly wrote her a most humble and affectionate letter which she did not even answer – she never saw either Ottilie nor any of her family, and nevertheless makes opposition against my choice with the most virulent vehemence. I cannot conceive at all why or wherefore. I cannot conceive at all why, for the family is a very good one and her individual character is most unexceptional – that she has no fortune is a drawback of course but it affects me only; Mamma ought to remember that when she married she had no fortune either, and that she was not as far as I am informed railed at either by your family on that account. However I will not say any more on this subject; I am convinced that I am acting rightly and that her opposition springs only from a diseased mind Pauline gives a very sad account of the changes which have come over poor Ma. in within the last year. I owe it however both to Tilly and myself to tell you that everyone else from Pauline to the most distant acquaintance most cordially approve of my choice. she has the sweetest most feminine disposition is at the same time highly educated but very simple domestic and without any pretensions she is very fond of country life & although she is very handsome and was always sought after very much at balls and parties still she assures me that she never cared for town amusements. she was 23 last January and as I am 35 her age too is in proportion to mine.[1] – I have not written to her that you intended to send a present to her so that it may come as a surprise – I think either a watchguard chain (for she has a nice little watch from her father) or a set of broche & studs for cuffs would please her best.[2] Pauline also wrote me dearest aunt that you had promised to send her £20 in case she got no dividend – thank you for this dearest aunt it will be a great help to her. Of our harvest prospects for this season I can as yet say nothing until the season is further advanced. Do try and take good care of your health; how sad and wretched is it that we must live so far apart the first trip I ever make with Tilly if we have a good harvest shall be to Pisa. Goodbye my dearest best aunt

yours affect
Willy

Febry 18ᵗʰ 1866.³
I have no photograph of Tilly to spare but I have asked her to send you one if she has any.
I reopened this letter in order to put Tilly's direction in

Ottilie's direction is:
Fräulein Ottilie Pichler
Beatrixgasse No 19⁴
Landstrasse⁵
Wien

Address: No envelope

Unpublished. Text: M.S., Pf. Coll., CL'ANA 0273

---

1 On 3 June, 1858, Wilhelm told Claire that Ada Ramsbottom was "12 years or so too old to be my wife" (see CL'ANA 0079). Ottilia was twelve years younger than Wilhelm, a fact Stocking interprets as Wilhelm's desire for a wife "twelve years younger than he" (*CC* II: 593).
2 Fashionable sleeves for women in the nineteenth century included the leg-of-mutton and the elephant sleeve. Sleeves were often cuffed with attractive studs.
3 Wilhelm cross-wrote the remainder of the letter. Wilhelm also included an insert with Ottilia's address.
4 The building today at Beatrixgasse 19 still stands and houses offices at the time that this collection went to print.
5 Vienna consists of twenty-three districts, known as "Bezirke" in German. The first district, Innere Stadt, is the most central of the districts. From there, the various districts "spiral out . . . in a clockwise manner" ("The 23 Districts (Bezirke) of Vienna". Web. 12 February 2015. http://www.tourmycountry.com/austria/districts-vienna.htm). Landstrasse is the third district and Beatrixgasse is about 400 meters from the Stadtpark, a city park that extends from Innere Stadt to the third district.

189 • Wilhelm Gaulis Clairmont to Claire Clairmont

[23 April 1866]

My dearest aunt.

I duly received your last letter although I have been in such a turmoil of business that I have until now not been able to find time to answer it. thank you dearest aunt for your anxious care for my interest – I have communicated to Pauline the substance of your letter I do not know whether she has written to you on the subject; she wrote me to say she had the persuasion that your fears were groundless – that it was not in Mammas nature even now in her altered state of feeling to attempt anything clandestine on the contrary she rather seems to delight in the open exercise of what she looks upon her good right in open defiance of the world – Pauline will nevertheless take your remarks into consideration & be on the watch –

I thank you much dearest aunt for your genuine kindness to Tilly – I am about to start for Vienna towards the latter end of this month. I shall stay about 4 weeks. If our harvest prospects continue as favorable as hitherto we shall very likely have our wedding towards the end of July – but this is as yet a secret; for if the prospects should turn out unfavorable we shall have to delay our wedding therefore it is not advisable to say anything about it now – I am very anxious to hear about your health; how your eyes are getting on if the distance were but not so great I would delight in making a trip to Florence with Tilly. I am sure you would like her very much – she is so gentle and so affectionate – I was much horrified at the account of the persecutions of Protestants in the vicinity of Florence – there will be no peace until they hunt all those Jesuits away[1] – Goodbye now dearest aunt; I have a great deal to do –

yours most affectionately
Willy

Csakova
April 23rd 1866.

Address: No envelope.

Unpublished. Text: M.S., Pf. Coll., CL'ANA 0274

---

1 The Waldensians, a Protestant sect, continued to experience discrimination in Italy in the nineteenth century. Bloody anti-Protestant riots occurred in Barletta in southern Italy in 1866. Danilo Raponi explains: "On 19 March 1866, a Catholic priest fomented a pogrom against the Protestant community. The mob set fire to the house of the pastor, Gaetano Giannini, who had moved from the Abbruzzi to Barletta in 1865 . . . six Protestants were murdered in 1866 in Italy, a country that wanted to fashion itself as a modern European power. Barletta highlighted, instead, the backwardness and fanaticism of some sectors of the Italian population, and even though the Italian peninsula would not host intolerant events of such gravity any longer, anti-Protestant attitudes remained in the Italian mind for a long time" (*Religion and Politics in the Risorgimento* [London: Palgrave Macmillan, 2014], pp. 152–3).

190 • Wilhelm Gaulis Clairmont to Claire Clairmont

[4 May 1866]

My dearest aunt.

I have arrived here a few days ago and have already been to Baden to see my Mama whom I regret to say I found very poorly, for she has had a fresh outbreak of the cancer and [illeg.] had to undergo a fresh operation on Monday last which however is luckily over and the wound doing well – but poor Mama has aged terribly in this year since I have not seen her – she looks as if she were at least 10 years older – I really believe it is only the uncommon energy and vitality of her mind which keeps body and soul together with her – although her person appears so decrepid still the vigour of her mind is as fresh as ever – I also read the two letters which you wrote lately one to Mama & one to Pauline – I thank you dearest aunt most sincerely for all the kind affection for me which those letters manifested so clearly – It will be a satisfaction to you to hear that your exertions have been successful and that Mama has been very kind and affectionate towards me and has consented to see and see Tilly tomorrow – So I shall go out with her and her sister Alma tomorrow – I am so glad of this on poor Tilly's account because she was fretting very much because of Ma's strange conduct. Perhaps I may retain this letter till tomorrow and post it in Baden to let you know how our visit went off – Also for what you wrote concerning Ma's will I was very thankful to you and I have no doubt that you will succeed in averting from us a very serious calamity – As to the hope which you held out to Ma of advancing her the money for paying off the saving Bank I could not exactly make out whether you meant this seriously or whether you only meant this as a stratagem to get hold of a motive why you want her will – In either case we (that is Pauline & I) must feel very thankful to you – But if you could in reality advance that money dearest aunt you would really confer a very great boon on us – you would obtain your 5 percent, and for us all danger of Ma's buying an annuity would be over, because being relieved of the yearly instalments which she has to pay back to the Sparcasse[1] now, she could make the ends meet very [illeg.] well and would no longer be under a temptation to buy an annuity, moreover you would have to be legally secured for the amount which would effectually prevent her playing any tricks even if she were inclined – I fancy she might then pay me also a small interest say 2 ½ percent on my 10.000f which she has had now for six years without paying me anything –

So dearest aunt if you could lend us that money you would indeed confer a great benefit on us all – and I think you would not be the looser yourself, for houseproperty is at all times safer than bonds or stocks only care must be taken that Mama shall have no power over it.

I am almost always with the Pichlers they are a very nice amiable family consisting of father, mother, one son of 18 and the two daughters Ottilia and Alma – the latter is 18 and a very nice younger sister she will be to me, she has a beautiful voice and sings very well – Moritz[2] is studying to be Engineer – their Mama has a most active brain and talks very much but quite harmlessly she is a person quite overflowing with sentiment but the father being quite of the opposite temperament their children have the just³ [illeg.] in this respect. Now Goodbye dearest aunt Believe me yours most affectionately

WGC

Vienna May 4<u>th</u> 1866
My direction is that of Hofrath Pichler I stop here till the end of May –
P.S. a point very much in favour of your sending the money now would be the rising of the discount in favour of foreign remittances in consequence of the impending war⁴ – You will in return of course have to secure yourself also to receive your interest not in Austrian but in foreign money so as to be sure of the fluctuations of the Austrian paper currency – If the war really does break out the discount will shortly amount to 40 to 50 percent again – so that about 700 instead of 1000 Pounds would suffice to pay off the debt of the savings bank which I believe 10.000f
Baden May 5<u>th</u> Mama has seen Tilly and is very much charmed with her, and so is Tilly with Ma – who was very kind towards her – we spent a very pleasant afternoon all together at Baden with Pauline. Mama is still very weak but getting on as well as could be expected after so serious an operation – Pauline and Tilly join in sending you their best regards. Believe me dear aunt yours most affect –

WGC

Address: No envelope.

Unpublished. Text: M.S., Pf. Coll., CL'ANA 0275

---

1 German for "savings bank". Today, the spelling is "Sparkasse".
2 Ottilia's brother.
3 Wilhelm cross-wrote the final paragraph, from the illegible word until "the end of May –" He began a new sheet of paper for the letter's postscript.
4 The Austro-Prussian War, also known as the Seven Weeks' War, began in June 1866 and concluded seven weeks later with the defeat of Austria by the powerful Prussian state under Otto von Bismarck (The Editors of Encyclopaedia Britannica. "Seven Weeks' War". *Encyclopaedia Britannica Online*. Encyclopaedia Britannica Inc., n.d. Web. 10 October 2015. http://www.britannica.com/event/Seven-Weeks-War).

191 • Wilhelm Gaulis Clairmont to Claire Clairmont

[22 May 1866]

My dearest aunt.

I was very sad at the receipt of your last letter complaining so much of the state of your eyes – I am very unhappy about it the more as I feel my utter incapability to help you in any way – it is so particularly unfortunate that we must be separated so much as a complaint of the eyes if not attended by pain could be alleviated so very much by the attendance of your relatives – Mrs Hauer[1] also suffers from weak eyes, it would be a great hardship to her to be alone for she cannot even read a letter but being with her husband who reads everything to her it is made comparatively easy – I am sorry the stocks are just now so low that you cannot send the money – but it does not matter in so far as I think the exchange will yet rise considerably in favour of foreign remittances for if war breaks out as now seems inevitable the austrian paper currency will sink down to nothing – but your interest will always be safe to you – as Mamma having had the profit in the capital can very well afford to pay the premium on your interest – I thank you very much dearest aunt for the presents you bought for Tilly – but I wish you could send them soon so that she may have them before the war breaks out – what sort of a chain did you buy? and how will you send it? the will you got sent was not drawn up rightly so I got Mama to make another one of the same tenor but worded differently so as to make apparent her debt to us children which was not the case in the last will. you will have received a copy of this last will and must please send the first back – I return to Csakova in June that is the first days in June.

Goodbye dearest aunt
yours most affectionately
WGC

Vienna
19 Beatrixgasse
Landstrasse
May 22nd 1866.

Address: No envelope.

Unpublished. Text: M.S., Pf. Coll., CL'ANA 0276

---

1 Probably Emily von Hauer, Ottilia's sister.

192 • Wilhelm Gaulis Clairmont to Claire Clairmont

[16 June 1866]

My dearest aunt.

I have since my last returned to my post in obedience rather to necessity than any inclination for I love Tilly most tenderly and found separation from her very hard – the [illeg.] money I got two days previous to my departure – £10 I transmitted to Mama at once for Tilly's £20 we got 257f. out of this we bought a nice gold watchguard[1] costing 58f then a silkdress undyed costing 30f. then our wedding rings costing 20f. so that about 150f are still left. this we put with common consent into the savingsbank in order to buy something with this money which may become desirable when we furnish our house – I wanted Tilly to have something for her person only but she is so extremely ardent and so self denying that she persisted in putting the money by, saying that we were not rich & must save and that for her the watch chain & the silkdress were more than enough. she is a dear creature and you would love her much if you could know her – I had the most agreeable surprise to find on my return here everything in the most promising state. Crops all look beautiful and with the war there is also a fair chance of there being a good price. the details you require regarding Mama's house are as follows –:

debt still remaining on the 9900f amount insured for the houses (that is which would be paid to Ma in case of these being burnt) _____ 4000f

amount of annual insurance paid by Ma for the houses   15f.

the amount which Ma insured the houses for 4000f. that is £400 is in my opinion too small – for you are of course aware that that is optional with the owner – the amount of insurance fee 15f. equal to 30f – is so small because the houses are all built of solid material and in a genteel vicinity where there are neither poor mens hovels nor manufactories endangering the safety of a building – the exchange in favour of England is now rising everyday – Goodbye dearest aunt Tilly has already the feeling of warmest attachment to you – Believe me yours ever most

affectionately
WGC

Csakova
near Temesvár, Banat.
June 16th 1866.

I hope our wedding will take place still the middle of July –[2]

Address: No envelope

Unpublished. Text: M.S., Pf. Coll., CL'ANA 0277

---

1 In what was possibly her wedding picture, it appears as if Ottilia was wearing the watch guard. See photograph of Wilhelm and Ottilia in this collection. The couple were married in Liebling on

8 August 1866. Wilhelm was listed as being a "Privatier" ("man of independent means"). Ottilia's place of residence was given as Vienna and her name was recorded as "Ottilie Caroline Anna Pichler". Wilhelm's place of residence was listed as Csákova. Alexander Bariss was the officiating clergyman while Ritter (Baronet) Rudolf von Hauer and Freiherr (Baron) Bernhard von Hauser were the witnesses. Liebling is 34 kilometers south of Timişoara and 25 kilometers north-east of Ghilad.

2 This final sentence was written on the back of the last page of the letter.

193 • Antonia Clairmont to Claire Clairmont

Baden 22 Dec. 1866

My dearest Claire.[1]

How can I thank you for the kind and affectionate letter which shows your sympathy with our loss, which came upon us so unexpectedly – dear Pauline did her duty in nursing him to the last, and I thanked God that every thing was done for him and a loving hand to shut his eyes, and put him to his last resting place;[2] you must excuse my long silence but I heard from Pauline that you are pretty well in health, and so the days passed on with us in trouble and uneasiness, the summer was bad for the houseowners – soldiery we had here the whole summer and we have just now done with cleaning all the rooms beddings and furniture they had in use which also kept me from writing for my head is growing so weak and I forget my English entirely which you will perceive in reading this: from dear Willy I had shortly a[illeg.] letter me, he is very happy with his young wife, and I hope they will remain so: the legacy from my poor brother was not so much as to clear the whole debt from the houses, only about half, but even that is a great benefit, for one in my narrow circumstances, but we cannot live so as you thought we could do as we are by no means sure what next spring will bring, if there is again war, and all its attending hardships it will go badly therefore Dear Pauline has taken a place again to help out, for she is the only one who can help if need be – I should be very happy to see you here next summer, you would find all the persons you know, but Mr Carl[3] he went to live in town, on account of his daughter I am very[4] to have lost his society Colonel B.[5] cannot recover the loss of poor George, he has been ill ever since, and makes himself a complete hermit to mourn his loss – they were such real friends – we have now a hard winter, snow and frost, but the cold never affects me, I do not go out more than beyond the court in the other house, and remain always alone, but that quiet does me good; Good bye my dearest Claire, if your health allows do write to me again, in [illeg.] shall write to you, and now let me conclude with my best wishes for your health and welfare in the next year.

ever yours affect –
A. Clairmont

Address: Mrs Clairmont/ 12. Corso dei Tintori/Signora Papiaroni[6]/<u>Florence</u>
Front postmark: AFF. INSUFF./ CRED. AUS. S 10[7]
Rear postmark: VENEZIA/ 2[illeg.]/₁₂ ; FIRENZE/ [illeg.]

Unpublished. Text: M.S., Pf. Coll., CL'ANA 0321

---

1 Antonia's initials "AC" are imprinted in the middle of the first page of the letter.
2 Antonia's brother, Georg Ghilain von Hembyze, died at the age of 64 in 1866. The *Wiener Zeitung* of 1866, number 252 (Austrian Newspapers Online, Österreichische Nationalbibliothek [Austrian

National Library, http://www.anno.onb.ac.at/cgi-content/anno?apm=0&aid=wrz&datum=186610 13&seite=9&zoom=2, p. 9]), records his death on 11 October 1866 in the afternoon. His name was recorded as Georg Ghilain v. Hembyze and his address was listed as Breitegasse 4. His profession was listed as k. k. Oberst (k. k. Colonel [kaiserlich und königlich, German for "Imperial and Royal"]).

3 See CL'ANA 0421, Box 1, bundle a, numbers 8–10.
4 Omitted word.
5 Colonel Becker. See CL'ANA 0421, Box 1, bundle a, numbers 8–10.
6 See CL'ANA 0208.
7 The number 10 was written in by hand.

194 • Wilhelm Gaulis Clairmont to Claire Clairmont

[11 March 1867]

My dearest aunt.

How is it you do not write us for such a long time – you give me great anxiety – Tilly is assisting her sister[1] at Csakova who has been confined of a daughter or else she would also add a few lines – we wrote to you both together some 6 or 7 weeks ago or may be even longer ago – your silence has caused us all great uneasiness – Pauline does not mention either having heard from you – it would be dreadful to know you ill among strangers – if your eyes are weak never mind writing long letters but write at least a few lines that we may know how you are off. You will be glad to hear dearest aunt that our crops are looking well; the season promises very fairly and so far as our prospects are formed for the present the[2] entitle us to the best hopes.

Goodbye dearest aunt Do write soon

yours most affectly
W. Clairmont

March 11th 1867.
Csakova near Temesvár
Hungary.

Address: La signora Clairmont/12 Corso dei Tintori/Firenze/Italia.
Front postmark: BANLOK/ 12/3; CRED AUS.S.
Rear postmark: VENEZIA/ 15/ MAR/67/5 S; DETTA/12/3/ARRIVO/16/MAR./67/FIRENZE[3]

Unpublished. Text: M.S., Pf. Coll., CL'ANA 0278

---

1 Emily von Hauer.
2 Probably "they".
3 See CL'ANA 0283 for information about Deta.

195 • Antonia Clairmont to Claire Clairmont

[22 June 1867]

My dearest Claire.[1]

How very amiable of you to write to me after my long silence to you; but I have suffered very much this last year as Pauline will have told you, my memory was so weak, and is so still, and my eyes also that writing is a difficult thing for me; I have a little recovered but am not strong enough to undergo the operation still waiting for me perhaps next month – we have a bad season this year what with the coronation[2] and the Paris exhibition[3] we let our lodgings very badly this year, but thank God I let them a little is better than nothing! Pauline is still in Vienna Miss M.[4] is not going to England at which poor P. is quite vexed, and if the Paris journey should also miscarry P. will leave her and come home, which I should be very glad off;[5] she is a very good daughter and helps whenever she can in paying off the instalments her misfortune is only that she is nowhere satisfied and cannot bear little things with patience. – of Willy I cannot tell you anything; since his marriage he wrote only once to say he is very happy with his wife and since then not a line not even last winter when I was so ill that the doctor hardly hoped for my recovery: I hear from [illeg.] P. and as she is gone, I hear nothing at all his wife's family have not much of my favour; of Otti:[6] I know so little that I cannot say I feel sure she will make dear W. happy. just now arrived a letter from W to P., but as I never open any of their letters I sent it off to her and must now wait what she tells me; you say, you are left much to your own thoughts and so am I, and so is poor old countess Auer[illeg.]sperg[7] who lives again here you will remember her? and so I think is everybody in old age; Mrs Fallenbock is always ailing I have not seen her since last year; how kind of you to think of her! Baden is now lovely so green and fresh, also the whether turns fine but we had a bad spring; I wish I could inclose in this the lovely bunch of flowers I had just brought in fresh from the garden; the trees and shrubs grow so finely; it is a pleasant thought that <u>we</u> shall leave the children such a nice home for their own; you also helped me on [~~illeg.~~] and so I way[8] <u>we</u>, and trust to give you a pleasant objects of your thoughts; if you could only come here and spend some time with us; though you would have little pleasure for I am dreadfully dull, cannot talk nor read hardly listen; my acquaintances dwindle of[9] one by one, I may not even at cards, it affects my eyes so badly. Pauline met with the Pulsky's[10] at Pest and she heard that they had been living 7 years at Florence have you not known them? but P. will tell you all about them; you wish me too much dearest Claire more than I can hope or expect health and strength I can never regain long life I can hardly expect, <u>prosperity</u> if granted to my children Im satisfied; if my eyesight is left to me I shall be grateful and wish no more; my head is also very weak. Now goodbye dear Claire take my best wishes for your welfare, and write to me again it makes me very happy. ever yours affectl

A. Clairmont

I shall thank you for the C Journal,[11] though I may not read small print, old Baron Reisner whom you perhaps know, as he lives at my house, calls sometimes and reads to me;

Baden 491. 22 June. 1867

Address: à Madame de Clairmont/Casa Barsantini alla Villa/Bagni di Lucca[12]/Italie.
Front postmark: Baden/ [22]/[6]/ 4.E.
Rear postmark: VENEZIA/24/ GIU.[13]/ 67/ 5 S;
BAGNI DI LUCCA/ 25/ GIU/[illeg.]

Unpublished. Text: M.S., Pf. Coll., CL'ANA 0320

---

1 Antonia's initials are pressed onto the left side of the paper.
2 In 1867, Austria and Hungary united to create the Austro-Hungarian Dual Monarchy. The compromise with Hungary (Ausgleich) meant that Emperor Franz Joseph I of Austria was also crowned King of Hungary and his wife Empress Elisabeth of Austria became Queen of Hungary. Under the Dual Monarchy, the countries shared military resources and pursued a joint foreign policy, but the two countries were governed separately for the most part, with separate capitals in Vienna and Budapest. The coronation of Franz Joseph I took place on 8 June 1867. See also Tóth, *A Concise History of Hungary*.
3 The Exposition Universelle (World Fair) of 1867 took place in Paris between April and October 1867 under Napoléon III, who "exploited the fair more efficiently as a means of communication to the public, and as an event susceptible to bring a political gain". The Exposition "was also the first World Fair to have pavilions, restaurants and amusement parks around the main building" (De Tholozany, Pauline. "The Expositions Universelles in Nineteenth Century Paris". Brown University Library for Digital Scholarship. 2011. Web. 24 May 2015. http://library.brown.edu/cds/paris/worldfairs.html).
4 Unidentified.
5 Antonia's spelling for "of".
6 Ottilia.
7 Countess Auersperg and Mrs. Fallenbock were friends of Antonia's. The author of *Picture of Vienna* described the palace of prince Auersperg with its "large garden, hot-houses, temple of Flora and private theatre" (p. 50). The House of Auersperg was an Austrian royal house ("Mediatized House of Auersperg". Web. 17 July 2015. http://www.almanachdegotha.org/id66.html). See also CL'ANA 0421, Box 1, bundle a, numbers 8–10.
8 Probably "say".
9 Antonia's spelling for "off".
10 See CL'ANA 0395 and CL'ANA 0289.
11 *The Court Journal*. See CL'ANA 0268 and CL'ANA 0298.
12 See CL'ANA 0291.
13 Abbreviation for "giugno," Italian for "June".

196 • Wilhelm Gaulis Clairmont and Ottilia Clairmont to Claire Clairmont

[1 November 1867]

WC

My dearest aunt.[1] It is a long time since I last wrote to you, so long that I hardly remember the date of my last letter, but we ~~have~~ often thought & talked of you nevertheless – you know this ~~wis~~ the farmer's busy season, when he is overwhelmed with work; the first spare halfhour I seize upon to ~~wt~~ write to you – Our harvest has on the whole been very good and the prices fair, so that we made a handsome profit; indeed we should have netted a very considerable return but for an unfortunate circumstance which robbed us of about 6000f that is £600. on the 4th Septbr during dinnertime fire broke out in our stockyard and burnt down wheat to the afore mentioned amount. We do not suppose that the fire was laid, but that it originated from a spark from the steam thrashing machine which was at work at the time there being just then an immoderate wind – You may fancy that this was a terrible blow to us all; but there was nothing for it but to rally and commence anew and so we are at it again – Now I have something to say to you with reference to yourself – Tilly and I were obliged the other day to unpack, dust and clean your letters and papers in your trunks for there are so many mice which got into the boxes lying apart and they dirty and destroy everything – While sorting the papers I found 2 printed forms dated January 18th 1853 signed by W.S. Parker and being receipts for the deed of Conveyance of fourty shares in the Waterford and Kilkenny railway Company[2] – I merely tell you this that in case these papers be still of value to you, you may know that they are in my safe keeping & that you can have them sent to you, any day you require them – I also read some of the letters ~~enclosed~~ contained in the box – among these I was particularly struck by a number of letters written in the same fine neat and elegant hand a father to his son the latter must have been a lad of 15 or 16 for his father talks to him about not smoking – I should like to know who these were – the letters are beautifully written, so full of fine manly sentiment and so much good paternal advice, yet so buoyant as if written between two young friends – there were also very neatly executed sketches mostly of a humoristical nature interspersed between the text of the letters. – Of Mamma there is good news with this one exception, that here head seems becoming always more unfit for business and that she will have to undergo a fresh operation on her breast, a proof that Dr Landesmann's[3] opinion which he gave to me was correct viz. that the cause of her cancer was not a local one, but in the blood and would always break out again – Pauline who has been away for some time has now rejoined her (at least she wrote to me she would do so on the 1st Novb) they look forward to the horrid operation soon – the Doctor declares he cannot this time allow of the application of chloroform on acct. of Ma's general state of health but dear Ma seems thank God quite courageous and f selfreliant; she has a wonderful character and constitution

Believe me yours affectly.
WGC

Novb 1ˢᵗ 1867.

OC[4]

Dearest aunt.

Many thanks for your kind letter which I should have answered long ago but for a number of delays I experienced – I was extremely glad to find that in point of health all but your poor eyes – towards which I trust the rendure of summer has done you some good We enjoy both of us excellent health for allthough this country is not entirely free from swamps and marshes these having been drained and dried all within the past 20 years yet there is still a little fever and ague[5] hanging about, but happily with common care and attention especially with respect to diet and by guarding against taking cold after sundown one can avoid these fevers very easily. The situation of Temesvar after which you enquire is also quite level in former days this too was surrounded by swamps and it was to these the fortress owed in olden times against the Turks its formidable reputation – now no trace of these swamps is left the country arround being cultivated up to the very walls of the fortress.[6]

Our puszta[7] is but three hours distant from Temesvar and Willy drives there to almost evry great fair – we intend to go there this week – as my unmarried sister[8] who joined us a few weeks since to stay some months with us does not know Temesvar at all – and we want to make all our Christmas purchases – Our daily provisions we get much nearer than Temesvar – for Csakova which is only an hour's drive from us – is a large village where we can get all sort of victuals. This is the place my married sister lives at – we therefore are in constant communication with it –

We generally spend the holydays at her house because she can't leave so often an account of her children. She was absent three months this summer to stay with our parents because the clima does not agree well with her children.

Otherwise one have hardly any society there are no nice people in our neighbourhood – an Willy is always so very busy that he can not well leave for any length of time –

Your question wether Willy drinks any wine I wanted to answer you already a long time ago.

We always drink wine and water for dinner for breakfast and supper we take tea –

Pray [illeg.] write me all particulars about your health for we are often uneasy about your hea when such a long interval elapses between your letters –

Please do write soon

your ever affectionate
niece Ottilie

Address: La signora Clairmont/12 Corso dei Tintori/Firenze/Italia.
Front postmark: CSAKOVA/^{5}/$_{11}$; CRED. AUS. S.
Rear postmark: [illeg.]

Unpublished. Text: M.S., Pf. Coll., CL'ANA 0279

---

1 There are raised red initials ("WC") interlocked on the upper left-hand side of the first page.
2 The Waterford & Tramore Railway line was opened in Ireland 1853 and the Waterford & Limerick Railway and the Waterford & Kilkenny Railway followed soon after ("Waterford & Suir Valley Railway". Waterford & Suir Valley Heritage Railway, County Waterford. Web. 13 February 2015. http://www.wsvrailway.ie/waterfordrailways.shtml). In a letter to the shareholders of the Waterford & Limerick Railway Company dated 24 September 1855, John Levy observed that the Waterford & Limerick Company was "much better than the Waterford and Kilkenny Company, whose misfortunes all arose from bad management; but now that the management is in better hands it is improving" (*History of the Mismanagement of the Waterford and Limerick Railway Board* [Dublin: P.I. Carroll, 1856], p. 20). W.S. Parker was the secretary for the Waterford & Kilkenny Railway Company. The secretary's office was located at 17 Gracechurch Street, London. The street was home to Mr. and Mrs. Gardiner in Jane Austen's *Pride and Prejudice*, the Bennet girls' aunt and uncle.
3 See note 2, CL'ANA 0268.
4 A blue, raised interlocking set of initials, "OC," is printed on the upper left side of the first page of the letter.
5 Ague is malaria, which causes fevers and chills.
6 István Deák notes that Hungary's fortresses played a "crucial" role in the war of 1848–9 and that "the saga of fortresses" is linked to Austrian history. In Temesvár fortress, he records, "an officers' assembly took power in October, overruling the commander and organizing for defense against Hungary ... Temesvar suffered continuous Hungarian siege during the war but never surrendered" (Peter Karsten (ed.), *The Military and Society: A Collection of Essays* [USA: Garland, 1998], p. 236). Note Deák's spelling for Temesvár.
7 Hungarian for "plain".
8 Alma von Pichler.

197 • Wilhelm Gaulis Clairmont to Claire Clairmont

[19 December 1867]

WC[1]

My dearest aunt. I heard ~~with~~ to my with greatest distress from Pauline that you have been severely ill – furthermore I saw a telegram in one of the Vienna papers from which I conclude – (for it was not explicitly stated) that Her Majesty's Theatre on the Haymarket was burnt down –[2] you may imagine how distressed I am at this news, as I am afraid it will seriously compromise your interest – You talked some years ago about selling your box; perhaps you have done so. I always shrank from asking you about your money affairs for fear of my so doing being misconstrued, but I now do wish that I ~~ha~~ knew how far you are dependent on the operabox for your income – but perhaps the whole news is not true at all – or perhaps it was the little Hay market theatre; do please relieve my anxiety as soon as you can – if you have not heard of it as yet be not unnecessarily alarmed for I saw the telegram already 2 days ago. Pray do also write to me about your health – I am well, but Tilly is not so – I am afraid she is of a nervous constitution[3] – We received a letter from Pauline today – she seems to rub along pretty pleasantly although she keeps railing at Austria and its climate – of Mama she writes that she is pretty well all but her legs which begin declining their services – she writes that Ma is nevertheless in good spirits and much more cheerful than she used to be – Your anxiety about our property are quite correct. poor M. has made away with a great deal of property latterly but I hope P.'s presence will put a stop to her proceedings without our being compelled to have recourse to measures aggravating to Ma. Tilly is too unwell to write to you herself; she is not exactly ill, but suffering from want of appetite and from general weakness and apathy – I think she wants a tonic and we are going to consult our medical man tomorrow – she writes with me in wishing you a happy merry xmas & new year –

Believe me dearest aunt
yours most affectly
WGC

Csakova
Decemb. 19th 1867.

Address: La signora Clairmont/12 Corso dei Tintori/Firenze./Italia.
Front postmark: [illeg.] The stamp has been removed
Rear postmark: TRIEST/26/12/[illeg.]; [illeg.]; [illeg.]

Unpublished. Text: M.S., Pf. Coll., CL'ANA 0280

---

1 See note 1, CL'ANA 0279.
2 Her Majesty's Theatre burned down in 1867.
3 Ottilia was, in fact, pregnant. Wilhelm would confirm her pregnancy in his next letter to Claire (see CL'ANA 0281).

198 • Wilhelm Gaulis Clairmont to Claire Clairmont

[25 February 1868]

WC[1]

My dearest aunt

I duly received your last in which you set my mind at ease with reference to your property or rather your income; it was a great load off my mind and you reap the fruits now of that circumspection and caution which you have practised all your life long – Nevertheless it is a heavy loss to you & I sincerely pity you and regret that you, who have been always so ready to give away and to share your surplus with your more needy relations should be thus curtailed in your income and in your capability of doing good – Of us I have little news to relate excepting that it seems now beyond a doubt that dear Tilly is in the familyway and will be confined as we hope in August. she is very much troubled with sickness & can keep hardly anything on her stomach which is very trying to her nerves and her temper – this is the reason she has not written to you for so long a time – I am exceedingly happy and grateful that it has come so for I hope this will put a stop to the hysterical fits which of late she has been subject to – In other respects we are doing pretty well – only I am just now in some what tightened money circumstances as I have to finish the building of my house this summer and there will be besides many farm expenses and the falling off of our income through last year's fire makes itself felt severely just now[2] – however I dare say we shall weather it – from Ma I hear through Pauline – physically she seems to be doing well but her mind is evidently going though at times she seems quite clearheaded and enterprising – Only fancy that she now has set her mind on engaging the money she got from U. George[3] in a farming enterprise – the farm has about 130 Engl. acres and is distant about 80 Engl. miles from Baden & Pauline is to manage it; of course she does what she can to drive this queer idea out of Ma's head – I have now after a consultation with a lawyer and in concert with P. written a very urgent letter to M. requesting her to yield up the property that is the title deed of it to us – according to the Austr. law she can do so with out [illeg.] resigning her claims to the interest – but she can not either sell it or make debts on it – We all hope that Ma will give her consent; the more so as she is most interested in the preservation of the property for P. & I can work for our living but she poor soul cannot and if she were chiselled out of it would be badly off. I hear nothing about Ma's impending operation – I do not like to ask about it because P. writes me that Ma reads all the letters – Goodbye my dearest aunt. Tilly sends you her best love – you have never told me whom those nice letters are from – in a neat hand with sketches on the margin[4] – I wish you could come and see us next summer –

yours affectly
WGC

February 25th 1868. Csakova.

28 MARCH 1861–24 DECEMBER 1889

Address: No envelope.

Unpublished. Text: M.S., Pf. Coll., CL'ANA 0281

---

1 There is a set of red, intertwined initials, "WC" on the upper left-hand side of the first page.
2 See CL'ANA 0279.
3 Uncle Georg, Antonia's brother (Georg Ghilain von Hembyze).
4 Unidentified. See CL'ANA 0279.

199 • Wilhelm Gaulis Clairmont to Claire Clairmont

[22 March 1868]

My dearest aunt[1] I was very much pleased to see your hand writing again after so long a pause – although I was very sorry indeed at what you write concerning Mama – It is a consolation to us to think that during the vigour of her mind nothing was more foreign to her [illeg.] than doubledealing and intriguing and that therefore we are entitled to look upon this sad change as a symptom rather of intellectual than moral decline –[2]

Pauline and I made two combined attacks on Mama now and I wrote her two letters to attain from her the transcription of the property but in vain – there is a law in Austria which enables holders of land or houses to transcribe the title of their property onto other people, but reserving to themselves for their lifetime the use or interest of the property this would have just met our case but Ma steadfastly refuses on the ridiculous plea that my mother in law would dispossess her – By signing the deed we want her she would for her whole lifetime remain in full legal possession and enjoyment of the property she would only resign the right of either disposing of the property or making debts thereon. I cannot therefore help suspecting that she means to play us some trick if she can – We have for this reason agreed that P.[3] must remain with her to prevent mischief – for this reason Paul. will also not be at liberty to accompany you to England – I could not accompany you; but if my personal presence in London could be of any service to you I would find time to take a trip there and arrange your business – I think however now a days such business matters are settled more satisfactory by letter – I have sought out the two books you require and will dispatch them by today's post – but a manuscript book in any other than your hand I was not able to find – I think you mistook my letter for I made mention of separate letters not of a book – In seeking through your papers I also found law deeds and a copy of Shelley's will[4] – please tell me whether these papers are still of a [illeg.] specific value to you if so I will[5] place them in my strongbox. I had a mind to send you the transfer certificates for the Kilkenny railway shares[6] – but I do not do so for fear of the parcel being lost – My dear Tilly is now half through the tedious period of pregnancy and I believe on the whole feels somewhat easier already – the event also causes me great pleasure and satisfaction for I am sure that she has one of those constitutions which require children for their perfect health; at the same time it gives me a great deal of anxiety and care both with [illeg.]reference as to how my dear wife will get through her first trial and also as to finances, for I have a great deal of domestic outfit to buy in preparation of the event and then I must complete the building of our farm cottage if we have but a good harvest this year –! I hope we shall not require a nurse for the child. if so it would be dreadful for such people are not to be found here – I hope dearest aunt you will succeed in getting your new operabox appointed – I am quite sure that it is of importance you should go there to London or at least urge the matter by letter – I scarcely think P. will be able to accompany you as M. wants continued attendance & watching and we have of late given up the idea we had at first that ~~Ma~~ P. should come down to help Tilly through her first confinement –

I have given my brother in law[7] a letter of introduction to you – he is a young man of 18 making his studies as civil Engineer at Zurich and is now on a hollyday trip through Northern Italy; he is however not quite sure whether he will go to Florence –

Goodbye dearest aunt; Tilly sends you a kiss believe me yours affectly

WGC

Csakova
March 22nd 1868.

Address: La signora Clairmont/ 12 Corso dei Tintori/Firenze/Italia.
Rear postmark:VENEZIA/ 25/MAR/68/[illeg.] S

Unpublished. Text: M.S., Pf. Coll., CL'ANA 0282

---

1 There is a raised imprint of Wilhelm's initials in the middle of the first page.
2 Antonia's symptoms seemed to suggest dementia.
3 Pauline.
4 Probably Percy Shelley's will. See note 3, CL'ANA 0404.
5 Wilhelm began a new set of pages and the "WCG" imprint was on the first page. There is consequently a blank gap between the word "will" and "place".
6 See CL'ANA 0279.
7 Ottilia's brother, Moritz von Pichler.

200 • Wilhelm Gaulis Clairmont and Ottilia Clairmont to Claire Clairmont

[24 July 1868]

WC[1]

My dearest aunt I duly got yours of the 11th inst. but as we are engaged in ~~the~~ harvesting our crops I could not find an hour's leisure until now – thank you dearest aunt for the many apprehensions and cares you have on my account. it is true I have suffered from the intermittent fever prevalent in this country, but of late I have kept strict diet and taken chinine[2] and I think I got pretty well rid of it at least I have had no further attacks for the last 6 weeks – the fever prevalent here is ague; most commonly the attacks commence with [illeg.] cold and end with heat, last about 12 hours and return once in 48 hours – with people who have disposition for fever the slightest indigestion on taking cold after sundown is sufficient cause to bring on a new attack – but if one is very very strict in refraining from melons cucumbers milk ~~and~~ bacon and such like things, cold drink and bathing; and if one makes a practice of putting on a warm clothe coat at sunset however warm it may be one can manage to keep out of harms way only it is very tedious to be so much bound by disagreeable restrictions – I have two more ~~points~~ questions to answer you first about the horse. Pauline told you the truth in so far that I have at present no saddlehorse but still she was not accurately informed when she says "I cannot keep one" – we have of course on so large a farm oats and fodder enough for a horse to keep on – the difficulty is that my saddlehorse died suddenly last autumn – and I have not been able to procure another one since – partly because I did not find one to suit me and partly because it is a serious expense for being so tall and heavy it must be a better kind of horse to carry me – which costs at least from £25 to £30. I have been very unfortunate with my horses of late – within the last 8 months I lost no less than <u>4 horses</u> all my own exclusive property – so I was rather disheartened about horses and did not care to buy another so soon – but now I must get one soon for I cannot do without it –

I am very happy to be able to relieve your mind completely as to any debts you seem to think I have – I owe not a farthing to any one excepting to Pauline who lent me 600f last spring for building my house – I shall pay P. out of this years harvest; the new house which I built in the course of this year cost me about 3000f that is £300 – this money is a very good investment for me as it must be returned to me according to our contract at the expiration of our lease – this year we have not a good harvest but still enough to rub through and carry us on till next year – It will be difficult for me to disengage myself here – moreover dearest aunt I should shrink from the responsibility of throwing myself and my family on your resources – I am married now; one child is under way; there is no telling how many more there may be coming so I think it would be imprudent to give up this enterprise which affords me at least a sufficient income unless it should turn out that my health absolutely requires change of climate – farms especially small ones do not pay everywhere in Austria and we would have to look very carefully about us before we engage any money or our existence in such an enterprise; there is time yet till winter to ponder over this in Tyrol³ I would not like to live because the people there are such bigotted idiots – my chief apprehension is that a small farm would cause more expense than it would fetch. Tilly is very well considering circumstances – we expect her confinement every day –

Goodbye dearest aunt. many thanks for your love and consideration for me. pray give me compts to lady Sussex⁴ and Fernando – I am surprised to hear that he is already married for he seemed very young but it is true that this is now 5 years ago since I saw him.

believe me dearest aunt
yours affectly.
WGC

Csakova near
Temesvár
Hungary
July 24ᵗʰ 1868.

My dear aunt⁵ – I must add a few lines to you myself because it is a very long time I could not write to you and tell you how pleased and happy I am when ever a letter from you reaches us –

Since my brother wrote from Florence what a kind welcome you gave him – I always intented to thank you very much for it – but then mama was here and afterwards we had to do a great deal with finishing the baby linnen⁶

Now every thing is ready and we are expecting the event almost every day.

I am so happy I have my dear sister⁷ with me not only for the sake of my household but because it will also be such a comfort to Willy who is so busy and occupied just now. We will begin thrashing to morrow – We had a few rains of late that damaged the crops a good deal the harvest will be something about the average.

After the harvest our new house is to be finished into which we intend moving in the autumn. From Pauline we have got better news about poor mama's state of health nevertheless it is very sad.

Good bye dearest aunt. I hope Willy will soon be able to give you some happy news

your's most affectionate
niece Ottilie

Tusokret⁸ 25ᵗʰ July

Address: La Signora Clairmont/Borgo alla collina/Cadentino⁹/ <u>Italia</u>. Toscana./
Front postmark: CSAKOVA/ ²⁵/₇
Rear postmark: FIRENZE/ 29/ LUG¹⁰/ 10 M/ [illeg.]; [illeg.]

Unpublished. Text: M.S., Pf. Coll., CL'ANA 0283

---

1 At the top of the page, in the center, are interlocking initials, "WC," printed in green ink.
2 Wilhelm meant quinine ("Chinin" in German). Quinine is used to treat malaria.
3 Tyrol (Tirol in German) is one of the nine *Bundesländer* (federal states or provinces) in south-west Austria. Its capital is Innsbruck, which is located 476 kilometers west of Vienna.
4 See CL'ANA 0378 and CL'ANA 0327.
5 Tilly's letter was included in this mailing to Claire. Tilly used the same writing paper Wilhelm had, with the interlocking green "WC" initials on the first page at center.
6 See CL'ANA 0282.
7 Alma von Pichler.
8 Wilhelm and Ottilia frequently wrote their dwelling location/farm's name as Tusokret, Tuzokrit, or Tuzokrét. Walter Clairmont listed his own birth: "Ich bin am 3. August 1868 auf dem Gute Tuzokrét meines Vaters in Banat beboren . . ." (English translation: "I was born on 3 August 1868 on my father's estate in Tuzokrét in the Banat"). See CL'ANA 0428, unpublished manuscript, Pforzheimer Collection. The "Local Heritage Book" of the town of Detta lists "Tuzokret, Gilad" as the birthplace of one of the residents of Detta in 1882. Her name was Catharina Szlatzky ("Online Ortsfamilienbücher". Web. 25 May 2015. http://ofb.genealogy.net). Detta (known as Deta in Romanian) is located 44 kilometers south of Timișoara, 5 kilometers west of Opatija, and 10 kilometers south of Ghilad ("Orasul Deta". Web. 25 May 2015. http://www.detatm.ro).
9 Wilhelm misspelled Casentino, a valley about 50 kilometers east of Florence.
10 Abbreviation for "luglio," Italian for "July".

201 • Wilhelm Gaulis Clairmont to Claire Clairmont

[3 August 1868]

My dearest aunt. I am most happy to inform you that Tilly was confined last night that is the Sunday the 2$\underline{nd}$ August. at half past eleven oclock although she suffered very much; the pains began on Sunday morning at 11a.m. we were fortunate in obtaining the services of a very excellent midwife. the baby is a boy with dark hair & blue eyes.[1] and they all say he is remarkably like our mother or like me – Goodbye dearest aunt. I trust you got my letter of about a fortnight ago – yours affectly

WGC

August 3$\underline{rd}$ 1868.

Address: La signora Clairmont/Borgo alla Collina/Casentino/Toscana/Italia.
Front postmark: CSAKOVA/ 5/8

Unpublished. Text: M.S., Pf. Coll., CL'ANA 0284

---

1 Walter Claire Clairmont (1868–1958). In 1933, Walter wrote an account of his family's heritage, probably to avoid charges of having had Jewish ancestors. In this document, Walter recorded that he was born in the Banat, was baptized as a Protestant in the Swabian area of Liebling, and that he studied and worked in Vienna, Hungary, Basel (Switzerland), Berlin and Russia. He earned a doctoral degree in Chemistry and worked for Agfa. He married Frida Zucker on 5 June 1913 in a Protestant church in Budapest. Walter informed the authorities that Frida's father was Catholic and that her mother was Lutheran (See CL'ANA 0428, unpublished manuscript, Pforzheimer Collection). Stocking reports that Walter severed connections with his sister, Alma Crüwell-Clairmont, as a result of his opposition to the National Socialist regime ("Miss Tina and Miss Plin," p. 373).

In *The Clairmont Correspondence*, Stocking identifies a portrait, formerly believed by some to be Claire (Mary Claire Bally-Clairmont identified the painting as Claire's likeness), as possibly that of Antonia. As the eyes of the sitter in the portrait are blue, Stocking concluded that the portrait likely depicted Antonia. Amelia Curran's portrait of Claire housed at Newstead Abby (see photograph in this collection) clearly shows that Claire had brown eyes. The donated papers to the Pforzheimer Collection include a photograph of what Mary Claire Bally-Clairmont termed "the Clairmont Corner," an arrangement of six paintings which she identified as likenesses of "Mary Jane Devereux" wife of "Charles Gaulis Clairmont (1st)", "Charles Gaulis Clairmont (2nd)" husband of "Antonie Ghylain von Hembyze (no picture, nor photo)", "Claire Clairmont", "Wilhelm Clairmont, young", "Wilhelm Clairmont" husband of "Ottilie von Pichler", and "Fanny Horstig (old)" married to Johann Franz Hofrat von Pichler (recently found – belonging to the family) great-grandmother of Mary Claire & Christoph". Mary Claire incorrectly identified the subjects of these paintings. The portrait identified by Mary Claire as Mary Jane Devereux-Clairmont is also probably Antonia, according to Stocking (*CC*, v. 2, photographic images).

202 • Wilhelm Gaulis Clairmont to Claire Clairmont

[12 October 1868][1]

My dearest aunt. I am happy to inform you that since my last letter which I am ashamed to say it is very long ago since I dispatched all has been going on well with us – Our dear little boy of whom I must speak at first is prospering visibly and growing stouter and longer every day – his features begin to develop into a very nice childs face in which bearing they all say a resemblance with mine he is remarkably good and quiet; Tilly maintains that he already begins to talk – I only hear him squall which he does in a manner bearing no discredit to the power of his little lungs –

Four weeks after his birth he was christened by the evangelical parson the same who acted at our wedding a nice old man with a large family living 20 miles from here.[2] We named the little pickanini Walter Claire – the latter of course in your honour – dear Alma /was his godmother, we showed her this little attention by way of recognition of the great services and sacrifices she brought us – for her parents in the mean time made a very pleasant trip of 3 months duration all through Germany & Holland where they have some distant relatives & of course Alma was to have accompanied them had she not been with us. I am immeasurably glad to day that dear Tilly has more than enough milk for her babe; she is now completely recovered and is looking very well & stout. Only I continue to have occasional attacks of intermittent fever, which although I always succeed in driving them off, return again at intervals – It would be very nice for us and especially for me if you were to carry out your intention and settle at Trieste[3] and we could visit you there; for the change of air would do me a great deal of good – Please write me in your next what you think about this project of yours & whether there is any likelyhood of your carrying it into execution – Our harvest would have been very fair this year, but there was contrary to the climate of this country much rain during harvesttime which did a deal of harm; in wheat we have a harvest somewhat better than a fair average crop – in oats and barley it was bad in maize extremely good, we receive 6000 Austrian Metzen which is equal to 1200 Engl. quarters[4] – this is however with the cobs – when these are removed the grain alone is hardly more than half the bulk of the what it was before so we calculate to have only 3000 Mtz for sale which will bring us about £600 – the cobs are good for burning as you li[illeg.]ving in Italy very likely know – last this year the cobs of our last years maize crop furnished the whole fuel requisite for our steam engine during the whole of the thrashing – the only principal drawback this year are the low prices; we have been obliged to sell wheat already at a very low price because we wanted money and I am not sure at all that we shall get for the maize what we hope – Pauline writes me she read in the newspapers that poor Col. Pringle[5] fell from a precipice some where in Italy and died immediately; pray tell me whether you know anything about it; this would be dreadful – I cannot believe that a man of his years would commit such a foolhardy act without inducement; perhaps it was another Pringle I should be extremely sorry for Mrs Pringle – P. writes of Ma

that she is in remarkably good health & spirits; but that her mind is wandering & that she is not fit to be left to herself at all – Have you been to England yet? or do you not intend going at all? and how ~~did~~ are your affairs going on about the operabox – I wish I could help you but I cannot – pray write me how your health is and especially how your eyes are getting on also how you are satisfied with your new appartements – we also built a new tract to our cottage the walls were already built in March – so that thank Heaven it is well dried – but now we have such difficulty in getting carpenters all is ready but the flooring to lay and the doors & windows to fix and we cannot get it done – and for this one comparatively insignificant job cannot move into the house –[6]
Goodbye dearest aunt believe me

yours affect
WGC

Octob 12<u>th</u> 1868.
Csakova near Temesvár –
P.S. Tilly was to have added a few lines but yesterday she had grand scrubbing & cleaning of the house and today she feels poorly – she sends you her best love I do not like to delay the dispatch of this letter any further

WGC

Address: La Signora Clairmont/ 83 Via Valfonda/ <u>Italia</u>. Florence
Front postmark: CSAKOVA/ $^{13}/_{10}$
Rear postmark: TEMESVAR/$^{13}/_{10}$; VENE[illeg.]; 16/OTT.^{7}/4 S
Written on rear: Luigi Romagnoli/Erbe vendolo/S. Michele. Casa Casimini/famiglia[8] Fiorti.

Unpublished. Text: M.S., Pf. Coll., CL'ANA 0286

---

1 This letter has a green, interlocking "WC" at the top of the first page.
2 The Evangelischen Gemeinde Augsburger Confession at Liebling. See CL'ANA 0284. The officiating clergyman was Alexander Bariss.
3 Trieste is 460 kilometers north-east of Florence.
4 "Metzen" refers to a dry measure, particularly for grain. *The Illustrated Catalogue of the Industrial Department* published for the International Exhibition of 1862, and under the heading English-Austrian "Measures of Capacity," recorded that one English bushel was equal to 0.59 Austrian Metzen and that one English quarter was equal to 4.73 Austrian Metzen (Foreign Division, London: Her Majesty's Commissioners, 1862), vol. iv, p. xliv.
5 *The Clarence and Richmond Examiner and New England Advertiser* (published in Grafton, New South Wales) of 3 November 1868 reported the death of Colonel Pringle in its "General Summary" from London dated 11 September: "Colonel Pringle, of the Coldstream Guards, was found dead, having fallen down a ravine near Geneva" (National Library of Australia, http://www.nla.gov.au/nla.news-article63667842, p. 2). It is unclear whether Pauline mistook the location of Colonel Pringle's death (Italy instead of Switzerland) or if the newspaper meant to report Genova, Italy (Genoa) instead of Geneva, Switzerland. Stocking quotes from Edward Augustus Silsbee's notes,

which recorded that Colonel Pringle fell to his death at Bex or elsewhere in the Rhône Valley. Bex is in Switzerland (*CC* II: 431). For Silsbee, see CL'ANA 0218.

6 The Pforzheimer Collection has five large photographic negatives in a folder marked "House in Hungaria (Czahora) or (Czakroa)". Each of the five images (only visible if held to a light source) shows the farm and the surrounding settings. The unidentified artist hand-drew these pictures on photographic paper.

7 Abbreviation for "ottobre," Italian for "October".

8 Italian for "family".

203 • Wilhelm Gaulis Clairmont to Claire Clairmont

[17 December 1868]

My dear dear aunt. I arrived here (Baden) and got your kind good letter to Pauline but which on an occasion like this was also a consolation to me and helped much to raise my spirits again – It is inexpressibly sad for me to return to this house which I have never seen or known without dear Ma and of which she used to be the center and the very soul and now to find her gone and the house empty no more questions to ask, no more recollections about bygone times of my early youth and so many details of my own life which I myself had already forgotten but which she with a mothers true & deep affection all stored up in her memory – and then I used to rally her about all sorts of funny queer ways & habits she had contracted and she used to take it in such good part and be so amused at my saucy remarks and call me "a kick into the world" who attempted to tutor his seniors and now all this is over –[1] It is very sad but Dr. Mülleitner[2] to whom we paid a visit yesterday said we should be glad that poor Ma found such a quiet peaceful death so without pain – he says that if the cancer had broken out again as it undoubtedly would had she lived longer she would have died the death of a martyr I was out at the cemetry with Pauline yesterday – she has a very handsome tombstone – already erected the inscription is in German – at the bottom is in English the verse which Pauline was just reading at Ma's death bed from the prayer for the sick when poor Ma [illeg.] expired[3] – I was very thankful to P. that she did not summon me up by telegram for I should have been too late to find Ma still in a state of sensibility and it would have been dreadful to leave Tilly behind to travel all alone with the baby – [illeg.] our little Walter is thank heaven hale & hearty he is a fats little baby with blue eyes and a soft little face. – his grand father & mother[4] are also extremely fond and proud of him – he seems however to have a preference for me of all others for whenever I bend over his little couch he smiles – he is the dearest little chap imaginable, all my wife's numerous friends and connexions have poured in on the news of our arrival and they all are, or pretend to be, quite charmed of with him – Our journey from the Banat to Vienna, was not quite without danger for the child, for the previous mild & springlike weather changed just the night before our departure; in the morning we woke with a roaring northerly storm whistling by our window and the ground covered with the first light fall of snow – On our arrival at Csakova both the Doctor and the midwife in my absence persuaded Tilly that it was dangerous to travel with a child in such bad weather, so that they succeeded in upsetting her completely and filling her poor maternal heart with fear & anxiety – as we could however not return to the farm where we had made arrangements to shut up our house for the winter I said we must start and start we did; and the good little fellow as well as his mother braved the storm & cold manfully; all he suffered was through poor Tilly's nervousness and anxiety [illeg.] together with the excitement of returning to her paternal roof which I suppose contaminated her milk but after a few days all was well again –

Tilly is still in Vienna I have come out to P. for a few days in part to cheer her up, in part to talk over all the business arrangements about Ma's will and the ~~testament~~ inheritance Ma it seems had altered her last will of which you got a copy, substituting a new one more to my disadvantage but P. good girl said she would not take advantage of it, so we agreed that I would drop the larger claim I had on the houses [~~illeg.~~] in consequence of my larger loan to ma and she resign the boon of the favours granted her by the last will and that we would share alike and so we are about to do. We intend not to sell the houses; but I have insisted already now on a clear & businesslike division of the property so that each should know what is his and that no harassing questions ~~between~~ of what should be mine & what hers should hereafter turn up to divide us or loosen our affections in after life – You will perhaps [~~illeg.~~] be anxious to hear something ~~more~~ about my health – the change of air has done me so much good I cannot say how much – I regained my colour & appetite since I am here and have had no more fever attacks – [illeg.] Dr Milleitner whom I consulted yesterday found my spleen still a little enlarged and ordered me to take more chinin[5] good living & plenty of exercise – I am in hopes that if I stop till spring I shall get over it Every season is not like this last was the oldest people do not remember such prevalence of ague[6] as there was this summer not only with us but all [~~illeg.~~] over Hungary – we had frequently more than two thirds of our men laid up with the same complaint and nearly all the women & children on the place – it was a mercy Tilly escaped it. perhaps it will not be so bad again in 20 years – I must correct an erroneous impression which you imbibed with reference to Tilly. it was me and not her who wished her to make use of her present sojourn ~~to~~ in Vienna to frequent a few balls – (of course previous to Ma's death) being if not a young, yet an inexperienced husband I never thought of the effects of dancing etz. on the poor babe and I kept saying to her how much I rejoiced that she would after 3 years privations have the enjoyment of a few balls in her own old circle of friends but when I explain to her the cause why I am sure she will resign all her girlish hopes, which were only raised through my ignorance with pleasure

Now Goodbye dearest aunt. I have chatted a good deal with you this time I shall remain here at least till the 15th February so direct to Baden.

Plin sends her love and will write to you in a few days. Tilly is in Vienna with Baby.

Believe me yours affectly
WGC

Baden
Decemb. 17th 1868.

Address: La signora Clairmont/ 83 Via Valfonda/ Florence/ Italia.[7]
Rear postmark: 9 S/FIRENZE/ DIC^8 19/ 68; 9s; UDINE-VERONA/19/[illeg.][9]

Unpublished. Text: M.S., Pf. Coll., CL'ANA 0285

---

1 Herbert Huscher confirms that Antonia died in her house in Baden near Vienna on 29 November 1868: "Antonia Clairmont starb in ihrem eigenen Haus in Baden bei Wien am 29. November 1868" ("Charles und Claire Clairmont," p. 101).
2 See note 3, CL'ANA 0268.
3 Antonia was buried in Baden.
4 Ottilia's parents, Johann and Fanny von Pichler, lived in Vienna. See CL'ANA 0184.
5 Wilhelm meant "Chinin," which is the German for "quinine".
6 Malaria.
7 Wilhelm was in mourning and his use of black-bordered stationary and envelope indicated as much.
8 Abbreviation for "dicembre," Italian for "December".
9 The word "Wednesday" was written on the rear of the envelope.

204 • Wilhelm Gaulis Clairmont to Claire Clairmont

[14 January 1869]

My dear aunt.

I just received yours of the 12\ts{th} inst. acknowledging the receipt of mine of the 9\ts{th} & saying you could receive me – I hope my dearest aunt I shall not cause you any convenience – of course I shall be satisfied with whatever accommodation you can afford me as long as I am confident you are not putting yourself to any inconvenience I shall start from here about the 18\ts{th} inst but I shall not arrive at Florence till the 22\ts{nd} or 23\ts{rd} inst as I intend stopping a day at Bologna[1] – from whence I shall give you news of my arrival there and when I expect to reach florence, so that you may not be taken by surprise – you might drop me a few lines to directed postoffice Bologna saying whether you are far away from the railway station – whether I must have a cab or whether I can walk on foot getting a porter to carry my small portmanteau – I shall have clothing enough against the cold – let me beg you dear aunt to drop all anxiety about my chest it is perfectly sound – the physician did <u>not</u> advise me a warmer climate only further change of air – to visit you was my own idea, because I had a great desire to see my dear good aunt again after so long a separation and because I should have known of no other place to direct my steps to so gratifying to my affection & feelings of all your plans dear aunt we shall talk when we meet – I got your letter of the 10\ts{th} –
Goodnight – I rejoice exceedingly to see you – my fever too has been much better these days –

yours affectly
WGC

January 14\ts{th} 1869.

Address: La signora Clairmont/ 83 Via Valfonda/ Italia. Florence
Rear postmark: VENEZIA/ 16/GEN²/69/ 4 S

Unpublished. Text: M.S., Pf. Coll., CL'ANA 0287

---

1 Bologna is 111 kilometers north of Florence.
2 Abbreviation for "gennaio," Italian for "January".

205 • Wilhelm Gaulis Clairmont to Ottilia Clairmont

Bologna Janry 26th 1869.[1]

My dear Titsle I arrived here this morning at 3 oclock – I slept till 8 and then sent to the post and got 2 letters one from Claire & one from you & Plin but of such a backward date that I thought there must be another one at the post so I went there myself and enquired but there was none – your letter is dated the 20th Since my departure I have written you 3 letters one from Vienna the 2nd one from Arensteins[2] the 22nd and one from Nabresina[3] the 24th I thought I should find a later letter here because I requested you in my letter of the 22nd (Arenstein) to write me to Restauration[4] Nabresina telling me all about how your birthday went off – and as I found no letter at Nabrsina[5] I hoped you would have written it to Bologna – I now hope to find the letter in question at Florence. if it is not there I shall be very angry with you and scold you very much – I shall get to Florence this evening at 7 o clock aunt Cl. expects me – I start in about an hours time it is now 11 a.m. I have therefore not die Ruhe[6] to write you a regular letter but I merely write a few lines to let you know how I am and where I am travelling adventures I had none – but I shall nachhohlen[7] the events of my journey sofar in my first letter from florence. thank you for your letter dear T. but it did not give me an jolly impression – that you will be compelled to wean poor Walterle is I think rather desirable for dawdling about so long could not have done him much good – poor little fellow I am so curious to hear how he is getting on – It is very cold even here and snow lies on the ground in the streets in the rooms in the hotels and I believe also in all private houses it is wretchedly cold – the only place where I am warm is in bed or in the railway carriage with my fuß[illeg.]ack[8] & big cloak. on – I was not cold even accross the semering[9] when it was 18 degr. of cold and all others were frozen to death –

I am afraid my going to the theater will meet with a heavy reverse as they tell me all the operas are closed during carnival – yesterday evening I went to see a circus as the letter is not full weight I enclose programme[10] – Miss Ella carried off immens applause – towards the conclusion she was called at least 20 times a simultaneously an regular shower of little papers was dropped down all round the circus from the top gallery the papers were of all colours so that it looked very pretty I caught one of them flying past me (for I sat in the 1st range) and found they contained poetical effusions. I enclose you my copy – she was is not at all handsome either in face or figur – she is in fact remarkably plain and owes her success only to her grace and art. I liked best Oscar mounted by Mad Adel – she rode not as a [illeg.]unstrei[illeg.]e[illeg.]in[11] but as a lady

She rode and leaped splendidly I thought how I would like you to ride like that. Goodbye my dearest T. do write soon. what you said about your resolution being confirmed I do not believe – I do not think that I shall wish it or that there will be any reason for you to wish it. Plin my love I do not answer her letter extra give Walterly a kiss from his pa – I already wish I was back – I have no idea whether

Alma is still at Baden or returned to Vienna – give her my love – now a kiss for you & believe me dear T. yours affectly

WGC

thank you Plin for the port manteux[12] it is just the fit – if it were but a little larger I could not get it into the shelves above the seats – as it is I squeeze it in and no one thinks of raising any objections otherwise I should have had to pay a great deal –

Address: No envelope

Unpublished. Text: M.S., Pf. Coll., CL'ANA 0133

---

1 This letter, and the next, are included in the collection and not in the appendix as they both shed more light on Wilhelm's visit to Claire.
2 The town of Arnstein is located 37 kilometers from Graz. Arnstein is 227 kilometers south-west of Vienna and 311 kilometers north-east of Nabrežina.
3 Nabrežina (in Slovene) or Nabresina (in Italian) is located in Italy about 17 kilometers north of Trieste. *Appleton's European Guide Book* of 1886 confirms that travelers have a "good view of the Adriatic below" as they approach Nabresina (London: Sampson Low, 1886), part 2, p. 601. The town's name was changed to Aurisina in 1927.
4 German for "pub" or "restaurant".
5 Wilhelm misspelled Nabresina.
6 German for "the peace" or "the silence".
7 Wilhelm misspelled "nachholen" which is German for "review".
8 Wilhelm may have intended to write "Fußsack" which means "footmuff".
9 Wilhelm probably meant to write the Semmering Pass. The Semmering Railway consists of four lines and was built between 1848 and 1854. The line between Vienna and Trieste was completed by 1857.
10 The programme is missing.
11 Possibly the word "Kunstreiterin," German for "circus or trick rider".
12 Portmanteau, a small suitcase or bag.

206 • Wilhelm Gaulis Clairmont to Ottilia Clairmont

Febry 2nd Florence
[1]869.

Dear Tilly.

I dispatched two letters to Baden yesterday one to you and one to Plin with enclosure to Zoepf I hope you duly received them both – this morning I got a short letter from Plin for which I am truly thankful to her as I love to hear from you everyday – It is a very good plan of yours to number your letters because I can then instantly see when one is missing. – Strange to say your letters from Baden all take 3 or even 4 days – counting of course not from the date in the letter but from the official date stamped by the postoffice on the stamp – whereas you seem to get my letters in 2 days –

I like when walking in the streets to watch the toilettes of the ladies – plaids are very fashionable here too and worn in the same way as in Vienna in the gayest colors & largest patterns – besides this they have also these fashionable new colours a dark red approaching to claret than a wonderful colour something between blue green and grey it is dark and sometimes looks like the sea not from when seen from a distance but when you look into it from above only it is not so decidedly green – they have a very nice coquette way of trussing up with large rosettes not only the skirt but also the paletot[1] [illeg.] (Kragen)[2] which comes down the shoulders over the waist which looks very nice; in this manner[3] I have not observed this fashion applied to the <u>upper regions</u> in Vienna. In general I do not find the ladies and women you see in the streets any handsomer than at Vienna but their hair is certainly more beautiful on an average than that of other women – but there is one great drawback which I gave expression to the other day at dinner and which was received with showers of disapprobation by the all the ladies young and old – I said that whenever a man was tempted to give full vent to his full admiration of any woman or any particular part of her moral or physical ensemble he felt him self chequed by the reflection oh who knows how much of this is genuine and how much is makebelief. now this applies more particularly to hair as this is a department in which women consider fraud and trickery of every kind even more admissible than in any other part of their <u>physical</u> disguise – the moral part offers of course a much more extensive field of operations to the ingenuity of a woman – they were all very angry & Miss Moulson[4] said she would write to you but I say I will not tell her your direction because she might write you anonymous letters. Now goodbye my child it is 10 oclock I have a rendezvous now to go with Miss Miller[5] to the Palazzo Piti[6] she is dreadfully learned in all matters of art and knows every picture or statue that is worth seeing in Florence.

Febry. 3rd Only think that I got a fresh attack of fever yesterday after writing the above and had to lie down all day – it came on much in the same way as that at Baden quite suddenly about 11 o'clock am – and lasted till about 1 oclock in the morning – when I fell asleep & slept well till the morning – the cold left me and heat [illeg.] came on about 9 or 10 o clock in the evening –

The attack was not so strong as that at Baden still I am weak today especially in the backbone – I am very unhappy about it, not of course that I care for this one attack but that I fancy I shall never get rid of the fever – I shall take a few doses of quinine tonight & tomorrow morning and then continue it in slight doses as Dr Milleitner advised me – I should like to write to you [illeg.] a nice gay letter for I have to sit at home any way as the weather is damp, but I know nothing amusing to write to you und immer raunzen & lamentiren will ich nicht[7]– dear Tilly I have already thought we should leave the papering and oilcloth flooring[8] of our house for the present. who knows how [illeg.] long we shall be able to inhabit it. it was the same in Australia I [illeg.] built a house there for myself and when it was all but ready I had to leave it – We have spent a great deal on this house already and perhaps it will be all in vain – so I would not like to spend any more on it. but perhaps I am cross now and shall see things in a brighter light by and by. –

February 4th 9.a.m. Here I am after having had my breakfast trying to scribble a few lines to you, but I am afraid I shall not be very successful for this is now about the time when the mail from Austria arrives and so I am nervous and zerstreut[9] always listening for the ring of the postman and then I had another fever attack yesterday – which has weakened me a good deal and acts on my spirits – It came on at 5 in the evening & lasted till about 12 in the night when I fell asleep & slept well till morning – I went to bed at 7 in the evening – and felt better at once; today I am well nur schwach und stark eingenommenen Kopf – On the whole waren beide Anfälle noch immer schwach zu nennen – Mein zu Bette gehen darf dich nicht irre machen in soferne du meine ich daraus einen Schluß auf die Heftigkeit des Anfalles ziehen könntest.[10]

I must go to bed for there is no couch or sofa where I might lie with any degree of comfort and then the Italian rooms are so cold that it is hard to bear when you are well; in fever the only possible protection are the blankets. I took quinine 12 grains[11] through the night and this morning weil heute erst der eigentliche Tag wäre – den gestrige Anfall war ein außer ordentlichen (glaube ich wenigstens) weil weder Tag noch Stunde stimmte –[12] I write you all these details about the fever much more explicitly than I would of any other illness because I am bearing in mind the influence which it may possibly exercise over our future – I am getting quite fidgety for time wears on and there is no letter. you ought to write me at least twice a week –

And now dear Tilly I want to talk some business with you – when you go to town get from Plin 100fl. of the money which Rudi[13] no doubt will have sent by that time and get all you want for your person – dont expect me to enter into details on this subject because I dont know what you want, but this I will say – get at least one pair of strong leather boots made a little larger than the exact fit so as to admit corksoles – and buy at least two pair of spare corksoles – and pray use your influence that Alma should do the same – for her it is a great deal more important than for you 1st on account of her weakness of the throat for which wet feet are the most injurious thing imaginable – 2^{ndly} because she living in town is constantly called on to go out in wet weather. which you are not – Now get all these things nicely for yourself and dont stint yourself – my good girl but the commissions for the house we leave till I return –

My patience was exhausted I did not want to wait any longer in vain, so I went out and had a palaver with the servantgirl and ascertained that the postman had been but that there were no letters for me – at which I am very much vexed with all of you – for I am dreadfully morose & low spirited and a letter would have done me good – yesterday evening aunt was sitting by my bedside & she asked me numberless questions all about you 3 sisters and your parents and your healths your characters your previous history and everything concerning you – she praised you very much for being so steady now and resisting the temptation of going out until the D^r would let you. but when she heard of Rippenfell Entzündung[14] she made a very grave face and said it was very dangerous her going out to skate so much in the bitter cold and she might easily bring on a similar attack by heating [illeg.] herself & then taking cold – and she likes you all very much already – she says Alma must come and stop a few months with her and that the mild climate of Italy will do her so much good[15] – and then she says she – aunt – will come to see us next summer because she is so desirous of knowing you – but on this I throw cold water because I know aunt would be very much disappointed of the Banat and would find it nasty and would get ill [illeg.] and be discontented for she makes a great many pretensions & has a great many faxen[16] – although she herself has no idea of it and believes herself to be the simplest most unpretensious person in the world – In this respect – that is the delusions in which she is befangen[17] regarding the spotless perfection of her character the sagacity of her mind etz. etz. she much resembles your Mama[18] although I believe in point of conceit this latter bears off the palm[19] – I hope dear Tilly you dont mind my writing all my letters to you in English – I have a double motive for so doing – first to prevent there being sent to Vienna and 2nd to improve my English if my present trip to Florence serves any one purpose it is this of freshening up my English – Goodbye now my dear Tilly give Walterle a kiss from me and do write to me all about him I do so rejoice to see him again I intend writing a few lines to Plin [illeg.] if the fever will let me

Goodbye –

February 5th this morning I got ~~the~~ your letter N° 5.[20] it was very good my child & made a deep impression on me you know I always did love you tenderly and do so now only dont endeavour to keep me within too narrow bounds and allow me to love others besides – I am writing this in a great hurry and without exactly thinking what I am writing for I want to get this letter away by today's post. so never mind what I say in it. – Only think dear Tilly that I had the fever yesterday too but not so strong as ~~yester~~ the day before yesterday – this is 3 days running I have had it; it has weakened me very much. but to day (it is now 3 oclock in the after noon) I feel very much better and I do not think I shall have it again not at least today. tomorrow would be my proper day but I shall take another lot of quinine tonight & tomorrow morning – I was out shopping with Miss Müller before dinner – she is very kind & useful to me – she helped me buying some little trifles for you – I hope you will like them – I shall answer your todays letter in full tomorrow & the day after – – it is mir sehr ungemüthlich[21] to [illeg.] know you in town – for I look upon that as the enemy's camp – tell me when you propose returning to Baden – I shall write to Plin about bringing you the money as you are separated now. I am sorry the skating is over – Enjoy yourself as much as you can while you are at Vienna for I do not intend stopping there long & you will have no more time to do so when I arrive – I am much weakened and dispirited by the fever – I shall leave this for Genoa on the 11th inst. on the 16th I expect to be at Turin on the 20th Venice – to all these places you can direct poste restante but deducting 2 or 3 days for the time the letter takes going there – after that direct to Sermage Oroslawje en Croatie[22] – but dont direct there till you have heard from me in a future letter that I am really[23] going there which I shall write to you as soon as I get his answer saying that he can receive me.

Goodbye my dear Tilly yours aff.
WGC

I got the second letter together with your N̄o 5 – it is the answer to [illeg.] I wonder what you mean by [illeg.] of what I wrote in this letter
At the receipt of this you write while have time to send the answer to Florence and if I should be gone it will be forwarded to Genoa.

Address: 8. Brief den 7. Februar/ Frau Ottilie Clairmont/ mit Briefen des Herrn Hofrath/Johann Ritt. v. Pichler/Landstrasse Wien./Salesianergasse N° 3. Italia/Austria[24]
Front postmark: FIRENZE/5/FEB/[illeg.]
Rear postmark: [illeg.]/WIEN

Unpublished. Text: M.S., Pf. Coll., CL'ANA 0130

---

1 A type of jacket worn over a dress.
2 Possibly "Kragen," the German word for "collar".
3 Wilhelm included a small drawing in the middle of the page, which depicted a woman's dress with flowers on the skirt and collar.
4 In her letter to Edward Trelawny of 25 December 1869, Claire informed him that Pauline was contemplating marriage to "an elderly Austrian retired Major" (*CC* II: 602) who would "lose his pension" if he left Austria. Claire indicated that she was deciding whether to return to Austria or continue living in Florence. She saw May Moulson, a "charming girl [who] likes me, and would have every care of me," as a possible long-term companion. Moulson, however, was to return home to England the following spring, and Claire expressed concern that she would be left "lonely and unprotected" (p. 602). On 23 April 1873, Claire told Trelawny that she received no revenue from her opera box and therefore had to take "two Lady inmates," i.e., boarders to provide her with income, one of whom was Miss Moulson. See also CL'ANA 0421, Box 2, bundle e, number 100. Herbert Huscher quotes from two unpublished letters which do not form part of the holdings of the Pforzheimer Collection and appear to have been lost. In the letters dated 30 January-1

February 1869, Wilhelm wrote to his family: "There is a housekeeper and two young ladies with Aunt Claire. One is Miss Miller, a German, who was with Mrs. and Mr. Pulsky, and one English lady, Miss Moulson. The latter is young, and good-looking and very coquette, but not in a designing way, quite innocently" ("Charles und Claire Clairmont," p. 102).

5 Miss Müller (sometimes spelled Miss Miller) as well as Miss Moulson resided in Florence with Claire at this time. On 3 August 1885, Richard Garnett wrote to Edward Dowden about Miss Müller. He recorded Miss Müller's impressions of Claire: "I have met Miss Müller, Miss Clairmont's friend. I did not learn much from her, but I hope that she will send me more particulars when she returns to Florence. She gives a very favourable account of Claire in general: though she suspects her of romancing and suppressing facts. She had the remains of great beauty, and must have been a deep brunette. She used to speak of Shelley with affection, but accused him of instability; she never, or rarely, mentioned Byron. Miss Müller feels sure that her love affair with the latter was the only one she had. She had about forty letters of Shelley's: which after her death were sold to an American" (*Letters about Shelley* [London: Hodder and Stoughton, 1917], pp. 142–3). See also CL'ANA 0421, Box 2, bundle e, number 100, for Alma von Pichler's description of her encounter with Miss Moulson and Miss Müller.

6 The Palazzo Pitti in Florence is a museum located adjacent to the Boboli Gardens. Originally owned by the Medici family and the Grand Dukes of Tuscany, it became a museum in the twentieth century. Today, the palazzo complex consists of six museums and displays an impressive collection of paintings by artists such as Titian, Raphael, Rubens, and Caravaggio ("Polo Museale Fiorentino". Web. 20 October 2015. http://www.uffizi.firenze.it/it/musei/?m=palazzopitti).

7 Wilhelm misspelled "lamentieren". The German translates as "I do not want to complain all the time".

8 A type of waterproof cotton cloth.

9 German for "preoccupied".

10 Translation provided by Ann Sherwin: "only weak and very giddy head – On the whole, both attacks could still be called mild – my going to bed must not mislead you, I mean, in the sense that you could draw a conclusion about the severity of the attack".

11 William Rothstein records that "quinine became a panacea for all ills in the 1870's and 1880's . . . in moderate doses it weakened the heart and pulse, caused gastro-intestinal irritation, and produced nervousness and giddiness. These side effects were accentuated by repeated doses of the drugs" (*American Physicians in the Nineteenth Century* [Baltimore, MD: Johns Hopkins University Press, 1885], pp. 188–9). Michael Flannery shows that dosages varied, depending on the severity of the fever, and that doctors might prescribe doses as high as twenty to forty grains (*Civil War Pharmacy* [New York: Haworth Press, 2004], p.161).

12 Translation provided by Ann Sherwin: "because the actual day would not be until today – yesterday's attack was an extraordinary one (at least I think so), because neither the day nor the hour was right".

13 Rudolf von Hauer.

14 German for "Pleuritis". Today, the word is spelled "Rippenfellentzündung".

15 Alma and her mother would indeed visit Claire in Florence in 1870. See CL'ANA 0421, Box 2, bundle e, number 100, and CL'ANA 0178.

16 German for "trouble".

17 German for "partial to" or "biased".

18 In a document entitled "Genealogical table of Mary Claire & Christoph's grandmother Ottilie lineage," Mary Claire Bally-Clairmont identified Ottilia's mother as Fanny Horstig von Pichler (CL'ANA 0428, unpublished manuscript, Pforzheimer Collection). Mary Claire recorded that Fanny Horstig (1805–1874) was the daughter of Carl Gottlieb Horstig (1763–1835) and his wife, Suzette von Engelbrunner (1768–1845). According to Mary Claire's table, the von Pichlers had five children. Letters in this collection confirm the identities of four of the five children: Ottilia, Emily, Moritz, and Alma. As Wilhelm wrote that Claire was interested in Ottilia's three sisters, the unidentified child was evidently a daughter. In CL'ANA 0221, Pauline

references the children of the unidentified Caroline. It is possible that Caroline was the fifth von Pichler child.

Stocking records that Caroline von Pichler had a salon in Vienna from 1814 to 1828 (*CC* II: 641) and suggests that she was perhaps a sister of Johann von Pichler. It appears unlikely, as Karoline von Pichler who kept a salon in Vienna was born Karoline von Greiner (1769–1843) (Jordan, S. "Pichler, Caroline, geboren von Greine". *Neue Deutsche Biographie*. 2011. Web. 26 October 2015. http://www.deutsche-biographie.de/sfz95796.html).

19 Hyamson defined the phrase "to bear the palm" as meaning "to carry off the prize" (Albert Hyamson, *A Dictionary of English Phrases* [London: Routledge and Sons, 1922], p. 262).
20 Wilhelm and Ottilia numbered their letters to one another.
21 The German colloquially translates into a statement that Wilhelm probably did not feel comfortable knowing that Ottilia was in town.
22 See CL'ANA 0246.
23 Wilhelm cross-wrote the remaining words in this letter.
24 German for: "8th letter from 7 February. Miss Ottilie Clairmont/with letters from Mr. Privy Councillor/Johann Baronet v. Pichler/ Landstrasse Wien./Salesianergasse N° 3. Italia/Austria".

207 • Wilhelm Gaulis Clairmont to Claire Clairmont

Oroslawje[1] March 5th
1869.

Dearest aunt.

I was at Görz and Udine[2] but I am sorry to say without any success the land on the seacoast is all subject to fever – this gentleman to whom I had a letter of introduction has already left his situation in consequence of fever – North towards the mountains there is no available land as there is no undulating country forming as it were the transition from the mountains to the plain – the rocky and sterile alps rise directly from the plains – moreover the country is so completely in the hands of the small farmers who hold from 5 to 10 acres & work it with their own hands, and who can afford to pay for such land a so much higher price thatn a gentleman farmer that these latter have no chance whatever of competing with th[illeg.] the small peasant farmer – there is however now a beautiful estate for sale in this vicinity and if you could make up your mind to invest part of your capital in it we might make all ends meet you would have from 4 to 5 percent on your money a most delightful residence – we should have the same advantages for our capital and we should all live together so as a good and loving family ought. I have here friends in the very best circles and we have an entrée at once to the best of society – the climate is very healthy, the scenery most beautiful. the celebrated watering place Rohitsch[3] close at hand – the winter is much milder than in Austria but if it prove too rigorous for you you have Trieste, Goricia, Venice or Fiume[4] all within easy reach from here – this latter especially will only be a few hours from here as there is now a railway in course of construction the a station of which will be only 3 or 4 miles (English) from the estate leading directly to Fiume – Varasdin[5] too is quite near and there are now already 4 lines of rail in working order – one to Vienna one to Triest one to Pest one to Sclavonia[6] and the 5th is the one to Fiume Richards father lived for many years at Fiume he says there is no fever there – Now for the financial part of the scheme. the estate comprises arable and forest land meadows vineyards all in all 454 acres Austrian measure that is equal to about 605 acres Engl. measure.[7] it is all in one plot and the farm stead in the center – there are no lawsuits hanging to the estate the former proprietor having during his lifetime settled all these questions with his neighbours in compliance with the forms of the law but by amicable adjustment – it is what they term here a noble's estate – the farm buildings are sufficient in number and size but very dilapidated; the manor house is a most interesting old castle with walls thick enough to stand a siege – it is situated above the high road (postal communication twice a day) on a hillside commanding a splendid view up and down the valley – a number of gentlemen's seats in view – the house is situated in a beautiful park with beautiful lovely walks; down in the valley there is a small lake the whole of the forest property joins on to the park so that it forms a most charming countryseat with lovely walks and the purest air – the castle is two stories high – the view from the upper rooms is something magnificent – there are numbers of nooks & corners in this old building rooms of all sizes and two large halls – with ancient wainscoating – I dare say there are no less than 20 rooms – one should have plenty of room all of us – it is however also very much out of repair – now for the money part:

the price of this estate would be in Engl money	£4500.
government tax on transfer of title deed	100.
repair of buildings	100.
stocking of the farm	300
total capital required	£5000.
Now I propose that you should invest in this purchase _____	£2000
and that Paul. & I. should sell our houses[8] and invest of the proceeds	£3000
this together would make	£5000

You would still have a good interest from the rest of your property to enable you to do in the winter as you pleased for about 3 mos – the rest of the year you would live with us – you can have your separate title deeds made out for your share of the property in proportion as you contributed to its purchase, you would consequently retain the hold of your property and the interest thereon just the same as if you had shares or any kind of stock – I would pay you say 4 per cent interest and you could then pay us for your board – or we would arrange that as you pleased – the estate bears now £264 annual nett revenue that is about 5 per cent – but that is not by farming it but only letting it in plots to the peasants. by having my own stock and farming it on improved principles myself, I should make 6 or 7 percent out of it. thus I could afford to pay you & Plin 4 percent for your shares of the capital – moreover we should get something on the other hand for your board. I should also make something from my Tuzokrit farm which I should sublet in small lots to the peasants for ready money so that I should have no anxiety of management there but should only have to go down there once a year to collect my rent – I think this is a plan that would suit all parties – you we all should have a comfortable home and live together in a beautiful & healthy country surrounded by friends and civilized society within easy reach of a mild climate for the winter – we should have no debts or business cares – you would still retain command of your property and the income therefrom – I should have between the new farm & Tuzokr. two strings to my bow. and make a plunge at once on to high and dry land from the uncertainties and difficulties which this cursed fever has thrown in my way – Only think that poor Alma is still and again suffering from fever – Poor Pauline would be the worst off as her share of interest would be small and if leaving with us she would not have the recourse left of earning an independence by giving a few lessons – the ins and outs of the estate I know that is of its revenue quality of soil etz. we are well informed of because some intimate friends of Richards' whose aunt formerly owned this property and who now died lived there and managed the property for many years – Richard who has a large castle also offered that myself and family should live there free of rent for half a year or so till everything were put into repair so that we could do it by degrees and it would cost much less – Now dear aunt tell me what you think of this plan – of course it is a bargain and if it is to be done must be done soon –

I saw aunt Mary at Görg.⁹ they both were very kind to me and invited to dinner & tea and insisted on my spending the whole day with them – I have not seen Tilly yet but have good news from her & the baby – compts to Miss Müller & Moulson. If you do [illeg.] write within 8 days from this that is to the 15 March direct Baden after the 15th Csakova near Temesvár –

Believe me dear aunt yours aff.
WGC

Address: La signora Clairmont/ 83 Via Valfonda/ Firenze/ Italia.
Front postmark: OROSLAVJA/ ⁶/₃
Rear postmark: AGRAM/ ⁶/₃/5.A.; 9 S/ FIRENZE/MAR¹⁰ 6/69/ UDINE-VERONA/ 8/MAR./69

Unpublished. Text: M.S., Pf. Coll., CL'ANA 0288

---

1 The estate of Richard von Sermage. See CL'ANA 0246.
2 Udine (Weiden in German) is in north-east Italy, some 54 kilometers north-west of Gorizia (Görz in German). Oroslavje is located about 260 kilometers east of Gorizia.
3 The town of Rogatec was known as Rohitsch in German. It is located in Slovenia today and is situated about 73 kilometers west of Varaždin. Murray's *A Handbook for Travellers in Southern Germany: Being a Guide to Würtemberg, Bavaria, Austria* describes Rohitsch as "a watering-place of considerable repute, from its mineral (acidulous) springs and baths. 400,000 bottles of the water are exported annually. Tolerable accommodation may be found on the spot, which lies close to the Hungarian frontier" (London: John Murray, 1867), p. 443. The town of Rogaška Slatina is six kilometers west of Rogatec (German: Rohitsch-Sauerbrunn), the location of the mineral springs.
4 For information about Trieste, see note 4, CL'ANA 0252. Wilhelm means Gorizia and not Goricia.
5 Varaždin is a city in Croatia, 81 kilometers north of the capital city, Zagreb.
6 Slavonia, a district in Croatia. Jim Harter notes that Archduke Johann conceived the idea for a "trans-Alpine route from Vienna to Trieste" in 1838. Construction on the Südbahn (Southern Railway) was completed by 1860 with the final portion joining the Lombardy-Venetian Railway at Udine. Harter also records the construction of a railway between Prague and Dresden in 1851 and the completion of the Kaiserin Elisabeth Bahn running between Vienna and Salzburg by 1860 (*World Railways of the Nineteenth Century* [Baltimore, MD: Johns Hopkins University Press, 2005], p. 160).
7 In *The Illustrated Catalogue of the Industrial Department* published for the International Exhibition of 1862, and under the heading English-Austrian "Measures of Superficies," one English acre is listed as equal to 1,124.93 Vienna Fathoms square" and one English mile equates to 804.86 Vienna Fathoms (Foreign Division, London: Her Majesty's Commissioners, 1862), vol. iv, p. xliv.
8 The houses Antonia left to them.
9 Wilhelm misspelled the town of Görz. As his handwriting is unclear, it is also possible that he wrote Görg. See CL'ANA 0401.
10 Abbreviation for "marcia," Italian for "March".

208 • Ottilia Clairmont and Pauline Clairmont to Claire Clairmont

Vienna 16th March [c. 1869]

My dear aunt: I waited for Willy's return to write to you, what a happy day was it our first meeting and how thankful am I for all the kindness you showed him.

I was deeply touched by the beautiful and charming present you sent me through Willy – many many thanks for it I have given you so little proof of my affection dearest aunt and you always load me with so many tokens of your love

Believe me my heart is truly thankful for any kindness and if it do not appear in my letters be sure it is not the want of feeling but the difficulty of expressing them in a foreign language.

How often have I wished to be with Willy to have stayed with you, it will be a long time till this ardent wish of mine can be realized

I sincerely trust it may be realized some day. I was delighted to hear that Willy found no change in you at all, that you look very well, and are in good health. I went to Baden at Willy's return to stay the first day with him. I dreaded the entire removal with baby to Baden too much for such a short time as I expect there will be till our departure for the Banat – therefore we resolved that I would remain with Wattie at my parents house and Willy at Baden to finish his business. Dear Willy looks a great deal better. I am sure the journey did him very good but still I look forward with the utmost anxiety to our return to Hungary.

If this bad fever would only leave him I am quite miserable about it. Our sweet little baby grows up splendidly both physically and mentally I am very happy with this dear little child may God guard this precious treasure of ours. About Willys stay at Croatia he surely wrote most explicitly himself it must be a charming place. Willy also remained a few day's at Graz.[1] to spent them with Alma. It is really extremely good and kind from you to have sent Alma too such a nice present she is an excellent dear sister and I miss her very much since she left.

Wattie is crying after his mama therefore goodbye dearest aunt I was not only very much rejoiced that you remembered me but the ring is most beautiful you gave me the greatest pleasure with it and I thank you from all my heart. Don't be vexed that I am such a prosy corespondent you really dare not judge my love and affection for you from my letters.

My parents want to be remembered to you – and please give my best compliments to Miss Müller and Miss Moulson

Hoping that you continue in good health I am dear aunt

yours most gratefully
Tilly.

Baden March 24.

My dearest Aunt[2]

Altho' I got your letter some days ago, I thought it better to delay answering till I could in a satisfactory way give you the information you want. You need be under no uneasiness concerning his[3] Lungs & Heart – they are perfectly sound the Doctor says – he never was ill till he got the fever – that is all the illness he has or ever had – he is perhaps the only one among us, whose lungs were perfectly sound – He suffered when a boy from bronchitis from which he was cured as you may remember by the sea – baths which he took while staying with you at Boulong.[4] My lungs are also good now but I may have had a slight inclination that way – when I was young but have outgrown it. About the houses[5] I can tell you I feel certain if we wanted to sell them they would fetch more than 3000 £. having been valued by the saving bank at 4200 £, & you know those people always set down the lowest price. These are the two important questions of your letter. They are answered. If you should have to go to England about the box – I am at any moment ready to accompany you – & if you wish to settle at Trieste next winter I shall also join you if you wish it – altho' I do not consider it a place climate suited to you. I might have wished to keep my house here – as it would have made me a quiet little home – but if it is very advantageous to W. I will give up the plan – besides if I think if you could live in W's house & feel that you were among friends who love & take care of you it would make you very comfortable.

Dearest Aunt I must close – the broach is admired by all;[6] & I thank you again for all your kindness to W. he quakes with delight of his stay in Florence – yours afftly

Pauline.

Address: La signora Clairmont/ 83 Via Valfonda/ Firenze/ Italia.
Front postmark: BADEN/[illeg.]/ 69
Rear postmark: UDINE-VERONA/ 26 /MAR/69; [illeg.]/[illeg.]/27/MAR; 95/ FIREN{stamped on side of envelope}

Unpublished. Text: M.S. Pf. Coll., CL'ANA 0203

---

1 Graz is the second largest city in Austria, about 200 kilometers south of Vienna.
2 Both these letters were included in the same envelope.
3 Pauline referred to Wilhelm's health.
4 Claire lived in France between 1842 and 1847. In 1844, Claire told Mary Shelley that she would not have any of Charles's children stay with her unless Antonia were dead, because she feared Antonia would blame her for anything that went wrong in their lives during such a stay. Further, if any of Antonia's daughters stayed with her they would come to appreciate a life of "leisure . . . and luxury" that Claire believed would render them "unfit" for the hardships of life (*CC* II: 390).
5 Antonia's houses at Baden.
6 A later photograph of Ottilia shows her wearing a large brooch. See the photograph in this collection. Mary Claire Bally-Clairmont included the following information on the back of the photograph: "I have this brooch and wear it occasionally – a brown/yellow big stone surrounded with pearls I got it in Geneva from Uncle Walter Clairmont in 1957 after the death of his wife Frieda Clairmont". It is possible that Pauline left her brooch from Claire to Ottilia and that Ottilia wore it when she was photographed. See CL'ANA 0179 and CL'ANA 0421, Box 3, bundle g, number 186.

209 • Wilhelm Gaulis Clairmont to Claire Clairmont

Baden March 24th
1869.

My dear aunt.

I duly got your letter concerning the purchase plan[1] – let me take this opportunity to disarm your ungenerous suspicion about the letter B; the name of the estate is Mirkovetz situated in the county of Varasdin in Croatia[2] – so you see not a single B. I should have answered your letter long before but I was very busy getting poor Tilly en route for Tuzokrit – she left on Saturday last. there were a variety of minor reasons which made it necessary for her to leave I remain at Baden for a few weeks longer to try the effect of cold water cure against the fever– for I have had more attacks although very trifling since my arrival here – Your suggestion to get a lease of Mirkovetz prior to purchasing it is very good, but it is not feasible because it is already let to a Jew and his lease will not expire yet for one year. I find it quite natural dear aunt that you cannot make up your mind so suddenly – especially now where you are beset by so many other cares – I read in the Vienna papers that all hope of H.M's theater being opened for this year is over – this is very painful – Tilly was exceedingly pleased by your present. she writes you herself – I tear off the second half of this sheet so as the letter may not become too heavy – My compts to Miss Moulson & Miss Müller. please tell the latter I have not yet been to Pest to deliver her present to Miss Pulsky.[3]

Goodbye dear aunt believe me

yours aff
WGC

Baden
March 24th 1869.

You can direct to Baden until such time as I shall write to you of my departure for Hungary.[4] Alma too was very much pleased with your attention for her – only think what an excellent girl she is – You know she is the God mother of our Wattie – I told her at the time that she must not think of making him any valuable present as is here the general custom. she accordingly made a beautifully embroidered babtizing dress for the baby which gave Tilly a great deal of pleasure – and there I thought the matter rested – fancy then my surprise when I heard that Alma had on her return from the Banat where she had been staying one year opened an account for Watties name in a savingsbank and there deposited to his act. the whole of the savings from her pocketmoney during that year – it amounted to 25f. that is £2.10.0d which is a great deal considering that she has not much pocketmoney allowed her and how many girlish wishes she could have satisfied with this money instead of devoting it to so generous and selfsacrificing a purpose – I thought it right to tell you this that you should see that your present was not thrown away on an undeserving person – all this she did quietly without telling anyone a word – it was only by chance I found it out.

P.S. I enclose you a stamp which I have left from my sojourn in Italy

Address: No envelope.

Unpublished. Text: M.S., Pf. Coll., CL'ANA 0289

---

1 Wilhelm hoped to purchase an estate with funds partially provided by Claire. His various attempts to secure an estate were well-documented in his letters.
2 The estate may have been located in Maruševec, about 15 kilometers west of Varaždin, in Majkovec (60 kilometers south of Varaždin), or in Mirkovec (54 kilometers south of Varaždin). See CL'ANA 0290.
3 See CL'ANA 0395 and CL'ANA 0320.
4 Unfortunately, Claire's letters to her family from 1869 have likely not survived. We only have her letters written to Trelawny, Cini, Emma Taylor, Charlotte Bennet French, and Margherita Cini Farina in the final decade of her life. Claire's only extant letter to Wilhelm from the 1870s, co-written with Pauline, dates to January 1879. Claire would die in March 1879.

210 • Pauline Clairmont and Wilhelm Gaulis Clairmont to Claire Clairmont

April 7th [1869]

Dearest Aunt

I received your kind note (I beg pardon letter) some days back, & mean to answer it most scrupulously in a day or two, but I must tell you that I have so much to do with letting the lodgings & all sorts of other duties that I have barely time to sleep – At first I was frightened seeing a stranger's hand – I am much obliged to Miss M.[1] for writing – it was very kind – Dearest Aunt I do hope your eyes are a little better now but the spring sun is very trying, I have a pair of green spectacles from poor Mama which would be just the thing for you shall I send them? There is one of the first occulists in the world in Vienna Professor Arlt[2] how I wish you could consult – He will operate Mrs Rismondo[3] who is blind on one eye – Poor thing! Dear W. is looking pretty well – but I am so sorry he is going so soon Dearest Aunt good night. I am very tired

your very aff^{te}
Plin.

Dearest aunt.[4]

I am about to leave this in a few days for Tuzokrét – previous to so doing I write you a few lines of wellfare from here and I at the same time send ~~the~~ you [illeg.] our photographs. Tilly's and one of mine which ever you may choose is for you, and of the other two one is for Miss Müller & one for Miss Moulson. the first I beg to remind that she has promised me but not yet given me her photograph and that I certainly expect to get it.[5] Miss Müller's present to Miss Pulszky I shall deliver now in a few days. – With reference to Tilly's photograph allow me to observe that it gives us the impression as if she looked very affected in it; but in reality she is anything but that. I have read the letter you last wrote through Miss Müller to Pauline. The questions you ask concerning distances from Mirkovez to sundry places it is impossible to answer prima vista[6] – at home I have a very excellent map of Hungary I shall there measure off with a pair of compasses all the distances you require and send you the result –

Of Tilly and Wattie I have pretty good news; she is in pretty good health and very busy putting her new house into perfect order but poor Alma is still suffering of fever poor thing – I am quite unhappy about her because she got the illness in saving and helping us – My water cure goes on steadily but the Doctor says I can not expect a result before 3 months. Goodbye dear aunt I used only one sheet to keep within the mark of a simple letter.

yours affection
WGC

Baden April 7th 1869.

28 MARCH 1861–24 DECEMBER 1889

Address: La signora Clairmont./ 83 Via Valfonda/ Firenze/ Italia.
Rear postmark: 9 S/FIRENZE/ APR⁷ 10/ 69

Unpublished. Text: M.S. Pf. Coll., CL'ANA 0202

---

1 Either Miss Müller or Miss Moulson.
2 Ferdinand Carl von Arlt (1812–1887) was an ophthalmologist at the Medizinische Universität Wien (the "new Vienna School"). In *The Standard American Encyclopedia of Arts, Sciences, History, Biography*, John Ridpath explains that Arlt was "an eminent oculist; Emeritus Prof. of Ophthalmology in the University of Vienna . . . He was the first to insist upon the necessity of having glasses prescribed and fitted by physicians instead of opticians" (John Clark Ridpath (ed.) [New York: Encyclopedia Publishing Company, 1897], p. 176). The archive of the Medizinische Universität Wien provides more details on von Arlt's career ("Universitätsbibliothek". Medizinische Universität Wien. Web. 20 August 2015. http://ub.meduniwien.ac.at/).
3 Antonia's sister. See CL'ANA 0401.
4 Both these letters were included in the same envelope.
5 These photographs are missing; however, there is a loose stamp inside the envelope.
6 Italian for "before seeing".
7 Abbreviation for "aprile," Italian for "April".

211 • Wilhelm Gaulis Clairmont to Claire Clairmont

[12 May 1869]

My dear aunt.

Pray do excuse me for having left. your letter so long without an answer – I was detained at Vienna and in Pest a great deal longer than I expected so that your letter was lying here waiting for me some time before I arrived – than I had a great deal to do and then I was absent again from home. I shall now make up for the delay by a most [illeg.] accurate answer to all your questions – I am extremely glad you are having good advice for your eyes. Graefe[1] is a most celebrated man no doubt his pupil will be competent to give you the best advice and it is such a comfort to know you in good hands – in this respect you would be well off too in the vicinity of Vienna as Arlt[2] of the Vienna school is also a great [illeg.] celebrity as occulist – I shall endeavor to write this in a large plain hand so as to give you no trouble in reading it – I have not been troubled with any attacks of fever of late I shall continue the douching here as soon as my apparatus which I got for this purpose from Vienna shall will be put up here – the our resident D^r here also thinks that a continuance of the cold water douching[3] is likely to do me good because he says almost imperceptible colds are mostly the immediate cause of all fever paroxisms and as the cold water hardens the skin and makes it less likely to take cold the use of cold water tends to remove one of the most frequent causes of fever – I do not think that your anxiety is justified that my life as a farmer gives me too much hard work or exposure to wheather and mental anxiety – on the contrary since work <u>I must.</u> for my existence I hardly know of any other condition in life in which I could earn so good a competency with comparatively so little trouble as I do now – I took the opportunity of my stay in Vienna to make sundry efforts to obtain a situation adequate to my knowledge in Vienna in case the fever should not allow me to continue here but people only promise and I could obtain nothing to rely on I am very unhappy too about your drawing no revenue this year again from your box.[4] I think partly from this reason, that is because you are thereby straightened in your money resources and partly on account of the uncertainty as to whether I can continue here or not and if not what I shall turn to next you should for the present continue quietly at Florence in your present arrangements – I give you this advice contrary to what I conceive to be my own interest for I fancy that if you were once settled some where in Austria you would more readily make up your mind to the purchase of an estate than while residing so far away, but I consider it better so for yourself – As to Pauline I think you are wrong with refference to the conclusions you say you have drawn regarding her – she will at all times be ready to fly to your assistance when you really need her – but for the present she evidently is under the impression that she is more necessary at Baden where our property must be looked after and where she can maintain herself than with you where she has no means of sustenance and would be thrown entirely on your resources. moreover she knows from me, that you have now a most comfortable establishment and are very well taken care of. I think it right that she should not disengage herself from her present duties ~~here~~ at Baden until you have an imperative and decided call for her services which for the present you have not – of Alma we must not think – her parents would not consent to part with her – she and Tilly both send their kind love and are most anxious to hear how your eyes are getting on – I am glad Till' photog. pleased you – Now I must answer your questions about Mirkovetz – it is not <u>dreadfully</u> cold – but certainly colder than you could bear – there is such a thing as a fortnights or 3 weeks snow of a stretch – the distance from ~~Agram~~ to

Agram[5] to Mirkovetz is		16 Engl. miles	
"	Fiume	100	" "
"	Trieste	140	" "

the above figures are however not <u>quite</u> reliable as the distances on my map are given by the now obsolete unit of posts – from Agram to Trieste the railway takes about 12 hours this however includes 2 ½ hours delay at Steinbrück[6] where one joins the Vienna Train in the direction of Fiume the rail is ~~only~~ completed only as far as Carlstadt.[7]

I enclose two transfer certificates N<u>o</u> 1522 & 1523. I am however not sure whether the aust. postoffice will register a letter for Italy – Goodbye my dear aunt – please give enclosed to Miss Müller & remember me to Miss Moulson & Miss Jones.[8] write soon about your eyes –

yours affectly
WGC

Csakova
Temesvar
May 12<u>th</u> 1869.

Address: Recommandirt./[9]La signora Clairmont./83 Via Valfonda./Firenze/Italia
Rear of envelope: WG.Clairmont/Csakova.

Unpublished. Text: M.S., Pf. Coll., CL'ANA 0290

---

1 Johann Hermann Baas provided names of the most celebrated ophthalmologists practicing in Vienna in the eighteenth and nineteenth centuries. Under the entry for Georg Beer (1763–1821), Baas opined: "it is upon his teachings that the fame of the university of Vienna in this speciality depends... Pupils are the best evidence of the importance of a teacher, and Beer's pupils were Ph. von Walther, C. F. von Graefe" (*Outlines of the History of Medicine and the Medical Profession* [New York: Vail and Company, 1889], p. 672).
2 See CL'ANA 0202.
3 Cold water douching was prescribed in the nineteenth century to cure typhus and typhoid fever.
4 Claire told Trelawny in her letter of 23 April 1870 that she had received no income from her opera box for five years and that she was living on £120 a year (*CC* II: 619).
5 Zagreb, capital city of Croatia, was known as Agram in German. Wilhelm correctly estimated some of these distances. The distance from Zagreb to Trieste is 230 kilometers which is about 142 miles. The distance from Zagreb to Rijeka (Fiume) is 165 kilometers or 102 miles. However,

Zagreb to Majkovec is 40 kilometers (25 miles), Zagreb to Mirkovec is 54 kilometers, while the distance to Maruševec is 100 kilometers (62 miles). See CL'ANA 0289.

6 Murray's *A Handbook for Travellers in Southern Germany*, published in 1857, provided information about Route 285, "Vienna to Warasdin, Agram, and Karlstadt". The railway passed through "Warasdin (Varasd) . . . a frontier town of Croatia" and "Agram (Zágráb), the capital of Croatia, and residence of the Ban, or Viceroy . . . Eilwagen daily to the Steinbruck Stat. of the Vienna and Trieste Rly. (Rte. 248), by Rann and Gurkfield. A Railway is in progress to Steinbruck" ([London: John Murray, 1857], p. 542). The term "Eilwagen" means a mail coach.

7 Karlstadt or Carlstadt is the German name for the city of Karlovac. The city is 54 kilometers southwest of Zagreb. Rijeka is 113 kilometers west of Karlovac.

8 Alma von Pichler would describe Mrs. Jones and Miss Moulson in her letter of 3 April 1870. Herbert Huscher quotes from the letter: "Mrs. Jones, die Haushälterin, begrüßte uns, und gleich darauf erschien Miss Moulson, eine ideale, elegante, nette kleine Engländerin mit langen, blonden Locken, mit blauem Band und elegantem schwarzen Schleppkleide. Sie begrüßte uns äußerst freundlich, und wir setzten uns in folgender Ordnung: Aunt Claire zwischen Mrs. Jones und Miss Moulson, und wir vis-à-vis von ihr . . . Miss Moulson sprach *lively* und nett, Aunt Claire ruhig und gute Lehren gebend und M[r]s. Jones machte die Honneurs" ("Charles und Claire Clairmont," p. 103). According to Alma (translated from the German), Mrs. Jones was the housekeeper. She described Miss Moulson, "an ideal, elegant, nice little Englishwoman with long blond curls, with a blue hairband and an elegant black dress with a train" greeting them in a friendly manner. They sat around the table as follows: "Aunt Claire between Mrs. Jones and Miss Moulson, and we opposite her . . . Miss Moulson spoke lively and nicely, Aunt Claire [spoke] calmly and provided good advice, and Mrs. Jones did the honors" (translations by Anja Reiner). According to Alma, the meal consisted of "rice soup, chicken with cauliflower, potatoes and pork, pastry, stewed fruit and biscuits, oranges and apples" (translated in Huscher, "Claire Clairmont's Lost Russian Journal," p. 43).

9 Alternative spellings include: Recommandiert, Recommandirt, Recommandiret. The word means "recorded". The use of the word indicates that Wilhelm sent the letter by registered post.

212 • Wilhelm Gaulis Clairmont and Ottilia Clairmont to Claire Clairmont

[20 August 1869][1]

My dear aunt.

I am afraid you will begin to be angry with me for not having written you for so long a time, however it was a very busy time with me and moreover I had little encouragement to write to you – as I have had bad news to give you of us. – nevertheless I seize the first opportunity a rainy day affords me of writing you these lines – Our harvest which promised so fairly has turned out the worst I have had yet (1863 excepted) it is so bad that it will not cover our own want for seed and the farmservants sustenance so that we shall be obligated to pay from our pockets or incur debts to cover the expenses of the farm for the impending year until the new harvest comes – the principal causes of this disaster was a cold rain which set in while the crops were all in blossom – besides this we had a very heavy hailstorm which did a great deal of damage, of this we shall recover [illeg.] the greater part having been insured – to crown our misfortune we had a fire which burnt down 4 wheat and 3 oatstacks – these were not yet insured; they having been just only carted in from the fields that very same day. the agent was to have come the next day to take down the depositions – the fire was very large and burnt an entire afternoon and night. I succeeded by dint of immense exertions to confine it to the stacks which were destroyed – in two places there was imminent danger of the fire being communicated to another row of stacks – but we happily warded off the danger – I was taken ill afterwards with a sort of gastric complaint which hung about me for a week or ten days but now I am quite well again I attribute it only to the fright and agitation consequent on that horrid fire – I was glad dear aunt to get better accounts of your health in your last – I am sure that the sojourn in the baths of Lucca[2] will do you good – poor Wattie is ailing I believe only in consequence of toothing. Tilly will ~~you~~ write you more about him and herself. She expects her confinement to take place about the middle of December – Pauline will I hope come to see us through this trying emergency. Goodbye my dear aunt I am sorry I must write you such a lamentable letter

Believe me yours affectly
WGC

Aug. 20th 1869.
Csakova Temesvár.

My dearest aunt.

Many thanks for your kind letter which I intented answering imediately to give you some satisfactory news concerning Willy's health. but ~~Watties~~ takes up almost all my time thus preventing me day after day from writing and I am sorry I can add to day even but a few lines to Willys letter as poor little baby is very unwell and requires great attention.

Soon after Willys return from Vienna he recovered remarkably and felt very strong and healthy till the beginning of the harvest and the extreme heat we then had.

He both physically and mentally over exerted himself as the harvest turned out worse than any one had suspected and besides we had again that great loss by the fire.

Willy could not stand all that and fell ill – he was obliged to lay in bed for a few days – now thank Heaven he is well again but still very low spirited.

Perhaps the indian corn will turn out better now as we have a very good rain since two days.

I am afraid there will be great misery this year all about in Hungary. – I enclose you my sister Alma's phothograph which she begs you to accept as a token of her affection – we all consider it a very [illeg.] [illeg.] excellent likeness. We were very anxious for her health till now. she too poor girl could not get rid of the inter mittent fever; now at last she seems to have shaken it off entirely and enjoys herself in the beautiful environs of Klagenfurth[3] where she is with my parents and my sister Emily[4] who went there with all her children to avoid the dreadful heat we are suffering here in the months of July and August.

Pauline very often writes to us and we are looking forward to her visit with the utmost pleasure. I only regret she will have so little amusement during the winter months, but she is a dear good soul and wants to share our trouble. Wattie is getting [illeg.] his teeth though very slowly, we celebrated his first birthday on the 5th of August his pa gave him a ducat[5] in his saving box. When he is in good health he is a dear little fellow and gives us a great deal of pleasure. he is very fond of his pa and quite delighted when papa plays with him – he is just learning to walk. Now good bye my dearest aunt we are very glad you feel well, and only hope your eyes are so too; that we may soon again get some news we always rejoice for them it.

Believe me dear aunt

B

yours most
affectionately Tilly

Tusokrét 20th August

Address: La signora Clairmont/ Casa. Pierini/ Bagni caldi di Lucca[6]/ Italia.
Written on the side of the front envelope: W. Clairmont
Front postmark: CSAKOVA/ 21/8 (three of the same over three 5 kr. Stamps)
Rear postmark: FIRENZE/ [illeg.]

Unpublished. Text: M.S., Pf. Coll., CL'ANA 0291

---

1 These two letters were enclosed in the same envelope.
2 Thermal baths in Tuscany, Italy. Bagni di Lucca is located about 100 kilometers north-west of Florence.

28 MARCH 1861–24 DECEMBER 1889

3 The city of Klagenfurt Am Wörthersee is located near Lake Wörthersee in southern Austria in the state of Carinthia (Kärnten). The von Pichler family vacationed there (see CL'ANA 0292). In a letter to Stocking written in 2005, Mary Claire Bally-Clairmont indicated that her great-grandmother, Fanny von Pichler, "made many trips and was enchanted of the Wörthersee (lake of Wörther), Austria, about 70 km west Graz, bought there a farmhouse, later changed to a Villa (still existing!); her son Moritz took it over. the Clairmonts were often there, as [illeg.] Christoph and I for summer holidays, the name of the village is Velden . . . The villa sold about 26 years ago" (CL'ANA 0428, unpublished manuscript, Pforzheimer Collection).

The *Amtsblatt zur Klagenfurter Zeitung* of 9 August 1865 records in its article "Kurliste aus dem Bade Vellach" (a list of names of people who arrived at Vellach since July 22, 1865) the arrival of "Fräulein Alma Pichler, f. f. Ministerialraths – Tochter von Wien" Austrian Newspapers Online, Österreichische Nationalbibliothek [Austrian National Library, http://anno.onb.ac.at/cgi-content/anno?aid=kfz&datum=18650809&seite=4&zoom=33&query=%22alma%2Bpichler%22~5&provider=ENP&ref=anno-search, p. 4]. Translation: "Miss Alma Pichler, Daughter of an assistant head of a government department from Vienna". Vellach is 49 kilometers south of Klagenfurt and is a spa town.
4 Emily Hauer.
5 Gold coin.
6 Thermal Baths of Lucca.

213 • Wilhelm Gaulis Clairmont to Claire Clairmont

[11 September 1869]

My dear aunt.[1]

Tilly sent me your letter of the 2nd inst. to this place Velden[2] a watering place in Karinthia[3] on a splendid lake a most rising place at which I am staying for a few days; Mrs Pichler having bought a few building allottments here which she proposes to distribute among her daughters on condition that we should each build on one of them – so I came to see the place and to consider whether by settling here and building a cottage with a few rooms to let in the summer season we might perhaps eak out a living and be liberated of the horrid Banater fever – but the difficulty is that we have after this bad year not money enough to build and if we had I do not see ~~how~~ what ~~I should~~ occupation I could find for myself; until I have found some other means of maintaining my family it is hard for me to give up the Banat – for the present I can tell you nothing definite about our immediate plans I do not think it will be possible to find an appointment for me here as everything is overfilled; one might perhaps undertake something but that I sha~~ll~~ould want capital for – I am very sorry dear aunt you give such a dismal account of your health – nothing would please me better than if you could live with us; I am sure you would like Tilly she is such a sweet disposition; if we settled at Velden this would perhaps for the summer months be possible for the scenery is charming & the climate most healthy only a little cold in winter – but in winter you might live at Trieste or Goritz[4] or Udine or Venice there is railway communication with all these places – and in a year when the new railway to Goritz will be completed it will be quite an easy distance I believe 5 hours to Görz. there are two English families here now (at Velden) the Ridells whom I believe you know from Baden and the Rev^nd Mr Tucker Engl. clergyman at Trieste;[5] he has a very nice family and has come up for a few months for mountain air – they are very nice people I questioned them a deal about Trieste with a view to your settling there – Mrs Tucker told me she found living in general very cheap at Trieste only house rent and butchers meat dear. she says it is very healthy no fever when the bora[6] rages she says invalid people must stay indoors.

I am away from home already a fortnight and am most anxious to return home because poor Tilly feels so lonely – I shall leave in a few days, do not answer me to this place anymore but to Tuzokrét. I have not looked at the box with your letters lately; but I know of no reason to suppose that they are injured; if we should move from the Banat you must please tell me where you want the box sent to. Alma has gone to Holland the Pichlers have some relations there and so she went to visit them and I believe is likely to stop the whole winter there – the fire of our stacks was not done maliciously but by sheer negligence; the man on whose mill all the others say the fire [~~illeg.~~] broke out & through whose carelessness the whole misfortune arose lost himself his whole wheat as it was not yet divided –

Goodbye now dearest aunt. as soon as we have ~~anything~~ decided anything as to our future movements I shall let you know.

yours most affectionately
WGC

Velden near
Klagenfurth Carinthia
Septemb. 11th 1869.

Give my compts. to your young ladies and to Miss Cini[7] when you see her I duly got her letter –.

Address: La signora Clairmont/Casa Pierini/Bagni Caldi di Lucca/Italia.
Written on the side of the front envelope: W. Clairmont
Rear postmark: LUCCA/ 14/SET./69/ [illeg.]; VENEZIA/[illeg.]/ BAGNI DI LUCCA/ 14/SET/69/[illeg.]

Unpublished. Text: M.S., Pf. Coll., CL'ANA 0292

---

1 The first page of this letter has a raised imprint consisting of a crown and the word "BATH".
2 Velden am Wörthersee is 23.5 kilometers west of Klagenfurt on Lake Wörthersee. Murray's *A Handbook for Travellers in Southern Germany* recommended that travelers visit Velden on the way to Klagenfurt as the town promised "agreeable promenades" and a variety of tourist sites to visit (pp. 421–2).
3 Wilhelm combines the German "Kärnten" with the Hungarian "Karintia".
4 Gorizia (German for Görz). See CL'ANA 0344.
5 Mr. Tucker was the Anglican chaplain at Trieste. *The Ecclesiastical Gazette* of 10 October 1871 records the death of Samuel Tucker, "formerly British Chaplain at Trieste" (London: George Cox, 1874), vol. 34, p. 64. *Crockford's Clerical Dictionary For 1868* lists Samuel Tucker as the chaplain at Trieste (p. 807) and notes too that he was made Deacon in 1848 and served as "Consular Chap. at Trieste" (London: Horace Cox, 1868), p. 664. The records of the National Archives (Surrey, England) affirm that he was chaplain at Coblenz, Germany, and at Trieste from 1861 ("Tucker, Samuel". The National Archives. Web. 7 July 2015. http://discovery.nationalarchives.gov.uk/details/rd/9d0939a5-1a06-4e16-a3cc-7e705de845b3). Gittings and Manton speculate that Claire went to Trieste where she resided with Mr. and Mrs. Tucker in 1871 in order to escape the harsh winter at Nikolaifhof (p. 232).
6 A wind.
7 According to Claire Tomalin, Bartolomeo and Nerina Cini had eight children, of whom only four survived by 1869. Wilhelm probably refers to Elena (1844–1921), the elder of the two remaining daughters. Margherita (1853–1914) was nine years her junior (C. Tomalin, Introduction and The Family Tree of Lady Mountcashell in Mary Shelley, *Maurice, or the Fisher's Cot*, pp. 48–65, 176–7).

214 • Wilhelm Gaulis Clairmont to Claire Clairmont

[29 October 1869]

My dear aunt.

I regret to say your last letter was mislaid in the disorder of packing and moving to Baden. so I cannot answer it as punctiliously as is my habit – however I remember that the principal part of it was about the safety of your letters and manuscripts. these are in perfect good order; Pauline who came down here from Vienna to help us packing and accompany Tilly up to Baden I being obliged to stop down here for another month repacked all your boxes – some things that would not pay for the freight such a heap of old Illustrated newspapers[1] she took out and left here so the remainder was packed by herself in the two large leather covered black boxes of yours – they are locked and await your orders whether to be left here or to be forwarded to any where – Tilly left for Baden with Wattie and Pauline on the 21st Octob. I shall follow about the 15th Novbr. so we are as yet quite undecided as to what to do with the farm, for this present year we sublet it after the Italian fashion to people who do all the work and share the profit with us, by this means one does not require to look so closely after ones farm as when one has labourers – I do not think that I can afford to give up my farm as I doubt whether I shall get another a situation, for it goes against me never having held a situation and consequently having no testimonials or recommendations However at any rate I am going up to Vienna now and I shall try what can be done.

We have sold part of our stock already I invested my share in railway shares of the line leading from Debrecin[2] to Fiume – as they are below pari[3] they yield 7 percent the interest is paid not in paper money but in <u>silver</u> and guaranteed by the Hungarian government.

As the interest being paid in silver is not liable to the fluctuations of Austrian paper money it would be a very appropriate investment for you – it is perfectly safe for besides enjoying a government guarantee it is sure to succeed as the only direct line of communication between Hungary and the sea – If I were sure I shall not require my capital for a fresh enterprise in the farming line I would perhaps think of building a house (part to sublet) at Velden[4] so as to secure Tillys share of her inheritance for her mother would give her a nice building allotment [illeg.] on the bank of the lake but as she is an impetuous flighty person there is no knowing what she may do with the property if we do not lay hold of our share now.

Goodbye dearest aunt please direct to Baden on or after the 13th Novemb

yours most affectly
WGC

Csakova
Octob 29th 1869.

Address: La signora Clairmont/Palazzo Orsini/ Via Valfonda/Firenze/Italia.
Rear postmark: [illeg.]/$^{30}/_{10}$/[illeg.]

28 MARCH 1861–24 DECEMBER 1889

Unpublished. Text: M.S., Pf. Coll., CL'ANA 0293

---

1 Probably *The Illustrated London News* which was published between 1842 and 2003.
2 Debrecen is a city in Hungary, about 231 kilometers east of Budapest and 822 kilometers northeast of Rijeka (Fiume). During the 1848–9 Revolution, Debrecen was Hungary's capital city.
3 German for "par".
4 See CL'ANA 0292.

215 • Wilhelm Gaulis Clairmont to Claire Clairmont

[8 November 1869]

My dear aunt. I duly rec^d yours of the 2nd Novbr. from which I saw that you returned to Via Valfonda. I hasten to inform you about Major Adams[1] and also about your boxes – The first I regret to say I do not know either personally or by repute so can give you no account whatsoever concerning him – but I believe you can make sure of Pauline's joining you in spring at least she has told me and Tilly that such was her intention, and what conversation passed between us on different occasions as to our plans for the future was all based on this supposition. I think it of course not only natural but even necessary for you that you should study the character of the person Plin marries (if she do so at all) I have even at the risk of appearing selfish & mercenary not concealed from Plin that I do not like the idea of her marrying – because she is a wilful independent disposition who has as you say of yourself been her own mistress for too long a time to sacrifice her independance readily to another. I think she is aware of this and that she will think twice before she does marry.

As to your boxes dear aunt we have plenty of room at Baden for them I shall take them there with my luggage. Pauline packed them when she was here – one contains your letters &papers; one the other sundry old novels and articles of hardly any value so that I question whether you should have this second box sent to you to Italy because the freight will amount to a great deal – if you send me no order to the contrary I shall dispatch them both to Baden – I expect or rather fear to be delayed here till the 20th of this month because we have had rain here for the last 3weeks which put a stop to all agricultural operations – Poor Tilly is very uneasy because she expects her confinement to come on about middle of next month and she fears I may not be back in time for it.[2] Our little boy is a dear little chapy, life has a new charm for me through him – I am sure you would be delighted to see him – He is already now so devotedly attached to me that he will not rest anywhere when he sees me anywhere from a distance or even hears my voice from outside the house. I have in my study an enormous writing desk his greatest ambition is to be placed on top of it – there he will sit for hours like a statue watching me writing or else examining with the greatest interest the different articles placed on my desk such as pen wiper notebooks pencils etc. – Pauline was quite charmed to see him at his favorite poste and said it was the most charming tableau vivant she had ever seen – he is a dear little soul with blue eyes like his ma; his hair is fair but they say it will be dark yet it is curly –

Pray give my best regards to Miss Mueller[3] & Miss Moulson I wish I could have been with you at San Marcello.[4] do give my compts to Mrs Cini Ellen & to Miss Dunn;[5] they all were so very kind to me – I have thank Heaven got rid completely of the fever. I am getting stout Goodbye dear aunt any directions concerning your boxes posted for me at Florence by the 20th or 21st of Novbr. are sure to find me still at Csakova.

Believe me dearest aunt yours

most sincerely
WGC

Tuzokrét
Post Csákova
Novemb. 8th 1869.

Address: No envelope.

Unpublished. Text: M.S., Pf. Coll., CL'ANA 0294

---

1 In her letter to Trelawny of 25 December 1869, Claire mentions an "elderly Austrian retired Major" who had proposed to Pauline but who could not leave Austria for fear of losing his military pension (*CC* II: 602).
2 Alma Pauline Clairmont was born in 1869.
3 Wilhelm spelled Miss Müller with "ue" which is an equivalent form of "ü".
4 San Marcello Pistoiese is located in the hills of Tuscany, about 69 kilometers north-west of Florence.
5 Mrs. Cini (Nerina Tighe Cini) and her elder daughter, Ellen (Elena Cini, later French). Miss Dunn is unidentified.

216 • Wilhelm Gaulis Clairmont to Claire Clairmont

[11 January 1870][1]

My dear aunt.

There I am again going to bother you with fresh financial proposals. Mirkovetz has been sold with a profit of £2000 – I have now been offered an estate for £4500 under most favorable circumstances which would if purchased double our capital in the course of two years – if you could manage to lend me £1000 on it for which I will engage to pay you 4 or even 5 percent I can manage the rest. The estate has been offered for sale privately to Count Bombelles (brother of the Charles Bombelles[2] who was the friend and adviser of Emperor Max of Mexico[3]) I spent a week at his house he would like to buy it him self but has not sufficient cash for the moment at his disposal – he would cede to us his offer of it – the price is very low the estate is situated about 2 miles from a railwaystation and 4 miles from Varasdin a fine road leading up to the very house door. a capital physician is a few miles off – the estate is called Petrijanitz[4] comprises 350 acres of arable land and 12 acres of firstrate vineyard – a fine on two story high family mansion with 15 rooms and every comfort of a well appointed country house. then a large barn con horse stables granary in short every thing complete all the buildings are new and most substantially built and will not require any repair for a long time to come – the revenue may be put at the present indifferent mode of its farming at £400.

If you can lend me the £1000 pray write me by what time I might calculate for certain on having the money – you can have drawn out a deed of mortgage on the estate like any stranger to me and thus be sure of your capital and interest – It would be a great pity to miss this chance of acquiring such a splendid property. which is only sold because the former proprietor died without children and there are 5 heirs to it who cannot agree among each other. I write this from Sermages place but pray answer me to Baden – whither I shall return in a few days.

Goodbye dearest aunt yours affect.

WGC

Oroslawje[5]
January 11th 1870.

the position of this estate offers great inducement to us – so near to Trieste where you will be settling and so near to Velden where my parents in law are likely to be in the summer – the climate is mild and the scenery beautiful – you might spend with us at least the summer months and return to Trieste or Fiume for a few months in the winter. it is only 8 hours railway travelling from Petrijanitz to Trieste.[6]

Address: No envelope.

Unpublished. Text: M.S., Pf. Coll., CL'ANA 0295

1 There is an interlocking set of initials, "WC," in red ink on the upper left-hand corner of the first page of this letter.
2 Count Karl Bombelles (Charles Bombelles, 1785–1856).
3 Archduke Ferdinand Maximilian (1832–1867), later Emperor Maximilian I of Mexico, was the younger brother of Emperor Franz Joseph of Austria. Charles Clairmont had been his English tutor before he died in 1850. Hubert Huscher quotes from the journal of Archduchess Sophie, the mother of Emperor Franz Joseph and Ferdinand Maximilian, and which Stocking incorrectly attributed to Countess von Schoenborn. Sophie described the effect of Charles's death on her children in her entry for 3 February 1850: "Nous allâmes chez L'Empereur et y trouvâmes Seeburg[er](?) qui venait d'apprendre la mort subite du pauvre Clairmont, le maître anglais de Maxi-Charles-Schoenborn, et des Mensdorff etc. . . . Je la cachais à Maxi lorsqu'il vint vers 6 h. $^1/_2$ chez moi accompagner son père à la première 'Faust'. J'allais un moment chez Charles qui fut très painé aussi de la mort de Clairmont . . . Je dis à Maxi la mort du bon Clairmont qui l'affligea beaucoup" ("Charles und Claire Clairmont," p. 65). Translation: "We went to the Emperor's place and found Seeburg(er) who had just learned of the sudden death of poor Clairmont, the English teacher of Maxi, Charles, Schoenborn, and some of the Mensdorffs, etc. . . . I hid it from Maxi when he came to me around 6:30 to accompany his father to the premiere of 'Faust.' I went for a moment to Charles's place who was also very pained to hear of Clairmont's death . . . I told Maxi of the death of good Clairmont which distressed him a lot" (translation provided by Sharon Joffe).
Maximilian was crowned Emperor of Mexico in 1864 because of a deal concluded by Napoléon III who wanted to assert French control in Mexico. However, Maximilian I was executed in 1867 after the French left Mexico (The Editors of Encyclopaedia Britannica. "Maximilian Archduke of Austria and Emperor of Mexico". *Encyclopaedia Britannica Online*. Encyclopaedia Britannica Inc., n.d. Web. 1 August 2015. http://www.britannica.com/biography/Maximilian-archduke-of-Austria-and-emperor-of-Mexico). See also CL'ANA 0402.
4 Known today as Nova Ves Petrijanečka, the town is located about 9 kilometers from Varaždin in Croatia.
5 The estate of Richard von Sermage, located about 67 kilometers south of Nova Ves Petrijanečka where Wilhelm hoped to live.
6 Trieste is 277 kilometers south-west of Nova Ves Petrijanečka.

217 • Wilhelm Gaulis Clairmont to Claire Clairmont

[13 January 1870]

My dear aunt. I just rec^d yours of the 8th Janry. It is out of the question to offer Dr Dominkus[1] less than 25.000 f. because he gave himself 24.100 at public auction and he has had some expense besides if we get it for that sum itis cheap enough. more I would not advise to give because I would not counsel you to another but a cheap bargain. It is now for you to decide and to write to me at once whether you are determined to give £2000 inclus of agio[2] for the estate and whether I can have you will positively engage to send me £500 at once – the remaining £1500 within 6 months of the day the purchase is concluded. If you resolve to do so and give me a solemn & positive promise that you will adhere to your resolution I shall go to Dr Dominkus at once – inspect and overhaul the estate once more and conclude the bargain with him at once more provided he will give it for 25.000 and provided I find the estate really what I suppose it to be – You need not disengage your investment capital from its present investment till the bargain is concluded but from the minute day I write that it is concluded you must be ready to send me £500 inclus agio at once – We have one great advantage in the purchase of this estate. that is that we cannot go wrong in as much as the price has been fixed at public auction by the competition of men who live in the vicinity and know the estate and its capabilities perfectly well.

Now for your questions.

If you purchase Nicolaihof[3] for 25.000f. you would have to add another 1000f. for lawyers and government fees. in all 26.000f. of this capital I would undertake to pay you 4 percent annually say 1000f in a round sum rent and I would stock it myself and pay the taxes and repairs of buildings myself. only for the first painting and refitting of the dwelling house – I would beg you for a small contribution – and of course your board and lodging you would if you were constantly with us (as I hope you would) pay us something. If we buy Nicolaihof I can make arrangements to undertake the management of it at once by subletting it in plots of an acre or two to the peasants for the first year. after the house at Nicolaihof were repaired we should then migrate from Beleci to Nicol.[4] at a convenient time in the summer so as tobe comfortably established in our new home by autumn – the management of Beleci for the remaining two years of my lease I can easily carry out. Dr Coles's[5] case is no parallel to this – if one purchases an estate in the Bakonyer wood[6] one can well afford to wait 3years; because buyers there are so rare that one runs no risk of being overbid by another buyer. but here in a fine scenery, an enticing property between 3 lines of railroad in a highly cultivated country equidistant from Vienna Treist[7] and Pest a competitor may be found over night. another reason why we must hurry the matter is that if Dr Dominkus retains the estate long enough in his hands. to be obliged to incur expenses on it he cannot give it so cheap as he would perhaps give it now. moreover the season for subletting it to the peasants would be past. and to have find stock and servants all of a hurry to farm it myself would be inconvenient to me – I think I have said every thing I had to say – I conclude as the post is just leaving. believe me dear aunt

yours most affecty
WGC

January 13th 1870.

Address: La signora Clairmont/ 83 Via Valfonda/ Firenze/ Italia
Rear postmark: FIRENZE/[illeg.]

Unpublished. Text: M.S., Pf. Coll., CL'ANA 0296

---

1 Dr. Dominkusch was the owner of Nikolaihof, a farm located in Marburg. Marburg is the German name for Maribor, a city in Slovenia on the Drau River. Today, Nikolaihof is known as Miklavski dvorec and it is located in the municipality of Miklavž na Dravskem polju on the left bank of the canal of the River Drau/Drava. The farm's address today is Nad izviri 8, Miklavž na Dravskem polju (Leopold Mikec Avberšek, Pokrajinski arhiv Maribor, Slovenia, personal communication: 3 November 2014). Records from the Pokrajinski arhiv Maribor (Regional Archives in Maribor) show the register of the farm dating back to its purchase by Claire. In the document, Mary Jean Clairmont (instead of Mary Jane Clairmont) was recorded as the purchaser of the Walcker estate. Dr. Dominikusch's name was also included. (The document reads: "Clairmont Mary Jean als Ersteh. der Walcker'schen /: D. Dominikus:/ [illeg.]" Translation by Ann Sherwin: "Clairmont Mary Jean as purchaser of the Walcker (D. Dominikus)". Source: Pokrajinski arhiv Maribor (Regional Archives Maribor, Slovenia). All three names are clearly visible in the record. The register depicts a negotiation deed. The property was apparently put up for sale in 1869 (sign C 1135 of the image) and the sale was concluded in 1871 (sign C 20506). Wilhelm's letter of 18 March 1871 documented that Dr. Dominkusch had purchased Nikolaihof from Mr. Walcker in order to recoup the money he had originally lent to Walcker. Walcker subsequently became insolvent.
   An article in the *Marburger Zeitung* of 4 May 1873 addressed bee keeping issues in Marburg and recorded the roles Wilhelm and Dr. Dominkusch played in the Bee Keeping Association: "Herr v. Clairmont, Gutsbesitzer auf Nikolaihof" (the owner of Nikolaihof) and "Herr J. Dominkusch, k.k. Professor und Bezirksschulinspektor etc". (royal and imperial professor and school district superintendent etc.) were administrative board members (Verwaltungeräthe) of the Beekeeping society (Bienenzucht-Verein). See "Einladung zum Beitritte an alle Bienenfreunde und Bienen- züchter". Web. 27 Ocober 2014 and 27 October 2015. http://www.dlib.si/
2 German and English for "agio," the premium for the difference in the exchange rate between the two currencies. "Inclus" from the Latin "includere" meaning "inclusive".
3 Murray's *A Handbook for Travellers in Southern Germany* describes Marburg as "a very dull town, although the 2nd in Styria; it has 4000 Inhab., and lies on the l. bank of the Drave . . . The women wear an ugly white cloth round their heads, allowing the ends to fall behind their back" (London: John Murray, 1873), p. 445. Sergej Vrišer notes that by 1880 "Maribor was a small provincial town with two faces: on the one hand the town houses and noble halls already formed a complete urban entity and revealed relatively advanced architectural ambitions, while on the other hand the overall appearance of the town was still distinctly agrarian" (*Maribor* [Ljubljana: Niro Motovun, 1984], p. 45). Vrišer explains that the opening of railway connections to Maribor from Ljubljana (1849), Trieste (1847), and Pragersko (1860) further positioned the town to take a more important role in the economic life of the Autro-Hungarian Empire. Marburg "almost wholly

resembled other German towns" in the nineteenth century, and the "policy of planned Germanization" was reinforced with the publication of the *Marburger Zeitung* (Marburger Times) in 1862 (pp. 48–9). Workers' unions appeared in the second half of the nineteenth century: "In 1870/2 Maribor journeymen and apprentices went on strike several times" (p. 89). Vogelnick explains that the Southern Railway selected Marburg as its preferred town for train repairs and railway maintenance owning to its location as a midway point between Trieste and Vienna. The town thus became fairly industrialized (Franc Vogelnick. *Maribor* [Lujbljana: Cankarjeve Založba, 1988], p. 76).

4 Wilhelm farmed on a number of farms in the Banat. At the time of writing this letter, he was living on a farm he called "Beleci" or "Belici". The farm was located in today's Belec, Croatia. The distance from Belec to Maribor (the location of Nikolaihof in Slovenia) is 86 kilometers.

5 Unidentified.

6 In *Hungary in 1851*, Charles Loring Brace described his journey through Hungary. He devoted a section to discussing the difficult lives (he termed it "wild") of Hungarian "cattle-drivers or herdsmen" who formed "formidable robber bands, such that the force of law could not easily reach them. It is only within five years such a band existed in the *Bakonyer Wood*, under *Rosza Sandor*" (New York: Scribner, 1852), p. 190. The Bakony Wald (Bakony Forest) is located near Lake Balaton (the Plattensee). See CL'ANA 0246 and CL'ANA 0254.

7 Wilhelm's spelling for Trieste.

218 • Wilhelm Gaulis Clairmont to Claire Clairmont

[24 January 1870]

My dear aunt.[1]

I received yours today and am very sorry indeed that the impossibility of your complying with my request should have given you so much concern – you are much too good hearted my dear aunt – I did not mean it at all in the light of a request which if not granted would hurt or injure me but in the light of a speculation which if entered upon would have benefited us both immensely – for you would have got 5 per cent. for your money and I should have got hold of an estate which would in a short time be worth nearly double of what I gave for it – Mirkovetz was sold for 44.000f that is £4400. the present proprietor was ~~offered~~ already offered £6000 but he asks £7000. there is a profit of £2600 – I shall very likely rent a small farm of 86 acres here in Croatia in Richards[2] vicinity – this would not be with a view of making money but merely to have a cheap comfortable dwelling – my revenue I shall derive from Tuzokrét – which by giving it out to people on halves like the contadini[3] in Italy I can manage by going there a few times in the year. Baden is so expensive a place to live in with a family that I can not afford it – Croatia is very cheap; and I got this farm at a bargain – I shall learn the language and peculiarities of the country and by the time my lease in the Banat is expired I shall find a larger and paying farm here – or if we sell in the mean time our houses and you were inclined to join us, we might wait our chance and buy a good estate at a bargain – but pray dont make yourself uncomfortable on that account – I shall be detained here another week. I long very much to see my poor deserted wife and the chicks – pray remember me to Miss Moulson and believe me dear aunt yours most

affectly
WGC

Oroslavje
January 24th 1870

Address: No envelope.

Unpublished. Text: M.S., Pf. Coll., CL'ANA 0297

---

1 The word "Oroslavje" is printed at the top left side of the first page of the letter.
2 Richard von Sermage.
3 Italian for "peasantry".

219 • Pauline Clairmont to unknown recipients

Naples March 7. [c. 1870]
~~Thursday~~
Monday

My dear Friends

This evening I got safe to Naples without the slightest accident excepting several pitched battles with the facchinis[1] in which I generally come off halfways victorious.

But I must begin at the beginning as tomorrow I shall have plenty to do lodging-hunting.

I left M[rs] P.[2] & Alma on Saturday last at Venice they going by rail & I per mare,[3] much to my delight but first I must tell you I spent a most delightful time at Venice with Prince. We trotted about all day long as poor M[rs] P's foot was rather weak & she was glad of rest. To see Alma find her way in the intricate labyrinth of calles[4] & vicolos[5] in Venice was more than wonderful – & how well she instantly understood the italian money while I was in a perfect state of bewilderment at the francs liras soldis & centesimi:[6] was equally wonderful – & she walked so fast that I had to keep up a constant little trot not to loose sight of her. talk of <u>my</u> being independant! We delighted in the Procuratie[7] & the beautiful shop windows I send you each a pair of studs for cuffs which I hope will please you being a specialité of Venice

On Saturday at 3 p m. I left by the steamer ~~Lucifer~~ Tomaso for Ancona.[8] I thought it safer to take my passage only thus far in case I should not like it. the passage was delightful the boat large & safe but the tea execrable. there were only 3 passengers an officer from Vienna a Baron Horneth & an Italian Marine officer who spoke german & so we spent the evening very pleasantly for I was not the least bit sick not even squeamish. those 2 gents landed at Ancona so I was glad I had not taken my passage any further as I should have been quite alone very dull – so I landed breakfasted & looked at Ancona which has only one beauty – its situation on the side of steep mountains I took my ticket to Foggio[9] & had nice company a lady with her 3 daughters who knew as much french as I do Italian & so we conversed tant bien que mal.[10] But I must tell you that Italian second class is next door to English second & austrian 3rd I got to Foggio at 9$_{pm}$ the same day in pouring rain there were no cabs but the railway guide was good enough to walk with me into town & look for a locanda.[11] It is a beastly little place subject to earthquakes & at last got housed in a trattoria[12] in a filthy room with disgusting beds & nothing but greasy macaroni & an apple for my supper – but being tired & hungry I eat the stuff & went to bed – the fiddling in the tap room went on half the night but I slept very well.

I should have gone on the same night to Naples but the railway is not yet finished & there is a pass across the Appenines to be done by vetturino,[13] with whom I was afraid to trust myself at night. It turned out however quite easy. the vetturinos are provided by the railway company & they send mounted police with every conveyance. at Starsi[14] we were six of us stowed into a small bus with 4 capital horse running a breast & 5 other similar vehicles following. the horses are small well made & well fed & harnessed without collars & only one wicker on the near side – so we rushed slap-dash thro' the mire the horses left entirely to their one guidance the reins dangling about their hind quarters – this was anything but comfortable but got safe to the other side entered the railway cars & passing thro' most beautiful scenery of large spreading hills & broad valleys reached Naples[15] at 9 pm. Fancy that they visit luggage nearly at every town ! Austria is most liberal compared to that! But I every where showed up my little packet of cigarettes which was the only objectionable article – was very civilly treated & payed nothing.

At the Hotel de Rome where we agreed to go there was no room I therefore went opposite to the Hotel belle vue – looking out on the port & Mt Vesuvius[16] but it is too dark to see anything I have a beautiful room but which is much too elegant for us & to morrow will go lodging hunting[17] – I had a new proof to day of how we in England & Austria eat a great deal too much – You know what a rush there is at the dining stations where passengers travel 10 hours a day – Well imagine that having all of us started at 10 at Foggio I was pretty hungry at 3 $^1/_2$ at San Spirito[18] on the other side of the appenines & eat a piece of roast veal with great relish – & I was the only one who eat anything – all the others took only a cup of coffee without milk – & waited for supper at naples –

Another curious thing I must tell you – the nacht kastle[19] in Foggio have a most peculiar shape – exactly like a throne with a vase standing on the seat, thus!

in ful view

Do please write to me soon best address Miss C. poste restante Naples – I have my passport & shall get them easily. I drank sweet Beebles[20] health in the first drop of wine out of the bottle you gave us – & prayed for him & you the first thing in the morning at St Marco in Venice[21] – May we all live to meet again. I hope you got my letter from Triest – about the Reise[22] Now good night dear friends it is midnight – I hear the tide rushing in long slow waves but it is a black night my journey including steamer from Triest to Venice cost 110 francs grub,[23] porters gondolas cakes sightseeing & other purchases. Very cheap I think. I must also inform you that there are italian steamers from Bari & Brindisi[24] to Naples for the very simple reason that the railway line what there is of it has only been very recently established & the steamers were the only communication between the east & west coast. I expect Alma on the 11th. Now I must close, breakfast & look out for an apartment – please write soon to your ever aff^t

Plin.

a kiss to my little goddaughter.

Address: No envelope

Unpublished. Text: M.S., Pf. Coll., CL'ANA 0228

1. "Facchini" is the plural Italian word for "porters". The singular form is "facchino".
2. Mrs. von Pichler, Ottilia's mother. Ottilia's sister, Alma von Pichler, would die in April 1870.
3. Italian for "by sea".
4. Italian for narrow Venetian streets. The singular form is "calle" and the plural is "calli". The plural form "calles" is also correct. The word is generally not used today.
5. "Vicoli" is the plural Italian word for "alleys". The singular form is "vicolo".
6. The Italian word "soldi" means "money," while "centesimi" means "cents".
7. On St. Mark's Square, in Venice. A series of connected buildings.
8. A seaport on the east coast of Italy, about 310 kilometers south of Venice.
9. She meant Foggia, a city 343 kilometers south of Ancona on Italy's east coast. *Cook's Tourist's Handbook for Southern Italy* of 1875 describes Foggia as a "rich mercantile city, presenting, however, in itself few attractions for the tourist" (London: Thomas Cook and Son, 1875), p. 174.
10. French for "as best as one can".
11. Italian for "inn" or "guest-house".
12. Italian for "tavern".
13. "Vetturino," Italian for "coachman" or "coach driver". The correct plural form should be "vetturini". The Apennine Mountains run north to south for about 1,400 kilometers.
14. Pauline misspelled Starza, located between Foggia and Naples.
15. City in Italy on the west coast, located 130 kilometers west of Foggia.
16. Mount Vesuvius erupted in AD 79, destroying the city of Pompeii.
17. Baedeker's *Italy. Handbook for Travellers* noted that the Hôtel de Rome was located "close to the sea" while the "Hôtel et Pension Bellevue" was listed as a "pension . . . for a stay of from 3–4 days upwards" and was "well spoken of" (London: Karl Baedeker, 1883), 3rd part, pp. 21–2. The *Handbook* also explained that warm baths were located near the Hôtel de Rome (p. 26).
18. According to *The Railway Times* of 1869, the railway line from Foggia to Naples would consist of 124 miles of functioning track when finished, and that it "comprised 41 ⅞ miles in working [sic] at the commencement of 1868 . . . In the course of last year the following sections were successively opened upon this line: . . . Benevent and Santo Spirito" (London: Railway Times and Joint-Stock Chronicle Office, 1869), p. 820.
19. "Nachtkastl," Austrian for "bedside table" or "night table". Pauline included a small sketch of it in her letter. The chamber pot sat on top of a chair, "in full view," as Pauline clearly stated.
20. Unidentified.
21. The Basilica of San Marco in Venice, a Catholic church whose construction began in the eleventh century.
22. German for "journey".
23. Food.
24. Towns on the east coast of Italy. Bari is 136 kilometers south of Foggia while Brindisi is 119 kilometers south of Bari.

220 • Alma von Pichler to Pauline Clairmont

[5 April 1870]
Florence $^5/_4$ 70.[1]

Dearest Plin!

Here in dear aunt Claire's saloon, I am sitting on her nice desk and writing you in her name about what she thinks and fears about you. It is not only that she should be <u>very</u> glad to see you as soon as possible and having your company, which she is wanting so much; but think only what she heard to day by accident and listen to me as her interpreter, as poor aunt is too weak to write herself feeling very anxious and agitated about you, having suffered so much of all the great losses and misfortunes in your family. In going out to day to the poste office, she met Mrs. Blanche Lyoleand[2] who told her quite accidentally that the english doctor of [illeg.] Florence had got so very bad news from Rome, where the typhus fever increases in a dreadful manner since a few days, so that the Hotel Europe[3] is quite shut up, as ten american ladies died there and where set off for Newyork. You may imagine yourself how very anxious she feel about you and so do I, knowing how little you think of your own health and happiness. Be good and listen. Aunt Claire implores you to come as soon as ever possible and not to pass Rome on no account. You shall wait for a fine, quired day and set off for Leghorn and come here by rail-way and she promises you, that you can visit Rom next year as well as you ever could now, as she learned too, that the whole easter – ceremonies would be reduced to very small terms, on the same account, as all the strangers are leaving in a hurry to get away of that dreadful sickly place. It is not the comon roman fever, but the real dreadful typhus fever. So you then see that dear aunt Claire is quite right fearing for your health.

We arrived here three days ago and spend many agreeable hours at aunt Claire's house, finding herself uncomonly well and healthy, she acquired inquired much about you and Willy and all the rest of our dear Badeners. We got here already three letters of Baden and Vienna. They are pretty well off only poor Bible[4] suffered still a little of fever and Tilly had much to do, as Wali was ill and the new children maid was to introduce. Good old W. still felt the fever in his veins, but it could not burst out.

Sie wollten am 3. od. 4 dieses schon verschiedenes nach Bélesci schicken, u. wollen am 15. Baden verlassen, wenn sich das Wetter bis dahin ändert, denn sie hatten jetzt noch Schnee von 5 Fuß Tiefe. Du ersiehst aus der vorstehenden, daß aunt Claire mich beinflußte; umsomehr, da sie mich bat ihr den Brief vorzulesen, aber ich kann Dir doch nur dasselbe sagen, daß Du Dich nicht das Gefahr aussetzen sollst u. komme direkt her, wenn ich auch glaube, daß es Dir sehr dawider läuft. Aunt Claire würde <u>sehr</u> böse sein, wenn Du dennoch nach Rom gingst, sie sagte, sie sei so agitirt so spränge aus dem Fenster wenn sie Dich in Rom wüßte. Ich ließ in Rom ein Brieferl für Dich, daher hörtest Du so lange nichts von uns. Wo steckst Du [illeg.] jetzt my good old girl? Miss Moulson is a charming person and rejoices your arrival very much. Mrs. Jones[5] makes us feel very comfortable and is a nice clever person, very personnable. Your room is prepared, your large box stands in it and you can gess, how much I must thinks about you and our old fellow here at Florense. We have been in the Uffizi to day and seen many beautiful things. Aunt Claire was as amiable as possible, we spent every dinnertime and yesterday evening with her. She gave me a nice coral comb and for Tilly a coral broche. Now good bye dear girl, write us either to Verona till the 12th, or Insbruck to the 16th of April. With the best love your old very stupid sister Alma.

Liebes herzens Paulinerl! Einen Gruß aus A Clairs göttl. Salon! o komme Du arme allein Irrende zu der lieben alten Tante u labe dich in Sie – die es so gut mit euch meint. Welch angenehmes Leben kannst du hier haben statt fremde Leute das Gute geneigten auf das Komfortabelste leben – wärend Du als Nichte dich so allein in d. Welt stehend plagst – Komme und [illeg.]zu laben für [illeg.] [illeg.] [illeg.] Ade mit Liebe Deine W Muller

Pray do not think its nonsense ore imagination and do not pass Rom and come here directly as aunt Claire is quite out of spirits for anxiety.

Thousand kisses and aunts best love.[6]

Translation (German transcription and English translation provided by Ann Sherwin):

They wanted to send various things to Bélesci as early as the 3rd or 4th of this month and want to leave Baden on the 15th if the weather changes by then, for still had snow feet deep now. You can see from the foregoing that Aunt Claire influenced me all the more, but I can only tell you the same thing, that you should not expose yourself to danger but should come directly here, even though I believe you will be very much against it. Aunt Claire would be very angry if you went to Rome anyway. She would be so agitated, she said, that she would jump out the window if she knew you were in Rome. I left a little letter for you in Rome; that's why you heard nothing from us for such a long time. Where on earth are you now, my good old girl?

Dear darling Paulinerl,

Greetings from A Claire's divine salon! O come, you poor lost thing, to your dear old aunt – who means so well for you, and let her refresh you. What a pleasant life you can have here, instead of with strangers, the gracious, most comfortable refreshment – while you, her niece, so alone in the world, slave away – come and [illeg.] refresh yourself for [illeg.] [illeg.] [illeg.]

Goodbye, with love, your W Muller[7]

Address: No envelope

Unpublished. Text: M.S., Pf. Coll., CL'ANA 0421, Box 2, bundle e, number 100

---

1 Alma's English skills were not that strong. This letter is also badly worn.
2 Unidentified.

3 Coghlan's *Handbook for Travellers in Southern Italy* recommended the Hôtel de l'Europe and described it as "a first-rate establishment in the Piazza di Spagna. The proprietor, Mr Melga, has established his prices, which will enable persons before entering to know what expense they are likely to incur" (London: Trübner and Co., 1863), p. 1. Baedeker's *Italy. Handbook for Travellers Second Part: Central Italy and Rome* suggested the "Hotel Europa" on the Piazza di Spagna and identified the hotel as among "the best and most expensive" in Rome (London: Karl Baedeker, Dulau and Co., 1886), p. 105.
4 Unidentified.
5 Huscher identified Mrs. Jones as Claire's housekeeper. See CL'ANA 0290.
6 Alma cross-wrote these last English lines on the first page of the letter.
7 The handwriting on this final section of the letter (from "Dear darling Paulinerl" onwards) appears similar to the writing at the end of CL'ANA 0231 and could possibly have been added by Miss Müller.

221 • Pauline Clairmont to Alma von Pichler

Florence Ap 16. [c. 1870[1]]

My dear Alma

I wrote to you to Verona[2] & hope you got the letter – I arrived here last night & found dear Aunt looking <u>very</u> well indeed & every body inquired after you most kindly. I left Naples by steamer Medeah & saw Procida Ischia a Cape Misene[3] to perfection. the latter has a fine lighthouse & Procida with a little swallows nest of a town stuck on to its rocks looked rosy & beautiful in the evening sun. The dinner on board the steamer was excellent the passengers few so I had a good flirtation with the Captain a Frenchmen which was only interrupted by my becoming sick – Before leaving Naples I went to see the Catacombs[4] & the Campo Santo,[5] & altho' it rained all day long I was very glad I went.

Abends

Theuerste Alma

Ich bin ganz unglücklich ich bitte dich nimm dir ein Beispiel an meiner elenden Characterlosigkeit, & wenn du je in der Stimmung der Selbstverachtung bist – so denke – es gibt <u>eine</u> noch elender als ich bin – bodenlose Vorwürfe nutzen jezt nichts mehr ich bin & werde ohne Verstand ohne Urtheil bleiben – & da ich mich Selbst nicht achten kann ist es ganz natürlich dass Ihr mich verachtet. Höre was geschehn ist – aber ich habe es verdient. Aus dem Koffer den ich damals ~~nach~~ von Venedig nach Florenz schickte ist mir fast alles gestohlen worden! der schöne schwarze Sannt leib meine neuen Hemden ein Schwarz seidner Kleider stoff – was noch von anderen Sachen abgeht werde ich erst entdecken. Also um die paar elenden Francs porto zu ersparen habe ich vielleicht 50 fl verlust. und kann nicht einmal reclamiren weil sonst Claire auch auf meine Betrügerei kommt & mit Recht sagt ich habe dich dringend gebeten diesen Koffer persönlich mit zubringen du hast es nicht getan geschieht dir Recht. Ihr habt mich damals in Venedig über meine unpraktische Pedanterie so ausgelacht & ausgespottet dass ich mir, mit meinem gewöhnlichen Mangel an Selbstvertrauen, ganz elend dumm vorkam, mich schämte so wenig Urtheil zu haben. Nach so vielen Reisen so unpraktisch zu sein einen werthvollen Koffer seinem Schicksal zu überlassen hat sich aber noch viel unpraktischer bewiesen denn dadurch habe ich meine besten Sachen verloren. Die Mutter wird natürlich dabei bleiben dass es so viel besser war – aber du bist noch jung Alma & kannst einsehen lernen dass auch andere Leute einmal Recht haben können – Ich kann mir meine Schwachheit gar nicht verzeihen um so mehr da es nicht das erste Mahl ist dass ich bereuen muss nicht meiner eignen Meinung gefolgt zu haben. Ich bin ganz untröstlich über meinen Verlust da ich gar kein anderes warmes Kleid habe & mir nicht so bald so etwas theures schaffen kann – & alles um die paar elenden francs zu ersparen. Das Schloss war ganz gut, die Kiste war von hinten aufgemacht die Sachen herausgenommen & wieder zugenagelt worden – & überdiess musste ich den halben Winter meinen Pelz entbehren! Let it be a warning to you dear Alma to know your own mind & follow it & not to be influenced by anyone who choses to call you a fool for having a different opinion. But I must try & bear my merited punishment as bravely as I can.

Yours truly
Pauline

Warum hat Paulin nicht gefolgt und den Koffer 6–8 Wochen allein am Bahnhof gelaßen – zum ausrauben das war Almas letzter Schmerz.

Translation (German transcription and English translation provided by Ann Sherwin):

<u>Evening</u>

Dearest Alma

I am very unhappy. I beg you, let my wretched lack of character be an example to you, and if you are ever in a mood of self-loathing, just think: There is one person even more wretched than I am – abysmal reproaches are of no use now. I am and will always remain mindless, with no judgment – and since I cannot respect myself, it is perfectly natural for you all not to respect me. Hear what happened – but I deserved it. Almost everything in the trunk that I sent to from Venice to Florence back then was stolen! The beautiful black velvet bodice, my new chemises, a black silk dress fabric – what other things are missing, I have yet to discover. To save a few miserable francs in postage, I sustained a loss of perhaps 50 gulden, and I can't even complain, because otherwise Claire will bring up my victimization and rightfully say I urged you to carry bring this trunk with you personally, and you didn't do it. It serves you right. Back then in Venice you laughed and scoffed so at my impractical pedantry that, with my usual lack of self-confidence, I felt woefully stupid and was ashamed at having so little judgment. After so many trips, being so impractical as to leave a valuable trunk to its fate has proven far more impractical, however, because it caused me to lose my best things.

Mother will naturally stick to her conviction that it was much better that way – but you are still young, Alma, and can learn to recognize that other people can also be right sometimes – I cannot forgive myself for my weakness, all the more so because it wasn't the first time I had to regret not having followed my own mind. I am utterly inconsolable over my loss, since I have no other warm dress and cannot get myself anything that expensive so soon – and all just to save a few miserable francs. The lock was fine; the box had been opened from behind, the things taken out, and then it was nailed shut again – and on top of this, I had to go without my fur for half the winter! [6]

Why did Paulin not follow but leave the trunk 6–8 weeks alone at the train station – to be plundered – that was Alma's last sorrow

Address: No envelope

Unpublished. Text: M.S., Pf. Coll., CL'ANA 0231

1 This letter dates to 1870, before Alma's death.
2 City in Northern Italy, 115 kilometers west of Venice.
3 Procida and Ischia are islands in the Gulf of Naples. Pauline misspelled Cape Miseno, the mainland town located across from Procida on the Gulf of Naples.
4 Baedeker's *Italy. Handbook for Travellers Third Part: Southern Italy and Sicily* describes the catacombs: "Descending to the left immediately beyond the bridge, and from the lower end of the street entering the winding Strada S. Gennaro de' Poveri to the right, we soon reach the large hospice or poor-house of that name, which contains several hundred inmates. At the back of the building is the Church of S. Gennaro (St. Januarius), with the entrance to the extensive Catacombs . . . of Naples, admission to which is obtained by applying to the porter of the hospice . . . The only entrance to the Catacombs is now at the back of this church. They consist of four galleries, of which, however, two only are now connected by staircases and accessible to visitors . . . The oldest part of the catacombs dates from the first century of our era. In point of architecture they far surpass the Roman, though inferior in every other respect . . . The bones which fill many of the chambers and corridors are generally those of victims of the plagues which ravaged Naples in the 16th century" (London: Dulau and Co., 1883), part 3, pp. 43–4.
5 In referencing the cemeteries of Naples, Octavian Blewitt explains that Campo Santo Vecchio is the "old cemetery of Naples. It is used only for the dead of the public hospitals, and for the poorest classes who cannot afford the expense of burial in the Campo Santo Nuovo or in the churches. The cemetery and the chapel at the entrance were designed by Fuga in 1763" (*Handbook for Travellers in Southern Italy* [London: John Murray, 1853], p. 145).
6 This final part of the letter appears in a different handwriting. It appears to be in the same handwriting as in the letter of 5 April 1870. Miss Müller may have written them both. See CL'ANA 0421, Box 2, bundle e, number 100.
7 The German word "Schmerz" means sorrow, anguish, hurt, distress, or pain.

222 • Alma von Pichler to Claire Clairmont

[30 April c. 1870]

[illeg.]
Sie selbst legte es auf die Bilder.[1]

Dear aunt![2]

At least here at Austrias frontier's but still in [illeg.] I find ~~time~~ a few moments rest, to send you my mamas and my best thanks for all your kindness and friendships which maid our stay at Florence to the most agreeable remembrance of our long journey. You were so exseedingly kind and friendly towards us that we realy do not know how to thank you. We hope your are quite well and the [illeg.] our good Pauline {ink} needless and she is with you since a good wile. We often spoke of you and her and we should have liked to know how things went on. We had lukly fine weather on our whole journey home spent one day at Genoa one other at Turin[3] and after having visited the famous lakes of Maggiones and Como,[4] were we spent quite a lovely day, we arrived on the 11th of April at Milan, visited the wonderfully dom[5] and the famous Scala.[6] At Verona we only staied one day and went on by Triest, Bozen – Meran and Insbruck.[7] On the Brenner[8] we found fully winter, had a great snowfall and found it still at Insbruck very cold. Poor Willy gave us again very bad news about Tilly and himself; the first got such a violent fever, that the doctor himself feared the typhus, but after cold [illeg.] during a few day's poltesess,[9] she felt better, but Willy caught again the hungarian fever[10] and felt very miserable, having a new childrens maid, which they could not yet be trusted. We will hope to get soon better news, as it is the more disagreeable for poor Tilly to be ill now, in the moment when they want to leave Baden. Once more our best thanks for all and our love; please give our best compliments to Miss Moulson and Mrs. Jones, and if Plin is with you, a hearty kiss. Tell her to write us as soon as possible. Mama sends her best love.

Ever your gratefully
Alma

Address: No envelope

Unpublished. Text: M.S., Pf. Coll., CL'ANA 0178

---

1 Alma's letter is badly worn. The first of these two lines is illegible. Translation of the second line: "She herself laid it on the pictures".
2 Alma von Pichler was not related to Claire, although called her "aunt".
3 Genoa is 230 kilometers north-west of Florence and is located on the Mediterranean Sea. Turin is 171 kilometers north-west of Genoa.
4 Lake Como, in Italy, is located 84 kilometers north of Milan. Lake Maggiore is about 60 kilometers west of Lake Como.
5 Alma meant the Duomo di Milano, a Catholic cathedral in Milan, Italy and considered a symbol of the city. Construction began in 1386 and continued for over five centuries.

6 Known officially as Teatro alla Scala, La Scala was commissioned by Empress Maria Theresia of Austria in 1776. La Scala today boasts both opera and ballet companies (The Editors of Encyclopaedia Britannica. "La Scala". *Encyclopaedia Britannica Online*. Encyclopaedia Britannica Inc., n.d. Web. 3 May 2015. http://www.britannica.com/topic/La-Scala).

7 Alma wrote the German names for the Italian cities she traveled through on her way back to Austria: Bozen (Bolzano in Italian), Meran (Merano in Italian), and Innsbruck (Austria). There are 154 kilometers from Verona to Bozen, 34 kilometers from Bozen to Meran, and 155 kilometers from Meran to Innsbruck. The southern section of the Brenner Railway (Brennero/Brenner line) was completed in 1859 and connected Bolzano to Verona. Service on the section connecting Bolzano to Innsbruck began in 1867 (See "Treno Alto Adige". Web. 3 may 2015. http://www.ferroviavalvenosta.it/). The Brenner Railway connected Innsbruck to Verona through the Brenner Pass.

8 The Brenner Pass enables one to travel from Italy to Austria across the Alps. The railway through the Brenner was completed in 1867 (The Editors of Encyclopaedia Britannica. "Brenner Pass". *Encyclopaedia Britannica Online*. Encyclopaedia Britannica Inc., n.d. Web. 3 May 2015. http://www.britannica.com/EBchecked/topic/78812/Brenner-Pass).

9 The words "[illeg.] during a few day's" are written in superscript. Cold poultices are compresses made from herbs or vegetables and are placed on the body to reduce fever or inflammation.

10 Typhus, transmitted by fleas and ticks from those living in close quarters. Symptoms include fevers, body rashes, and chills.

223 • Ottilia Clairmont to Claire Clairmont

Beléci[1] 19th July 70

My dear aunt.[2]

I must ask your pardon for not having written to you for such a long time and not even having thanked you for the beautiful present you sent me. Both the comb and the broach[3] is in my possession now – how happy should I be could I share it with my dear sister.

I am so full of thanks towards you that you were one of the last who was kind to her. I dare not hope ever to find consolation and become reconciled to the heavy loss we all sustained through the death of my dear sister – time only can soften the pang of such grief.[4]

I am quite ashamed not to have answered Plin's letter – but writing is particularly painful to me and full of bitter remembrances.

We get on very well at Beléci it is a charming place and I hope you will come and see it. I shall be delighted to make your acquaintance and to make you feel comfortable in our small dear little house

The situation is lovely – in the midst of a very extensive beautiful garden very healthy on the summit of a hill.

The farm is but small just a sufficient occupation for Willy as long as he is still engaged at the Banat

The children are in very good health and also Willy had no more fever.

If we had not that heavy burden on our hearts we would feel very happy and quite satisfied.

We have most amiable neighbours and a lovely scenery.

Pray excuse my want of facility in expressing myself in English which makes my letters appear very much colder than I feel at heart and believe me my dear aunt

yours affectionately
Tilly

I send very best love to both of you – I have no time to write on acct of the harvest Is Miss May not coming back any more? she will never send me my Roman girl –[5]

Address: No envelope

Unpublished. Text: M.S. Pf. Coll., CL'ANA 0179

---

1 Belec.
2 The name, "OTTILIE" (written in capital letters) is pressed into the paper on upper left-hand side.
3 See note 6, CL'ANA 0203 and CL'ANA 0421, Box 3, bundle g, number 186.
4 Alma von Pichler died earlier that year.
5 Wilhelm added these final sentences. Miss May refers to Miss May Moulson, who returned to England by July 1870. See note 4, CL'ANA 0130.

224 • Wilhelm Gaulis Clairmont to Claire Clairmont

[30 November 1870]

My dear aunt.

I re^{cd} yesterday yours of the 24th; I am extremely pleased to find you have such energetic plans for the future because I accept them as a proof of your good health & spirits. I need not tell you that I should feel much gratified if you did purchase something in Austria as I agree with you that landed property or houses are the safest [illeg.] investment and it would be a great consolation to me to have another bit of solid property added to my share of the Baden property which I might look upon as sure to go to my children – for as I advance in years – I shall be attain the ominous number of 40 on my next birthday – the conviction becomes more settled in my mind that the hope of saving up a small capital for my children by my own exertions is a-a delusive and that all I can do is to hold my own that is to struggle through the exigencies of life in a respectable manner but nothing beyond – therefore I repeat that the acquisition of some landed property by you in Austria especially when made with the avowed intention of leaving it to my children would give me the great satisfaction, but still great caution is necessary for you in the purchase of a property because small properties labour under two great disadvantages. 1st they are comparatively (d.h. neun man den Preis pr. Ioch repartirt.)¹ much dearer than larger farms 2^{ndly} their management is much more difficult and very much more costly than that of small larger farms – the why and wherefore of those two reasons; is very simple but to explain it would lead me too far – If you really make up your mind to purchase some land, we must wait our chance till something like Mirkovetz or Petrijanitz turns up again – I would not advise you to split your property by having both land and a house I would rather propose that we should endeavor to sell our Baden houses, club add the proceeds to your capital and buy a larger farm which under my management and provided we had not paid too dearly for it might yield us a handsome return. the purchase of Beleci would not be a good speculation for 4 distinct reasons:

1st the soil is bad and the fields are not in one block but in detached pieces in among the peasants' fields which exposes one to theft and to much damage from cattle and pigs which constantly keep trespassing –

2^{ndly} the house although it will do our time is not solidly built and will require to be almost newly rebuilt within 10years which would cost at least 5000fl.

3^{rdly} the whole of the neighbouring country although a beautiful mountainous country very healthy has no Zukunft² that is : it has no rising prospects. agricultural land is bad – the population poor. no railway – no traffic a general stagnation of everything – the value of land which you purchase in such a country is just as likely to fall off as to improve – Very different from this is the country about Varasdin – at the junction of 4 lines of rail (Vienna Pest Trieste & Fiume) with a much better soil an intelligent agricultural population and generally more civilized Zustände –³

4^{thly} Belleci is the sole property of a poor widow who of course wants to make the most out of her estate. she would like to sell it – but although she devastated all the forests by selling all the wood out of them she asks for Belleci 18.000fl. while its real value is certainly not more than 10.000f – her husband bought the whole concern some 12 years ago for 5 or 6000fl. it is true he built the farmbuildings all new – adding thereby to the value of the estate, – on the other hand the trees in the woods have all been cut down & sold since then – Mirkovetz was offered to Richard Sermage for 10.000f about 10 years ago. its present proprietor asks 70.000f for it. there was a farm offered to me in the neighbourhood of Rohitsch[4] price 35.000f. but further details about soil size etz. I know not excepting that there is a fine house ~~with~~ 2 story high on the estate and that the proprietor a man of near 80 yrs. of age wants to sell it because he has no heirs and fears the estate will go to rack & ruin after his death. perhaps he would give it a great deal cheaper – his name is Mr Honyez. the estate is called Wissnewetz.[5] the country is mountainous and very healthy Now I shall proceed to answer all your questions –

Land in Croatia Styria or Austria does on an average not yield more than 4 or 5 percent. but when bought at a bargain – that is by waiting one's suitable opportunity. and when well managed it will yield from 15 to 20 percent thus for instance if you invested say 30.000f in land [illeg.] and give me the management of it it would yield under favorable circumstances 4500f. this would be distributed in the following manner:

2%. for the interest of capital for stocking the farm (which I as tenant would furnish)	600f.
6%. rent which would go to you	1800.
7%. my remuneration & profit for farming the farm	2100
total proceeds	4500f

you would get your 6 percent all in ready money but my 7 percent I would not get all in ready money but also in kind for instance poultry vegetables flour free lodging etz. all this would be as it were included in my 7% – supposing we had bought Petrijanics for 40.000f. you would have paid 30.000f and I 10.000 (proceeds of Badner house). I leave Plin purposely out of the calculation because she may someday wish to marry and therefore her capital should not be bound up – I would pay you rent for the farm amounting to 5 or 6 percent on your share of the contribution enjoying the entire percentage on my share of the contribution myself. thus we might although clubing together our capital still preserv a distinct account of it, have each our distinct revenue, have a comfortable home and be much better off than we are at present – the silver agio has for the last year or two been varying from 20 to 25 percent, at present it is 22 percent. that is as much as £10 are worth 12[illeg.] florin. but as there are certain expenses attending the exchange of money it is better not to calculate on more than 20 percent. which would be equal to an increase of English capital imported into Austria of one fifth. I do not believe that foreigners are prohibited to possess land in Croatia but I shall enquire – long leases like in England for 50. 60 or 100 years are quite unknown here. Houses in Agram are like those in Vienna of brick and mortal with tile roofs – our Beleci house is one half of wooden slabs the other half of brick and morter a tile roof over the whole. houseproperty entails as we know from Baden a good deal of looking after and a good deal of expense for repairs and after all the interest is very small. and unless it be a fine large house with [~~illeg.~~] appartments suitable for the higher classes of society there is a great deal of trouble in getting in the rent. I am going next week to Varasdin – perhaps I shall hear there of some suitable estate for sale. for the present I think I have said all my say and answered all your questions – thank you very much dear aunt for the court journal[6] it is very agreable to us both to have it Tilly sends you her best love – I regret much & she too that you were kept in suspense so long – but I do not intend to be ill any more – I put on a new pair of trousers yesterday which I bought at Pest on my way home from the Banat, only think that I got so stout since my recovery from the fever – thanks to Tilly's feeding up – that I could not get the buttons of the aforesaid inexprs to meet – I should rejoice very much, if you really came next summer – if it were but to show you our dear children – Wattie has large pensive melancholy looking eyes of a light blue with a slight tinge of grey – little Alma will have dark eyes. very piercing and lively – Goodbye dearest aunt. I send a kiss both to you & Pauline

yours affectly
WGC

Beleci Novbr. 30th 1870.
Rec^d avis[7] this minute of arrival of your parcel at Poltschach but it is not yet at hand.[8]

Address: La signora Clairmont/ 83 Via Valfonda/Firenze/Italia.
Rear postmark: FIRENZE/[illeg.]

Unpublished. Text: M.S., Pf. Coll., CL'ANA 0298

---

1 Wilhelm wrote that one has to allot nine (times) the price for one Joch of land. Wilhelm appears to spell "Joch" with an "I". A Joch is the equivalent of 1600 Quadratklafter (square Klafter). A Lower Austrian Klafter was equivalent to 189.6484 cm. See CL'ANA 0367.
2 German for "future".
3 German for "conditions".
4 See CL'ANA 0288.
5 Probably Višnja Vas, a small town about 38 kilometers from Rogaška Slatina. Both towns are in Slovenia today.
6 See CL'ANA 0268 and CL'ANA 0320.
7 French for "notice".
8 The sentence was written on the side of the fifth page of the letter. Murray's *A Handbook for Travellers in Southern Germany* lists Pöltschach station as one of the stops on the railway line to Trieste. The station with its stone viaduct is located 9.5 English miles from Pragerhof Junction Station which is about "15 m. S. E". from Rohitsch (London: John Murray, 1873), pp. 445–6.

28 MARCH 1861–24 DECEMBER 1889

225 • Wilhelm Gaulis Clairmont to Pauline Clairmont

[10 January 1871]

Dearest Plin.

Your last of Christmas day we received some 10 days behind time, owing to the interruption of the postal service to Italy in consequence of heavy snowfalls on that line. I have hitherto delayed answering yours that our letters may not cross each other as you say in your last that you will write again in a few days. if you have written another time your letter was lost. I herewith enclose you the answer from Mrs Svágel the proprietor of Beleci to my application concerning its sale – the figure she asks is most ridiculous – no one would dream of giving more than 10 the utmost 12.000f – having already expressed my disapproval of A. Cl.[1] project of the purchase of Beleci I have nothing more to say on the subject excepting that I feel certain that you both will agree with me when you come next summer and see everything with your own eyes.

With respect to Nicolaihof the estate near Marburg I enclose you a letter received from Dr Dominkusch who purchased it at the last auction for 24.100f and wants to sell it again. he asks 28.500. but will of course give it much cheaper. the house is substantial, the buildings all new, the scenery is fine, the situation between 3 railwaystations very favorable the country civilised – it is always a very saleable property which you can get rid of without loss at any time whereas Beleci you could never sell. With £2000 (which inclusive of Agio would make about 24.000f.) ready money I would advise A.cl. to buy the Nicolaihof and if A.Cl. really and seriously thinks of such an investment I would go there once more and spend a few days in the thorough inspection of the property previous to any other decisive steps. but this would cause me expense which it would be unreasonable to incur unless I had the positive assurance from A.Cl. that she will buy if my final examination proves satisfactory in which case I would have to pay down immediately 5000f as Angabe.[2] or else someone else might slip in and buy snatch it away before our noses. What Dr Dominkush says about the price at which Nicol. h. was sold at on previous occasions I know to be true it is a proof that the property would be cheap at 25.000f. A.Cl. says she will not carry all her eggs to one market – she will buy an estate for 20.000f and a house for the other 20.000f. this is very good principle for <u>selling</u>. but not for buying. In buying one always fares cheaper by purchasing more on a large scale – thus if you buy 1000 acres in one plot you will buy them for less money and have consequently a better investment than if you bought 10 different plots of 100 acres each. If a.Cl. insists on buying a house for you let her buy my Baden house – I would sell it for [illeg.] 18.000f. and it would be of such importance not to split the property. I would then join this 18.000f with 2000f of my own to A.Cl. 20.000f (which she has destined for the purchase of an estate) and we might then purchase an estate for 40.000 instead of 20.000f. which would enable me to live more comfortably myself and pay a much better rent to Aunt. besides the properties would not be split. If A.cl. buys Beleci with the intention of leaving it to me or Wattie (in case I were to die before her) and a house in Agram with the intention of leaving it to you as she wrote to me – I would have an interest in Baden and Beleci you in Baden and Agram. Aunt in Agram and Beleci – there would be such a splitting of interests that no one knew which way to look for his revenue. if aunt bought Beleci or any similar small property and I succeeded in selling my Baden house to a stranger and bought another small farm for the proceeds, what would be the consequences – I should have two small farms to look after neither of which paid for the trouble it gave; you would have two small houses one at Agram one at Baden. and the latter a joint property with a stranger. Is it not evident that my proposal is much more practical and leads to better results. and aunt would still gain her object of dividing her property between the purchase of a house and that of a farm. please read this letter to Aunt and let us hear what she thinks on the subject. We spent the holydays with the Sermages. we also drank your and A.Cl's health and to your safe journey to Beleci next summer. à propos of this I dont know how we shall do for a fireplace in A.Cl.'s room for you know that such a thing does not exist here; but I fancy A.Cl. will not want it in the ~~winter~~ summer. Wattie is the dearest little chick – the Sermages both are quite in love with him. I must tell you more of him in my next. Give my and Tilly's best love to aunt and believe me dearest Paulin

       yours most affectly.
       WGC.

Zlatar pr. Pöltschach[3]
January 10th 1871.

please return me both the enclosed letters.

P.S. I do not enclose M^{rs} Sv. letter as it would make this letter too heavy if A.Cl. wishes it I shall send it next time
she asks 18.000f.

Address: No envelope.

Unpublished. Text: M.S., Pf. Coll., CL'ANA 0299

---

1 Aunt Claire.
2 German (used in Austria) for "deposit".
3 See CL'ANA 0298. Zlatar is in Croatia. The distance from Zlatar to Belec is 8 kilometers.

226 • Wilhelm Gaulis Clairmont to Pauline Clairmont

[25 January 1871]

Dearest Pauline.

At the risk of our letters crossing again I write, before receiving aunt's answer to my last addressed to her concerning the purchase of Nicolaihof. first of all I must say I was not a little astonished to find you ask what you are to do with the power of attorney inclosed in my money letter to you – for I gave you along with it all the necessary instructions – You must please go to the Austrian Embassy – (mind not the English) and there sign the power of attorney in presence of the person appointed by the Embassy who will add his signature and the seal of the Embassy – the Power of attorney thus signed and attested /: legalisirt:/[1] you must return to me along with the printed receipt /:on yellow paper:/ which you hold from the Bank as a receipt for the deposit of your debentures (Prioritäten).[2] in a registered letter. The purpose of this proceeding is to enable Postl[3] to pay for you the ~~prolongation~~ fee for the ensuing year which is due some time in February I wanted to pay it for you in December last when I was at Vienna – as the clerk would not receive the money I demanded to be shown to the chief of the department. – I explained to him that I was your brother that you were in Italy – and above all things – that I did not want to claim either capital or interest on your behalf – but that I simply wanted to pay the fee for you which would become due in the course of february. I wound up my oration with the rather ironical remark that my limited knowledge of bankingbusiness did not enable me to perceive how the Bank would run any risk by <u>receiving</u> money albeit from a stranger – but that if the circumstance of my being a stranger were the difficulty I might inform the chief of the Department that I was well known to no less a person than their own Secretary General Mr Luccam[4] whose office was next door. the said chief waited patiently till I had done then blandly informed me that his instructions were positive that he could accept the renewance of deposit fees from no one but the proprietor in person or any one furnished with a power of attorney from the proprietor.
I repeat all this tedious story to you to show you that I left nothing undone to save you the trouble and expense of the power of attorney but you see it is positively impossible –

I am expecting aunt Claire's decision with reference to Nicolaihof with great Spannung.[5] if she does buy it she will make a capital bargain (provided of course Dominkus gives it up.) the property is of so prepossessing a character that I have not the slightest hesitation in saying that when farmed by me for a few years it will fetch 40.000f provided we wanted to sell it again – I saw a gentleman from Marburg the other day, from whom I learnt quite accidentally that Mr Walker the former proprietor of Nicol. had been offered 42.000f but then he would not sell it – now he failed and was imprisoned and of course the property went to the dogs. you must call Aunts attention to this that I do not propose to her any but the most favorable purchases. but with such one must be quick and pop in when a chance offers. or else another buyer seizes the opportunity and pops in before us – so it was with Mirkovetz and so with Petrijanitz, which latter is worth 60 or 70.000fl. if aunt thinks she can wait till May she is grosely mistaken. if we do not buy Nicolaihof at once if[6] will go into the hands of speculators who will wait for the favorable season when everything looks to more advantage and rich people from town will buy it more readily. at any rate it would under the present prospects be more prudent to have part of one's capital in landed property than all in shares – if the present congress in London do not succeed in adjusting matters everything will go down and aunt will not be able to realize excepting at a heavy loss – the dwelling house and farm buildings alone are worth 20.000f in Nicolaihof. also its situation is wonderfully advantageous for us. as the migration from here to there would cost us next to nothing and as it is near enough to enable me to continue the supervision of Beleci as long as I have it still[7] – also the Südbahn is so convenient as facilitating communication with Baden and with the South provided A.Cl. found it necessary to go southward during the winter months – then the protestant church & school at Marburg.[8] and the facility of finding a ready market there for all our produce.

there is one more circumstance which makes the purchase of Nicolaihof just now particularly desirable for me – I met accidentally the physician who treated me during my last illness on my return from the Banat. he insisted on examining my spleen although I assured him I was perfectly well – he found it double the size it ought to be, he said that my return to a fever country even though it were for a temporary sojourn might prove a dangerous experiment – In consequence of this and yielding to Tillis ardent wishes I made overtures to Rudi (from whom I concealed my true motive viz health) to buy my share in the concern. he immediately entered on my proposals. negotiations are still pending, but as the difference between us is only 750f. I make no doubt that we shall come to terms. thus I would have the illeg. not only the 5000f ready money to stock Nicolaihof but also have my unencumbered time to give my full attention to the concerns of Nicolaihof. on the other hand I cannot wait ins Blaue hinein[9] – I must look out for another farm if aunt does not buy the Nicolaihof as Belici yields no revenue and I cannot live without income – I am not a man to be done by lawyers – I make them show me their books and inspect the registers in the tax offices – when I see a really first rate chance I grab at it. but I repeat that it is necessary for Aunt to follow in my wake with equal speed or else other people will be as smart as we are and smarter and snap the prize from us. – my rent of 1000f. annually would begin from the day the bargain is concluded and I take possession of the estate – if Beleci is worth 14.000f to Aunt Nicolaihof is worth 50 or 60.000f. but if we go on corresponding much longer this chance too of a capital investment and a union of all our family under one roof will be lost – love to Aunt. yours affecty

WGC

Zlatar January 25th 1871.

One[10] great reason why we must decide about Nicolaihof at once is the necessity of ploughing and sowing the fields in the early Spring. In May it is all over Zoepf sold his estate near Linz[11] which he bought for 25.000f 4 years ago to a prinz Chatoriski[12] for 35.000 and the harvest extra amounting in all to 40,000f for the like result we might look at Nicholaihof

Address: No envelope.

Unpublished. Text: M.S., Pf. Coll., CL'ANA 0300

---

1 Archaic spelling for the German word "legalisieren" which means "legalize".
2 There are two possible meanings here. Either Wilhelm referred to the paper that provided Pauline with security for special rights (i.e. in case of default) or he asked Pauline to register the letter as priority mail.
3 Unidentified. It is possible he worked in the Ministry of Finance, which would explain the connection with the Austrian Central Bank (Claudia Köpf, Österreichische Nationalbank, personal communication: 9 June 2015).
4 Banker Wilhelm von Lucam (1820–1900) worked for the Austrian National Bank (Österreichische Nationalbank). The bank was founded in 1818 with the "exclusive right to issue banknotes" ("History of the Oesterreichische Nationalbank". Web. 7 June 2015. http://www.oenb.at/en/). In 1857, von Lucam became Secretary General of the bank (Kernbauer, Hans. "Lucam, Wilhelm Ritter von" in *New German Biography* (1987) 15, p. 269 f [Online version]. Web. 7 June 2015. http://www.deutsche-biographie.de/ppn13299190X.html). In *A History of Banking in All the Leading Nations*, Max Wirth notes that von Lucam was "removed" from office in 1878 because of "his firm adherence to the correct and solid principles which he had ever applied in the management of discounts and interest. For this he was especially unpopular in Hungary . . . When the new Bank Act of 1878 went into effect, the strenuous opposion to Von Lucam in Hungary succeeded in removing this inflexible man from office" (New York: *The Journal of Commerce and Commercial Bulletin*, 1896), vol. iv, pp. 87–8. See CL'ANA 0226 and note 2, CL'ANA 0311.
5 German for "tension," "suspense" or "excitement".
6 Probably "it".
7 Maribor to Belec is 75 kilometers.
8 Christ's Church, constructed in 1869.
9 German for "haphazardly" or "randomly".
10 Wilhelm cross-wrote the following paragraph in red ink on the first page.
11 Located on the Danube River, Linz is a city in northern Austria about 30 kilometers south of the Czech Republic.
12 Probably from the House of Czartoryski.

227 • Wilhelm Gaulis Clairmont to Claire Clairmont and Pauline Clairmont [1]

[9 February 1871]

Dearest aunt.

Many thanks for your letter. I much regret both in your and in my own interest that you could not buy the Nicolaihof as you would have had a safe investment, an agreeable and genteel residence 5 percent for your capital and a clean profit of 10.000 to 15.000f besides in the course of a few years – It is not likely that such a favorable chance will turn up in a hurry again, but if it should I shall let you know. I hope however that this failure of our project of a purchase will not prevent you from carrying out your original design of visiting us in the course of next summer. Belici is a very cheerful place with a beautiful view, as a summer residence I think you would like it very well. and the journey taken in easy stages would be a pleasant change. it would give me the greatest pleasure to have you know Tilly and see the children especially Watty is such a dear little chick – and it would give such a fresh impulse to our English – I am afraid Wattie will grow up without learning it. Goodbye dearest aunt – pray take care of your health so that you may be strong and able for the journey

yours affectly
WGC

February 9th 1871.

Dearest Plin duly rec'd yours with documents – forwarded the same to D'r Postl. and hope this matter will be all right. I regret you had so much expense and inconvenience but it could not be helped – If you write to the Pichlers mention nothing about the plans we had for Nicolaihof – My negotiations with Rudi respecting his purchase of my Tuzokrate share have not yet led to an issue, we are sure to come to terms the only difficulty likely to be is whether he can command the requisite funds for this purchase

Goodbye my dear old woman

yours affectly
WGC

february 9th 1871.

Black is well and hearty as always in winter – but just now in Tilly's bad books because he bit her finest turkey to death. Wattie is growing more and more into my most especial pet. his heart is so soft and tender that it gives me apprehension for the future. he has the greatest passion for horses to stand on the fensterbrettel[2] and see a cart or carriage pass by is to him the greatest treat. the hour in the evening from 5 to 6 I generally pass in the nursery and play with him – his favorite game is "Häuserl bauen"[3] – I build little make believe houses of toy bricks. each house is then appropriated to a member of our household and I then must tell him a tale how the lucky proprietor of the house goes in there and sleeps and how comfortable it is etz. etz. to all of which he listens with the greatest interest. If he is naughty in the day time a threat that I wont come Häuserl bauen makes him good and obedient at once.

Address: La signora Clairmont/ 83 Via Valfonda/ Italia. Firenze
Rear postmark: MIHOVLJAN/$^{11}/_2$;[4] UDINE-VERONA/[illeg.]/ 71

Unpublished. Text: M.S., Pf. Coll., CL'ANA 0302

---

1 Wilhelm's letters to Pauline and to Claire were written on the same bifold sheet of paper and both have the same CL'ANA number (0302).
2 German (Austria) for "window ledge".
3 German for "building houses".
4 Mihovljan is located in Croatia.

228 • Wilhelm Gaulis Clairmont to Claire Clairmont

[23 February 1871]

My dear Aunt.

Notwithstanding your refusal to have anything further to say concerning Nicholaihof I could not disengage my attention from it as I think it such a pity that such a prize should again slip away from us into the hands of strangers. As you say that you would be satisfied with everything but the price which exceeds by 5000f the limit which you have set to yourself I propose to overcome this difficulty by adding 5000f out of my own money to your 20.000f thus completing the requisite sum of 25.000f.

the terms of payment are very easy – 4000f. would have to be paid at once – on concluding the bargain – this 4000 I would pay of my own money. in 4 or 5 months another 10.000f would become due and the for rest they would give us one or two years time – thus your first payment would become due on the 1st of August 10.000f – giving you plenty of time to come here and pay the money yourself if you wont trust bankers or the post-offices – Now dont throw this chance away of acquiring a beautiful little property – if you make up your mind to buy and can realize at the stated terms viz. 10.000f on the 1st of August 1871. and 10.000 more on the 1 August 1872

So please write to me at once but you will have to furnish me with a power of attorney written in German. vise'ed[1] by the Austrian Embassy empowering me simply to purchase for you the estate Nicolaihof situated near Marburg in Styria. Pauline can write this quite well. If you could only see the place I feel assured you would not let it slip from you – you would be proud of such a fine and manorial country seat. Goodbye dearest aunt believe me yours truly

WGC

february 23rd. 1871.

Address: No envelope.

Unpublished. Text: M.S., Pf. Coll., CL'ANA 0301

---

1 Wilhelm creates a word from the French for "viser," which means "to notarize".

229 • Wilhelm Gaulis Clairmont to Pauline Clairmont

[18 March 1871]

Dearest Plin.

I duly rec^d. your letter of the 28 Febry with postscript from Aunt herself and of the 6th March. Many thanks both to Aunt and you for the explicit manner in which you explain the obstacles in the way of Aunts purchasing Nicolaihof – it is particularly pleasant to me to be informed not only of the dry fact – Aunt will buy or will not buy – but also of the motives that guide her steps – the difficulties she has to contend with, the particular aim she has in view etz. etz. as a knowledge of all these collateral circumstances enables me to meet her views for the future. It would be silly indeed were I "vexed" as [illeg.] Aunt supposes at her not purchasing when she explain in full why she cannot purchase – on the contrary I repeat that I am very glad to have her decided answer respecting Nicolaihof which prevents my entering any engagements with the proprietor.

Aunts plan of hiring the Nicolaihof is not feasible as the proprietor only bought it to get at his money, which he had lent to Mr Walker[1] – he wants to sell Nicolaihof again as speedily as possible and will not encumber it with a lease to a tenant as this would diminish the chances of selling it – Respecting aunts two other questions whether there is any mortgage on it and whether I had it valued this is my answer – there is no mortgage on it. it is now passing through the insolvent court its former owner having declared himself bankrupt. an estate passing through the insolvent court is as a matter of course in all due form cleared of all its encumbrances – the legal form gone through is this: the estate is sold by public auction – the proceeds of this auction go to satisfy the claims of the mortgagees & creditors – the estate it self is handed over pure and clean (in a legal sense of the word) divested of all encumbrances like the soul of a sinner emerging from purgatory to Heaven to the hands of the new owner (this would have been in the case of Nicolaihof Aunt Claire) – therefore if there is no better title to land than that from an insolvent court – because it positively and unquestionable annihilates all provision claims on the land be they real or sham legal or illegal – Nicolaihof was sold by the insolvent court on the 12th Decemb. 1870. as I informed you – it is now going through the aforesaid cleansing operation there can be therefore no question as to the validity of its title and freeness from mortgage –

N° 2 question concerning valuation: Nichof. was valued by the insolvent court officially at 39.900f. it was sold twice within the last 10years at 36.000 and at 40.000f. Mr Walker was offered 42.000f for it. I spoke with a man of business at Marburg concerning its value. previous to the auction – he told me there was now in the winter not much demand for such estates that it would be very likely sold much under its value and that 25.000f would be a very safe price to give for it – I should of course have valued the estate myself more in detail previous to concluding the bargain – the answer to these two questions I look upon as einen überwundenen Standpunct[2] I merely give this to clear myself from any interpretation of having acted carelessly in this matter.

I have succeeded in bringing my negotiations with Rudi Hauer concerning my his purchase of my share in the Tuzokrét farm to a satisfactory conclusion – he pays me 3500f now and 3500f in a year and I am quit of the beastly fever country. as I am now without a revenue and as expenses nevertheless go on – I must look for a new farm – I am trying to find something in the neighbourhood of Varasdin which offers this advantage that there are a number of nice little properties about so that if A.Cl. wishes to buy we may still hope to find something. I should have preferred Nichof. as it is in Styria a German country – which when Austria comes to be divided would very likely go to Prussia, whereas Croatia will go to Hungary or worse than that to Russia.

If Aunt does purchase in Austria I am quite agreable to acceed to her proposition to pay her 5 percent for the money invested in halfyearly instalments from the day the money is paid. only ithe interest should not be paid in advance from other stock or shares she would also not get the interest in advance either –

Tilly is just now absent in Vienna whither she went to get her teeth stuffed.[3] and make sundry purchases for the summer. I hope dear aunt has got rid of her Rheumatism and lumbago – Do not let our present unsettledness (I mean my looking for a new farm) interfere with your coming – the chances are I shall not find anything in so great a hurry but if so we shall have room for you wherever we are – I had a letter from Dr Postl, he paid the prolongation fee for your Ostbahn prioritäten[4] – his total expense expence[5] amounted to 6f50 which sum as well as the interest due for your house on April 7th (120f) I shall deduct at our next settlement. Mrs Werner[6] has not yet sent me any money since December. please write in your next whether you want the tin sent you or whether I shall keep it till you come.

Please tell A.cl. that she owes me still 15f. that is inclus agio in a round sum 30 francs for frght of her boxes from Tuzok to Ditta[7] from Ditta to Vienna and thence to Baden – as I owe you 40 frcs. which you gave to poor Prince please keep these 30 frcs and I shall pay you for the remaining 10 frcs. 5f. at our next settlement. the weather has changed since a few days – we had the most beautiful spring days – now there is sleet and snow and a northerly blast.

Give my love to dearse aunt and believe me my dear Plin

yours most affectly.
WGC

March 18th 1871.
Zlatar
pr. Pöltschach.

I have to inform you of the death of two people of our acquaintance first Mr Plunket[8] the late Sollicitor General in Australia I saw his death in an Australian paper which Richard Sermage's brother gave me who is just returned from a long voyage round the world – he is naval officer in the Austrian service – then the death of Rudolf Schuretton[9] who was killed in the first battle fought under the walls of Paris – another brother (not Richard who was also in the Banat) was also killed in the same war –

Address: Miss P. Clairmont/ 83. Via Valfonda/ Firenze/ Italia.
Rear postmark: UDINE-VERONA/ 22/MAR/71

Unpublished. Text: M.S., Pf. Coll., CL'ANA 0303

---

1 See CL'ANA 0300.
2 German for "an attitude/point of view of the past".
3 By the mid-nineteenth century, dentists began to fill cavities using amalgam fillings which were made from mercury and metals such as "silver, tin, and copper". French dentists pioneered the practice (John Waller. *Health and Wellness in 19th-Century America* [California: Greenwood, 2014], p. 168.
4 Probably shares Pauline owned in the Ostbahn, constructed in the 1850s (Royal Prussian Eastern Railway). "Prioritäten" refers to "priority" shares or bonds ("priorities").
5 The word is repeated twice.
6 Unidentified.
7 Misspelling for Deta, a town about 17 kilometers south of Ciacova. There are 567 kilometers between Deta and Vienna.
8 John Hubert Plunkett (1802–1869). Born in Ireland, Plunkett was educated at Trinity College, Dublin, and was admitted to both the Irish and English bars. He was named solicitor-general of New South Wales in 1833 and attorney-general in 1836. He died in Melbourne (Suttor, T.L. "Plunkett, John Hubert (1802–1869)", *Australian Dictionary of Biography*. National Centre of Biography, Australian National University. 1967. Web. 11 May 2015. http://adb.anu.edu.au/biography/plunkett-john-hubert-2556/text3483).
9 Unidentified.

230 • Wilhelm Gaulis Clairmont to Pauline Clairmont

[5 August 1871]

Dearest Plin.

Yesterday we re~cd~ yours of the 31st July announcing Aunts' intentions about Nicolaihof and which must have crossed ~~with~~ my last letter to you – Tilly and I are both much pleased at the prospect of going there but we will not rejoice too soon – My first impulse was to telegraph to ~~Nicol~~ Marburg (Dr Dominkus) at once to enquire whether he had it still [illeg.] and was still inclined to sell it. but on second thoughts I have decided on going there without any previous intimation to him – in order to be able to reconoiter ~~the~~ everything about the property. whether he has any people desirous of purchasing, how this year's harvest was, whether the management of the farm has given him a good deal of bother and trouble and in short whether circumstances have rendered him anxious to get rid of it or not – Much cheaper than the sum proposed at first – he will not give it because he would else have to suffer a loss which he is not likely to be willing to – at any rate I shall shape my offer according as circumstances will allow and aunt may depend that I shall act with the utmost circumspection – but anyhow my offer to Dominkus will not be binding on her until she has indicated her agreement to it by paying the first instalment ~~iof~~ the purchase money agreed on – that is the "Angeld"¹ for a purchase in Austria is no purchase until the Angeld has been actually paid down – If Aunt has the 10.000fl. lying ready in the Bank without interest on them. and if she is decided to buy Nicol.hof and finally if (there are three "if"s) she is ready to [illeg.] trust me with the 10.000f it would be much safer that is more to Aunts advantage to send the 10.000f at once to me – /:that is after we had ascertained that Nicolhof is still to be had :/ for 1st I would pay aunt her interest on the 10.000f from the day it was paid into Dominkus' hands. She might thereby save 2 months interest on the money – 2^ndly^ with 10.000f ready cash in hand I shall knock much more favorable conditions out of Domink because he will see that this time we are in earnest; the sight of ready money will tempt him at once to the utmost concessions, whereas if a longwinded correspondence is in view he will think ~~there~~ there is again to be no result and wont go in with a good will for even though I explain him the details about Aunts selling out her papers he wont believe it. besides there is a great risk of losing the money when bringing it personally whereas the postoffices "sta bun"² for it – I shall leave for Nichof on the 11th inst and write to you from Marburg the result of my mission. If Aunt buys the Nichof than I shall not want the loan of your money because the farm is small and I think my capital will be quite sufficient for stocking it.

I must of course agree to farm the farm myself for it would have no sense [illeg.] to buy the farm and then leave A. Cl. to fight the battle out with a strange tenant. who would also deteriorate the estate very much. I can take charge of Nic.hof in October only it would be much more convenient to me to do so in September, because the 1st half of October is the vintage and the second half is too unsettled

to move because ~~the~~ it is a two days journey for a cart loaded with furniture and traps and the risk of being cought by rain the latter end of October would be serious – I am willing to pay aunt 5 percent by way of rent she paying the taxes – but I would also require a promise that the arrangement shall be one of a certain duration as the cost of moving there stocking the farm etz. etz. would not sich auszahlen[3] for a short term of tenure – I have formed a scheme for the adjustment of these points to mutual satisfaction but I must first consult a friend versed in law matters besides it will be time to submit these details to Aunts consideration when the main point the purchase is agreed on. You may expect a letter from me in about a weeks time
With best love to aunt believe me dear Plin
                            yours affectly
                                WGC

Zlater
August 5th 1871.
Just spoke a gentleman from Marburg Nichof is not yet sold – he is anxious to sell provided he have no loss – [4]

Address: No envelope.

Unpublished. Text: M.S., Pf. Coll., CL'ANA 0304

---

1 Archaic term for "deposit".
2 Italian for "is good". Wilhelm misspelled "sta buon".
3 German for "be worthwhile".
4 Wilhelm wrote this final sentence on the side of the page.

231 • Wilhelm Gaulis Clairmont to Claire Clairmont

[23 August 1871]

My dear aunt. I have no doubt you will be vexed at my having left you so long without news, however Dr Dominkus did not answer my letter – so there I was waiting for his answer day for day and it never came – so at last I set out for Marburg a second time and here I am now coming to write you the result of a days bargaining – He will give the estate for 25.000 and the stock and crops for 6.500 I consider it cheap at that price, I am sure that if you like, you can by waiting your chance sell it for 40.000 therefore I counsel you to buy it at once send me say only 4000f by post to pay the Angeld[1] and you are the proprietor – you will find it a better investment than the operabox or railway shares – I still stick to my share of the agreement to add 5000f to your 20.000f to complete the purchase money and to buy the stock out of my own funds and to pay you 5 percent on your 20.000f by way of rent you paying the taxes. the necessary repairs and improvements I will also pay for myself contrary to custom – provided you will guarantee me eventual ownership of the estate or reimbursement of my expenses on that score in case you should otherwise dispose of the property.

Under any circumstances do please dear aunt write to me at once whether or no you intend to embark in this enterprise because I have dropped all my other negotiations and if not this I must have something else by autumn. If you write now at once that you will purchase we might have completed our moving to Nichof by the time you come and you might come to Nichof direct – instead of first – to Belici than to Nicolaihof which would involve a most fatiguing land journey.

Please dear aunt get Plin to write the answer to this in duplicate direct one to Zlater as usual one to Clairmont poste restante Marburg so that I shall get one wherever I am – but please do answer soon – I close now for it is already one oclock at night and I start tomorrow at daybreak. Give kiss to Plin and Believe me dear aunt

yours affect

WGC

Marburg
Aug. 23rd 1871.

Address: La signora Clairmont/ Strada Casentino/ Toscana Italia.
Front stamps: Three 5 kr. stamps, each with a postmark: MARBURG/^{23}/$_8$/71

Unpublished. Text: M.S., Pf. Coll., CL'ANA 0306

---

1 Archaic term for "deposit".

232 • Wilhelm Gaulis Clairmont to Claire Clairmont

Nicolaihof Septb. 14th 1871.

My dear aunt. I recd yesterday yours of the 5th inst. and am much gratified to find that you approve of all. all details we shall settle on your arrival here. We both rejoice much at the idea of having you here so soon – We have reserved for your use the best room in the house only as to furniture I am not quite sure whether we shall be able to meet all your wants – as regards all your other comforts it would have been a great ~~comfort~~ assistance for Tilly to have had Plin first to put her in the way of everything but if it cant be we must manage without – I should be very happy if Plin married well only I have a great distrust against the choice she is likely to make (I mean not in this special instance of which I know nothing, but in general). however I want to stick to business –

As a matter of course I shall be most happy to come to Trieste and accompany you from there to Marburg if you require it – You must in this case telegraph to me to Nicolaihof Marburg. stating the inn where you are stopping and the day on which you want to leave for Marburg. from Trieste to Marburg. is just a days railway travelling. Now about money. – If you take the whole of the 20.000f from the bank at once you need not bother sending me a blank cheque for the £400 extra let the money be transferred all in a lump instead of in two lots –

Now about your realizing the money [~~illeg.~~] at Trieste – If you know the Consul there and he gives security for you they will no doubt give you the whole amount at once; it is however an unusual favour for the consul to grant and for you to ask of him – I would therefore advise for you to place your draft on London in the hands of a banker at Triest whom the consul may advise you and wait at Trieste for the money till the telegrafic news from London is returned of ~~the~~ sufficient funds being in the bank to meet the amount of your draft. this I fancy will not take more than 48 hours time and that much you must allow yourself any how at Trieste for rest after the long journey from Florence – If you wish for my assistance to bring the money here I repeat I am at your service. Now dear aunt I must conclude for the windows are all open, there is a draught enough to sweep the hair from my head and masons and carpenters making so much dust and row all about me that I cannot collect my ideas any more than for the most pressing questions – We hurry to have everything snug by the time you arrive – I do not think dear aunt that you will have reason to regret this purchase. you will have a nice snug home with us especially if you can make up your mind that is if your health will allow you to stop here also the wintermonths.

Believe me dear aunt

yours affectly
W.G. Clairmont.

Nicolaihof
Marburg.[1]

form of telegram to be used in case you want me at Trieste.
Clairmont. Nicolaihof Marburg.
Erwarte dich schwarzen Adler (or any name of hotel) Triest
zur farth nach Marburg 28 September (giving the date) (früh (or evening)[2]

(Signature: <u>one name</u>).

the date you give in the telegram must be the one on which you want to leave for Marburg I shall time my journey according to it – the train leaving Triest at 7 a m. arriving in Marburg at 7 p.m. there is also an express train leaving Trieste at 7 a.m. reaching Marburg at 2.37. p m. but it costs just <u>double</u> the fare of the slow train –

Address: La signora Clairmont/ Strada Casentino/ Toscana Italia.
Rear postmark: VENEZIA/ 15/ SET[3]/71/6 S; [illeg.];[illeg.]

Unpublished. Text: M.S., Pf. Coll., CL'ANA 0307

---

1 Wilhelm wrote the following on a separate, two-sided insert. The second side begins with the words "the date".
2 As this was a telegram, Wilhelm's word choice was not grammatically correct. The insert reads as follows:"Expect you Black Eagle (or any name of hotel) Triest for the journey to Marburg 28 September (giving the date) (morning (or evening) (Signature: <u>one name</u>)".
3 Abbreviation for "settembre," Italian for "September".

233 • Pauline Clairmont to Wilhelm Gaulis Clairmont

Nov. 4. Florence [c. 1871]

Dearest best William

How glad I was to see your dear hand writing again and very sorry all the same time that poor Tilly is suffering from gout – how ever is that possible so young – it must be rheumatism and a summer at Baden would do her good. And poor little Walter dear little darling I hope is quite well now – here dyptheria has also been very bad. I cannot at all account for A. Claire's behavior to me, not writing at all – I am very much hurt indeed not knowing at all, how I have offended her – I offered to come and stay with her if she was intent upon leaving you, and she has not even answered.[1] About buying an estate I leave it quite to you – if you think it advisable & if it is any use to you & any advantage do so by all means. Sooner or later I must have sold the shares as those sort of investments do not hold good many years, therefore if you like to do so I give you carte blanche, as Dr. Postle has got a power of attorney it will be easily managed.

I was going to write to you and ask your advice about the disposal of my fortune – which I will state in a few words & you will think over and tell me what you think. It is about this marriage. Lady Sussex[2] is the person who has made it and who advocates it. – Aunt said – Please yourself I would have any responsibility – But now all my other friends who know the details advise me not to marry that man – so that I am rather frightened of going against everybody. Even the lawyer said repeatedly male[3] – male – those people have debts – In short every single person I have consulted says without hesitation "No" –

But the thing is this – suppose I do marry him & suppose I do have a child – the law of the country assigns to the husband in case of my death the interest of my whole fortune & a third of the capital. Now this I could never agree to – I do not even know if a will would suffice to leave my fortune to those I wish to leave it to. I am thinking therefore of getting a deed of donation/ Schenkungsurkunde[4] drawn up in your favour which would have to be dated and signed before my marriage making you Georgina's guardian and leaving me the interest as long as I live. 5000 fl have been insured Georgina's name on my house, and there are 4000 debts on it, leaving about 15,000fl (including the shares) to dispose of. If you can think of any other way of securing my property against the attack of Italian husbands please tell me.

With best love to Tilly & the chicks believe me yours ever

Plin

Address: No envelope

Unpublished. Text: M.S., Pf. Coll., CL'ANA 0225

---

1 Claire arrived at Nikolaihof in September 1871 but left for Trieste to spend the winter. By March 1872, she had returned to Florence. This letter probably dates from 1871 when Claire was

still with Wilhelm and his family. Stocking writes that Walter Clairmont remembered meeting his great-aunt Claire ("Miss Tina and Miss Plin," p. 373).
2 Lady Mary Margaret Sussex Lennox. See CL'ANA 0327 and CL'ANA 0378.
3 German for "many times".
4 German for "deed of gift".

234 • Wilhelm Gaulis Clairmont to Claire Clairmont

[8 November 1871]

My dear aunt.

We were both of us much relieved at the receipt of your post card, it is such a comfort to know that you got through this troublesome journey all right. I only hope that Mrs Tucker[1] will succeed in making you comfortable and that the house and garden as well as the climate at Trieste and other circumstances attaching to the locality will suit you – Do please assure us on this point in your next. I redirected a Morning Post to you yesterday it must have been mislaid for Pauline acknowledged the receipt of the letter to me in which I communicate ~~her~~ your new address to her. Dr Dominkuch showed me a letter written to him by your lawyer.

I wish dear aunt you would consent to deposit the money with the court of insolvency – so as to put a stop to this uncertainty which is ruinous not only to your peace of mind but also to my interest because I cannot go on repairing improving and sowing as I must and ought when under the pressure of such uncertainty – the money once deposited the whole affair must be settled in 2 or 3 weeks but if it lasted a year it would be of no consequence as the registry of your name on the government book is a mere form – your paying the money into court establishes your title to the [illeg.] <u>estate free from all debt</u> and prevents any other person from encumbering the estate with debt during the interval until the forms of court are gone through with and you are registered as proprietress. Please put this question to Mr Raities (I believe the name of your lawyer). I am sure he will pronounce this [illeg.] the simplest means to get out of this difficulty. You are unsettled in your mind and loose one percent on your money besides it is therefore clearly your interest to bring this matter to a conclusion – and the [illeg.] proceeding I propose to you is both speedy and safe. Mr Tucker[2] arrived safely, he is a very nice gentlemanly lad and very willing and pains [illeg.] taking only I fear he will be disappointed in as much as I gathered from some of his chance expressions that he looks upon his sojourn here more as a visit to a friend in the country than as a course of learning and drudgery.

I had a letter from Plin – she seems hurt at your not writing to her.[3] Goodbye dearest aunt

Believe me yours most affectionately
WGC

Nicolaihof
Novemb 8th 1871:

Address: No envelope.

Unpublished. Text: M.S., Pf. Coll., CL'ANA 0305

---

1 See CL'ANA 0292 and CL'ANA 0421, Box 3, bundle g, number 186.
2 Willie Tucker, the son of Reverend and Mrs. Tucker. See CL'ANA 0421, Box 3. bundle g, number 185.
3 See CL'ANA 0225.

235 • Wilhelm Gaulis Clairmont to Claire Clairmont

[19 June 1872]

My dear aunt.

I got your that is Plin's letter of the 12th as she says that you cannot go to the country unless you get my rent and that your health absolutely requires it I sold my working bullocks and send you the proceeds ~~illeg~~.f – the details I give in a separate account – I now enclose.[1] for the remaining 100f I can perhaps make arrangements with Pauline. – she writes "I <u>should understand I must go on paying the rent till you have found another tenant</u>". of course I am quite aware that my lease puts me under this obligation but when I shall have sold all my cattle or even part of them I cant work the farm and then I <u>cant</u> pay – it is for me a most unhappy speculation which has ruined me quite – I do not think I shall be able to go to Venice to meet you there because even ~~all~~ a personal interview is not likely to help us out of our difficulty as this is not a question of what can be done by mutual accommodation – you have a right to – and want your rent – the difficulties I have in meeting my engagements lie elsewhere and cant be obviated by any understanding we might come to – In this misery it is a consolation to me that T. & the children are well and that you have quite recovered from your frightful accident and are in a position again to walk albeit with crutches.[2] – we must be all thankful to God that you have so bravely got over this severe trial

Believe me dear aunt

yours affe
WG. Clairmont

June 19th 1872

account.

Rent due on July 1st 1873.		312f50
Balance from last quarter coppers not remitted.		82
total.		313f32
Deduct:		
freight for box		5f 22.
stamp on declaration to savings bank. –		.50
Correspondence with savings bank. _____		95 6.67
		306.65

Enclosed _____		206f.
Transfer for next quarter because copper unremitable _____		.65
Rest due (perhaps by Plin)		100f
		306f65 306f65

Tilli sends her best love

Address: No envelope.

28 MARCH 1861–24 DECEMBER 1889

Unpublished. Text: M.S., Pf. Coll., CL'ANA 0308

---

1 Wilhelm left a significantly sized space between these two sentences.
2 In her letter to Charlotte Bennet French of 14 June 1873, Claire commented that her foot was healing and that she was able to walk with crutches (*CC* II: 623).

236 • Wilhelm Gaulis Clairmont to Claire Clairmont

[22 July 1872]

My dear aunt

Enclosed I return you D̲ͬ Dominkusch's account which on closer inspection proved to be 80f too much as the 80f interest which I paid at your order to D̲ͬ D. out of the April rent had not been taken into consideration – He begged me to give you his best compits. & thanks for settlement of his bill and rest of purchase money which is now all settled –

Agreably to your wishes I add a statement of [illeg.] how the rent due on July 1st went:

I owed you on July 1st rent for April May June 312/50x
<u>deduct from this:</u>

balance by which you overdrew your April acct.	20f54.
fee for delivery of Grundbuchsanschreibung[1]	1.5.
postage to you in forwarding you the above	.70
dto. in forwarding Dr. Domik. bill	45
fee for delivery of official notice that franz & Maria Scribe[2] could not be found	35
D̲ͬ Domikusch's bill	203.91.227.
Leaves balance in your favour of ———	85f50

this balance of 85f50. I ought to remit to you now after settling D̲ͬ Dominck. bill, but I cannot do so because I have got ~~the~~ government order for the payment of two sums of which I have written to you already 127f for the waterworks against inundation of the Drau[3] and 145f for an additional tax on the purchase money – against both these orders I gave in a protest to government – (the first myself – the second through D̲ͬ. Dominkusch) but as the protest may not be acknowledged by government and the order of payment enforced I must retain the 85f 50 to cover at least part of these payments – I am very unhappy dear aunt that you have so much to pay – I do my best to defend your interest, I am 10 times worse off myself and very dejected about the heavy expenses.

I enclose you the postage receipt for 70x.[4] also the receipt of the amtsdiener[5] who delivered the documents concerning Mary & franz Scribe. for the 45x. I got no receipt but you can see the postage stamps on the letter; for the 1f5 the receipt was on the document then forwarded –

Goodbye dear aunt Believe me yours affectly

W.G. Clairmont

Nicolaihof –
July 22nd 1872.

Address: No envelope

Unpublished. Text: M.S., Pf. Coll., CL'ANA 0309

1 Documents from the record of deeds.
2 Unidentified.
3 Drau River.
4 Abbreviation for Kreuzer.
5 German for "usher".

237 • Wilhelm Gaulis Clairmont to Claire Clairmont

[29 December 1872]

My dear aunt.

Enclosed I forward you 200f of the rent due on the 1st January. the remainder 112f 50x. I shall remit as soon as ever I can – I hope in four weeks perhaps sooner. I was disappointed in my hope of selling some corn which I got ready for sale there is just now a glut in the market and owing also to a momentary stagnation of business during the holidays no one would buy. I hope you will not be vexed. I could not have sent you so much if I had not got some money from Mrs Werner. You must excuse my long silence, I could not write to you without touching on the principal topic the progress of the farm and as I shrank from the idea of giving you pain by an unfavorable report I preferred not to write at all. but now I cannot conceal from you any longer that things are going very ill with me and that it is only Paulines generous aid which gives me a hope to battle through. and even with this it is more than questionable whether I can keep my head above water. the expenses are terrific. rent and taxes are 1600f. household 1200f. wages 1400f. seed manure fodder and sundry expenses 800f repair of buildings purchase of material 200f blacksmith wheelright etc. 300f purchase of fuel 200f wine for labourers 250f this is in round numbers a total expense of 6000f. the proceeds come nothing near this mark and are uncertain besides – however as long as I can – as long as I have means to do it I shall go on manfully – you thought that I could dispose of the lease but this is not possible not only because the rent is very high but also because the lease being limited ~~by~~ to my lifetime no one can take it from me on the chance of [illeg.] being turned out when I die – You may well fancy that with these heavy cares hanging about me we did not spend a very pleasant Christmas – however we were both of us happy through the joy of our poor dear children who knowing nothing of the anxieties that weigh us down were bright and happy. Wattie who insists on accompanying me all over the fields in every kind of weather got a pair of big boots half way up his little leg. it would be quite in vain to attempt to picture his delight. then he got a set of ninepins and two balls[1] ~~which~~ very large and fine which Baron Hauer a friend of mine who is an amateur turner turned himself & sent him – Baby got a doll and a large box of splendid cooking apparatus pots and pans which Countess Sermage sent her as they were sent to her daughter by a distant relative who does not know her and Countess Sermage found (and justly so) that her daughter was past such childish toys – Tilly made up some old cloths for some of the children of our farmservants and we also had a tree which pleased and astounded all the children very much. We also thought a great deal of you & Plin and little Georgina I hope you spent pleasant holiydays together – I wish you dear aunt a happy new year and a great many returns of it and may you live a long long time yet to enjoy your handsome property here. If the seasons had been reversed – that is if this present winter had been last year you would very likely not have left us so soon – this is quite like an

Italian winter. we have had frost only twice – in the beginning of Decemb. now we have fine sunny days interrupted only by occasional fogs – in the morning we have 6 degrees warmth R.² at noon in the shade 10 to 12 + R.

I sincerely hope dear Pauline will find it possible to come & see us in the summer – we should be also very glad to see you here and of course I need not say that your pay for board would be a very welcome assistance but nevertheless I do not invite you to come because I think travelling does not agree with you and also we live on too poor a scale to make you comfortable. but if you will nevertheless come we shall be delighted to see you.

Goodbye dearest aunt we are all well I hope you are so too.

Believe me yours
most affectionately
W.G. Clairmont

Nicolaihof
Decemb 29th 1872.

Love to Plin. got her letter and will answer in a few days – no acts. yet from Mrs Werner – Tilly began a letter to aunt but it is not ready & this letter cannot wait. She sends her best love to all.

Address: No envelope.

Unpublished. Text: M.S., Pf. Coll., CL'ANA 0310

---

1 To play ninepin bowling.
2 See CL'ANA 0377.

238 • Wilhelm Gaulis Clairmont to Claire Clairmont

[25 March 1873]

My dear aunt.

I feel much distress in forwarding you a paper which caused me the greatest indignation ; it is a demand from the Gru[illeg.]er Savings Bank[1] to pay from the 1st January 1873, 6 percent instead of as hitherto agreed 5½ percent, If you do not agree to the demand you are called upon to return the capital 4000f by July 1st if you do agree to pay the 6 percent interest you are to [illeg.] sign (and get signature legalized at the Austrian Embassy) the enclosed declaration and return it to me to put a stamp on – the savings bank say they will give time for decision only till March 30th. I wrote to them to say that this was impossible as you lived at Florence and that their letter although dated December 30th 72 bore the postmark of yesterday. and was received by me only today. so I begged them to give you time for decision till 30 April – the more as the interest is already paid up till then. I must wait for your decision in this matter before I can undertake anything.[2]

Believe me yours affectly
W. G. Clairmont

Nicolaihof
March 25th 1873.
this is a mere business letter – personal matters in Plins letter –

Address: No envelope.

Unpublished. Text: M.S., Pf. Coll., CL'ANA 0311

---

1 Unidentified.
2 Wirth refers to the "crisis" of 1873 in which "the feverish over-haste in railway enterprises and the stock-gambling in bank shares and other securities were attended with unfortunate consequences . . ." The Austrian National Bank "resolved, in 1872, to retire fifteen million florins in railway priority bonds from the reserve fund and sell the bonds. By the close of 1872 there was an addition of ninety-four million florins to the discount and loan transactions . . . The maximum of bills and loan transactions occured in 1873 (the crisis of that year declared itself in Vienna in on May 12th)". As a result of the banking crisis, the bank's charter was discontinued. However, as Wirth notes, von Lucam assisted in implementing a plan that literally saved the bank from financial ruin (*A History of Banking in All the Leading Nations* [New York: *The Journal of Commerce and Commercial Bulletin*, 1896], vol. iv, pp. 81–3). In June 1873, the Bourse in Vienna crashed, which resulted in worldwide economic problems. See CL'ANA 0300.

239 • Wilhelm Gaulis Clairmont to Claire Clairmont

Marburg 29th May 1873.

My dear aunt

Just now I received yours of the 27th which I answer at once from Marburg in order to do so by return of post. I cannot say how distressed I am at the account of the sufferings you have had to go through at your age too and with so much illhealth and constitutional weakness constantly preying on you. however I sincerely trust that you have over come the worst and that now with the fine season before you, you will speedily get round. We have often talked of your trials and both of us join in most sincere commiseration of you but I am always weighed down by such heavy cares and anxieties and I see difficulties which must soon provoke a crisis closing round me always closer so that I am not in spirits for letter writing.[1] but now to business. I got Plins letter which you mention but I could not answer it because I did not then know and do not now what the future would bring. moreover she wrote me another letter a few days after stating that you were in a most precarious state of health. that you could not think of hearing business letters read and that on no account I should write any bad news just now because your health and nerves were not in a state to hear it – so what could I do? of course I had no option but silence – and so I would continue now but for your personal and express desire to have information on business matters. You ask whether another Drau installment will be called upon to pay. – this is as yet not the case then whether I shall be able to pay you your rent on July 1st this I cannot tell – from the farm I shall <u>not</u> get the money, the rent is much too heavy. but I shall endeavour to make a debt. and to pay you by this means. Paulines papers (I mean stock or bonds) are unsaleable in consequence of the crash at the Vienna exchange of which I believe you must have heard. many 100 thousands of people are ruined. we suffer indirectly in as much as ~~nothing~~ no loans are procurable now.[2]

Do not dear aunt be vexed at Tilly for not having written to you she has an excellent heart and ingratitude is truly not her failing – but she cannot write alone in Engl. and she bothered me once or twice but I had not time; she is now (I believe for I am not in the secret and am against it on account of the expense) preparing a surprise for you and when this is ready she will write. I envy her her pure confiding mind which carries her better through our difficulties than I can struggle through so do not dear aunt be vexed at a neglect which I can assure you is only apparent. Please give my love to Plin and Georgina and believe me dear aunt

yours most affct.
WG Clairmont

Address: M<u>rs</u> <u>Mary J. Clairmont.</u>/ 83 Via Valfonda/<u>Firenze</u>/<u>Italia</u>.
Front post stamps: Three 5 kr. Stamps, franked twice with KLAGENFURT/30/5/
Rear postmark: FIRENZE/ [illeg.]/ 7 M

Unpublished. Text: M.S., Pf. Coll., CL'ANA 0312

---

1 Wilhelm's letter of 2 May 1873 to the *Marburger Zeitung* suggests the extent of his "heavy cares and anxieties". Writing from Nikolaihof, Wilhelm recorded the "näher rückende Gefahr" ("fast approaching danger") of Rinderpest (cattle plague), a highly contagious disease in livestock (www.oie.int). He explained that a fellow farmer in Croatia had warned him that Rinderpest had killed cattle in Agram and Oroslavje, and that the military had been called in to assist with the destruction of disease-ridden livestock. Wilhelm wrote to warn readers that the disease was a serious threat to farmers in the Styrian border area and he urged them to take appropriate precautions ("Die Rinderpest". Web. 25 October 2015. http://www.dlib.si/).
2 Peter Drucker attributes the collapse of worldwide stock exchanges to the crash of the Vienna Stock exchange in 1873: "Short-lived panics in Paris, London, Frankfurt and New York" ensued and "although the economy of the Western world had recovered 18 months later, politics – which would now seek security and protection from the upheavals associated with the Industrial Revolution – was changed forever" (*Managing for the Future* [Oxford: Routledge, 1993], p. 2). See CL'ANA 0311.

240 • Wilhelm Gaulis Clairmont to Pauline Clairmont

[8 June 1873]

Dearest Plin

I got yours of the 4$^{th.}$ – Something must be done that is clear to me too – the best thing would be to sell Nicolaihof while we are still living on it, because hereafter when not inhabited & not kept in proper trim it will not sell so well as it would now – If aunt does not consent to sell we must think of something else – Your offer to let me have the rent of yr Baden house for a year is just like yourself – always considerate and selfsacrificing but it is no radical cure – it will involve me in debt more and more and finally I must come to a stand. it would only defer the catastrophe for a year or so – your idea of subletting the house only is quite unfeasible because you would find no one to take it – there is in Nicolai neither butcher baker grocer post office etz. etz. there also no decent people living here – for everything appertaining to creature comforts as well as for all social intercourse you have no nearer place than Marburg so that you could not live here without keeping a house and chaise,[1] this only well to do people can afford but such would not come to a solitary place like Nicolaihof.[2] I am therefore quite convinced that we shall never find a tenant for the house and garden alone – I have already made efforts to sublet the whole farm I have given commission to this effect in Vienna and Graz. but hitherto without result. – If Dr Dominkurch as you say told Aunt over and over again that the estate would let for £180 I am quite willing to cancel the lease – let aunt give Dr Dom instructions to relet the farm and she is most welcome to whatever more she will get than I now pay. You need not imagine that I would be vexed at your advice to take a more humble dwelling and let the house. In the position in which I now am I should be glad to make money out of any thing but I see no possibility of letting the house.

Pray give my love and Tilly's to aunt. Tilly wanted to make Aunt some work but she could not as she was confined to her bed so long and then she was weak and unable and there were so many arrears of mending etz and making summer clothes for herself & the children so it was and is still utterly impossible to make any work for aunt but she got Wattie photographed for Aunt in his new suit given by her – but the wretch – the travelling photogr. does not send the likeness – Excuse my candour but the only sensible thing you said in your last was that you would perhaps come to talk over all this complicated matter with me – by letter will never come to a result – dont neglect to call aunts attention to my advice to sell the property. Thank you dear Plin for your dear kind heart towards me believe me yours affect

WGC

June 8th 1873.

Address: <u>Miss P. Clairmont</u>/ 83 <u>Via Valfonda</u>/ Italia. <u>Firenza</u>/

Unpublished. Text: M.S., Pf. Coll., CL'ANA 0317

1 A small carriage, usually for two passengers.
2 Nikolaihof was not without its attractions. In the article, entitled "Einladung zum Beitritte an alle Bienenfreunde und Bienenzüchter" and which appeared in the 4 May 1873 edition of the *Marburger Zeitung*, Herr v. Clairmont and Herr J. Dominkusch were identified as two of the five "Verwaltungsräthe" ("administrative board members") who had invited all beekeepers to join the Lower Styrian Beekeeping Society in order to learn new methods of beekeeping, following the example the Royal Imperial Agricultural Association in Graz had set. The Society offered free classes as well as colony evaluation, the provision of economical hives, and a newsletter. The article explained that the bylaws were approved on 10 March 1873 and that the society had 100 members. Wilhelm and Dominkusch were elected as administrative board members. (Web. 25 October 2015. http://www.dlib.si/). See also CL'ANA 0296.

241 • Wilhelm Gaulis Clairmont to Pauline Clairmont

[15 July 1873]

My dearest Plin

I enclose you 133f. the proceeds as you will perceive from Dr Postl's letter to me of the 17 coupons of your Obligations due on July 1st 1873.
I duly rec^d your note with postscript from Aunt. I am extremely glad she can walk again albeit with crutches.[1] anything better than being confined to bed for good – I hope dear aunt will soon recover entirely.
I was quite prepared to ~~pay~~ find aunt disinclined to pay me my investments. at the same time my cancelling the lease would ~~be~~ account ~~to~~ a forfeiture of my ~~lease~~ claim which I cannot forego we shall therefore rub on the best way we can. –
Got and read the S.M. Herald[2] with best thanks. intend trying to write a German article on it. put the articles from the Times on poultry ~~to~~ into translation for a German paper got 5f for it. I joined an excursion last Week to Wittingau (prince Schwarzenberg)[3] by invitation to Arenstein.[4] special train first class all free gratis for nothing. Wrote article on the excursion to "Times" just watch whether you find it – would like to know whether they accepted it or not – please if you keep the Times look out for it – I sent it them July 5th –
Glad you are at fiesole[5] hope you & Aunt will be better there – Best love to aunt and you all – T. & children well yours affect

WGC

Nichof
July 15th 1873

Address: No envelope.

Unpublished. Text: M.S., Pf. Coll., CL'ANA 0421, Box 1, bundle a, number 12

---

1 See CL'ANA 0308.
2 *The Sydney Morning Herald.*
3 German for Třeboň, a spa-town in the Czech Republic today located some 425 kilometers north of Maribor. Třeboň is known for the Château Třeboň, an impressive castle that the princely von Schwarzenberg family owned. The Château Třeboň dates back at least to the fourteenth century and was reconstructed as a Renaissance palace after a fire destroyed most of the original building in the sixteenth century. In 1660, the von Schwarzenberg family purchased the property, which remained in family hands until 1940 when the Nazis appropriated it. Today, the castle and the surrounding gardens are a state-run tourist attraction ("Státní zámek Třeboň". Web. 11 May 2015. https://www.zamek-trebon.eu/cs).
   The author of *Reports on the Vienna University Exhibition of 1873* described different products resulting from the distillation of peat: "They were all prepared from the peat of Wittengau, near where the peat works of Prince Schwarzenberg are in operation" (p. 312). The report also stated that "the peat bricks produced on Prince Schwarzenberg's estate . . . are in all respects said to be equal to the best lignite. The peat plant at Wittengau has now been at work for three seasons, the

first being the spring of 1870". The author noted too "the general success of the enterprise" (London: George E. Eyre, 1874), part. ii, p. 205.

In *Picture of Vienna*, the author lists the palace of Prince Schwarzenberg on "neuen Markt" as one of the palaces in Vienna (p. 46). The author also describes the summer palace belonging to Prince Schwarzenberg as one of the "remarkable buildings and gardens in the suburbs" and notes that it has a "large garden on the Rennweg; built in 1725 by Fischer" (p. 49). The library of Prince Schwarzenberg on neun Markt had 30,000 volumes, "chiefly old classics, history, politics and natural history" (p. 71).

4 Wilhelm could have meant the German town of Arnstein, located 450 kilometers north-west of Třeboň or the Austrian town of Arnstein, located 370 kilometers south of Třeboň.
5 A town, about 10 kilometers north of Florence. Nestled in the hills above Florence, the town enjoys a more moderate climate than that of Florence, and Claire would repair there to avoid the heat of summer.

242 • Pauline Clairmont to Wilhelm Gaulis Clairmont

Florence Oct 14 [c. 1873]
8 Via delle Terme[1]

My dearest William

I cannot tell you how sorry I am to think of your leaving beautiful Nicolaihof[2] – if you could but have remained there if we could but have weathered thro' another year – I know nothing of particulars or details the why & the wherefore & cannot expect you with so much business as you have on hand to sit down & write long gossiping letters of how the two ends wont meet & why they wont meet & that is principally why I wanted to come & see you but all that is past & gone now – so we must see what you can do next. Of course you will not fail to send Aunt's rent exactly on [illeg.] or about the first of January 1874 as she cannot do without it & even then will be very short of money. I must say I tremble at the idea of going to Vienna to get something to do – it seems to me almost an impossibility & I can think of nothing else but writing a petition to the Archduke William[3] – Aunt asked you in one of her letters to give her a list of the English directors of the Anglo Hungarian Land – company[4] & if she knew any of them she would write to them or get some of her friends in England to do so that they might if they knew you would be sure to employ you – Is not Alfred Klein one of them – but then he is a Jew, & will only help a Jew or a beggarly Count, but not an honest man.[5] I will also write to Cts. Koll. – we must leave no stone unturned, & not despise little means.
I wish I was in Vienna I would go straight to Prince Nicholas Esterhazy he knew poor Papa & me & now that Mr Smallbones is dead perhaps he might someone.[6] Dearest boy let us not despair – You have been on Prince Schwarzenberg's estate this summer – his mother died lately the beautiful Lori Schwarzenberg[7] He was my pupil once upon a time – but I am afraid it is too long ago besides I believe his Father is still alive. That is all I can think of.
Please tell Tilly that I have had much to do with the moving & could not write & if she could send me a paper pattern of children's socks I will knit some, now I am knitting for you, & will send you them to Vienna at Xmas. Dearest boy do not stint yourself in food in Vienna such saving does more harm than good. A kiss to Tilly & the children & believe me yours faithfully

Plin.

Aunt sends her best love to you all, she has not been so well lately for want of exercise but the foot is pretty well.[8]

Address: No envelope

Unpublished. Text: M.S., Pf. Coll., CL'ANA 0421, Box 3, bundle g, number 185

1 The letter's reference to 1874 suggests Pauline wrote it in 1873. This letter, and the following two letters, were bundled together in a single envelope, possibly by Christoph Clairmont.
2 It is unclear from the records whether Wilhelm sold Nikolaihof or whether he continued to own it and to administer it from Vienna. However, by 1874, he had reestablished himself in Vienna. Stocking records that Wilhelm served as a "consultant on agriculture to a government office" (*CC* II: 640). An address book from 1889 listed Wilhelm as a Güter-Schätzmeister des Obersthofmarschall-Amtes (Treasurer of Commodities in a court office). It also places Wilhelm at the same address as Ottilia's father, Reisnerstrasse 40 (Image provided from the address book, Heraldic-Genealogical Society Adler, Vienna, 3 May 2015). The *Wiener Zeitung* would list this address for Johann von Pichler when he died on 24 February 1892 (Austrian Newspapers Online, Österreichische Nationalbibliothek [Austrian National Library, http://anno.onb.ac.at/cgi-content/anno?aid=wrz&datum=18920301&seite=10&zoom=29, p. 10]). An article in the October issue of *AJR Information* (Assocation of Jewish Refugees, vol X, number 10, p. 2) identifies Reisnerstrasse 40, Vienna, as the location of the British Embassy in 1955 ("Property, Rights and Interests of Victims of Nazism". 1955. Web. 26 October 2015. http://www.ajr.org.uk/journalpdf/1955_october.pdf).
3 Probably Archduke Wilhelm Franz (1827–1894). Born in Vienna, he died at Weikersdorf, Austria (Lundy, Darryl. "The Peerage". Web. 7 June 2015. http://www.thepeerage.com).
4 *Accounts and Papers: 1875* for the House of Commons lists the following jointly held Anglo-Austrian Companies: The Anglo-Austrian Gas Company and The Anglo-Austrian Water Supply Company (London: Great Britain Parliament, 1875), v. XIII, p. 394.
5 See CL'ANA 0404.
6 See CL'ANA 0343 and CL'ANA 0255.
7 Pauline referred to Prince Adolf Joseph Johann zu Schwarzenburg (1832–1914). He was the son of Johan Adolf II (1799–1888) and Eleonore von Liechtenstein (1812–1873). Eleonore died at Třeboň–Wittingau ("Mediatized House of Schwarzenberg". Web. 11 May 2015. http://www.almanachgotha.org/id101.html). The celebrated art critic, Anna Jameson, recorded meeting Princess Schwartzenburg at the home of the French ambassador. She described the princess as "a famous Austrian beauty" (*Sketches of Germany* [Frankfurt: Charles Jugel, 1837], p. 169).
8 Pauline cross-wrote this last sentence on page one of the letter. See CL'ANA 0308.

28 MARCH 1861–24 DECEMBER 1889

243 • Pauline Clairmont to Wilhelm Gaulis Clairmont

Florence Oct. 16.
8. Via delle Terme [c. 1873]

My own dearest William

This morning I got yours dated Oct. 4. I have much difficulty in getting out by myself & I do not want to let G.[1] see that I get letters P. restante.[2] I should have to make the child tell stories which she is only too happy to do – or else Aunt would find it out – for she sends G. with me to find out all that I do & where I go, etc. (to exercise G's memory & ~~her~~ cultivate her power of observation.)[3]

However I got your letter & am so far relieved of <u>some</u> of my anxiety to know that you are in good health all of you.

I got all your letters also the one about Heine which shocked me very much as M^r H took much pains with their education & sent them to the best school. Both the boys were clever the eldest a perfect Jew of unconcealiable descent the younger one who misbehaved himself was one of the handsomest boys you could see & most aristocratic in appearance Pale grecian features black hair & blue eyes – probably not his father's son. He had nothing of the Jew about him & the sister's marriage with a pennyless Count quite upset the whole family with glory & convulsed them with ambition & such is the end of their pride.[4] this other sheet here enclosed is the "official".[5] the 100fl german money that I told you of I have still got & will give it to you for the January rent but "she wont take Charity from me" – & wants me to send it to you & you send it back to her. So you had better send the January money to me <u>minus 100 fl</u> which I will add & she must then send you a receipt for the <u>whole sum.</u>

Dear Tilly says she cannot imagine the circumstances & difficulties that <u>my</u> energy could not have over come! If I had chosen to part with Aunt of course I could have come, but at that price I would not do it – She makes her health a pretence & says, Surely you would not leave a poor helpless cripple like me to the care of paid servants – in my precarious state of health! it would be barbarous! If I had a person near me to take care of me during your absence if Miss Miller[6] was her or if I knew of a good nurse but I cannot afford to pay any one. then I said – Do you mean to say that as long as you live I am not to see my brother & his family? – She – well I cant say, all I can say is that I cant be left alone. It is only her intense selfishness but that one must expect in old people – but her all-devouring Envy – the bare idea of my enjoying a little trip seeing you all & above all going to see the ex hibition has cost her many a sleepless painful night. Now she is to a certain extent sorry because she knows so little about your proceedings & all the Nicolai affairs & is in active correspondence with Mrs Tucker to out something thro' her son Willie[7]

I myself am deeply grieved to think of your going away from Nicolai Sweet little Walter what a darling he must be the hot tears came into my eyes when I read your letter to think that many dreary years will have to pass before I can see those dear children & you all – & then Aunt who has lost all perception of human kindness says in her cold sneering cynicism – Yes – your brother – you like him because he is a man well there is the Post office why dont you write your effusions! – I told the Ctss Dini[8] of this speech & she said – that is very hard. So it is – but she cant hurt me – even by abusing you for I think then how our Saviour was reviled & how patiently he bore <u>his</u> heavy cross – & I know that you & Tilly believe in my love & devotion to you both & your children & that gives me courage Aunt said the other day that God would some day punish me severely for my wickedness towards her & I said – He wont do me much harm in that respect – Ah! she cried You defy God! – upon which I answered with unfeigned surprise – I? defy God!?

When I thank him everyday for the courage he gives me to bear my heavy cross – And so it is – the idea & consciousness of fulfilling my duty towards her – & being some use to you & yours gives me health & strength to bear it all.[9] About Mrs Werner's bad tidings I am much concerned but let us hope they will be satisfied with one instalment for some time to come & that next year we shall be better off. I have not yet touched my July dividends – please send me the January coupons (at least the money for them) along with Aunts' money & have no scruple in selling some of the shares if you are in want of money.

Believe me yours ever
Plin.

Address: No envelope

Unpublished. Text: M.S., Pf. Coll., CL'ANA 0421, Box 3, bundle g, number 185

---

1 Georgina.
2 Poste restante. See CL'ANA 0398.
3 In April 1873, Claire wrote to Trelawny about Georgina, describing her, falsely, as an orphan (*CC* II: 620). Stocking records that Pauline had told Claire about Georgina's birth by 1871 and that she had brought Georgina to Florence to reside with her. In 1876, Claire told Bartolomeo Cini she intended to sell the Shelley letters in order to educate Georgina: "For myself I would not sell my letters – but to benefit Georgie I will" (p. 634). In her letter to Margherita Cini Farina (daughter of Bartolomeo and Nerina Cini) of 15 November 1877, Claire described Georgina as a "comfort" to her (p. 638). Her will mentioned Georgina. She planned on leaving the interest on her shares, which she hoped would be purchased from the proceeds of the sale of the Shelley letters, to Georgina upon Pauline's death (p. 661).
4 See CL'ANA 0404.
5 This sheet is missing.
6 Pauline meant to write "if Miss Müller was here".
7 See CL'ANA 0421, Box 3, bundle g, number 186.
8 Probably Countess Maria Teresa di Serrego Alighieri Gozzadini (also known as la Nina). An article in *The Nation* of 29 September 1887 described Countess Gozzadini as "charming . . . one of the last descendants in the female line of Dante Alighieri" and who "numbered among the Florentine aristocracy". The article recorded too that "during the last ten years of her life la Nina's letters relate chiefly to literary matters" (New York: The Evening Post Publishing Company, 1887), vol. xliv, p. 251.

9 By 1877, Claire informed Margherita Cini Farina that Pauline's feelings towards her had improved somewhat (*CC* II: 638). She believed that their past disagreements stemmed from differences in opinions. She attributed these differences to a lack of "sympathy" between them, noting that they both came from different cultures.

244 • Pauline Clairmont to Wilhelm Gaulis Clairmont

Oct 19. [c. 1873]
8 Via delle Terme.[1]

Dearest William

I wrote to you I think on the 15<u>th</u> or 16<u>th</u> & think that you will to day or tomorrow be setting off to Klagenfurt & that you will find this on your return to Nicolaihof. the day before yesterday was poor Mama's wedding day in the year 1824 almost half a century at W-Neustdt[2] & think that M<u>rs</u> Aunt wants to make out that they never were married & we are illegitimate – because she never associated with respectable people – I think her life must have been very bad – intemperance of <u>all</u> sorts.[3]

Also of <u>your</u> wedding day I thought of you & pray God that neither of us may become such a nuisance as that old woman. Dear Bill you must tell me now (in a <u>private answer</u> of course) whether you think of going to Klagenfurt for the Xmas holidays or whether T. will come to Vienna because I am going to make a winter frock for Baby & would like to know where I am to send the parcel. I shall also have 6pr. socks for you if you want them if not I will keep them till there are 12 pair – but perhaps you may want even 6 pair as T. wont be there to mend them for you. Also for dear Walter I mean to send a suit but I'll take it a good size as he is so tall – another thing I want to mention to you that if T. should have spasms again try <u>Dr. Collis Browne's Chlorodyne</u>.[4] In small dark blue bottles. it is very strong & I would not give more than 10 or 15 drops in a small wine glass of water & never more than 25 drops at a time – It did me a great deal of good but acts slowly. Tell me do the children want socks or at least Walter he will have outgrown his.

Aunt says she will be very glad to see young M<u>r</u> Nadler[5] & will ask him to dinner – she delights in having young men (& old ones too) round her only they <u>must</u> not talk to me.

I have a very dear Xmas present for you dear boy that I know you will value – only A¹ must not be told of it. it is poor Papas portrait I had a Photo taken from the picture A¹ has – but as she would not have it I had it copied while I was doing all the emigration into the new house. It is a very good apartment much better than the other only no view. Close to the Lungarno. I shall call for a letter at the end of the month – Yours ever truly

PC.

Address: No envelope

Unpublished. Text: M.S., Pf. Coll., CL'ANA 0421, Box 3, bundle g, number 185

---

1 The letter "P" is printed in blue ink and surrounded by leaves on the upper left-hand corner of the first page.
2 Abbreviation for Wiener Neustadt. Walter Clairmont corroborated the information contained in Pauline's letter in a note written in 1933 describing his family's heritage: "Er heiratete 1824

Antonia Ghislain d'Hembyse, eine Wienerin, die einer alten walonischen Familie entstammte. Ihre Mutter, also unsere Urgroßmutter war eine geborene Schönbichler" (CL'ANA 0428, p. 1, unpublished document, Pforzheimer Collection,). Translation: "In 1824 he [Charles] married Antonia Ghislain d'Hembyse, a Viennese who came from an old Wallonian family. Her mother, our great-grandmother, was born a Schönbichler".

3 Pauline surely knew some of the stories of Claire's past, particularly the history of her relationship with Byron and the birth of Allegra in 1817.

4 Dr. John Collis Browne (1819–1884) patented Chlorodyne, a medicine that was used to treat cholera and later diarrhea, and which contained laudanum. Advertisements from the time attest to the efficacy of the medicine. In their 1974 article, "Chlorodyne Dependence," Parker, Cobb, and Connell describe the contents of chlorodyne, which they explain are "opium-based" and can cause dependency. They conclude with the warning that "the prognosis in terms of giving-up the drug seems to be very poor . . . In the light of our findings we recommend placing the supply of chlorodyne under some form of control" (*British Medical Journal* [I: 1974], pp. 427–9).

5 Probably one of Ottilia's "Nadler" relatives. See CL'ANA 0184.

245 • Pauline Clairmont to Wilhelm Gaulis Clairmont

Florence Oct 31.[1] [c. 1873]
N[r]. 8. Via delle Terme

Dearest William

I suppose by this time Tilly & children are safely lodged at Klagenfurt & she will have to get reconciled to the separation which she will think very hard – I begin to see that life is not a path of roses. But you must not loose courage – it may seem foolish at this moment to say hope on for the best – but you must keep your spirits up it is like eating when you dont feel hungry one must eat to keep up ones strength & that reminds me to beg you most earnestly not to neglect your food when at Vienna. Drink as much of the excellent Vienna beer as you can & above all eat meat plain simple roast meat & no puddings. I wish I could see you – if I had a magic mirror walking with Walter by your side as I once saw you with W. Hauer – he too is a dear little boy.[2] I do hope the winter wont be very hard or else they will suffer tremendous cold up at Kl.[3] Do you remember how rosy Walter used to look that winter at Baden when I used to take him out in the snow to see the little birds & the gee-hoss!

Aunts foot is pretty well at least the walking is much improved only there are occasional other ailments – but altogether I think she may be very thankful for her general good health & strength.

The rainy season has begun & we have been very fortunate in getting all the snowing over in good time – we have a very nice apartment close to Piazza St. Trinità[4] which you may remember. I will write to Tilly as soon as I can.

Yours ever
Plin.

Dearest William[5] I open this letter to say that Aunt sends her best love & says that she has received an unexpected present of 10£ from England (Mr Mitchell)[6] & she most kindly and generously says she will give it to us. So therefore in January you will send instead of 312fl only 262fl. & take the 5£ towards the payment of that dreadful installment of the Vienna Saving bank.

A[t] says that without M[r] M's kindness she could not have done it, & in April she must have her full rent, at least such part of it as is due to her.

You have also 27fl to deduct for yourself.[7]

Address: No envelope

Unpublished. Text: M.S., Pf. Coll., CL'ANA 0421, Box 3, bundle g, number 188

---

1 Christoph Clairmont dates this letter to 1873.
2 The son of Rudolf and Emily von Hauer. See Appendix, CL'ANA 0421, Box 1, bundle a, number 85.
3 Klagenfurt.

4 The Piazza Santa Trinita in Florence. The square (piazza) is named for the Church of Santa Trinita (St. Trinity Church), which is on the square. The Medici family once owned the church, which contains works by Luca della Robbia and Ghirlandaio.
5 Pauline included the following paragraph on the same page.
6 See CL'ANA 0071, CL'ANA 0393 and CL'ANA 0421, Box 3, bundle g, number 186.
7 Pauline cross-wrote the final sentence.

246 • Pauline Clairmont to Wilhelm Gaulis Clairmont

the enclosed is official[1]

Florence Nov 2ⁿᵈ [c. 1873]
8. Via della Terme

Dearest William

I got yours Oct 23ʳᵈ a few days ago & send this P. rest.[2] to Vienna Dearest boy I cannot tell you how I take the failure of Nicolaihof to heart, I did so hope it would be for years an elegant & comfortable home for you – it must be a great disappointment both for you & Tilly – & dear little Walter even! You may imagine how distressed I am to think that I can not help you by word or deed, & am tied down here in prison. I am glad to think you will at least spend the Xmas holidays at Kl.[3] & I will make up the parcel & send it there: addressed to Tilly. I am very glad you got rid of Master Tucker's visit which was only to spy.[4] Of course you cannot take another farm having no money to stock with – & am quite at a loss to think what you will do & how & where you will live. Only do not stint yourself in food.

I can manage to get on till the spring with the dividends only – & what comes from the houses in spring will help you for the April rent to Aunt. Now I must tell you that a Mʳ Mitchell[5] a friend of Aunt's in London has sent her a <u>present of 10£ to buy coals</u> & she will give us this she says as she does not want it at present – the agio is very high in our favor 2f50[illeg.] for a german florin. 5£ therefore are to be deducted or rather 50fl from your rent & 27fl. besides which she owes you therefore instead of 212fl you will have to send only 135 [illeg.] & I will add the 100fl in german money that I have kept for you. This will help you a little & must write her a nice letter for it. I was quite surprised at this sudden burst of generosity I suppose her conscience smites her for bullying me so.

God bless you dear boy & give you courage – I mean to send my darling Walter a cloth suit for the winter (would an overcloak be more useful?) & socks – & a nice frock for baby but no hats they are sure never to fit. It is my only pleasure to make up these little things – Baby shall have a Poplin frock on the newest English pattern. You – dear Bill must always be fobbed off with a few shabby neckties – for Tilly I got a mosaic brooch – a white bouquet on dark ground[6] Dearest Bill I must close now – ever yours faithful

Pl.

Address: No envelope

Unpublished. Text: M.S., Pf. Coll., CL'ANA 0421, Box 3, bundle g, number 186

---

1 The enclosure is missing.
2 Poste restante.
3 Klagenfurt.

4 Pauline clearly believed that Claire sent Willie Tucker to Nikolaihof to "spy" on Wilhelm and his family. See CL'ANA 0421, Box 3, bundle g, number 185.
5 See CL'ANA 0071, CL'ANA 0393 and CL'ANA 0421, Box 3, bundle g, number 186. See also CL'ANA 0360 for information about coal mining in Austria.
6 See also CL'ANA 0179 and CL'ANA 0203.

247 • Pauline Clairmont to Wilhelm Gaulis Clairmont

Florence Dec 8. [c. 1873]
8. Via delle Terme.

My own dear Bill.

I got your letter dated 2 ^{d}. containing the news of M^{rs} R's death[1] – I do not suppose you will get any answer from R. as he makes a lawyer convey the news, perhaps you had better write to the lawyer – I would ask Battistes advice for if Mrs R. died without a will I think her property revolves to her family & not to her husband – she having left no children & <u>never having had</u> any by him But I suppose R. took good care to secure to himself all there was to grasp.

We have not heard from Dr Miklauz[2] altho' Aunt sent him 3. austr. fl. I suppose there was nothing to say.

Dear boy I am very sorry to hear about your eyes being weak you must not read in the evening – mine are also getting unsteady therefore I do nothing but knit the whole evening – I have finished your socks they are rather coarse I am sorry to say but hope they will do for the winter. I find now that they have very good English stuffs here for man's clothes – but very dear – – however I got Walter a suit of mixed stuff – <u>all</u> the boys wear sailor's suit in all colors – so as he had marine blue last year I got heather color this year I do hope it will turn out well & not be too heavy, but it must be awfully cold up at Klagenfurt & poor dear little Baby having the croup – I hope she has got over it & that you will spend a jolly Christmas – & my thoughts at least will be with you & my best wishes. Aunt says your weakness of the eyes is only low living – so pray eat as much as ever you can & keep up our spirits in spite of adversity.

Aunt is exceedingly well & sometimes walks quite alone, but it is a dangerous experiment. It is very cold here & a terrible Tramontana[3] blowing

Dear Bill are you comfortable or do you go to bed without fire & have a sloppy breakfast? Dear boy take care of yourself

Plin.

Address: No envelope

Unpublished. Text: M.S., Pf. Coll., CL'ANA 0224

---

1 Antonia's sister, Marie Rismondo. See CL'ANA 0401.
2 Unidentified.
3 North or north-east wind.

28 MARCH 1861–24 DECEMBER 1889

248 • Pauline Clairmont to Wilhelm Gaulis Clairmont

Florence Dec 14. [c. 1873]
8 Via delle Terme

<u>Behalte diesen Bf.</u> weil darin steht was <u>öffentl was privat zu bedanken.</u> ich muß ihn selbst erst beantworten. – [1]

Dearest William

I your last letter about Mrs R.[2] immediately – & do not suppose you have had any further news. Mr R. evidently wishes to keep in the background for reasons best known to himself.

We have not heard from Dr Miklauz either. He thinks the 3 fl a clear gain & would not even spend a postage stamp.

Dearest boy I wish you every success in this new year & a merry Christmas with your family – to morrow is Baby's birthday & I hope the frock I made will fit her. the box went off yesterday & I trust Tilly will have no difficulties about getting it. I sent Walter a Top-boot full of sweets & a box of bricks to build houses with as he is so fond of building Dear little fellow – he inherited that inclination from his poor Grandmother what a pity she could not see him! I remember how dear little baby tried to say "Plin" in her little voice when I was at Bellecé. God knows when I may see them again! The suit for Walter did not turn out quite what I wanted as the tailor made a blouse jacket to be worn over the pants, & with a belt he said it was more suitable to the material & the season.

at all events it will be warm & large enough. there are also two "serious" neckties & a "serious" waist coat for you. But remember please to mention nothing to Aunt <u>but the sock</u>s the <u>frock</u> for Baby and <u>the toys</u>. of the other things she knows nothing. – Aunt has a very bad cold from sitting in the draught & with windows open. the sun shines bright but there is a treacherous cold wind now tramontana now Eastwind – that undermines more constitutions & brings more illness than 10 degrees of cold.

I hope you are pretty well & your eyes none the worse & tell me also what you done in the way of employment – how sad you could not remain at N.[3]

Ever yours affte
Plin.

Address: No envelope

Unpublished. Text: M.S., Pf. Coll., CL'ANA 0223

---

1 Transcription and translation provided by Ann Sherwin: "Save this letter, because it contains something public for which thanks must be expressed privately. I must first answer it myself".
2 Marie Rismondo. See CL'ANA 0224.
3 Nikolaihof.

249 • Wilhelm Gaulis Clairmont to Claire Clairmont

[25 December 1873]

Christmasday 1873.

My dear aunt.

I cannot let this Christmas pass dear aunt without expressing you Tilly's and my own very best wishes for the ensuing year may God preserve you in health and strength & may he have still a great many returns of the new year in store for you. All the news there is to tell relating to us I have told in Plins letter so that I have nothing more to say I will only thank you dear aunt once more for the generous present of £5 you made us and I hope the way in which part of it was spent will meet your approval – for Wattie Tilly bought a very handsome toolbox for 5f containing every kind of carpenters implements (he is using them now much to the detriment of the application of my mental facilities to the writing of this letter) for Alma T. bought a nice little dolls bed with sheets and matrass etc. compll.[1] and a doll to put in – the children got these presents in your name and so did Tilly a half a dozen new pockethandkerchiefs. for which she also thanks you very much. & [illeg.] I gave T. 3f (that is 6/-) to buy a trifle for me – for this money she got the childrens photo taken (of which we send Plin a copy.) this was a most pleasant surprise to me as I think it very good. and I am now so much separated from the children;[2] also so many friends and acquaintances ask me about our children I can then show them their likeness. Now goodbye dearest aunt pray do take care of yourself you want nursing I am so glad you have quite recovered from the injuries your leg sustained Tilly sends you her very best love she is so sorry she has nothing to send either for you or Pauline

yours most affectly
Willy.

Address: No envelope

Unpublished. Text: M.S., Pf. Coll., CL'ANA 0313

---

1 Possibly an abbreviation for "complete".
2 After Wilhelm and his family returned to Vienna, he took a position as a government employee. His responsibilities included spending many days on the road assessing the value of various farms.

250 • Pauline Clairmont to Wilhelm Gaulis Clairmont

Florence Jan 20. 74.
8. Via delle Terme.

I hope you approve of the letter. I will also write to his wife[1]

Dearest William

I duly received your letter this morning containing 135 fl. Dear boy I wish you would never say anything to A[2] about <u>our</u> affairs between you & me. It quite aggravated her to think that I spend any money in my own way. I dare say I shall have to send the money to you in April & you send it back to her – from my hands she wont take it – We had a considerable scene the other morning – she in bed – draping herself majestically in an old shawl looking at me scornfully over her shoulder – – Take alms from <u>you</u> – <u>you</u> – indeed! I never was a burden to my family! She is a ridiculous poor old person I am happy to tell you that I have <u>385</u> fl in German money at this moment here therefore you are quite welcome to the 150 in April – & I insist on your having it my own dear boy only do me the favor not to mention it to Aunt – she has very little feeling left, which is to be expected at her age – ~~but~~ & therefore cannot understand the delicate & sweet happiness of <u>giving</u> & <u>taking</u> among hearts that love eachother. Would you & T. not help me the same you would I know – indeed you <u>both</u> – pure & spotless yourselves have not spurned me – & what money could or can ever pay for feelings? About your conduct towards me I say nothing – for nothing can equal <u>your</u> Christian charity – but also Tilly behaved like a loving sister to me – I wrote to her some days ago & begged her never to mention the word <u>sacrifice</u> How can there be sacrifice where there is love – To help you to save for you is my happiness – <u>If</u> there is any sacrifice on my part – it is my being & staying <u>here</u> in this house that <u>is</u> a sacrifice – but as it is for you I do it as cheerfully as I can, besides being a real duty to her, poor old thing.

I have studied thro' B's[3] letters & wonder how you made them out they are perfect hyrogl~~y~~iphics[4] – He is coming here at Easter – & A[1] has taken quite a fancy to him – & <u>he</u> will help her, & <u>he</u> will advise & if I dont marry him, <u>she</u> will. What a man of feeling! Such sweet sentimental letters for a lawyer! He is profoundly unhappy; I dare say he is very glad to have got rid of her, & her principal charm was her having left <u>him</u> all her money.

I remember R.Wrbna[5] very well He must be a man of about 40 now & was always on very good terms with poor Papa who gave him lessons. (& I to his sister, Resa[6] who was my first pupil when I was 17. & she about 12.) They had no mother, but an old governess Fraulein Habercorn, & a French tutor M. Henri. ~~His~~ The Countess Resa married one of C[t] Kinsky, proprietors of ~~our~~ the house we lived in at Vienna (Landhausgasse. 31.) this Resa was always a very kind friend to me & Clari & I will try & get her address & write to her. I will also ~~get~~ write the letter for C[t] Fries[7] & enclose it here. Now dear boy I must say one more thing – would you like me to write to C[t] Karoly[8] for you? Or would it be disagreable to you – of course they, the people in the house would put two & two together. He is a most kind & generous man – & rich & his brother of Foth[9] is a great deal richer. You would have to go to Pest about it (I believe but you could first inquire if by any chance they are in Vienna then all their estates are in Hungary which is a great drawback.

Your article is truly beautiful so concise so clear & such good round phrases just like poor Pa. used to write – I had the greatest pleasure in reading it – it seems impossible that you should find no situation But you have plenty of time before you dear boy Keep up your courage – How very kind of Ctss Sermage to send the children some toys – she is an excellent Lady & of high principles to judge of her countenance. I hope she is happy with her husband.

I got a letter from M[rs] Suttor & two Sydney papers which I sent you yesterday. She says Lottie (M[rs] William Mayne) has a second child a little girl[10] – & Little Herbert whom you may remember is engaged to his cousin Emily Suttor of Wyagdon.[11] – Do you remember Allowaybank house the residence of old M[r] Suttor[12] – that is pulled & a new fine house built & it is called <u>Cangoura</u>[13] a native name, & Willie & his beautiful wife Adelaide are coming to live there.[14] He is 39, already. How time does pass – I wish we could go back there! But as long as Aunt lives of course it is impossible – does it not seem to you reading those Australian papers as if you met a tall lanky longlimbed lad whom you had known as a little boy. M[r] Suttor seems in ill health & is suffering from a bad chronic cough.[15]

Dear Bill I have read you letter at least ten times about Walter's instinct of knowing of your coming before he could even see you. Dear Tilly & you too how happy you must have all been – tell me that marriage is not that sphere where a woman finds her greatest happiness! – Selfish nonsense only pray dont give your daughter a highflown education – for then she is sure to remain an old maid. Look at all our highly educated ladies – Aunt, Miss Müller; Baroness Hein[16] (Stein) Betti Paoli[17] – they get proud & argumentative & adieu happiness. As for Georgina – Aunt says very mysteriously I have my plans with that child – or – she is to be a telegrafista[18] – or a governess – her mind must be enlarged she must be made independent. etc – And then she makes her learn astronomy greek philosophy & read Shakespear not yet 10 years old[19] – The poor child is in despair sometimes & has good sense enough to see that she ought to learning grammar multiplication table & writing – & says to me, I wont be a governess I'll do anything for you at home, but dont make me a governess – I have promised her that she shall always remain with me – & indeed I am determined to get her married if I possibly can – & that must be your aim with your daughter For Walter's education every sacrifice must be made but the little girl must <u>above</u> all things not be tormented with music if she has no ear G. has no ear whatever nor hand either – & I accordingly do not teach her. needleworks of all[20] kinds & housework & cultivate her judgment – Our age is practical let our children be early initiated but there is an immense deal to be said on this subject & no sooner – It is very cruel of Aunt to separate us she is always saying to me as she did last summer this summer you will see them — but I dont go into her trap anymore I shall not see you nor the children for years — but never love you any the less. Believe me ever yours truly

Paola[21]

Will you mind to show C^t Fries your article on Australia — I am now writing to the Countess & tell her of it. Do you remember a clergyman of the name of Alworth at Twofoldbay? & a daughter Clelia Celia — she married one of M^{rs} Ch. Suttor's sons (John)[22]

I wanted to remind you of going to see Gustave Schauer[23] — he is an old friend & lives 18 Paniglgasse Wieden.[24]

What death has occured in the H. family? that Rismondo speaks of.[25]

Address: No envelope

Unpublished. Text: M.S. Pf. Coll., CL'ANA 0421, Box 3, bundle g, number 201 bis

---

1 Pauline wrote this sentence on the upper left-hand corner of the first page of the letter. She drew a line around it. She referred to Adelaide Agnes (Bowler) Suttor.
2 Aunt Claire.
3 Unidentified.
4 Spelling for hieroglyphics.
5 Rudolf Wrbna (1831–1893). He was the son of Maria Konstanzia, Gräfin Chorinsky Freiin von Ledske (1807–1831) and Rudolph, Graf von Wrbna und Freudenthal (1802–1874). His sister was Therese, Gräfin von Wrbna und Freudenthal (1828–1905). She married Christian Josef, Graf Kinsky von Wchinitz und Tettau (1822–1894) ("Geneall". Web. 8 June 2015. http://geneall.net/de). The author of *Picture of Vienna* lists the palace of "prince Kinsky, Herrngasse" as one of the Viennese palaces (p. 45).
6 Shortened form of Therese.
7 Unidentified. Probably the von Fries family. The family owned homes in Vienna and Bad Vöslau
8 See CL'ANA 0358, CL'ANA 0340, and CL'ANA 0315.
9 Fót is a town in Hungary, some 25 kilometers north-east of Budapest. The Károlyi family had a home in Fót which Count István Károlyi (1797–1881) inherited. Count István Károlyi "played a decisive role in Fót's social, economic and cultural life . . . In the Reform Era, the Károlyi mansion of Fót was a significant meeting place for all the progressively thinking politicians and aristocrats of the age . . . On his Fót estate Count Károlyi established a thriving farm" ("Fót". *National and Historical Symbols of Hungary*. Web. 9 June 2015. http://www.nemzetijelkepek.hu/onkormanyzat-fot_en.shtml).
10 Genealogical tables in *Dear William: The Suttors of Brucedale* (Judith Norton) provide information for the family relationships mentioned in the following notes. Charlotte Augusta Anna Suttor (1848–1926) was the seventh child of William Henry and Charlotte Suttor. She married William Colburn Mayne (1838–1901) in 1870. They had five children. Their second child, Eleanor, was born in 1874 and died in 1958.
11 Herbert Suttor (1850–1939) was Willie Suttor's younger brother and eighth child of William and Charlotte Suttor. He married Emilie Henrietta Suttor (1854–1929), daughter of John Bligh Suttor (1808–1886) and Julia Bowler Suttor. John Suttor was the younger brother of William Suttor. Julia Bowler Suttor was Adelaide Suttor's sister. Herbert and Emilie had seven children. Judith Norton notes that the Brucedale land grant was rather small and that George Suttor applied for another

grant at Wyagdon, an area close to Brucedale. In his daybook entry for 24 July 1835, George Suttor (father of William Henry and John Bligh Suttor) recorded applying to buy some land at Wyagdon. On 9 December, he confirmed purchasing 864 acres. Norton cites Bernard Greaves who states that Wyagdon had increased to almost 10,000 acres by the time it was sold in 1890 (*Dear William*, pp. 70–1). In his will, written in 1856, George Suttor bequeathed all his land at Wyagdon to John Bligh Suttor (p. 291).

Herbert and Emilie's son, Roy (1888–1982), was the father of John Herbert Suttor (1930–2011) and the grandfather of David Suttor (born 1961), who farms at Bathurst today.

12 Alloway Bank was originally owned by Captain John Piper. He sold it to the Suttor family in 1845. In his will, dated 31 August 1876, William Henry Suttor left his Alloway Bank estate of two thousand acres to Charlotte Suttor and, after her death, to his sons Horace Melbourne Suttor and Norman Lachlan Suttor (*Dear William*, p. 301).

13 In his will, William Henry Suttor Senior left Cangoura to Willie Suttor: "I give and devise to my said son William Henry Suttor the younger All those five hundred acres (more or less) of land adjoining Alloway Bank which I purchased from the late John Savery Rodd and was conveyed to me by Indenture dated the first day of October One thousand eight hundred and fifty two and now known as Cangoura and upon which my said son William Henry Suttor the younger has lately built a house" (*Dear William*, pp. 301–2).

14 In 1862, Willie Suttor married Adelaide Agnes Henrietta Bowler, who had been one of Pauline's pupils when she was a governess at Brucedale. They had six children (see introductory notes to The Australian Sojourn and CL'ANA 0220). Stocking states that Willie and Adelaide named their first daughter Pauline (*CC* II: 568). However, Judith Norton's genealogical table lists Willie and Adelaide Suttor's daughters' names as Dora Henrietta, Isabel Adelaide, Grace Agnes, Lilliane Charlotte, Kathleen Francis and Una Leonora (*Dear William*, pp. 322–3). Adelaide's sister, Julia, married John Bligh Suttor, Willie's uncle (see note 11).

15 William Henry Suttor died in 1877.

16 Baroness Marianne von Stein, Abbesse of the Cloister of Wallerstein in Germany. She was arrested in lieu of her brother, Baron von Stein (1757–1831) who escaped the wrath of Napoléon I in 1809. Baron von Stein was a Prussian political figure who instituted major reforms in Prussia (*The Living Age*, New York: E. Littell, Littell, Son and Company, 1856), vol. xlix, pp. 332–42.

17 Austrian poet, Betty Paoli (1814–94).

18 Italian for "telegrapher".

19 The words "not yet 10 years old" were written above the line.

20 The remainder of this letter was cross-written.

21 Pauline included a two-sided insert in the letter. Side one begins here until "M^{rs} Ch. Suttor's sons (John)" and the second page begins with "I wanted".

22 John George Suttor (1841–1887) was the son of Thomas Charles Suttor and his wife, Mary Anne Grosvenor Francis. He married Celia Allworth and they had seven children. See CL'ANA 0020. Celia was the daughter of the Reverend William Allworth. *The Twofold Bay and Maneroo Telegraph* of Friday 14 September 1860 records that the members of the Church of England Building Committee met Reverend Allworth who had arrived from Sydney earlier that week under orders from the Bishop to commence the building of a church at Eden (National Library of Australia, http://nla.gov.au/nla.news-article106755242, p. 2).

23 See CL'ANA 0383.

24 Wieden is the fourth "Bezirk" (district) of Vienna.

25 Pauline's uncle, husband of Antonia's sister, Marie Rismondo.

251 • Pauline Clairmont to Ottilia Clairmont

Feb 13.[1] [c. 1874]

My own dearest Tilly.

How can I express all I feel at the sudden & painful loss you have experienced in the loss of your poor Mother! I have still too much in mind the loss of my own poor mother, & know what your kind heart must feel – & so very sudden & unexpected – I at least was prepared & poor Ma died quite unconscious but for you it came like a thunderbolt. & you had not even time to realize that she was ill – & that long dreadful lonely journey at night & in this dreadful cold season – oh my dear child may the Almighty give you strength to bear it all – but you were such a good daughter – & death is so often a release for those who go on before, that in my opinion those left behind are those who are to be pitied.

Aunt also was quite upset by this sudden dreadful news – she sends her best love & hopes you will bear up in the idea of the great duties you have on hand.

What a comfort it would be to you at this time not to be separated from Willy – but also this is denied!

We have hard to times before us just now my dearest sister could I but be with you to comfort you! When you feel able please write a few lines to say now[2] you are – I am so glad that <u>she</u> spent her last Christmas among her children & grandchildren! & with love to Emily[3] please believe me your ever

loving sister
Pauline.

I reserve answering your last letter for another time.

Address: No envelope

Unpublished. Text: M.S., Pf. Coll., CL'ANA 0229

---

1 This letter dates to 1874. The *Wiener Zeitung* of 12 February 1874 recorded the death from inflammation of the lungs ("Lungenentzündung") of Francisca von Pichler, aged 69, on 8 February. Her address was listed as Marokkanergasse 22 (Austrian Newspapers Online, Österreichische Nationalbibliothek [Austrian National Library, http://www.anno.onb.ac.at/cgi-content/anno?apm=0&aid=wrz&datum=18740212&seite=18&zoom=1, p. 18]). Documents in the Clairmont Collection include Mary Claire Bally-Clairmont's family tree of the von Pichler family. According to this genealogical table, Ottilia's mother, Fanny Horstig von Pichler, died in 1874. She was 69 years old. The year 1874 has been written on this letter, possibly by Christoph Clairmont. See also CL'ANA 0275, CL'ANA 0292, CL'ANA 0184, CL'ANA 0130 and CL'ANA 0291.
2 Probably "how".
3 Emily von Hauer.

252 • Wilhelm Gaulis Clairmont to Pauline Clairmont

[11 January 1875]

$^{11}/_1$ 1875

My dear Plin. I hurry to in form you that T. was confined yesterday evening at a quarter to 7 of a fine healthy boy. – the midwife ~~was~~ had been sent for already during the preceeding night – towards morning the $^{10}/_1$ the pains subsided – but towards noon they recommenced steadily increasing till the act took place – we were lucky in getting a very good experienced Madam. Now 1 oclock p.m. both Tilly & the child are progressing very favorably and I hope every thing will go off well. the children are bursting with excitement Wattie wanted to know whether it would be sure and remain a little boy and whether we would keep it or send it away again – both were anxious to know its name – I think it will be Paul.[1] Rec^d yours 8/inst. answer in next now in great hurry

Love to Aunt & Gg.
Yours affectly
WGC

$^{11}/_1$ 1875.

Wattie was to have acknowledged the receipt of his nice presents himself but now that T. is in bed I am afraid it wont do.
Dont we wish you were here now to help us!!

Address: Miss P. Clairmont/ Villa Laughier Via Barbaconna/ San Domenico/ Firenze/Italia.

Unpublished. Text: M.S. Pf. Coll., CL'ANA 0316

---

1 Given the political climate in Austria during the Second World War, it appears that the Clairmont family was keen to prove its origins. In her "Herkunft der Familie Clairmont" ("Origin of the Clairmont Family"), written in the 1930s, Alma Crüwell noted that her brother Paul was born in Vienna and that he attended both school and university there. Alma asserted that neither she nor her siblings were of Jewish origin: "Unser Familienblut stellt sich also als eine starke Mischung guten deutschen, romanischen und englischen Bluts dar und enthält keinen Tropfen semitischen Bluts, wie es böswillige Gerüchte verbreiten wollen. Der brünette Typus, den Paul Clairmont, sein Bruder Walter und ich aufweisen ist vor allem ein immer stark durchschlagendes Erbe der wallonisch-belgischen Rasse, ein Familienzug, der an den letzten Vertreterinnen dieser Familie, zweier in Linz lebenden Damen Ghislain d'Hembyse auch wahrzunehmen ist". Translation provided by Anja Reiner: "Our family blood represents a distinct mixture of good German, Romansh, and English blood and does not contain a drop of Semitic blood, in spite of malicious rumors. The brunette characteristic of Paul Clairmont, his brother Walter and myself is a dominant trait of the Wallonian-Belgian race, a family trait, that can be perceived in the last representatives of this family, two Ghislain d'Hembyse ladies living in Linz" (CL'ANA 0419, unpublished manuscript, Pforzheimer Collection). The "brunette characteristic" refers to the brunette coloring of the three Clairmont siblings. See also CL'ANA 0221.

28 MARCH 1861–24 DECEMBER 1889

The Pforzheimer Collection also has a notarized document dating to 1940 which certified that William Godwin and Mary Clairmont were married in 1801 in London. The Reichsadler (Imperial Eagle seal of the Nazi regime) is visible on the document. There are eleven notarized document copies from the 1930s, some with the Reichsadler stamp, tracing the family's heritage back to the eighteenth century (CL'ANA 0422, unpublished manuscript, Pforzheimer Collection).

253 • Pauline Clairmont to Wilhelm Gaulis Clairmont

Feb 2^d [c. 1875]

Dearest Bill

After I had written to you yesterday I occurred to me that I had not sufficiently impressed on your mind that staying here will be <u>no</u> sacrifice at all if I am sustained by the idea of helping you & doing something for your children. The amount of comfort I c^d have afforded you by being at Nice is very much compared to the assistance 12 fl or more will be to you in the work you have undertaken. And as I said yesterday the comparative lazyness I sh^d indulge in at Nic was very well when I thought I had nothing else to do, but now I feel positive that money is more use to you & that idea is sufficient to me. If we were, either of us in ill health I sh^d say my place was near you but we both enjoying good health & good spirits & courage to work, let us do so, & let me enjoy the consciousness of being of real use to you – & dearest boy let me hear nothing of interest or anything of that kind or else you will spoil all my pleasure.

And above all do not torment yourself with the idea that I am making myself miserable – on the contrary – if the work was 20 times more it w^d be no sacrifice – <u>Nothing</u> I c^d do for you or yours ever c^d be a sacrifice only if you are too proud to accept my years income then I sh^d feel very much discouraged.

I enjoy the idea of work & am proud of being able at my age still to earn so much money Very few people cd do as much.

I shall be very anxious for your answer & very much hurt if you do not accept, always supposing <u>first</u> that the Count[1] renews his offer of my staying here & 2^d that you consider the sum I am able to contribute as <u>more</u> useful than anything I c^d achieve by my personal presence at Nice.

I feel much relieved having told you all this. This is poor Papa's anniversary of his death – you & I we must help each other as much as we can.

Every your's faithfully
PC.

Address: No envelope

Unpublished. Text: M.S., Pf. Coll., CL'ANA 0217

---

1 See CL'ANA 0218.

254 • Alexander Knox to Pauline Clairmont

[9 February 1875]

91 Victoria P.
Westminster
Feb 9/75.

My dear Pauline. I have carefully read over yr. note and inclosures – and I am sure what you want from me is a business opinion, and not fine protestations. Your statement of facts is in many points imperfect – but I fancy I gather from it that Sir Percy F Shelley is at the present – moment intending to publish a life of his grandfather; – and, further, some hitherto unpublished m.s. of his called his "Sermon of Xtianity". Now I would begin by saying that I more than doubt if, commercially speaking – there is the value of one sixpence involved. He, or S, or A, B, C (I mean, the whole world)
has a perfect right to ~~publi~~ write and publish a Life of Godwin, as much as he would have to write a Life of Shakespear. No doubt he has no right – nor has any one – to use papers which are the property of another person – but you would find, I think, in his case that it would be a very hard job, and would require a great outlay of money in Chancery Proceedings to make out that his right lay in the Exors[1] and Administrators of the late Mr Charles Clairmont. – You may be right, or wrong, but the case is surrounded with technical difficulties. As for Godwin's Sermon of Xtianity I, for one would cheerfully pay a considerable sum of money to have nothing to do with the venture. I think you are disquieting yr.self about shadows. But – I cannot write too plainly that I will not in any way mix myself up with family disputes between the Shelley and Clairmont Families – These things are to me intermixed with the most exquisitely painful recollections of my life; and, indeed, you must not expect me to take any part in them. I had not the faintest or remotest idea, until I got yr. note, that anything like the publication you mention was intended – for of late years I know nothing about Shelley and his proceedings – I see him very rarely – once or twice a year – and then in the most formal way. If you think your rights of any account your only plan is to put yr. interests under competent legal safe-guard – but I had rather not advise upon such a matter. I wish you could have written more cheerfully about poor Willy and yourself – but, believe me we all have troubles, and enough.

affectionately yours
A. A. Knox

Address: No envelope

Unpublished. Text: M.S. Pf. Coll., CL'ANA 0200

---

1 Executors.

255 • Pauline Clairmont to Edward John Trelawny

Villa Laugier
10 Via Barbacane
S. Domenico[1]
Florence
June 24. [c. 1875]

Dear Mr Trelawney[2]

My Aunt have been very unwell for some time & is still quite incapable of writing to you to acknowledge the receipt of your packet of letters which she has duly received thro' Maquay[3] She thanks you very much for them, & desires me to say that she will write to you a <u>long letter</u> as soon as ever she can.

Believe me yours very truly
Paola Clairmont

Address: No envelope

Unpublished. Text: M.S. Pf. Coll., CL'ANA 0431

---

1 Claire gave as her address 10 Via Barbacane San Domenico, Firenze, in her letters to Trelawny of 1875.

2 See CL'ANA 0056. In Claire's correspondence with Trelawny, written between 1869 and 1875, she documented her observations of past events concerning Byron and the Shelleys (see *CC* II: 597–633). By 1878, Claire had hoped to sell the Shelley letters she owned, and she sent copies of them to Trelawny whom she believed would help her sell the originals.

3 In his letter to Claire of 17 June 1875, Trelawny confirmed that he had sent the letters to Florence: "My writing now is to remove one of your great wrongs that has been rankling in your mind so long "the letters, the letters! !! they are in Florence at last and you will sleep the sounder: you can have them by sending to the inclosed address 'Messrs. Maquay' I can't read the address, so I inclose it" (*Letters of Edward John Trelawny*, H. Buxton Forman (ed), [London: Forgotten Books, 2013], pp. 248–9).

256 • Pauline Clairmont to Wilhelm Gaulis Clairmont

Put your next letter into one of your official envelopes.[1]   Palazzo Cruciato[2]
27. Feb. [c. 1877][3]

My dearest boy – I began a long letter to you some days ago, but I was in such low spirits, owing to the press of business & new duties in this house that I did not send the letter hoping I should soon get over my troubles & indeed so I did, & feel much better now & am falling more comfortable into harness. It is hard work just now as the cameriere[4] (as I told you before I think) had to go to Livorno & I was left alone here with the dirty old cook & am Reader, secretary, housekeeper, companion, housemaid, ironer, needlewoman in short Jack of all trades, if there are any visits I must do the lady & play on the Piano – All this would do very well, & I do easily if I could only get enough sleep – but these nervous fidgetty old people who cannot sleep, he wont go to bed & I must read to him sometimes till 1 o'clock a m. he being really sleepy & tired & dozing & nodding all the time & starting up again – only like Aunt he won't go to bed. & as the cameriere is not here & sometimes wants his fire lighted at 7 in the morning I must go down stairs & fetch the cook. All this made me very uncomfortable for want of sleep which to me is terrible – He & A[i5] call it laziness as they cannot sleep – because of irritation & illtemper.

I must however not be hard upon him & thank God that I have such excellent nerves (which however A[i] can not forgive – like she could never forgive poor Mama her irreproachable moral conduct.)

My dearest boy for heaven's sake. do not take a dislike to letterwriting what should I do if you dont write to me – & Tilly even less – as I look thro' your last letter of Feb 24 you say you are glad that I & my old gent agree – but that you dont look upon{ink} as lasting. You are quite right there & I have the same impression – but I suppose I should find other situations if I [illeg.] was obliged to leave here. His temper is very bad, & there is a <u>fond</u> of meanness that is very aggravating, besides my health may not be able to stand – as at my time of life I ought to have no moral worry & not too much fatigue. But however sufficient for the day is the evil thereof – & I will therefore communicate to you a little hope of future happiness that will also please you – Of course I have spoken to ~~you~~ M[r] G.[6] of you & he asked all sorts of questions about you & me & Aunt. He went to see A[i] once or twice & asked her to dinner – but she did not come as it is too far out in the country.

We will probably stay here till the 1st of May & then go to Leghorn – we are here about a mile out of town a pleasant walk when there is no Northwind & no dirt. We have a spare room – to the north it is true but there is a stove & one might make a fire – there are double doors & double windows so it can be made comfortable & M[r] G. said that if you could come here & stay a week or 10 days he would be very happy to make your acquaintance & talk German with you which he is studying hard now – with a very pretty German teacher & I sit by to chaperone. He is always sorry when he has been in a rage & spiteful & tries to make up for it afterwards – & he very soon found out that the greatest pleasure he could give me would be to have you here. If it was more convenient to come when we are at Leghorn, there is <u>there</u> equally a spare room ~~bed~~ for you. Now my dear boy think it over well & write soon what you think & <u>when</u> you could come – but I am sorry very sorry you could not bring dear little Walter as he does not like children never having had any himself.

Would it not be delightful if you could come & stay with me – Mr Silsbee[7] is with Aunt & she is quite happy & delighted I am not there to watch her funny ways with men – when she plays the <u>Gurli</u>, or the imbecile which she does to perfection. I shall expect your next letter with impatience as you do not want the 200 fl I will exchange them & put them in the saving bank. & all that you say about money matters – sta molto bene[8] – Yes my dear boy altho I like Italy very much Germany is also beautiful & here I am quite alone – so I certainly mean at all events to make a trial – but where is there such a kind generous & gentle brother as you are & such a kind sister as T. & shall I never teach your children to love me (particularly if poor little G.[9] should not live, which sometimes I have serious fears about.) Doctor Bottare Aunt's present doctor, knowing of course nothing of the family circumstances said that G. could not live as she was scrofulous & it would attack the chest when she left off growing[10] – she is such a serious melancholy child & her education is so unfavorable that she cannot be any thing but unhappy – & for her it would be a hundred times better to die than enter upon a life full of troubles – having no name no health no talent, & nothing but bad habits & absurd ideas in her head.

However,[11] let us hope for the best & be resigned to the worst
Write soon my boy when or what arrangements you can make.
And with love to T & the children

believe me your affect
Sister

Address: No envelope

Unpublished. Text: M.S., Pf. Coll., CL'ANA 0218

---

1 Pauline drew a line around these words.
2 The Via del Palazzo Bruciato is a road in Florence, Italy. Claire's letters from 1876 were written from 43 Via Romano.
3 In March 1877, Claire told Emma Taylor that Pauline had taken a new position the previous July. Georgina continued to reside with Claire, who complained of having to do all the housework as well as assist with Georgina's education (*CC* II: 636).
4 Italian: "cameriera" is the feminine form for "maid". "Cameriere" is masculine form for "domestic worker".
5 Abbreviation for Aunt (Claire).
6 Stocking identifies Pauline's employer as M. Gautier (*CC* II: 654). However, in her letter to Claire of 30 June (c. 1877), Pauline identified him as both Mr. Garetier and Mr. Gautier (see CL'ANA 0211).

7 Stocking provides an excellent description of Claire's interactions with Edward Augustus Silsbee (1826–1900), an American-born adventurer who became fascinated with the Shelley circle. Stocking records that Silsbee thought of Shelley as "the Christ of Literature" (*CC* II: 654). Silsbee began visiting Claire and Pauline in Florence, alternatively paying attention to them both; he probably was Pauline's lover in the mid-1870s. His aim was to secure the Shelley papers in Claire's possession and he vied for the attention of both aunt and niece. After Pauline inherited the papers in 1879, she sought a suitable buyer, recording her endeavors in her journal. Stocking records that she may have suggested marriage to Silsbee in exchange for the letters. Hebron and Denlinger affirm: "It is clear from her journals that she [Pauline] did propose marriage to him [Silsbee]. When Silsbee refused – one suspects she sought respectability more for her daughter than for herself – they became, briefly, lovers" (*Shelley's Ghost*, Oxford: Bodleian Library, 2010), p. 170. Pauline did not marry Silsbee nor did he acquire the papers, his inability to pay for them having ended the relationship. See *CC* II: 664–60 and *Shelley's Ghost*, pp. 168–74. Henry James later immortalized the events in his novella, *The Aspen Papers*.
8 Italian for "is very good".
9 Georgina, Pauline's daughter.
10 See CL'ANA 0077.
11 Cross-writing from "However".

257 • Pauline Clairmont to Claire Clairmont

Palazzo Cruciato
Jun 30. [c. 1877]

Dearest Aunt

Thanks for your dear note which I got yesterday along with the one from my friend Caroline.[1] I am very sorry to hear you have had spasms again & would recommend my Bismuth[2] powders or the new form of them – in a liquid state – but the doctors dont seem to know what your complaint really is. One thing is certain & that is that both cold & heat & damp hurt you very much – & as we cannot get away from Florence which is hot & cold & damp occasionally we must endure what cannot be cured.

I should have written to you yesterday but we had some company at dinner which took up a good deal of my time & I did not get to bed till nearly one o clock.

These were two German ladies perfect specimens of opposite types of education & [illeg.] its result – You will say it is my prejudiced eye, my one sided view, my narrow mindedness, my love of opposition, my desire of contradiction that induces me to form judgements without any visible or invisible relation to real facts – but in this case without any coloring of my own no opinion of any sort or kind I could not help seeing facts there they were as big as life personified in these two ladies they were both middleaged, between 30 & forty. One of them (Spinster) prussian reminded me forcibly of a <u>friend of ours</u> Tall, stout with a snowy complexion & teeth & lovely features gave one the impression of a lily in a storm – This handsome woman evidently formed by nature to be the mother of a large family – has studied all the "Ologies" & "Ographies" under the sun – 4 languages, drawing, music, & so overstrained her brain & her nerves that she at times loses all command over them & gives way to such fits of Pride rebellion Anger & passion that she cannot stay in any family; – being poor & obliged to earn her bread – this is an unfortunate circumstance.

She had been Mr Garetiers[3] governess for two years but he could stand no more – & she was sent away then she went to Rome with another family but after two months was sent away again & now is on her way back to Germany to give lessons. She is a most interesting woman to[4] because of her beauty her good moral conduct & her misfortunes. At dinner the conversation was highly interesting on history & antiquity the Rights of man – human & Divine laws – but when they got from Rome to the cause of her leaving it she went off into such gusts of anger – she could not eat any more she ended in crying & leaving the table. I talked of the cat & the weather & the Rhine all the commonplace I could think of & then she got a little better.

The other one is also pretty a nice smiling Dolls face so kind so pleasing so sensible no latin no greek no "ologies" but a happy wife & Mother began her married life with 3 bits of furniture – now has a nice apartment with 5 spare rooms thinks her husband an angel sends her two boys to school – E sa Signora" said the little boy Babbo mi comprato un libretto di cassa di risparmio e ho quasi cento lire!⁵ The Father is a maestro di casa⁶ – & how happy those people are! Comparisons are odious! –

I continue very comfortable only have too little to do. I said to Mr. Gautier I was sorry I had it not in my power to do more for him & he said Cela viendra⁷ I also expressed my regrets at not being so learned as the former companion – but he said that did not matter as at his age he did not want to learn only to be taken care of –

Dearest Aunt I hope the weather will soon change & you will be able to get out & with best love to all

believe me your ever affte
Paule.

Address: No envelope

Unpublished. Text: M.S., Pf. Coll., CL'ANA 0211

---

1 Unidentified. See CL'ANA 0221.
2 James Carlin explains that, in 2011, "bismuth usage in pharmaceuticals included bismuth salicylate (the active ingredient in over-the-counter stomach remedies), and other bismuth medicinal compounds used to treat burns, intestinal disorders, and stomach ulcers in humans and animals" ("Bismuth," *United States Geological Survey Minerals Yearbook – 2011* [US Department of the Interior, 2012], p. 12.1).
3 See CL'ANA 0218.
4 Misspelling for "too".
5 Italian translation: "And you know Missus," said the little boy, "Dad bought me a savings book and I have almost a hundred lire!" (Translation provided by Beatrice Ferrari).
6 Italian for "butler".
7 French for "that will come".

258 • Wilhelm Gaulis Clairmont to Claire Clairmont

29.30.1877[1]

My dear aunt.

I was so very much rejoiced to see your dear hand again, I cannot tell you what pleasure it gave me ; it is very natural that while living with Pauline under one roof you did not write yourself so that a letter from your own hand has become an extreme rarity – I am very sorry to hear that you have been unwell again ; I hope that this ailing, like the cause from which it proceeded – Georgie's inflamed eye – was only temporary and that you are by this time quite restored – I am also sorry that you had besides the trouble of mind so much expense with poor little Georgie it would have been so much better to let her return to Countess Ky.[2]

Of P. I have not heard lately but I believe she is well off in her new home – of Nichof I write nothing because it is unpleasant to tell bad news – I would have answered yr. letter at once but I put it off in accordance with your wish till I knew for certain whether I could send the money or not – I write this from an estate of Baron Sina's which I have to value[3] – he was so rich he inherited £ 7.000 000 from his father 25 years ago and now he died without a son so that the whole of his splendid property goes to his sons in law all as it were strangers one a french man this duke of Castries. – two Greeks – prince Ypsilanti and prince Maurocordato – [4] Till. and the children are well at least I have not heard anything to the contrary and hope to find them well on my return to morrow – the children are all very good and give us both much pleasure little Paul is a most lively intelligent little fellow quite out of the run of the former ones. – I wish you could see them all – I think they would please you – Goodbye dearest best aunt take care of yr health and believe me ever yours

WG. Clairmont

Rappoltenkirchen[5]
29.30.1877.

Address: No envelope

Unpublished. Text: M.S. Pf. Coll., CL'ANA 0315

---

1 Wilhelm recorded the date in this manner. I have placed this letter at the end of the letters from 1877.
2 Georgina was raised for the first seven years of her life in the home of Countess Károlyi in Hungary. Pauline was a governess in the home of Countess Károlyi in Rakičan (see CL'ANA 0340, CL'ANA 0358 and CL'ANA 0208). Stocking notes that she traveled "once or twice a year" to visit Georgina and that she deemed her daughter "unlike" herself (*CC* II: 621). By 1871, Pauline had brought Georgina to Florence where she resided with Claire. Stocking also recounts that Countess Károlyi proposed taking Georgina back to Hungary in 1873, but that Claire would not grant permission.

3 After his return to Vienna in 1874, Walter Clairmont recorded that Wilhelm worked as a "landwirtschaftlicher Berater des Obersthofmarschallamtes" (CL'ANA 0428, p. 2, unpublished manuscript, Pforzheimer Collection). He was an agricultural counselor or consultant. Although Wilhelm's son Paul was born in 1875, Wilhelm registered the birth with the British Consulate in Vienna on 3 January 1881. A record of the birth lists Wilhem's profession as "valuer of estates" (see CL'ANA 0408, unpublished manuscript, Pforzheimer Collection).

4 Baron Simon von Sina or Baron Sinas, (1810–1876). On the death of Baron Simon von Sina's father, George Sinas, the *Annual Register* of 1856 recorded that he was "one of the largest landed prorietors, and one of the richest men, in that part of the world. The deceased is said to have left property to the enormous amount of 40,000,000 fl. (4,000,000l.)" (London: F.& J. Rivington, 1857), p. 256. Helene, Baron Simon von Sina's daughter, married Prince Gregorios Ypsilanti of Greece, while her sister Irene married Prince George Maurocordatos. A third sister, Iphigenia, married Edmond Charles de La Croix, Duke of Castries ("The Hôtel de Castries". Web. 13 May 2015. http://www.developpement-durable.gouv.fr/IMG/pdf/L12003-1_MLETR_depliant_Castries.pdf). In *Reports of the Commissioners of the United States to the International Exhibition Held at Vienna, 1873*, the editor records that Baron Sina displayed "the products of his forests at Baan and Teplieska, and from Simongät he had galls, deciduous and evergreen plants, and logs" (Robert Thurston, (ed.) [Washington: Government Printing Office, 1876], vol I, p. 38).

5 The estate of Baron von Sina, located some 41 kilometers west of Vienna. Today, Reitstall Rappoltenkirchen (a horse riding stable) is located on the grounds of the Schloß Rappoltenkirchen ("Reitstall Rappoltenkirchen". Web. 13 May 2015. http://www.rappoltenkirchen.at/).

259 • Pauline Clairmont to Wilhelm Gaulis Clairmont

[9 June c. 1878]
Florence Whitsunday[1]

Dearest William

I got your letter the day before yesterday – I could not answer it directly, being in the midst of packing to go to the country & we were to have gone tomorrow morning, but today is not at all well & so we shall be detained, surrounded by half packed, gaping trunks & empty drawers. I expect the doctor this evening to decide whether she[2] can bear the journey & if change of air will do her good. I am so truly sorry to hear your affairs are going so badly – but we must have patience & bear privations another year or so, now the peace is settled it is to be hoped things will look up. For my part dear boy I shall be quite content if in July you will send me only 50 fl instead of 150 as I really at present do not want more – I have sold a good many superfluous things & good Mary Dratschmid sold a piece of antique lace for me,[3] which is also a little addition to my income, so that you are quite welcome to keep the 100 fl & <u>not</u> put them down to my credit – because I intend as a little comfort for you – & no loan.
If you send the money to Aunt next month pray direct:
Mrs Mary Jane Clairmont care of <u>Mssrs French &</u> Co <u>Bankers N^r 14 Via Tornabuoni Florence.</u>[4] <u>To be called for.</u> Racomandirt[5] as usual. I have already told them of it & they will keep our letters till I fetch them.
We are going to a villa Michelozzi[6] about 1½ mile out of town, an old medieval place (I dont know how to spell this hard word) up on the hill of Bellosquardo which you may remember was the old convent of San Miniato with a most superb vue over the town;[7] dearest boy – how sorry I am you cannot come there would be a spare room ready for you – but they are all idle hopes & I am sorry to say that I dare say we shall not meet as long as poor Aunt lives. She may drag on a long time yet. I begin to perceive that her excessive ill-temper is much owing to nerves. This last attack has been very severe – For 5 or 6 days she disliked her food slept little & scolded everybody that came near her – then she began to have pains in her loins & in the back & this morning she had a great flow of blood followed by whites – so that I had to put ice on her & laudanum[8] injections upon which she got better, & the scolding ceased – Other women have hysterics, crying fits, & convulsions, but her nervous attacks all fly to the tongue & her brain always having been active she vents her irritation in a most copious, bitter, cutting use of the tongue.[9] You will see by my photo how stout I am getting – my troubles seem to agree with me, & I certainly have been very well the whole winter. because I have left off drinking the red wine which caused all my indigestion – If you have turned grey – in the course of years (which is better than being bald) I have lost my teeth which is much uglier than grey hair.
   Marie Dratschmid says she is surprised how I keep up my spirits & it is a case of Heine's famous "Aber fragt mich nur nicht wie"[10] We must not despond my

dear boy — times will get better soon & as for M⁻ⁿ Werner I think she is a thoroughly honest person there is nothing to fear

The papers I will send in a few days.

Pray[11] give my love to dear Tilly & the dear chicks & Grandpapa[12]

<u>Pray ask my dear nephew Walter</u> to <u>write</u> to <u>me again</u> now when his holidays come on — he will have more time. When I think — good Heavens! <u>Is it possible</u> that I should treat your children like my Aunt treats <u>me</u>! No it is a moral impossibility — but <u>if</u>

I[13] should — pray kick me out of the house at once —

Your own true affte
Sister
Paola

Address: No envelope

Unpublished. Text: M.S. Pf. Coll., CL'ANA 0421, Box 3, bundle g, number 207

---

1 Whitsunday is celebrated seven Sundays after Easter. In 1878, Easter Sunday fell on 21 April. The letter therefore dates to 9 June 1878.
2 Claire.
3 See CL'ANA 0234.
4 The *Handbook for Travellers in Central Italy* documented Via dei Tornabuoni as the address of the banking firm, French and Company. The listing also recorded that French and Company and the firm of Maquay and Hooker (see CL'ANA 0431) had branches "in Rome, at the Baths of Lucca and Pisa, and are agents for the despatch of parcels to England and the United States" (Octavian Blewitt, London: John Murray, 1875), p. xviii. The *Handbook* also names Mr. French of French's Bank as the British Vice-Consul (p. xvi).
5 See CL'ANA 0290.
6 Michelozzo di Bartolommeo (also Michelozzi) (1396–1472), Florentine sculptor and architect. Michelozzo designed and restored villas for the Medici family.
7 The Basilica of San Miniato al Monte, named for St. Minias, a Florentine martyr. The Basilica is located on the hill of Bellosguardo, one of the hills near Florence.
8 Containing opium, it is highly addictive.
9 Pauline cross-wrote the next few lines (until "grey hair") on page 1 of the letter.
10 Heinrich Heine (1797–1856), German poet. The English translation is "but do not ask me how". The line is from Heine's *Buch der Lieder*: Lieder, VIII (Book of Songs, Song VIII), published in 1827. Composers Schumann and Schubert wrote the music to accompany Heine's poetry. Cross writing on page 2 of the letter from "Marie" until "days".
11 Cross-writing on page 3 starts here.
12 Johann von Pichler, Ottilia's father.
13 Cross-writing on page 4 starts here.

260 • Pauline Clairmont to Wilhelm Gaulis Clairmont

Villa Michelozzi
Bellosguardo[1]
Florence
July 1. [c. 1878]

Dearest best William[2]

I got your letter to day including the two dear little notes from the children,[3] sweet little things – you have a great treasure in those dear young souls, all your own – & no selfish gratification old bachelors or old maids can indulge in, comes equal to the sweet faithful trusting love of children. Let us have patience my own dear brother & be thankful for what is given to us. I am glad I had not written to you since our arrival here as now I can give you more details. I will not enter into the painful details of Aunts long illness – she is better now, but she was very uneasy about herself – no one so frightened of death as she is, & saying it was all her exquisite sensibility that made her dread to die, as only unfeeling brutes did not care whether they lived or died.

I think I told you what her illness began with – losses of blood from the womb. The doctor & we all feared a cancer or tumour – ~~but~~ & we had a consultation with one of the first doctors for female diseases, but he pronounced it to be varicose vains in the vagina which occasioned the blood to flow & the subsequent humours. You may imagine what a Sister of Charity I have become in nursing, administring pills powders, frictions with all sorts of waters spirits & pomatums,[4] clisteri,[5] injections etc, cooking besides, letter-writing & book keeping This illness has reduced her very much indeed –

Her nerves are in such a state of irritation for which her only vent is scolding – & I do not know what I should do without a new valuable & rather expensive remedy called <u>Codeina</u>[6] the finest possible extract of opium a little pill at night makes her sleep & be a little calmer next day – Formerly she took 2 a week, but now every day. We are going to stay 3 months June July & August up here but you may as well send all letters to French's bank at <u>14 Via Tornabuoni</u>.[7] About Mr Luccam,[8] I can not tell you much – I saw him sometimes at Baden He is a cousin of those Luccams that lived in the Schottenhof,[9] one of which married a painter but I have forgotten her name, & I think it was there I first saw him He had some friends at Baden & one summer he used to come out there every sunday & once or twice, he came to see us –. poor Mama was still alive but you know her dislike to strangers. I dont think she ever saw him – & then I lost sight of him. He was, or is very clever witty & sharp – but being a plain little man, I believe he had not so much success in ladies society as he might have had – had he been handsome. You know I have <u>never</u> had any chance of cultivating mens'[10] society – neither as a governess nor with Mama nor with Aunt; I think your best plan would be to cultivate his cousins the painter's wife & get her to recommend you to Mr Luccam – She is clever & ambitious & fond of men's society & has always kept her humbler sister Maria in the background – I have tried in vain to remember the name of that Miss Luccam that married the painter – I have lost all memory for names, tho' not for other things it begins with a D. & she lives somewhere near the old Postoffice. I think she could be of more use than I could in this matter, as I saw little of Mʳ L He was very friendly & agreeable. & showed evidence with to see more of me – but as I said before, I had no opportunity of cultivating as the only similarity that ever existed between Mama & Claire was their endeavours to cut me off from society – when living with them – They had different motives it is true, but the result was the same.[11]

Pray dear boy – do not think anything about the 100 fl I assure you I do not want the money. Claire envies every pair of gloves I wear.[12]

Address: No envelope

Unpublished. Text: M.S., Pf. Coll., CL'ANA 0226

---

1 See CL'ANA 0421, Box 3, bundle g, number 207.
2 The information provided in the letter dates it to 1878, the year before Claire's death.
3 Walter and Alma Clairmont.
4 Pomatum: another word for pomade (a scented ointment applied to the hair or scalp).
5 "Clistere" is the Italian word for "enema". The plural form is "clisteri".
6 Italian for Codeine. Codeine is an opiate taken to reduce pain. The regular use of codeine can lead to a dependency on the medication (U.S. National Library of Medicine. Web. 2 May 2015. http://www.nlm.nih.gov).
7 The bank's address is underlined in blue pencil.
8 See CL'ANA 0300.
9 The Schottenhof is located 14 kilometers outside of Vienna. Today, the property is used for educational purposes ("Schottenhof". Web. 2 May 2015. http://www.schottenhof.at/).
10 The words "never" and "cultivating mens'" are underlined in blue pencil and a blue question mark has been inserted next to the word "mens'".
11 Pauline probably believed that Antonia wanted to protect Pauline's virtue. Pauline may have believed that Claire was jealous of her.
12 These last two lines were cross-written on the first page of the letter.

261 • Pauline Clairmont to Miss Taylor

Florence Septb 5. [c. 1878]

Dear Miss Taylor[1]

Altho' I have not the pleasure of knowing Mr Trelawney personally I write a few lines to thank him most sincerely for his kind attention to my poor Aunt.
The enclosed letter is her dictation & you may perceive how much altered she is or she would have said more – she was so very glad when she got the money Mr T. so kindly sent her. What I feel to see her suffer such severe pain at her age I cannot describe – neuralgia is so painful & there are so few remedies, indeed none that will cure – only some that relieve.[2]
It is cruel – she says so many times – to have to suffer such pain – I had much rather die at once – & so often do the words in Trelawney's book on his Greek campaign come to my mind that Ld Byron said in his last illness – "Not Death do I dread – but long sufferings".[3] – How long this dreadful illness will last no one can tell – We have had two consultations with some of the most eminent medical men here & their opinion was that there was no real danger from illness but – he said – there is no more oil in the lamp. When she is free from pain her mind recurs to scenes of her youth & she shows a wonderful memory of names places & events & she often recalls Trelawney & his deeds & manner & words so that he seems quite an old friend to me – & sometimes, she so longs to go back to England & her mind wanders back to sweet English Country scenes – & then to Pisa & Leghorn in the year 1822 when the dreadful catastrophe of Shelley's death happened[4] – then I feel glad I came to stay with her & nurse her for who would take any interest in events of half a century ago! I thought you would like to hear these details but have not told Aunt I was writing to you, as she of course does not think that she is in any real danger.
With kind regards to Mr Trelawney believe me

your's very afftely
Paola Clairmont

Address: No envelope

Unpublished. Text: M.S. Pf. Coll., CL'ANA 0432

---

1 William Michael Rossetti explained that "the lady who kept house" for Trelawny was "Miss Emma Taylor, currently termed his niece: this however was only a phrase adopted for convenience sake, as there was no blood-relationship" (*Some Reminiscences of William Michael Rossetti*, New York: Charles Scribner's Sons, 1906), vol II, p. 373.
2 Nerve damage, often caused by diabetes, shingles, or multiple sclerosis (www.healthline.com).
3 In his *Recollections of the Last Days of Shelley and Byron* (1858), Trelawny described both Byron's and Shelley's deaths. He quoted Thomas Gordon who wrote of Byron in his *History of the Greek Revolution* (1832), "His health declined, and we cannot be surprised, considering what he had suffered, and was daily suffering, from the deceptions practised upon him" (Boston: Ticknor

and Fields, 1853), p. 234. In Trelawny's *Adventures of a Younger Son* (1831), he cited directly from Byron's *The Corsair* (1814): "No dread of death, if with us die our foes,/ Save that it seems even duller than repose; / Come when it will, we snatch the life of life;/ When lost – what recks it – by disease or strife?" (London: T. Fisher Unwin, 1890), p. 280.

4 By October 1821, Percy and Mary had moved to Pisa where Byron joined them. Edward and Jane Williams were also in Pisa, as was Teresa Guiccioli, Byron's lover, and Thomas Medwin, Shelley's cousin and author of *The Life of Percy Bysshe Shelley* (1847). Claire was in Florence, angered by the fact that the Shelleys were consorting with Guiccioli and Byron. By 1822, Trelawny arrived in Pisa and Claire joined the circle in April; thus, the Pisan Circle was complete. By March 1822, Mary was pregnant again. But the excitement of the Pisan sojourn soon took a fateful turn. In April 1822, Allegra Byron died, leaving Claire bereft. Then, on June 16, Mary miscarried. On July 1, Percy and Edward Williams sailed to visit the Hunts, who were in Leghorn. On Percy's return voyage to Casa Magni (where the Shelleys and the Williamses had been living since April), he and Williams were caught in a storm, their ship capsized, and both men drowned. Mary's letters to Maria Gisborne written shortly after Percy's death are particularly poignant. See *LMWS*, volume I.

262 • Wilhelm Gaulis Clairmont to Claire Clairmont

[22 December 1878]

My dearest aunt.

Christmas is approaching and affords me a welcome opportunity of writing to you, for I confess with great regret that I have fallen off greatly in my good quality as correspondent so that it needs an outward motive to drive me to letter writing – but I hope dear aunt you will not draw disadvantageous conclusions from my remissness in correspondence on my affections – those are the same as ever they were – but care and anxiety of all kinds generally oppress my mind, so that I am not in a fit state for letter writing for who would like to receive a doleful lamentable epistle? I rejoice to say that with reference to yourself at least we have reason to congratulate both you & ourselves – the last letter we had from Plin was about 5. or 6 weeks back and I was excessively relieved to hear that you had got over the frightful illness from which you had suffered so long. of course we cannot expect to hear of your complete recovery so soon such a heavy trial and especially at your time of life takes a long time to get over; you will perhaps suffer under the consequences of this severe affliction ~~for~~ the whole winter yet – but it is an enormous consolation for us, to think that you have got over the worst and are on the way of recovery. With reference to ourselves I do not want to mention unpleasant subjects, thank Heaven I have one theme in which there is not the slightest discord – I mean my wife & children – the latter you would find very much altered – Walter is a big boy, tolerably goodlooking but not so handsome as I thought him as a child, but he has a frank and good natured expression of countenance together with a certain mildness & gentleness of manners which makes him friends everywhere – In point of ability he is not brilliant but a fair average – his ambition is perhaps only moderate but his conscientiousness, ~~tis~~, for his tender age strikingly powerful, he has consequently a very steady application to his studies – He commenced the 1<u>st</u> latin school on the 15<u>th</u> of Septbr. last and passed his examinations very well his new teachers <u>all</u> speak very highly of him[1] – Alma[2] will I think be handsome she is very dark and promises to be most like my sister Emy. in character she is very different from Walter – she is most talented in every respect especially in intellectual perception – but she is a little lazy. her inclinations run towards reading & studying; manual accomplishments or household concerns are a horror to her she will sit a whole evening over a book lost to and for every thing about her. Tilly complains that she cannot even dress herself yet and is utterly useless in attending little Paul while dear Walter waits and attends on him with truly maternal care and also aptitude – Alma has the very best heart and very warm affections but true to the Hembyze nature it lies deep and does not show on the surface besides she is shy, reserved and prone to occupy herself with a book hence no one appreciates her really excellent heart and she makes comparatively no friends – neither among her associates nor her superiors – Her manifestations of affection towards me with whom she has no reserve are truly touching. Paul is an impertinent little scamp. – in appearance he is decidedly the plainest of the three but I think he will prove the cleverest. he has not so much of the Hembycze type as Wattie & Alma but still he is more like me than like Tilly (as I believe all the children are). In consequence of his continued infirmity he is a good deal of a spoilt child – he has a good heart, but he is by far not so soft and impressionable as the other too.[3] he shows symptoms of a great deal of reflection and spirit. his grandpapa he domineers completely – and it is truly ludicrous what cunning this little 3 yr old child displays. Mr P.[4] is extremely fond him, when Paul has a wish he is sly enough never to utter it in public before us because he knows he would meet with a rebuke – he waits till Grandpa goes to his room follows him there, climbs up his knee, meets him eye to eye, shakes his little raised finger to his face, and assures Grdp. that in the most solemn manner that he could not love him any more unless he brought him chestnuts or lolypops or anything else that he may desire – Grandpa is so awed that he never dares to disobey. of course spoiling the child to an awful extent – In point of health Paul is better at least this is the first winter that did not bring on a violent relapse. but of course it may come yet. –

Tilly is the same as you know her – a true pattern of a mother and an excellent wife – Like all women she is a little trying when her hysterical fits come on, but those she cant help & as I often tell her in joke if it were not for that one thing she would be a complete angel whom I could not approach otherwise than on my knees and as this mode of locomotion would in the long run also involve a considerable degree of discomfort its better as it is – Now goodbye dearest aunt I wish you and Pauline & Georgie a very merry Christmas and many many returns of it and believe me ever

yrs affectly.
Willy.

Csaba[5] 22.12: 1878.

I write this from the estate of a Count Toni Appony who just married Princess Mary Montenuovo a charming creature of 19. grand daughter of Empress Maria Louisa.[6]

Address: Briefe [illeg.] an aunt Claire über die Kinder 1878/aufgehoben[7]

Unpublished. Text: M.S. Pf. Coll., CL'ANA 0314

---

1 Walter Clairmont attended the Franz Josef Gymnasium in Vienna. He studied Chemistry at the University in Basel where he also earned his doctorate (CL'ANA 0428, unpublished manuscript, Pforzheimer Collection).
2 Alma Crüwell. See CL'ANA 0316 for Alma's explanation of her dark coloring.
3 Wilhelm's spelling for "two".
4 Johann von Pichler. He would die in 1892. His death notice in the *Wiener Zeitung* recorded his death on 24 February 1892 at the age of 92 years (number 49, page 10). His address was given as

Reisnerstrasse 40. He died of "Herzlähmung" (heart paralysis). See CL'ANA 0421, Box 3, bundle g, number 185.
5 Békéscsaba, Hungary. The town is about 453 kilometers south-east of Vienna.
6 Archduchess Marie Louise (1817–1847) was the second wife of Napoléon I and therefore Empress of France. She later became the Duchess of Parma. She married Count von Neipperg after Napoléon's death and then, after von Neipperg's death, she married Charles, Count de Bombelles (The Editors of Encyclopaedia Britannica. "Marie-Louise". *Encyclopaedia Britannica Online*. Encyclopaedia Britannica Inc., n.d. Web. 15 May 2015. http://www.britannica.com/EBchecked/topic/365097/Marie-Louise). Her son with Count von Neipperig, William, Prince of Montenuovo, was the father of Marie who married Count Apponyi. See also CL'ANA 0295.
7 The envelope has German words written on it. Translation: "Letters from [illeg.] to aunt Claire about the children 1878/preserved".

263 • Pauline Clairmont to Wilhelm Gaulis Clairmont

[c. 1878]¹

there is one box full of crockery & glass. One box full of kitchen utensils a bronze tea urn & a bronze clock of Greil² a very good one. one box full of linen & books. All these things may be useful to you & you had better use them instead of letting them rot. One box I should like to reserve to myself – an old sea chest. containing trashy old things but of value to me. Old books old papers – odds & ends – those I wish to be left untouched. In one box there is a little wooden case containing a small sowing machine. If you could when you return to Baden, I mean if you like to take all these things away & come upon the sowing machine & send it me as roba usata³ or second hand, I should be very glad of it.

Now dear boy, do not forget that all your letters coming here are fished up by Aunt & pray do not say anything of that dirty Pest affair. She would lay hold & publish it then & there – & rejoice in my ruin.

I know what the <u>zweiter Satz</u>⁴ is – they would not be bothered borrowing money – they would sell the house as you say over my head – & I will allow no such thing – in some way I must get {ink} out of it. Aunt was advising me yesterday to take G.⁵ to Australia to marry her there & that seems to me a very good plan. For there no one will ask any questions about birth or money.

If you have anything particular to say write to Brini the banker 4 Via Rondinelli – But pray write all your letters so that she may see them.⁶

She never goes to the Banker herself besides they would not give her any letter addressed to me.

I think I will write to Mary Dr.⁷ about the lace.

Now dear Bill, I have worried you enough – your poor eyes must be tired reading as mine are writing so with best love to all believe me your ever affec

Paule.

I dont mind Aunt hearing about the changing hand of the boxes – only the Pest affair you must not mention on any account.⁸

Address: No envelope

Unpublished. Text: M.S., Pf. Coll., CL'ANA 0234

---

1 This letter is a fragment. There is an orange line drawn around the first paragraph, which ends with "I should be very glad of it". Context suggests Pauline wrote it to Wilhelm when she was living with Claire in Florence.
2 Probably the French clockmaker, Griel and Morterea.
3 Italian for "used goods".
4 German for "second rate".
5 Georgina.
6 Octavian Blewitt in *A Handbook for Travellers in Central Italy* provides a list of Florentine bankers. Among them, "Brini, Via Rondinelli" (London: John Murray, 1874), p. xviii.
7 Mary Dratschmid. See CL'ANA 0421, Box 3, bundle g, number 207.
8 This final sentence was cross-written on the second page.

264 • Pauline Clairmont to Miss Taylor

Florence Mch 23^d [c. 1879]
43 Via Romana

Dear Miss Taylor

About a fortnight ago I wrote to you a long letter by poor Aunt's desire asking news of her old friend Trelawney; & now I have to give you the sad tiding that she is no more. She expired on the 19th most calmly without agony nor suffering nor previous illness – which was a blessing for her as she so feared death. She is one of the last, as Mr Trelawney says in one of his many interesting letters of the Pisa society of 1821.[1] I hope to hear from you soon & also how Mr Trelawney is & pray tell him how happy I should be if he sent me his photograph If I could afford it I should take a trip at once to England where I have not been since 1862.

I feel quite lonely now since poor Aunt's death, I seem to have nothing to do but I expect my brother to come & stay with me

Believe me yours very cordially
Paola Clairmont

Address: No envelope

Unpublished. Text: M.S. Pf. Coll., CL'ANA 0433

---

1 See CL'ANA 0432.

28 MARCH 1861–24 DECEMBER 1889

265 • Pauline Clairmont to Miss Taylor

Florence April 25 [c. 1879]
43 Via Romana

Dear Miss Taylor

I thank you & Mr Trelawny for your kind sympathy as indeed I have suffered much the last 9 years of my life that I have spent in Florence – & as the rude spirits of youth are curbed with years, one values sympathy & friendship more. Pray tell Mr T. that I was just now reading his Adventures of a younger son,[1] which was one of my dear Father's favorite books & I find in it many an echo of what I was in my youth – & many an energetic cry against tyranny – so dear to weak & ignoble minds – I am thankful I am poor – better that, than the meanness & the love of despotism that money inevitably produces – À propos of money, I must tell you that Aunt left 2 wills – one open in her drawer (which most likely she thought I would be sure to look at which I never did) in which she left me everything & another one secretly made by which she leaves all to my brother & only 1/5 to me.[2] Fortunately I served & nursed her for 9 years not for interest but for Christian Charity & human kindness – but human ingratitude became evident. She left everything here in the hands of an Executor saying no respect would be paid after her death (textual in her will) & verbally she said, she would be kicked into a ditch like a dog – Query? Did she feel she did not deserve respect? & would she have been capable of kicking a dead relative into a ditch?
– I may say without vanity that all my friends here have admired my devotion & attention to my Aunt during 9 long years & that I do not deserve any of the insinuations she made against me – I tell you all this to explain why I cannot at present send Mr T.'s letters – He has a moral & legal right to have them & if I can manage it – he shall have them. I could tell you many more incidents & psychological observations – but you would simply smile & say – Excuse me if I take you for mad. As soon as these testamentary proceedings are at an end I will write again – I shall remain here all the summer & if I can go to England I shall be most happy to come & see you – & with best love & admiration to M^r T.

believe me yours
very sincerely
Paola Clairmont

Address: No envelope

Unpublished. Text: M.S. Pf. Coll., CL'ANA 0434

---

1 *Adventures of a Younger Son* (1831).
2 The second will has not been found. Claire instructed Cini to purchase shares with the money she hoped to earn from the sale of the Shelley letters so that Pauline could live off the interest. Claire wanted Georgina to inherit the capital after Pauline's death.

266 • Pauline Clairmont to Wilhelm Gaulis Clairmont

Sz.[1] Mch 18. [after 1885]

Dearest William

This afternoon I got yr letter & understand it all, & am quite einverstanden.[2] I beg you to have the annuity deed prepared & also the will. As to the latter I have no observation to make for you know that I wish you to be the heir of all & everything I possess.[3] If you think it necessary to send me the will you must send it to Hostiz[4] but if not I will sign it when I come to Vienna. But if you think it advisable – send it to Hostiz only tell me if it must be legalized & signed before witnesses.

I have several things more to say – Do you not think it w^d be advisable to sell the Egyptians[5] & buy Steuerfreie Rente[6] & make up the 1000 revenue fl with the proceeds of the Egyptians, the Koll money[7] & the 250 Leibrente?[8]

If then in case of an accident of the taxgatherer pouncing upon me I c^d say boldly There are my Steuerfreie bonds – from there I derive my income – go & look at them, & I c^d give the Doctor the same information and cut him short. (I trust no slave)

I think that c^d be safely & easily done, as my name is not on the house, (a real comfort) & as you have thought of selling the Egyptians on acc^t of the couvertirung.[9] The Koll money is 420 a year

The Leibrente   – 250
                 ─────
                  670

& I sh^d think the revenue of the Egyptians turned into Steurefrei Rente w^d make up the 1000 fl. More I do not want – I have always told you so.

I began my letter by saying that I agreed to the preparing of the annuity deed – but in thinking of this subject the latter plan occured to me.

In this case you w^d at my death have only to pay legacy tax on Koll money & the capital of the Egyptians – it w^d be a good deal at 8% - but then you w^d be relieved of the heavy annuity of 750 fl & I c^d say to any wretch that tried to frighten me – about my not paying taxes, there are my bonds – look at them & hold yr tongue.

The doctor said last year already (on the chance of hitting the truth/ Sie wissen gar nicht was das Leben kostet Sie zalen ja keine Steuer[10]– I recollected the Koll papers & said – ich habe steuerfreie Rente[11]] – & he said (again haphazard) aber doch nicht alles steuerfrei.[12] Now if I had my 1000 fl all Staatsrente[13] & y^r 250 Leibrente[14] I shd give him as smart an answer as he deserved he is as curious as an old woman.

Another thing I wanted to ask – Must we take any legal steps about Claire's legacy to me of 250?[15] As you said in yr letter before last that the will is there & they might stir it up – Let us be safe of that monster of iniquity the law. I am very tiresome dear W. with all my ifs & ands but I wish to do what I can to make things advantageous to you – Now I also understand that you have paid my tax for the 250 from Claire – I cd not make out what you meant by

Pauschaltaxe[16] but now I understand it all Dearest W. you are doing too much for me – & I wont have it you slave & work only for others & all these years you paid the Gratz saving bank & I had the capital in my pocket – no dearest boy that cannot go on so anymore – I feel like an idle goodfornothing & help to fleece you.

I know there are difficulties in selling the Egyptians therefore perhaps we shall have to wait a little.

Now I have reflected the whole evening on this annuity deed & if it is any advantage to you we will have it done.

I can only repeat that my object is to relieve you of the legacy tax after my death. As I understand it you would then not have to pay any tax of that sum that was p named in the annuity as capital (13000 fl but you w^d have to pay for the Koll money?

It is all very difficult to combine. What I said about selling the Egyptians & buying Steuerfreie would make it very safe for me but then you w^d have to pay legacy taxes on the Koll money & on the Egyptian money (say 5000) that w^d be 15,000 fl as 8% makes a heavy sum.

But suppose the tax off. did come down on me, how dreadful if all was not square, & they might go into the matter & I might have damages to pay no end. Of course everybody here from the Countess down have asked me how much income I have & I have always said 1000 fl that was before the Koll money came in.

Now they know that I have 1400 & I still think that it will be bad to have an amount of Steuerfreie Rente to show up.

Suppose we dont go to law about it at all. Suppose I say I have 10,000 (Koll money) Steuerfreie & perhaps 5000 more Steuerfreie that gives me an income of 600 fl. & for the rest I am dependant on my brother's generosity he makes me a present when he can. I think that w^d be the best thing to do, for when I come to look things closely in the annuity plan there is not only the legalization of 80 fl, but as the annuity does not comprise my whole fortune you will afterall have legacy tax to pay. – There is no getting out of it – un vrai cercle vicieux[17] I have got so tired pondering these questions – I have been nearly 3 hours writing these few pages I shall expect another letter from you – shall we leave the law alone shall we make the annuity – I have a good mind to say I have given away all my money except 600 fl income – only nobody w^d believe me – can you sell the Egyptians? Shall we leave it all till I come in May?

You[18] will say like Mr. Peacock[19] Heaven help one if one had business to do with women

yrs ever
PC

Address: No envelope

Unpublished. Text: M.S., Pf. Coll., CL'ANA 0222

1 Unidentified.
2 German for "in agreement" or "content".
3 As Georgina died on 21 February 1885, Pauline decided to leave all her money to Wilhelm and his family. Georgina's death certificate, recorded in Italian and issued in Florence, stated that she was a 21 year old, unmarried woman. Her name was recorded as "Giovanna Maria Giorgina Hanghegyi," and her occupation was noted as "donna da casa" (a woman who stayed at home). The document confirmed that she was born in Pest and a citizen of Austria-Hungary. It listed her parents as unknown. On 5 May 1885, the Austro-Hungarian consul in Florence certified her death certificate (CL'ANA 0318, unpublished manuscript, Pforzheimer Collection).
4 Hostiz is located in Lower-Austria (Niederösterreich) near Rabenstein, some 84 kilometers west of Vienna. Hostiz could also have referred to a person (unidentified).
5 *The Fortnightly Review* of 1889 includes an article called "The Spoliation of the Egyptian Bond Holders" in which the author (the anonymous J.R.) discusses the Egyptian Five per Cent, bonds which were issued in 1876. Between 1876 and 1880, the bonds fluctuated enormously. J.R. believes that the Egyptian bondholder "is neither more iniquitous nor more disinterested than any other investor. He placed his money at high rates . . . oblivious or careless of the fact that high interest means proportionate risk, and he endeavours to make the best of the by no means bad bargain he has made" (Frank Harris (ed.) [London: Chapman and Hall, 1889], vol. xlv, p. 874).
6 German for "tax free pension or annuity".
7 Possibly Pauline's abbreviation for Kölner Mark (the Cologne mark).
8 German for "life annuity".
9 Pauline created a German noun from the English word, "Coverture". The German ending, "ung," identifies a word as a noun. In English, the noun "Coverture" refers to the status of a married woman whose property and person her husband legally controlled.
10 German for "You do not even know how much life costs. You do not pay taxes".
11 German for "I have tax-free pension/annuity/income".
12 German for "But not everything tax-free".
13 German for "Federal security" or "state retirement pension".
14 German for "life annuity".
15 In her will, Claire left Pauline twenty-five bonds from the Trieste Municipality in addition to the Shelley papers. She wanted Pauline to have the interest from the bonds, but not the capital, which she left to Georgina after Pauline's death. Claire also left 1,200 lire to pay for her own funeral expenses (*CC* II: 661–2).
16 German for a "general tax".
17 French for "a real vicious circle".
18 This final sentence and the signature were written in pencil.
19 Thomas Love Peacock (1785–1866), friend of the Shelleys and Claire and author of *Nightmare Abbey* and *Melincourt*. He published the "Memoirs of Percy Bysshe Shelley" in *Fraser's Magazine* (1858–61) in which, Sunstein notes, he altered many aspects of the Shelleys' lives (p. 391). He also proposed marriage to Claire as well as to Pauline. On 5 June 1856, Claire reminded Antonia that Pauline would be living on 1,200 pounds a year had she married Peacock (*CC* II: 551).

267 • Pauline Clairmont to Wilhelm Gaulis Clairmont

Sz. Ap. 16. [after 1885]

Dearest William

I put off writing as I understand you were not at home. Now I think you must have returned. Your last concert of which you send me the program must have been charming & I am glad that the popular concerts so <u>long opposed</u> in Vienna at last assert themselves. Also the Septuor[1] you must have enjoyed & the very next Sunday I played it (duet) with Mr Corrompai [2]who really plays very well is very fond of music & has a very good piano

Please tell Walter I have not sent him so many papers lately as c^d I. was away but now he will get some more. The family P. have settled to spend the summer months at Reichenau Payerbach[3] & I wish very much to go & see them there. & will combine my trip there according to Caroline's[4] proceedings. I shall be very glad to spend a month with her either before or after her Mother's visit. And remember that if T. takes the journey (of which she was disappointed thro' her sister's death) later on in the autumn I will come & stay with Paul in Septb.[5] Tell T. that I got her card only yesterday 15th & it was 5 days on the way as the Vienna postmark was <u>10th</u> She seems still in a great flurry & must miss Alma very much I hope she will soon get back home. Fearing that T. had not time to talk to Caroline – I wrote to her directly. perhaps <u>you</u> c^d talk it over with Caroline About the money I am glad to see how much I have at my banker's. & shall be glad to have <u>50 fl. 200 fl I mean to give to Walter</u> for his <u>English journey –</u> which plan I hope has not been dropped. Have you any ideas for him for next year?

I like your idea of the Méridionaux[6] – I think they will answer – but the Egypt. [7]were not a bad spec[8] either. Goodby dear Bill thanks for paying my bill at [illeg.]. I hope to play[9] something to you when I come to Vienna my old fingers are not so stiff as I feared.

Ever yrs
PC.

Address: No envelope

Unpublished. Text: M.S., Pf. Coll., CL'ANA 0221

---

1 Pauline referred perhaps to Camille Saint-Saëns' "Septuor, Op. 65", which debuted in 1881.
2 Unidentified.
3 Possibly the Palffy family. Payerbach is a municipality in Austria. The towns of Payerbach and Reichenau an der Rax are located some 93 kilometers south of Vienna. Reichenau an der Rax is located beside the Rax mountains and was a famous nineteenth-century resort.
4 Unidentified. See CL'ANA 0211.
5 Wilhelm and Ottilia's son, Johann Paul, was born in 1875. His first wife, Alexine Clairmont, died in 1920 at the age of 36 (see her death announcement in the *Neue Freie Presse Morgenblatt* of 30 March 1920. Austrian Newspapers Online, Österreichische Nationalbibliothek [Austrian National

Library http://anno.onb.ac.at/cgi-content/anno?apm=0&aid=nfp&datum=19200330&seite=13& zoom=2, p. 13]). The death announcement refers to Alexine as a "Universitätsprofessorsgattin" (university professor's wife) and it records that she died on 27 March 1920 in Zurich, Switzerland, after a long illness. Paul Clairmont is identified as "Prof. Dr. Paul Clairmont". Paul later married Emmy Koller (1893–1986) in Zurich on 7 July 1921 and they had two children, Mary Claire and Christoph.

6 *The Economist, Weekly Commercial Times, Bankers' Gazette and Railway Monitor* (London: The Economist, 1893, vol. li, p. ii) identified the Meridional Railways of Italy as a company engaged in business. The "Report of the Board of Directors of the Meridional Railways of Italy" published in *The Economist* of 16 July 1892 confirmed that "the results of the year 1891 may be looked on as satisfactory" (vol. l, p. 931). The term "Méridionaux" probably indicated shares in the Meridional Railways.

7 See CL'ANA 0222.

8 Possibly spec or spea. "Spec" could be the shortened form of "speculation".

9 On the piano. Pauline was an accomplished pianist. See note 11, CL'ANA 0405 and CL'ANA 0210.

268 • Pauline Clairmont to Alma Clairmont[1]

Zdislowitz[2] July 20 [c. 1887]
Post Zdounek[3]
Mähren.[4]

Dearest Alma

I was so surprised to get a letter from you, it quite took my breath away & I was very glad to see (after I had recovered myself) that you have not forgotten me. I am very sorry you had such bad weather on your trip in the mountains, but here it is the same & they say that the oldest people dont remember such an abominable month of July, But I like to hear such patriotic excuses – it shows the esprit de corps of the inhabitants in trying to make out an every day case as an exception. However the country is not poor in fruit & we have had strawberries in abundance cherries ditto eaten off the tree a whole large cherry tree is sold here for 20 x[5] (the fruit only) melons prodigious (not to be compared to the persian melon however) & as for rhaspberries white & red they are endless – & one tree we have here that grow gooseberries & currants on the same stem.

We breakfast at 8. That is breakfast comes on the table at that hour & I make the tea – at that early hour only the piano teacher & 2 gentlemen come in to breakfast. C:t Dubsky[6] the master of the house takes only fruit & cold milk at that hour. All the others come in later. At 10 I play on the piano with the young ladies at 11 $1/2$ I give an English lesson to young Ct Dubsky the son of the house just Walter's age – at 1 we go to bathe & at 2 we dine. I am surprised to hear that you liked Olmütz[7] – I thought it a very dreary place – it was a fortress at that time & just after the revolution of 48 I went there with my dear Father the Court[8] had taken refuge there & I had a great many lessons to give I was there the whole winter & we lived in a very pretty little loding[9] near the gate & heard the music every day. But it was a sad break up of all our family – Willy your Papa went to England & my sister also – she married the year after,[10] & my poor Father died the year after that, & so the world goes round & round & is always the same – only altering the fashions a little

I only wish I cd come back after 2 hundred years to see what will be the fashion then – not only the fashion of dress.

Please tell your Ma that I got her letter last night – & the spirit moved me much to write to her immediately – you know my dears that I love you all tho' we dont always have the same way of thinking – but if one does not loose one's temper, argument is very refreshing – but in one thing M.[11] & I. are perfectly like – love becomes warmer & judgement more generous when we think a friend is suffering.

So the idea grieves me much that poor Paul[12] is ill again that your stay at Pl. was spoiled by rain – & that Caroline's[13] children are also in danger – Do you see now why married women & mothers stand deservedly in higher esteem than single ones.

Goodbye my dear give my love to Dora, Stevy & Irma[14] – & in two or three years when you write again tell me if any of you are married.

Yrs ever
PC.

Address: No envelope

Unpublished. Text: M.S., Pf. Coll., CL'ANA 0230

---

1 Alma (later Crüwell) was the daughter of Wilhelm and Ottilia.
2 Pauline incorrectly spelled Zdislavice, a town in the Czech Republic today, 154 kilometers from Lysice (see note 6).
3 Possibly Zdaunek. *A Gazetteer of the World* from described Zdaunek as "a town of Austria, in Moravia, in the regency of Brunn . . . WNW of Ungarisch-Hradisch. Pop. in 1834, 937" (Royal Geographical Society [Edinburgh, Fullarton & Co, 1859], vol. 7, p. 626). Brünn is the German name for the Czech city of Brno. Hradisch is known today as Uherské Hradiště and is also located in the Czech Republic. It is located 150 kilometers north of Vienna and 77 kilometers east of Brno, the capital city of Moravia.
4 Mähren is the German word for Moravia. After the Revolution of 1848, Moravia came under the rule of the Austro-Hungarian Empire until 1918, when it became part of Czechoslovakia. Moravia was further subdivided in the twentieth century until 1993, when it was included in the newly created Czech Republic (The Editors of Encyclopaedia Britannica. "Moravia". *Encyclopaedia Britannica Online*. Encyclopaedia Britannica Inc., n.d. Web. 2 May 2015. http://www.britannica.com/EBchecked/topic/391877/Moravia).
5 Abbreviation for Kreuzer.
6 Lysice Castle, located 39 kilometers north of the Moravian capital city of Brno, was purchased by the family of Count Emanual Dubský (1806–1881) who, together with his son Ervin Dubský (1836–1909) would fill Lysice with artworks acquired from all over the world. Lysice Castle belongs today to the Czech Republic and is open to the public: "The opulent and richly furnished interiors give visitors an idea of the lifestyle of the family of Dubský from Třebomyslice" ("State Chateau Lysice". Web. 2 May 2015. http://www.zameklysice.cz/).
7 See note 1, CL'ANA 0402.
8 See note 11, CL'ANA 0402.
9 lodging.
10 Clara Knox.
11 "M". refers to Alma's "Ma," Ottilia.
12 Paul Clairmont was born in 1875 and Georgina died in 1885. This letter dates to after Georgina's death.
13 See CL'ANA 0221.
14 Possibly some of the children of Rudolph and Emily von Hauer. Wilhelm referred to Dora in his letter to Ottilia of 7 February 1866 (see appendix, CL'ANA 0421, Box 1, bundle a, number 85). Stevy is the shortened form of Stefani.

269 • Pauline Clairmont to Wilhelm Gaulis Clairmont

Sz. July 2^{d1} [c. 1888]

Dearest William – Enclosed is very interesting – what a shocking bad hand – shows a weary spirit in spite of what he says to the contrary There is a great deal in handwriting a legibele hand proves a clear mind. Not a word about his wife[2] – she is a nonentity as to mind – a beautiful animal as Mr Gladstaner used to call her. Nor does he mention me, tho' I wrote him shortly after reception of his book[3] – before you – perhaps he never got it owing to our stupid post here. Pray mention that I wrote to him when you answer his letter. There are few words that I also can not make out. Having time just now I will enclose you a copy & original.[4]

My dear Mr C. I was very pleased to have yr letter for with it many old associations were revived. I have seen yr old friend T. S. M.[5] & have sent him yr address. Mrs Buchanan, my sister's sister in law is in England with her husband.[6] They are not likely to return to the colony. Her daughter is married to a broker Schwartze a German or of German family I believe.[7] B. is managing Mess. M. & Co.[8] business in London. If you were to come out here you wd not recognize the colony as the same place you left it. Sydney has improved in a wonderful way, in buildings in population & in every way. When you left we were only commencing our railways. Now in N.S.W. alone we have upwards of 2000 miles open to Traffic. Brisbane Sydney & Adelaide are directly connected by rail & our western line from Sydney via Bathurst ends at Bourke on the Darling river 503 miles from Sydney.[9] The whole of the county is fenced into large paddocks. No shepherds are now employed, & our sheep will number if all goes well after the lambing now going on over 50 million all the land on the Murr. & indeed all the River has been purchased & formed into large estates. this will give you some idea of our prospects as a County. Our Parliament is the only blot upon the scene, but the fault lies in human nature, & somehow or another in most men there is a good deal of human nature. All the same it is a pity that nature could not be somewhat altered. At Brucedale a younger brother Herbert is living, he married a cousin, one of Wyagdon Suttors. At Mount Grosvenor my uncle Charles an old man of 85 & my Aunt Mary are still living.[10] I am located near Alloway Bank. The last place was left to my two younger brothers.[11] they have quite lately sold it to strangers & not nice people, much to my sorrow & regret. My sister Caroline (Mrs M.)[12] has just left us, having been here on a visit; she is getting a grey-headed young woman, but she has not lost her vivacity, notwithstanding she is the mother of 12 children. The slim lad you knew in myself has grown into a stout, portly elderly gentleman of great girth & weight some 15 stone 7 lb. with grey beard & alas I fear, a little bald patch on the top of his crown is beginning to show itself. However I do not feel much older thank to a good constitution & our healthy climate.

Do you ever feel any desire to take a run out to Australia? It can be so easily done now & so quickly. Just now we are in the usual condition of hoping for rain, after two years of almost continued wet weather. Have you anything to do with sheep now? & do you know where any first class ones are to be had? I almost think there are better sheep in Australia now than Saxony can boast of. Our best flocks here tho' are supposed to be the descendants of a Silesian[13] ram imported many years ago by one of the Mess Cox of Mudgee.[14] My family consists of 6 girls & one boy three of the girls are over 17 & the only boy is about 10. the youngest child is 8.[15] A second cousin of mine, a daughter of Maria Suttor[16] who was a very pretty little girl at Alloway Bank is married to the son of y^r friend Mr J.S.M.

with kindest regard
yrs very sincerly
W.H S.[17]

I still have the little fox paper weight to remind me of you.

Address: No envelope.

Unpublished. Text: M.S. Pf. Coll., CL'ANA 0220

---

1 See note 4 for the date of the letter. As Willie Suttor wrote that his uncle was 85 years of age, the letter can be dated to 1888.
2 Adelaide Agnes Henrietta Bowler Suttor (see CL'ANA 0405, CL'ANA 0325, CL'ANA 0421, Box 3, bundle g, number 201 bis, and the introduction to the Australian Sojourn).
3 Probably Willie Suttor's *Australian Stories Retold, and Sketches of Country Life* (1887).
4 The Pforzheimer Collection has in its archive the original letter from Willie Suttor to Wilhelm (CL'ANA 0198). Written from Cangoura on 11 May 1888, it is almost identical to the letter Pauline has copied for Wilhelm. At the top of the letter are the words "return this to me WGC" in blue ink and underlined. See CL'ANA 0421, Box 3, bundle g, number 201 bis.
5 Thomas Sutcliffe Mort. See CL'ANA 0210, CL'ANA 0065, CL'ANA 0075 and CL'ANA 0355.
6 Benjamin Buchanan (1821?–1912) married Louise Harriet Manning, daughter of Edye Manning (1807–1889). Edye Manning's son and Louise Manning's brother, John Edye Manning, married Caroline Suttor, Willie Suttor's sister (see note 12). See Niland, John. "Buchanan, Benjamin (1821–1912)", *Australian Dictionary of Biography*. National Centre of Biography, Australian National University. 1969. Web. 10 June 2015. http://adb.anu.edu.au/biography/buchanan-benjamin-3098/text4591
7 Mary Buchanan married Charles Eric Rudolph Schwartze (Niland, "Buchanan, Benjamin").
8 Benjamin Buchanan managed Mort & Co. in 1883 in London: "Five years later when this company amalgamated with R. Goldsbrough & Co., he became a director on the London board of Goldsbrough, Mort & Co., at a salary of £1000" (Niland, "Buchanan, Benjamin").
9 Bourke, New South Wales, is located on the Darling River, 800 kilometers north-west of Sydney.
10 Thomas Charles Suttor (1804–1889) was Willie's uncle and the older brother of William Henry Suttor. He married Mary Grosvenor Francis (1808–1889), sister of Charlotte Suttor. They had seven children. Mount Grosvenor was located in the town of Peel. In 1837, Thomas Suttor purchased 769 acres of land on Clear Creek which, together with the original grant of 300 acres promised to him in 1824 by Governor Brisbane, was known as Grosvenor Farm. The estate was later called Mount Grosvenor (*100 Years of Peel and District*, pp. 3, 170).
11 Horace Suttor (1861–1924) and Norman Suttor (1864–1928). All genealogical information in the following notes comes from the genealogical tables in Norton's *Dear William: The Suttors of Brucedale*.

12 Caroline Elizabeth Suttor (1841–1921) married John Edye Manning (1831–1909) in 1859. They had twelve children.
13 From Silesia, a region located today in south-western Poland.
14 Mudgee is located 261 kilometers north-west of Sydney and 128 kilometers north of Bathurst. The Cox family received land grants in the Mudgee area. William Cox (1764–1837) was the superintendant responsible for the construction of the road over the Blue Mountains (see CL'ANA 0209). Edna Hickson documents that, on their station in the Mudgee district, Cox's sons and grandsons "formed studs from William's flocks which became famous for the fine quality of their wool" (Hickson, Edna. 'Cox, William (1764–1837)', *Australian Dictionary of Biography*. National Centre of Biography, Australian National University. 1966. Web. 10 June 2015. http://adb.anu.edu.au/biography/cox-william-1934/text2309).
15 Willie's eldest child, Dora Henrietta, was born in 1866. Isabel was born in 1868 and Grace in 1871. All three of his daughters would therefore have been over seventeen years of age by the time he wrote to Wilhelm. His son, William Henry, was born in 1878, which serves to confirm the date of the letter. His youngest child, Una, was born in 1879.
16 Maria Suttor was the daughter of Sarah Cordelia Suttor (aunt of Willie Suttor) and her husband William Beverly Suttor (son of Henry Suttor). Maria's daughter, Edith Gore, married William B. Mitchell in 1887. William's father, J. S. Mitchell had been a partner in the firm of R.and F. Tooth & Company since 1860. G. P. Walsh notes that, in 1873, after the dissolution of F. Tooth & Co. (there had been some changes in ownership over the years), Mitchell and Robert Lucas Tooth conducted business as Tooth & Co, importers of wine, beer, and spirits (Walsh, G. P. "Tooth, Robert (1821–1893)", *Australian Dictionary of Biography*. National Centre of Biography, Australian National University. 1976. Web. 23 November 2014. http://adb.anu.edu.au/biography/tooth-robert-4731/text7851). In 1853, Thomas Mort, J. S. Mitchell, and Thomas Rowntree started the Waterview Dry Dock Company in New South Wales (Walsh, G. P. "Rowntree, Thomas Stephenson (1818–1902)", *Australian Dictionary of Biography*. National Centre of Biography, Australian National University. 1976. Web. 10 June 2015. http://adb.anu.edu.au/biography/rowntree-thomas-stephenson-4518/text7393).
17 Willie Suttor (William Henry Suttor, Junior).

270 • Pauline Clairmont to Wilhelm Gaulis Clairmont

Nice Feb 1. [c. 1889]
Hotel de la Gare[1]

Dearest William

Last night on receiving yr & Ts letter I wrote off at once to let you all know that I had arrived here all right, found a room & was so far domiciled. I am very happy that T. was pleased with the fur cloak & that it will be useful, I was only afraid that it is not good enough – there were better ones with silk outside with the same fur – but those are more for wearing in the day time & I thought that T has too youthful a figure to walk about in a rotonde.[2] I wd have liked to send one also for Alma but she is already provided & very handsomely. In Florence it was bitterly cold – it is still quite a northern climate, & not agreeable but the good Powers did all in their power to make me comfortable & so I was quite satisfied. I really dont know if I shall stay here long – Nice is not much to my taste there is too much of the large town most elegant shops & southern fruit very tempting – Specialité of Nice is preserved fruit baskets labelled Prix 10 fr rendu en Angleterre 15 fr rendu en Russie 18 fr en Autriche 13 fr.[3] etc all the geography of Europe. Therefore I dont think I shall get my tickets prolonged & they are due at the end of Feb. Abbazia[4] wont cost me so much as the Palffys[5] will surely invite me to dinner & I shall not stay longer than 2 nights. Now I am going out for a walk & will finish my letter in the evening.

Feb 2nd

I cd not finish my letter last night having had an attack of cramp. I can't think what cd have given it to me – but almost think it was taking coffee several times which in the long run is not good for me – not that the tea is so bad but the milk! skimmed boiled milk in your tea is too bad – so I took coffee which was rather good to take but not good in its effects.

To day I am all right having fasted a good deal. In the afternoon I wandered out in search of the old town & with my usual luck in such things found not only the queerest little old streets & steep stairs but suddenly found myself on a little terrace where I heard rushing of waters & presently found myself at one of the sights of Nice – the cascade – a modern affair but picturesk & in very good taste. A river turned aside & brought to throw itself down the rocks thus supplying the town with water.[6] I was very much pleased at this discovery & when I got down to the sea side sat down to watch the sunset I had been in rather low spirits all day – To day as you remember is the anniversary of our dear Father's death whose memory will live in ous till our last day & I cannot help remembering what troubles & privations both he & dear Ma underwent to educate us all & that mostly what I enjoy now, is owing to their our education & how little they enjoyed in this life. that one great satisfaction they had of being loved & honored by everyone. He wd be now 93! & Ma 89.[7]

Is it possible that all things will be as much changed in another 93 years as they have changed from then to now?

I think of going to Cannes on Monday & there I believe ends the Riviera – la Cornice[8] they call it in french – At dinner I heard a gentleman say who had just come from Paris that he left that town in drizzling rain & here we have day after day the most lovely sunshine – I bought photos to day that will interest you & if I c^d only send T. a nosegay of flowers every day – <u>Tossatti</u>[9] everywhere & the fruit Bananas fresh dates Jerusalem oranges – & such preserved fruit. But everything very dear.

I dread to think how you are immersed in snow & fog but I hope to hear of your soirée how it went off & all the other gaieties. I am a little dull in the evenings that is true but one must always pay in some way for the pleasures one has. Please address still to Nice poste rest. till I am on my way back. The Cognac is excellent here & so cheap a large bottle A 1 only 5 fr. I wish I c^d bring you a bottle. but it is so hard & heavy to carry. It looks so funny to see mules harnessed to Tram cars & donkeys as small as dogs drawing children.

yrs ever
PC.

Address: No envelope

Unpublished. Text: M.S., Pf. Coll., CL'ANA 0216

---

1 This letter, and the three that follow, all date to after 1888.
    Karl Baedeker's *Italy. Handbook for Travellers* suggested hotels "near the station" in Nice. While the Hôtel de la Gare (French for "Station Hotel") was not mentioned, the guidebook recommended the Terminus Hôtel, "a large new house, with café, opposite the station; a little further off, in the *Avenue de la Gare*, Hôt. National, also with café, less pretending, both frequented by passing travellers" (Leipsic, Karl Baedeker, 1889), p. 109.
2 Archaic term for a shawl.
3 French for "made in" ("rendu en"). The words "Angleterre, Russie, Autriche" are French words for England, Russia, Austria. "Fr" is the abbreviation for "franc".
4 Known today as Opatija, a town in Croatia on the Adriatic Sea.
5 Noble Austrian family whose home, the Palais Palffy, is located in Vienna and has served since 1969 as the headquarters of the Austrian Cultural Center. Wolfgang Amadeus Mozart performed at the Palais Palffy in 1762 ("Kulturzentrum Palais Palffy". Web. 30 April 2015. http://www.palais-palffy.at/). In *Picture of Vienna*, the author notes that the palace of Prince Palffy was located "back Schenkenstrasse" (p. 46). House numbers on "Hintere Schenkenstrasse" were numbers 49–51 and 55–57 (p. 110).
6 The Gairaut waterfall (la Cascade de Gairaut) was constructed in 1883 to provide water to the citizens of Nice. Water from the Vésubie River is still funneled today through a channel that terminates in the Gairaut waterfall and where the water for the city is oxygenated ("Cascade de Gairaut". Département des Alpes-Maritimes. Web. 26 October 2015. https://www.departement06.fr/nice/cascade-de-gairaut-2101.html).

7 Charles Clairmont was born in 1795 while Antonia was born in 1800. The letter therefore dates to 1889.
8 Pauline meant la Corniche de l'Estérel or la Corniche d'Or (the Golden Coast), a 30-kilometer stretch which runs from Saint-Raphaël to Mandelieu and Cannes, France, through the Côte d'Azur, and which provides views of both the Mediterranean Sea and the Massif de l'Estérel.
9 Unidentified. The first letter is either "f" or "t," but the word is unidentified either way.

271 • Pauline Clairmont to Wilhelm Gaulis Clairmont

Nice Feb 4th [c. 1889]

Dearest William

This evening as I came home from a nearly 8 mile tramp up in the mountains I got y^r letter I went to the Post off. immediately after dinner & got 3 letters – no wonder I have time to write, the evenings are long & they say it is not adviseable to be out about sundown, so I come home before 6 & get ready for dinner & rarely go out afterwards – but this evening I went to the P.O. Yesterday sunday it rained all the afternoon – I went to Villefranche[1] & had to sit in the dirty little station waiting for the next train to go back to Nice.

But to day turned out lovely no dust no wind & the rarest of blue sky. Drove to St André[2] about 5 miles out of town then when I had seen the old castle & wondered at the immense quantity of water that is let to run to waste, visited a small stalactyte grotto & then wandered away into the mountains – my intense delight only the road smooth as a table ran along between towering rocks at the bottom of a cold valley – at last I espied a goat path leading up into the sun over rocks & brushwood. There a peasant showed me the way to the next old castle Falicone[3] where I had a good lunch of new eggs milk & bread & had such a panorama This place is out of the region of vegetation – nothing but rocks a regular [illeg.] – far away Nice & the sea to the north Monte Calro,[4] the ruins of Castelnovo[5] on another mountain top the observatory[6] on another a madhouse right down under me, the castle of St André from where I had started – the air was sharp & cold up there & so clear you c^d see every rock every window in the little houses perched here & there. A shepherd girl told me I cd take a short cut down the precipitous mountain & I determined to do so – but somehow I mistook the path & suddenly found myself on the top of a tremendous stonequarry It was fortunate that I found it out in time – to turn back was impossible as it was already 4 ocl, (I had started from St André at 12) so I had to edge down over rolling stones & thorns letting myself down on my hands in steep places throwing down my shawl & parasol before me & so at last reached the blessed high road at St André & found no carriage nor diligence & had to tramp all the 5 or 6 miles to Nice. I was really glad to get to dinner – but to think back it was a splendid walk. but to look up at those rocks of the quarry it was quite marvellous how I scrambled down without tearing my dress.

The extract you sent me about poor Murska[7] is very interesting What a voice she had & what real talent & how I enjoyed studying Schuman songs with her. She was very clever but not always ladylike.

She always when on the stage passed herself off for Mlle tho' she had been married & had 2 children, she anxiously concealed her age & her daughter Hermine who in 1867 was already 15 w^d have betrayed her age. & therefore she called her Aunt. Her (Murska's) husband was an Austrian officer one of Uncle George's best friends & was called Eder – [8]it was just such a case as Mrs Wild[9] – when she would take to the stage her husband separated from her & the children were put to school.

Poor little Hermine the daughter was a good child & implored her mother to go back to her home she was not pretty but had a splendid voice – she had a harelip and perhaps that is the operation mentioned in the article. Poor things – they are at peace! I dont think I can stay here much longer it is a very expensive place – only I have not settled which way to come back – To morrow I will go to Cannes & Antibes & then I dont see why I sh^d not run down to Marseilles[10] & come back by steamer to Leghorn & then I sh^d have a few days more in Florence. On the 26th of Feb I must positively be in Florence. So I think you had best write there. I have asked them to keep my letters.

Yrs ever
PC

Address: No envelope

Unpublished. Text: M.S., Pf. Coll., CL'ANA 0215

---

1 Villefranche-sur-Mer is 8 kilometers east of Nice.
2 Saint-André-de-la-Roche is 7 kilometers north of Nice.
3 Falicon is 6 kilometers north of Nice.
4 Pauline misspelled Monte Carlo, which is 21 kilometers north-east of Nice.
5 Pauline perhaps meant to write Castle Park, "also referred to as the Castle Hill (Colline du Château)... where the ruins of the former Château de Nice can be spotted" ("Nice". Web. 9 June 2015. http://www.nice-tourism.com/en/).
6 L'observatoire de Nice was designed in 1883 by Charles Garnier, who also designed the Palais Garnier for the Paris Opéra. The observatory is known as l'Observatoire de la Côte d'Azur today ("Observatoire de la Côte d'Azur". Web. 1 May 2015. https://www.oca.eu/).
7 Ilma di Murska (1836–1889), a famous Hungarian opera singer who sang for U.S., Canadian, and Australian audiences in 1874 and 1875, and whose daughter committed suicide when she learned of her mother's death. Murska's birth name was was Ema Pukšec, she was born in Ogulin (Croatia) and her husband's name was General Auditor Eder (Batušić, S. "Pukšec, Ema". Österreichisches Biographisches Lexikon und biographische Dokumentation. 1815–1950. Web. 1 May 2015. http://www.biographien.ac.at/oebl/oebl_P/Puksec_Ema_1834_1889.xml). According to an article about Murska published in the New York Times of 3 March 1889, after suffering financial losses in the United States in 1876 ("the bloom had then departed from her celebrity"), the "once-petted prima donna" went back to Germany in poverty (http://query.nytimes.com/gst/abstract.html?res=9402E6D6173AEF33A25750C0A9659C94689FD7CF). The Press (a New Zealand newspaper) reported on 18 December 1888 that the former "Lovely Hungarian Nightingale" was found "starving" in New York (p. 3, http://paperspast.natlib.govt.nz/cgi-bin/paperspast?a=d&d=CHP18881218.2.6).
8 The New York Times documented that Murska was married to an Austrian officer, that she was the daughter of an Austrian colonel, and that she had a son and a daughter. It also stated that she had commited polyandry with two additional men (http://query.nytimes.com/gst/abstract.html?res=9402E6D6173AEF33A25750C0A9659C94689FD7CF).
9 Unidentified.
10 Cannes is located 34 kilometers south of Nice; Antibes is 12 kilometers north-east of Cannes; Marseilles is 180 kilometers south-west of Cannes. Marseille is 576 kilometers west of Livorno (Leghorn).

272 • Pauline Clairmont to Wilhelm Gaulis Clairmont

Ajaccio[1] Feb 14 [c. 1889]

Dearest William

Here is a jolly go – Snowbound in Corsica! It is a heavenly day & we wander in streets planted with orange trees admiring the beautiful port & the towering mountains. Yesterday I took the railroad to Bagognano[2] about 2 hours from here & there we expected the diligence to take us over the mountain pass called la Foggia[3] to Corte[4] from where there is rail again to Bastia.[5] But no diligence[6] came – it stuck fast in the snow & the passengers 2 ladies & 2 gentl. had to get out & spend the night in a charcoal burner's hut. In the morning they left the diligence in the snow loaded the post bags and passengers on the horses & came down to Bagognano. I took a walk in that splendid scenery high mountains & precipices & old old chestnut trees & at 10 ocl. p m we all came back to Ajaccio. I am staying at Hotel D'Europe[7] & there is very pleasant company. A lady very pretty from Paris with her brother a corsican doctor & many other people. I wanted to go round on the Eastern coast of Corsica to Bastia by diligence but it is a long & troublesome road travelling all night so I preferred to wait a day or two & try the Foggia pass once more. These Corsicans are most interesting people full of energy spirit & courage & the wine here is so good & cheap & does not hurt me at all.

Yesterday at dinner at Bogonano there sat near me an officer captain of gendarmerie[8] in the mountains he was quite an interesting person pale & melancholy looking – & on the other side what do you think again a protestant missionary. He took up a good deal of my attention – he spoke so beautifully & had such dark soft eyes – just like W.[9] He said you see even in Corsica I travel without arms – I am under the protection of the Lord!

Ma foi[10] – said the Captain if I had children the first thing I shd teach them w^d be the use of the pistol & the sword – life is a battle I am a Catholic but I wont give my cheek for a second blow – I did not like not[11] egg on the conversation in that direction – but in my heart I felt like a Corsican Capt. said C'est une affaire de temperament – missionary said – mais il faut gouverner le temperament

<u>Capt</u> – mais jamais subir l'insulte!

<u>Missionary</u> mais notre Seigneur a subi l'insulte!

Capt – Et il en a subi l'ignorrance[12]

Fortunately we were interrupted here by the arrival of the travellers of the diligence & all their adventures – Of course there are plenty of Raubergeschichten[13] – but I believe it is principally personal vendetta that prompts them to murder.

There are plenty of English living here & an English counsel whom I shall go to see this afternoon.

this letter will perhaps have to go round by Marseille to Nice – I will write again tomorrow – it is very jolly

yours ever
PC.

Address: No envelope

Unpublished. Text: M.S., Pf. Coll., CL'ANA 0214

---

1 The coastal city of Ajaccio is also the capital city of Corsica (La Corse). The island is located 90 kilometers from Italy. Napoléon Bonaparte was born in Ajaccio (The Editors of Encyclopaedia Britannica. "Corsica". *Encyclopaedia Britannica Online*. Encyclopaedia Britannica Inc., n.d. Web. 30 April 2015. http://www.britannica.com/EBchecked/topic/138780/Corsica).
2 Pauline meant Bocognano, 40 kilometers east of Ajaccio.
3 Pauline appeared to have recalled incorrectly the name of the pass. The Foce del Poggio is a mountain pass, south of Ajaccio.
4 Corte is 42 kilometers north of Bocognano.
5 Bastia is 111 kilometers north-east of Bocognano.
6 French for a type of stage-coach, typically pulled by a team of four horses.
7 Karl Baedeker's *Italy. Handbook for Travellers* listed the Hôtel de l'Europe as being located in the Cours Napoléon in Ajaccio (Karl Baedeker: Leipsic, v. 1, 1874), p. 372.
8 A "gendarme" is a French police officer.
9 Walter Clairmont.
10 French for "my faith".
11 nor.
12 Translation: "Capt. said It is a matter of temperament – Missionary said – but it is necessary to rule temperament Capt – but never to suffer insult! Missionary but our Lord suffered insult! Capt – And he suffered the ignorance of it" (Translation provided by Sharon Joffe).
13 Probably "Räubergeschichten," German for "stories about robbers or thieves" or "an unreliable or unbelievable story".

273 • Pauline Clairmont to Wilhelm Gaulis Clairmont

Ajaccio Feb 17 [c. 1889]

Dearest William

Times goes so quickly & one is so happy here – I can not get away Every body is so kind so hospitable as if I was a valued friend. The weather is so heavenly the country so beautiful I have had to promise to come & spend a whole winter here. And I feel so sorry that I am so happy. when there is such sorrow in Vienna. I heard of the dreadful misfortune that happened in the Imperial family only a few days ago thro' a gentleman that arrived from Paris & I was thunder struck – my first idea was a revolution & my impulse was to rush off fearing for you & yours, but then they told me it was an accident & not a political demonstration & my fears were calmed but the misfortune is none the less[1] I am going away from here tomorrow to Bastia where I hope to catch the Leghorn[2] steamer which leaves at 10 p m. & reaches Leghorn in 6 hours & be in Florence on the 19th I will write as soon as I land in Leghorn. The weather is beautiful & the sea smooth. It is so warm here in the day time quite overpowering & the moonlight on the bay & snow capped mountains beautiful. Yesterday we went to visit the gardens of C^{hs} Haggard an Englishman an original who lives here all by himself & has a splendid orangery & his little house is covered with creepers all in flower.[3]

Today I was invited to a picnic i e. I brought nothing but myself at the country house of a gentleman here we were a large party & lunched under the pine trees and wandered along the shore picking up shells & climbed the rocks & sat watching the soft waves till a little girl dropped her cautshuck[4] ball into the water & it floated like a nautilus out in the bay till a larger wave brought it back & we fished it out – then we went to lunch & began by a basket of ursins,[5] I am quite french now & dont know the English of it in Italian they are called castanie di mare – they are dark brown & prickly just like chestnuts – they are opened & inside is a delicate yellow star shaped fish.[6] Then we had saucissons de Corse grillés[7] then merles rotes[8] & the richest desert possible & excellent wines liqueur & Cognac. Then we took a walk up the mountain where we had a lovely view of the bay & walked home to the hotel where we arrived just in time for dinner. My friend a french lady with her brother invited me to come & see her in Paris for the Exhibition[9] – & vous Trouverez une chamber prête et des bras ouverts pour vous recevoir [10] – Is that not charming

It is 12 ocl at night & I must get up at 4 as that odious train starts at 5 & I am afraid they wont wake me early enough so I must say goodnight Yrs ever PC.

Address: No envelope

Unpublished. Text: M.S., Pf. Coll., CL'ANA 0213

---

1 On 30 January 1889, the bodies of lovers Archduke Rudolf of Austria and Baroness Mary Vetsera were found at Mayerling, not far from Vienna. Although their deaths were termed suicides,

"theories that the apparent suicide pact was in fact a political assassination have been in circulation for over a century" (Mark Everist, *Mozart's Ghosts*, Oxford: Oxford University Press, 2012), p. 235.
2 There are 212 kilometers between Livorno (Leghorn) and Bastia.
3 In *Murray's Handbook to the Mediterranean: Its Cities, Coasts and Islands*, Robert Lambert Playfair described Colonel Haggard's gardens: " . . . further on still are the beautiful garden and villa of Barbicaja, belonging to Colonel Haggard, celebrated for its oranges" (London: John Murray, 1890), v. 2, p. 453.
4 Probably "caoutchouc," French for "rubber".
5 Pauline referred to sea urchins ("riccio di mare" in Italian), a delicacy from the Mediterranean Sea.
6 Misspelling for "castagna di mare," Italian for "chestnuts of the sea".
7 French for "roasted/grilled Corsican sausages" which could have been made from boar meat or from liver.
8 French for "roasted blackbirds," a game bird considered a delicacy. Pauline misspelled "rôtis".
9 L' Exposition Universelle of 1889 (World's Fair). La tour Eiffel (The Eiffel Tower) was built for the fair.
10 French for "And you will find a ready room and open arms to receive you".

274 • Pauline Clairmont to unknown recipients

>Porto Ferraio
>Isola d'Elba[1]
>Hotel Api[2]
>Dec 24 [perhaps after 1888–9]
>Xmas eve

My dearest friends

At last my wish is fulfilled & I reached Elba with a good deal of trouble but no mishaps.

On Saturday last I left Florence & went to Leghorn – at the station of Fl. I met a very nice young woman with a baby who went to see her parents at Leghorn. Her husband put her into the train & recommended her to my care. So we made the journey together very comfortably – On the way she told that her Father was head waiter at the best inn in Leghorn, so I resolved to go there – the Falcone[3] excellent restaurant, & next morning being Sunday went to Church, posted 2 cards & thence to station, (always in the rain) There are two ways of getting to Elba – one by steamer from Leghorn, & one going by train to Piombino & thence by steamer to Porto Ferraio – short passage & sea being very rough I chose the latter which gave me an opportunity of seeing the Maremma[4] And I was not sorry – the Maremma is lovely at this time of the year the air as soft & balmy as madeira fields green all the sheep & cattle grazing & rosebushes in full bloom. I travelled 3ᵈ class & the train was very full. But I was not surprised to find that these poor people are human beings just like high classes & serve my desire of the study of human character much better than the varnished conventional high classes, & I have generally found that education & cultivation before bringing us to its highest attainable point a Christian Philosopher, generally stops short at the intervening stations & produces pride love of finery, ostentation & uncharitablness I suppose it is something like the fermentation of wine – only that wine ultimately does reach perfection – but we do not. I was quite satisfied with my humble surroundings – Near me was a servant girl going to service at Naples – & 3 students full of glee going home to their parents for the holidays. After we had travelled for about an hour I asked one of the students when the train reached Piombino. He looked at his time table & said. It does not go to Piombino! Good gracious I said then I got into the wrong train. & wanted to get out but was informed by the two other students who were also going to Elba that Piombino was not a station but the place to get out at was Campiglio & there a diligence wᵈ take us to Piombino – Altogether there were 8 travellers for Porto Ferraio so we could not go wrong. So after much changing of diligence & loading & unloading of luggage to took a boat & reached the steamer at 6a m The sea was very rough & the wind bitterly cold & the sails were all reefed – but thank goodness I was not sick & at 8 p m we landed at Porto F. I took a porter & went to the Hotel Api where I found a very good room – ditto supper ditto the celebrated Porto Ferraio wine[5] & went to bed at 9. It rained all night – I have

not yet seen the Italian sun. The island is lovely as I saw this morning after breakfast went up to the lighthouse from where there is a lovely view – as it began to rain I had to come home. It is so warm here I c^d scarcely bear my cape – orange trees with fruit in the open air geraniums cactus & palm trees – the port is like that of Genoa an amphitheater with an old fortress & villas scattered all over the hills. I can scarcely realize that this is Xmas eve – & you all perhaps surrounded with snow, but preparing for this evening's festival I wish you all a happy Xmas & merry New year, my thoughts are all with you, as yours I am sure are with me.
Now I am going to see the Villa Napoleone which unfortunately belonged to Pr.[6] Demidoff who carried away all its treasures & sold the villa – I am very glad I came here – because it is so warm.

yrs ever
PC.[7]

Address: No envelope

Unpublished. Text: M.S., Pf. Coll., CL'ANA 0227

---

1 Italian for the Island of Elba, an island off the coast of Tuscany in the Tyrrhenian sea. The largest town is Portoferraio which is located some 130 kilometers from Livorno (Leghorn). There are just ten kilometers separating the port town of Cavo from Piombino on the Italian mainland. In 1814, Napoléon Bonaparte was exiled to Elba for 300 days. John Murray's *Handbook for Travellers in Central Italy* estimated the voyage between Leghorn to "Porto Ferrajo" to take five and a half hours by steamer (London: John Murray, 1889), part I, p. 231. See also "Elba". Web. 2 May 2015. http://elba.org/. This final letter's date is unclear from its context and has therefore been placed at the end of the collection.
2 Pauline mistakenly wrote the inn's name as "Hotel Api," which translates to "Bees Hotel," instead of "Hotel Ape" ("Bee Hotel"). Today, the Hotel l'Ape Elbana continues to welcome visitors to Portoferraio. The hotel itself was constructed during Napoléon's exile and was originally known as the Bonroux Inn. From the hotel's website: "ed è proprio in quel periodo che il nostro albergo inizia a divenire tale,fu infatti l'imporvviso afflusso di tante personalità in un periodo nel quale il turismo era cosa lontana, a decretarne la nascita, si chiamava a quel tempo: Auberge Bonroux" (Translation provided by Beatrice Ferrari: "It is in that period when our hotel started to become what it is. In a time when tourism did not exist, the unexpected flow of many personalities determined the birth of the hotel, that at the time was called Auberge Bonroux"). See "Hotel Ape Elbana". Web. 2 May 2015. http://www.ape-elbana.it/
3 Baedeker's *Italy. Handbook for Travellers, Northern Italy* of 1886 provided the following recommendation for hotels in Leghorn/Livorno: "In the Corse Vittorio Emanuel: . . . FALCONE & PATRIA, No. 62; both in the Italian style with trattorie. – Those who make a prolonged stay will easily obtain private apartments" (London: Dulau and Co, London, 1886), part i, p. 348.
4 The coastal region of south-western Tuscany.
5 Elba is well known for its Biancone di Portoferraio, a white grape used in wine production.
6 The Galleria Demidoff was named for its owner Prince Anatole Demidoff, who purchased Napoléon's Villa di San Martino in 1851 and turned it into an art gallery. Located about 5 kilometers from Portoferrai, the villa was Napoléon's summer residence. Unfortunately, after Demidoff's death in 1871, the property and the art collection were sold, an event Pauline attributed to Demidoff himself ("The Galleria Demidoff on the Island of Elba". Web. 2 May 2015. http://www.napoleonsites.

eu/en/default/521/the-galleria-demidoff-on-the-island-of-elba.html). John Murray's *Handbook for Travellers in Central Italy* described the Villa: "it was purchased by Count Demidoff in 1851, by whom it has been converted into a Napoleonic Museum, a separate handsome building being erected near the Imperial residence for the purpose. It is open 4 times a week ... The contents all relate to the first Empire, and to the members of the Imperial family; the greater number having belonged to Jerome, ex-King of Westphalia, and purchased from him by Count Demidoff on marrying his daughter, the Princess Mathilde; they consist of statues and busts of the princes of the Bonaparte family, portraits and historical paintings, objects that belonged to Napoleon I, medals and coins, with a collection of engravings, and other relics" (London: John Murray, 1889), part i, pp. 232–3.

7 Pauline would die from a fall in 1891 in Öblarn, Steiermark, while walking with her nephew, Paul Clairmont. On 4 September 1891, Willie Suttor wrote to Wilhelm from Sydney: "I was terribly shocked today to see in one of our papers here an account of the death by accident while ascending the Sonnenberg at Ohlarn the account is as follows. 'A mountain accident in Upper Styria cost an English lady her life. Miss Pauline Clairmont was ascending the Sonnenberg at Ohlarn only the day after her arrival when she slipped & rolled down the mountain side. Her lifeless body was found next day Is this true. I am you with kind sympathy W. H Suttor" (CL'ANA 0199). Willie Suttor misspelled Öblarn.

Wilhelm would die on 26 December 1895. He was buried in the the family crypt in Matzleinsdorf on 27 December. Ottilia would survive him until 1913.

APPENDIX

This appendix contains nine letters written by Wilhelm Clairmont to Ottilia von Pichler (later Clairmont) after their engagement in February 1866. The Carl H. Pforzheimer's holdings include an additional 250 letters from Wilhelm to Ottilia that have not been included in this collection. Most were written in old German script (Kurrent), although there are some English-language letters interspersed as well as letters written in a combination of German and English. The relationship between Wilhelm and Ottilia is beyond the scope of this collection which has focused primarily on the correspondence written to Claire Clairmont. This appendix provides a sample of some of Wilhelm's English language letters to his future wife.

1 • Wilhelm Gaulis Clairmont to Ottilia von Pichler [later Clairmont]

[7 February 1866]

Wednesday evening 7$\underline{\text{th}}$
February

My own sweet Tilly. I hope you duly rec$\underline{\text{d}}$ my last letter from Tuesday; it was rather late when it was sent away; and to my great horror I found Master Seppel[1] still dawdling about the courtyard when I thought he had left already long ago – So do not think I was at fault if it was one day behind time – Yesterday evening we did not even play at chess for Emily is now always more sleepy than even Rudi[2] – this morning Rudi & I left tolerably early for Puszta,[3] for the weather is so fine that ~~our~~ the field works are already about to begin – tomorrow we shall commence ploughing and harrowing and in a few days we shall sow the first fields – today we accomplished another nice bit of work; do you remember the straight broad road leading from the corner of the Offsenitzaer[4] common up to the farmstead; well this road is now all ploughed with trees on both sides from 4 to 4 [illeg.] and looks very even now; when the trees grow to be any size it will look very nice – there is now already so much to do at the Hodaja[5] that I ought to live out there altogether but I am as yet afraid that we will yet have a Nachwinter[6] for it is too early to last – We did not come in for dinner at all today but took some meat with us and dined at my house in Offsen. in returning at night I said to Rudi "In Einer Beziehung ist es jetzt beinahe gut daß die Tilly nicht hier ist, es würde sonst schwach mit der Arbeit gehen".[7] he immediately made a face as if he felt the weight of the labour and discomfort which would have devolved upon him in this case and said; ja ja es wäre fatal gewesen.[8] My poor dear Titsy! what nasty people we are; you thinking and dreaming of none but myself and I expressing my satisfaction that you are not here – never mind my dear goldenhaired Titsy, when you do come down here, then you shall prove that you do not keep me from being active and delinquent but on the contrary you shall assist me and then everything must go well.

On our return in the evening we found Emily quite in a state of animation for she had had a pleasant visitor; a M:rs: Korzo[9] from [illeg.] had been staying with her all the afternoon and as she is a very clever and talkative woman at the same time an excellent housewife who manages all her estate by herself for she is widow since many years, so she managed to shake Emily out of her humdrum vegetative existence; she was quite pleasant and animated and even looked handsomer in consequence. It would do her a great deal of good to mix a little with the world; she would be more sensible too in the management of her children if she had intercourse with other mothers, that are equally affectionate towards their children but more experienced in their management. Emily's world is too confined on the one side it is bound by Willy's cradle and on the other by Dora's white earthenware throne[10] – Now she has taken [illeg.] to spinning with great eagerness; she is very frightened that M:rs: Rittmeister[11] will learn it sooner than she. – Ich freue mich schon sehr auf den Brief den mir die morgige Post von meinem lieben hübschen Mädchen bringen wird; aber wie wenn keiner käme; ich traue schon kaum mich zu freuen.[12] Titsy if ever a letter from me does not come on the appointed days, be assured that it is not me but the post or else some untoward accident which has prevented the letter reaching you; and do you also sweetest Tits be equally punctual and careful in dispatching your letters to me, for twice a week is already quite little enough and it would be such a deep bitter disappointment to me not to get even that. Goodnight sweet, dear Titsy I hope for a nice letter form you for tomorrow.

Thursday evening. 5oclock. Today I was at the Puszta all day we returned only at 3oclock where I found your nice long letter and one from Alma. dearest best Titsy I am happy to think that you always still love me as before, nay perhaps even better – Titsy you are a real jewel I cannot tell you how I love my little girl for I have no words to express it. I hope you have got over your sadness about my last but one letter today illeg. you will have got my letter from Tuesday last & that will have set you up. I shall never again write you anything sad I feel, if you take it so much to heart you noughty girl oh my Tilly what an excellent invention letters are how wretched would I be without yours! you will now also know that I got your Sunday letter all right; it is only the letter from Pest that came two days behind time and there your cousin was in no way to blame for the letter bore the postage stamp of the day on which you sent it to post – I do not understand from what circumstance you concluded that I had not received your letter – this evening ~~the~~ we go to the Rittmeisters to have our accustomed game of whist when we return I shall write you more; this I only wrote hastily on Emily's desk with the seamstress sitting on one side of me and Dora crying back on the other; Goodbye for the present my handsome dear bride du fragst mich ob ich dich noch mit derselben treuen Liebe wie in den ersten Tagen unserer Trennung liebe, ja mein einziges Mädchen ebenso und nochmehr, Alma's Brief hat heiße Pulsschläge durch meine Adern gejagt doch hiervon später mehr wenn ich Muße habe mehr gesamelt zu schreiben; hier ist alles voll Lärm und es laufen ewig Leute durchs Zimmer –[13]

Thursday night. We are returned from the Rittmeisters I am in my room again and now write to you in peace and comfort. oh my sweetest little Tilly if you know what happiness I derive from your love you would be satisfied; I am often angry with myself but even Alma's & your account of your sadness and dejection has something soothing to me – But now my handsome sweet beloved Titsy let us talk of the subject that interest us most – will you supposing that the plan of finishing the house must be given up for this year, will you consent to have the marriage in June or say the [~~illeg.~~] beginning of July? Now dont be guided by any false notions of modesty but say the candid truth. it will depend as far as you are concerned on two circumstances, first the wishes & feelings of your heart & those I hope will be in favour of an acceleration of the day which is to make you mine for life – Secondly can you get all your outfit ready by this time ? but as it is settled ~~anyway~~ that you should anyway spend July and August in travelling your outfit would under any circumstances have to be finished by the time you would start for your Ferienreise[14] so instead of going to Switzerland or some other distant country, you may as well come down here to your poor puszta house at once. I talked it over with Emily she said of her own accord the following words – Es ist unnatürlich ja sogar peinlich daß Ott. auf dieser ganzen Reise sozusagen gegen ihre Neigungen mitgeschlept werden soll während doch ihr Herz und alle ihre Gedanken immer bei ihnen sein werden; und was die Eltern betrifft so wäre es ja für sie viel ~~practis~~ angenehmer nach der Trennung von Ottilie, wenn nähmlich die Hochzeit noch im Juli stattfindet zur Zerstreuung die Ferien reise vor sich zuhaben, als daß auf die Hochzeit und Trennung von Ott. unmittelbar das langweilige Ausziehen und den traurige einsame Herbst folgen sollen.[15]

I think these words of Emily's very sensible and that you and your parents must agree with them – as far as myself is concerned you know that my motto always was the sooner the better – and you will surely feel yourself how happy I would be to have you 3 months sooner than I expected. only there are two obstacles in the way; first I am not sure whether we can get even hired lodging by the 1st of July. Secondly my promise to your father but above all my deep love for you my Titsy require that we should be sure of the results of this harvest before I can claim you as my own – You are aware that if we openly proclaimed the time for our wedding to be the end of June it would not only be very painful to ourselves to have to put it off on account of the harvest perhaps turning out badly but it would also give rise to a good deal of lieblosen Tratsch[16] – To avoid all this I therefore propose that we keep our plans strictly secret (even from your Mamma who is not quite safe in this respect) till I come up in spring; by that time we shall know all about the lodging and the harvest – if things go well I have no doubt we shall persuade your parents to give their assent then to the acceleration of our wedding and then we shall be married quickly and snugly for all the disagreable people will be out of town. Nun schreibe mir in deinem nächsten eben aufrichtig und erhlich mein aller liebstes Mädchen was du über alles dieß denkst, schreibe ganz offen, ohne Rücksicht auf meine Wünsche und aber auch mit Beiseitelegung deiner allzu großen mädchenhaften Schüchternheit die für ein kleines Frauchen wie du schon nicht mehr am Platze ist. Küße mir Alma und sage wie ich ihr danke, daß sie diesen Gegenstand berührt, sage ihr auch daß ich denselben absichtlich in ihrem Briefe vermeiden werde weil ich nicht wünsche daß die Andern davon wissen sollen – Ja mein Mädchen welch ein Glück wäre das dich schon im Juni oder Juli zu haben.[17] About the harvest we have less apprehensions every day; it is true the wheat has suffered a great deal through the frosts, but if a favorable spring comes it will improve yet. We have had a heavy soaking rain to day again and it looks as if we are likely to get more. I do not know how Bernhards[18] crops look and cannot therefore make a comparison between his and ours. Dear Titsy this is a very imperfect letter for I am so much wrapped up in the one thought I ~~do~~ can not think of anything else – tell me whether you found my last letter sufficiently [illeg.] and whether I answered all your questions. I would like you to write me more of what you do all day & where you go to – Dearest Titsy spare your health, dont run about to much, but do not grieve if you should not look quite so well; you know by what sign I shall know my sweet pretty girl again ; in your future home you will have plenty of rest and fresh air to fetch you round again – Titsy I tremble about your visit to the horrid dentist's but I know once its over you will thank me for having urged you[19] write to me the moment its over if only a few short lines; I shall be in great uneasiness till this matter is disposed of Goodnight sweet Titsy tomorrow I have no time to add anything for I am off to the Puszta and do not return till night. Give my love to your parents; if you have any conversations with your father write it me for it interests me I hope you will still go on playing at Chess. how is it with the English Your loving affectionate Willy. has Pauline not yet been to see you?

Address: No envelope

Unpublished. Text: M.S., Pf. Coll., CL'ANA 0421, Box 1, bundle a, number 85

---

1 Unidentified.
2 Rudolf and Emily von Hauer. Emily was Ottilia's sister.
3 Hungarian term for the "plains" or "prairie".
4 Ofsenița, town in the commune of Banlok, Timiș County, Romania. See CL'ANA 0270.

APPENDIX

5 Term used in the Banat for "a [small] farm in the field, outside the village" ("Hodaja". *Hungarian-English Dictionary*. Web. 25 June 2015. http://www.genealogy.ro/dictionary/hun_eng_h.htm).
6 German: "more winter weather" or "another cold spell".
7 German: "In one respect it is now almost good that Tilly is not here; otherwise not much work would get done" (transcription and translation by Ann Sherwin).
8 German for "Yes, it would have been disastrous" (transcription and translation by Ann Sherwin).
9 Unidentified.
10 Emily's children. See CL'ANA 0230.
11 Unidentified.
12 German: "I am already looking forward to the letter that tomorrow's mail will bring me from my dear, pretty girl. But what if none should come? I hardly dare get my hopes up" (transcription and translation by Ann Sherwin).
13 German: "You ask me whether I still love you with the same true love as in the first days of our separation; yes, my only girl, just as much and even more. Alma's letter sent hot pulse beats through my veins, but more about this later when I have leisure to write in a more composed state. Here everything is noisy and people are constantly passing through the room" (transcription and translation by Ann Sherwin).
14 German for "holiday trip".
15 German: "It is unnatural, indeed, even embarrassing that Ott. should be dragged along on this whole trip, against her inclinations, as it were, while her heart and all her thoughts will always be with them; and as far as the parents are concerned, it would be much more practic pleasant, after the separation from Ottilie, if the wedding is in July, for them to have the holiday trip head of them as a diversion rather than that the dull setting out and the sad, lonely autumn should immediately follow the wedding and the separation from Ott". (transcription and translation by Ann Sherwin).
16 German for "unkind gossip".
17 German: "Now, my very dearest girl, in your next letter, tell me frankly and honestly what you think about all this; write very openly, irrespective of my wishes, and lay aside your all-too-excessive girlish shyness, which is no longer fitting for a little woman like you. Give Alma a kiss for me and tell her how grateful I am that she touches upon this subject; tell her also that I will intentionally avoid mention of it in my letter to her letter because I don't want the others to know about it – Yes, my girl, what a joy that would be to have you as early as June or July" (transcription and translation by Ann Sherwin).
18 Probably Freiherr (Baron) Bernhard von Hauser. See CL'ANA 0277.
19 Wilhelm cross-wrote the rest on the final page.

2 • Wilhelm Gaulis Clairmont to Ottilia von Pichler [later Clairmont]

Saturday 10th February 1866.

My own dearest Titsy. Two more days have passed away in my dull monotonous life since I wrote you last, two more days of which there are so many yet to pass before I can again embrace & kiss my dear handsome sweetheart to my soul's content; oh how cruel & sad is it that we have been thus obliged to separate. Do not however give yourself any uneasiness on my account dearest Titsy, I am not of course what I was when you were here, but I am not any longer so sad & wretched as I was at first after your departure and you must do the same dearest Titsy you must not give way to grief but console yourself with the idea how entirely we shall possess and enjoy each other when you come down here to be my own sweet gentle wife – Yesterday I was all day at the Puszta I took some dinner with me in the evening we played at chess – this morning I went to Rittmeisters to enquire about some young trees – then I came home & wrote letters to Pauline & Zoepf ¹then dinner; after dinner finished my letters read newspaper went a little out on business – till coffee; after coffee sat in the dusk thinking of my dear nice girl – Emily was enjoying the squalling of her two hopefuls while bathing them & Rudi was sitting in his room reading – When Emily came I had a talk with her about our future house and the little wify that is to be in it; then I teased her about having imaginary ailings – I also told her I already foresaw that she would not come to visit us and that then we would not come either till I had the satisfaction of getting her quite into a fit. after tea we [illeg.] played at chess & then Rudi drove us to bed. at this latter I am now glad because I can sooner get to my letter writing – I can tell you that we are much lazier now since my sweet Titsy is not here any more to make us rise early – I told Emily so today; she immediately denied it but at last she admitted that the barking of the dogs would not allow her to sleep and that that is why she could not rise in the morning for which I of course laughed at her and said it was a good excuse.

I would give something to see my darling play chess with her papa; do you play often and who wins generally ? I suspect poor Tilly will be the loser; do you know I now also play so badly that I should be ashamed to play at the club in Vienna – I am very glad to hear that your papa is always in such a happy mood; did you have any conversations with him on the subject of our future? if so write it to me, for it interests me – If Mel[illeg.] Hauser still remembers me pray give her my compts. when you see her next, also to Judith – aber daß Bernhard dich bei mir verklagen will wird mir "nachgerade" verdächtig! was hast du denn gemacht du böses Kind? mit wem hast du denn schon wieder coquettirt? ich bin rasend eifersüchtig wie Bernhard kommt fahre ich auf die Gefahr hin bei einem zweiten Eröthen ertappt zu werden nach [illeg.] und frage ihn haarklein über alle deine Vergehen aus. Das ist mir das verdächtige daß du selbst mir gar nicht sagst <u>warum</u> Bernhard dich verklagen wolle! ah wenn ich wieder auf die Welt komme suche ich mir kein so hübsches Schätzchen mehr aus – man steht damit gar zu viele Angst aus zumahlen wenn man selbst schon graue Haare hat –²

I am anxious to know whether Pauline has not been with you yet ? also whether you have not yet received an answer from my mother; my dearest Tilly if [~~illeg.~~] her letter should fall short from what you expected dont show it to any one dont complain to others who do not understand the circumstances, but burn the letter and think of it no more; I could relate you circumstances, but they occupy too much space in a letter from which you would perceive, that her head is quite gone although P. writes me that her health is more than ever improved. du mußt auf ein liebevolles Benehmen von Ihrer Seite ohne Murren verzichten und ich werde dafür in dir einen Grund mehr sehen, dich, die ich schon über alles liebe noch mehr zu lieben. Sag mir mein Titsle kommt es dir noch immer nicht recht vorn [~~und~~] daß ich du zu dir sage; und erscheint es dir von deinerseite noch immer fremd und ungewohnt du zu sagen? findst du das Sie noch immer herzlicher und natürlicher? Mir komt es aus deinen Briefen so vor als ob ich in dieser Beziehung einen Umschwung der Ansichten in dir wahrnehme.[3] I am glad you liked Sermage's & your admirer Zoepf's letters there was no note enclosed from Flora.[4] Richard cant bear her since his marriage although he was all there at flirting with her before his marriage – I wonder whether I shall also become so virtuous through you my Tilly? About the secrets in my desk you can be quite easy; there are now no more for you at least; nothing would have given me greater delight than to have shown you everything for then I should have had a protracted visit from my Titsy in my room – Oh my sweet little girl how often do I look quite sorrowfully at the spot where you stood in my room the last time and where you shed your last tears before parting – I wonder how my dear moonlit face will look when I see it next.

Sunday 4 oclock afternoon – My dearest expectations were realized I got such a nice letter from my Tits who says she still loves me a little and I of course am silly enough to believe her – but your letter also made me sad dearest Titsy especially the first part written some days sooner, it was sad and dejected and bore the unmistakable stamp of weariness of mind and unsoundness of body. But dearest Titsy how shall I sufficiently praise you for having been so good and fulfilled my most anxious wish in going to the dentist's – I wish I could shower a heap of rich presents on you for this; in default I will endeavor to make my sweet Tits[illeg.] a slight surprise by sending this letter away so today as a [illeg.] but with the express condition that you shall not expect one constantly on Tuesdays from ~~the~~ [~~illeg.~~] Offsenitza especially it will be difficult to write because the post office is not so conveniently at hand. – Titsy your todays letter gave me great pleasure from one reason because of conjecture from it that you will not be averse to shortening the period of our separation and that consequently the wish I urged on you in my last letter will meet with a favorable reception – oh do my Titsy write to me very soon what you think on this subject – it seems now already pretty well decided that we shall not get the house built for this year Goodbye dearest sweetest girl remember me to Alma, take care of your health & believe me yours affectly

Willy.

APPENDIX

february 11ᵗʰ 1866.[5]

I shall begin this evening to answer your letter & post it as usual on Tuesday tell me how is it you always fancy I do not get your letters I hitherto got all and at the right time too excepting the first from Pest. Titsy I want more details about what you do everyday – something like [illeg.] Emily sends her best love to all of you, she and the children and Rudi of course are all well –

Address: No envelope

Unpublished. Text: M.S., Pf. Coll., CL'ANA 0421, Box 1, bundle a, number 16

1 See CL'ANA 0354.
2 German: "but that Bernhard wants to file a complaint with me about you is starting to sound increasingly suspicious! What have you done anyway, you naughty child? With whom have you been flirting again? I am madly jealous. When Bernhard comes I risk being caught blushing a second time. I will go to [illeg.] and interrogate him down to the last detail about all your transgressions. That's what I find the most suspicious, that you yourself have no wish whatsoever to tell me why Bernhard wants to file a complaint about you! Ah, if I am ever reincarnated I won't choose such a pretty sweetheart – it just causes too much anxiety, especially when one has gray hair – " (transcription and translation by Ann Sherwin).
3 German: "You must forgo a loving demeanor on her part without complaint, and in return I will see in you one more reason to love you even more, whom I already love to pieces. Tell me, my Titsle, does it still not seem right to you that I address you as *du*? and does it still seem strange and awkward for you to say *du*? Do you still find *Sie* more heartfelt and natural? It seems to me from your letters as though I detect a reversal of sentiments in you" (transcription and translation by Ann Sherwin).
4 Richard von Sermage (see CL'ANA 0367). Flora is unidentified.
5 Wilhelm cross-wrote the paragraph that follows the date.

APPENDIX

3 • Wilhelm Gaulis Clairmont to Ottilia von Pichler [later Clairmont]

Saturday 17<u>th</u> February 1866.¹

My dearest Tilly. Yesterday Rudi & I were at the Pusta all day; We set 6400 Rupfen² with the plough in eight rows all along the northside of the homestead so as to give a shelter against the bleak northwinds. Do not however rejoice too much at all our planting of trees; for if these meet the usual fate, which all plantations in the Banat have to contend against they will all go to destruction as there is too great a prevalence of drought to allow young trees to get past their tender age. I also began to plough up the spot on which our future garden is to be, but we had to leave off again as it is still too wet. We returned at six in the evening. I was most agreably surprised by the receipt of a letter from my dear aunt in Florence³ who wrote me a most kind warmhearted letter in reply to my announcement of our engagement; I read it to Emily and she was very much pleased with it. My aunt also requested me to send her your direction written in English characters that she may write to you – As ~~you~~ I know your excellent heart my Titsy I think you might be desirous of forestalling her intentions I therefore give you her address "La Signora Clairmont 665 Piazza della Fontina, Pisa, Italia" – If you do write to her take pains my dear girl to write in a little larger and more legible hand than usual as she is old and has very week eyes –

This morning I spent all at the Hambar⁴ and in the afternoon I have to go again so I have only comparatively little time to devote to writing and will hurry to answer your last Thursday letter – [~~illeg.~~] What you wrote directly in the beginning in German my Tilly was very sweet and delightful to me to read how happy am I to think that I have such a dear treasure of a girl who is so fond of me and whose wishes coincide so completely with mine only you deserve a slight punishment because as you admit yourself you had not den Muth es zu gestehen!⁵ as if that required any Muth⁶ on your part; as if it were not the sweetest music I could hear to have such confession whispered into my ear from the pretty lips of my Titsy. I said already in my last if it <u>cannot</u> be, why it cannot, and we must only make bonne mi~~n~~ne à m~~e~~auvais jeux;⁷ we are in this respect as in respect to building dependent on circumstances and we must be guided by them; we must resign the privilege of the rich to mark out a certain course for ourselves to be followed a tout prix⁸ but we must take things as they come and turn them to our best possible advantage. therefore I also shrink now from the responsibility of the promise given in my last to tell you something decisive about the building of our house. but I feel that you must wish to know something in order to communicate ~~with yo~~ to your parents. So much I believe we can say for certain that if we adhere to the plan of the nice and more expensive house of which Inspector Meyer made the estimates that it will not be finished this year but that we shall do well if we get up the walls and the roof still this year – but if we were to be contracted with a smaller and less handsome house may be it might be got ready still this year of course even that would depend on the harvest. So turn it as we will I do not see that we can already now fix on a certain course but we must be contented to be guided by circumstances when I come to Vienna then I trust everything will be settled – I am also quite einverstanden[9] with your parents' wish that you should not sit up so late at night and write; I would almost rather make the sacrifice of having shorter letters than that my Titsy should loose her nights' rest over them – Pauline continues to write me very nice letters; she writes that Mamma has so far recovered as to put all danger of a relaps out of question, but still she cannot get away as M's state of[10] health would not permit her to leave her alone; she assured me that she is very unhappy at it but she cannot alter it however she hopes to come and see you very soon – she will then also explain to you, why being prevented from coming herself she has not invited you and Alma to come and see her – Pauline also writes me that M. was just on the point of answering your letter when she was prevented by the attack she got. My dear Tilly do me the favour not to think of her and her whims – I believe I am old enough to choose a wife for myself without any one's interference and as I receive no money assistance from her, but it is on the contrary me that is assisting her she has not the shadow of a right to meddle with my affairs – With any other being I would resent such conduct most determinedly but with her I prefer to pass it over in silent contempt – to save myself such irritation and pain I must endeavour never to think of her – and of you my Titsy I must beg the same thing – I shall love your parents not exactly on their own account, but because they are your parents – through and with you and on your account and you my dear must do the same thing to me; forget my mother because I want to forget her and let us not mention her any more in our correspondence unless it be with reference to any facts concerning her –

Saturday 7 oclock evening. Today two incidents occurred, the fact of their being worth mentioning proves how monotonous a life I lead, but also how faithful a correspondent I am to report such trifles – first I had eine Staatsvisite[11] today and whom do you think from? The Rittmeister the first I ever had here in Csakova – and what do you think he came for? to invite me for dinner tomorrow – I of course accepted the invitation very politely but unless we contrive to play a Strohman[12] between the Rindfleisch[13] & the pudding I hardly know how the time will be made to pass and what we shall talk of. the second event is a letter I got from dear Pauline; she writes that now M. is already a great deal better & she hopes to be with you very soon – I am very glad you heard such a favorable account of poor Pauline – you must know that when she was young she was very much gefeiert[14] for her beauty, but also subsequently on account of her great many and vielseitigen[15] accomplishments and also on account of her richly endowed mind and excellent heart – she was a universal favorite everywhere; at Australia they all were so fond of her they would not let her go at all but with the understanding that she was to return again –

I must thank you dearest Tilly for having observed my request that you should be more explicit about ~~my~~ your everyday life you have no idea how much everything interests me – When I read your letter to Emily I asked her a hundred questions about all the people whom you went to and how the evening is spent there, what people frequent there etz. etz.

the favorable opinion you give of Bernhart pleased me very well, I also have and always had a friendly and sympathetic feeling for him although I fancy him to be a person in whose continued and intimate intercourse I would not find much resource. his remark about the house is very true, but the account of discomfort entailed by the diminution in breadth would not be in proportion to the saving of the expense. Emily and I debated a good deal today as to how one could build a simpler smaller but cheaper house – Our debates did not however lead to any practical result. I laughed very much at the account you give of Julchen[16] and that she gave such romantic interesting Steggreif[17] descriptions of me and my past life – I am very much afraid, that you are doing me a grievous harm, for everybody's expectations will be raised to such a pitch that they will be quite disappointed by my actual appearance. This however gives me little concern; my thoughts are now centered on one dear [18]sweet little girl and as long as she will but love me I feel indifferent as to what all the rest may say & think – Tits its long yet till the end of April! Wont you change in the mean time? oh Tilly I do so long to press you to my heart again and to hear you tell me those dear, nice little things which you wrote in your last letter – But why did you not write me something too about Alma [illeg.]; you know I have a veneration for her since the clever sensible letter I read from her to you – did you not tell her how we laughed at her for supposing that I would follow you so quickly.– About the two new rivals you discovered you can be quite easy – one that Zoepf mentions I have never seen; the other I am not very likely ever to see again. and now I must answer your business questions – the measures of the [illeg.] I cannot yet send in this letter but I positively will in the next. About matresses I have already written to you in my last, but I will make further inquiries both here and at Temesvár – about feathers which I believed you asked of Emily I also think you are giving yourself needless anxiety – for I have already 3 or 4 featherpillows and I shall get lots more feathers from my geese in the course of this summer moreover we are not likely to have any guests yet the first winter – unless Alma should after all make up her mind to keep her promise to me. aber das wäre viel zu gut um wahr zu sein[19] – And now my dear Tilly I want to give you a hint with reference to your mother but that must remain strictly between ourselves Alma excepted who is also concerned in it – from a letter of your Ma's to Emily of which Rudi read part aloud I gathered that your mother has a feeling of something like jealousy towards your father and Alma with reference to you – I do not remember the exact words but they were something to this effect: Ottilie und Alma genügen sich so ganz für sich allein[20] as much as to say they don't think of asking or consulting me about anything. and then there were also the words: die geringste Gunstbezeugung vom Vater geht ihnen über alles.[21] this was put in connexion with other remarks, which left me to infer that your mother regretted to think that you loved your p.[22] more than her – this may be so my dearest Tilly perhaps even without your. being conscious of it. but dont give your Mamma a sad impression by showing it, be more than particularly attentive and dutyful to her for the few months you have yet to be in your parents house. it will leave her an agreable impression of you – and you too, for in proportion as you are gentle and conciliating with her, she will also relent towards you –

Sunday morning. 8 oclock. Oh how do I rejoice for a letter from my dear little girl how dreadful if I were to get none; I do not of course suppose that you would not write, but that some delay occurs at the post I have measured one of the fremden Betten[23] it measures precisely 6 feet Austrian measurement in length and 2ft. 10 inches in width – this is of course not the outside but the inside dimension what is called in German "die innere Lichte" so that the Strohsäcke[24] must be exactly that 6ft long and 2ft 10 inches wide – the measurement of the other bed I will give you in my next. I should prefer federn Strohsäcke.[25] I like them very much but I am afraid they are too expensive – if we have them these too had better be made down here as the packing and sending down of them would be very expensive –

Sunday morning 11 oclock. this minute I got your nice long double letter – oh was hab ich doch für ein prächtiges liebes süßes liebchen[26] – oh my Titsy would that I could kiss you a 1000 times for your excellent affectionate heart but really you must not write me such long letters it will wear you out completely – listen to/and obey your parents' injunction not to sit up so late at night. Wie freue ich mich auf die Photographie und das Journal Wenn du eine Photog. zu entbehren hast so bitte schicke sie an aunt Claire berufe dich hiebei nur auf mich, wenn es dir sonderbar vor käme dieselbe gleich zum ersten Mahl zu schicken – Meine Tante interesirt sich für so was sehr stark und ich habe ihr in meinem heutigen Brief versprochen zu vermitteln daß sie ein Phot. von dir bekomme.[27]

Sunday afternoon. This minute my sweet girl I return from Rittmst's where I dined today and for fear of forgetting it I will tell you at once that they both send you & your parents "Alles Schöne"[28] Mrs Rittmst also rc^d the parcel from the Bauernmarkt[29] and I believe it was to her satisfaction – We were very jolly at dinner and there was no lack of conversation at all. the new Oberlieutenant[30] made the 4th of the party tonight they come to whist – Now I have also a little more on to say on business – I spoke with the Csakovaer [illeg.] upholsterer he told me that he made beds all sorts of furniture in short every thing in this line for all the gentry in the neighbourhood – his price is 2f pr Stück Matraze fürs Heften d.h. bloß seine Arbeit dann 70 xr pr Pfd. fürs Roßhaar und den Stoff. Er sagt eine gute Matraze brauche 20 Pfd. Roßhaar. es soll besser sein wenn man sich die Matrazen 3theilig machen läßt. Auch fragte ich ihn wegen feder Matra Strohsäcken die sind aber so theuer daß wir sie wohl fahren laßen das Paar käme inclus Arbeit und Material auf 32 f. dafür meint er käme dann höchstens 14 Pfd. Roßhaar in die daraufgehörige Matraze so daß man de an den beiden Matrazen 12 Pfd Roßhaar d. h. 8 f 40 erspraren würde, aber es ist doch noch theuer – Ich denke in Wien muß das Pfd. Roßhaar wenigstens 1 f kosten, so daß wir pr Pfd. 30 xr. die fracht, Emballagekosten und außerdem das Risico ersparen daß auf dem transport alles gerissen und gestohlen werde. Überdieß arbeitet ein solcher Arbeiter Handwerker der einem in der Nähe ist viel besser, weil er schon weiß daß er liederliche geschleuderte Arbeit nachbessern muß – Ich bin also entschieden dafür alles derartige herunter machen zu laßen – Laß deine Eltern nur ja kein Geld auf Federn ausgeben, denn es sind schon da und wir bekommen noch fort. Zum Überfluß kannst du dir noch einige lebende Gänse in die Polster hineinschopfen, denn sie sind mir schon zuwider da sie viel Schaden auf der Pußte machen.[31] I was much pleased at what you wrote to me about the linen you got that your grandmother made – wont it be a lucky hour when we unpack it all! But now lazy Titsy its time you began about your outfit – I gather more from the other letters than your own that you have done nothing yet in this respect whow knows whether my despised July plans will not be realised yet, inspite of my wise, reflecting bride – and then how sorry would you be not to have finished yet. Ich komme schon nicht mehr dazu deinen lieben, heutigen Brief noch in diesem zu beantworten;[32] but I will begin another for Tuesday it will not however be so long as we begin tomorrow to sow in good earnest and I want to be at the Pusta all day – One thing I must tell you which particularly pleased me, that you said you liked my last moralising letter, you know I did not say that merely in joke but I really feared you would think the letter langweilig[33] because it was all serious and although I know my Tits likes serious conversation still in a letter it sounds so much more dull. Goodbye my dear girl give Alma my best love tell her I wanted to write to her today, but I have no more time. If you write to Claire mind you write a good legible hand. Goodbye my dearest sweetest pet Immediately after sending away this I will read over your letter again

                  yours most affectionately
                           Willy

Csakova
february 18th 1866.

Schon wieder hab ich keine Zeit den Brief [illeg.] durchzu lesen Rudolfs including both the enemies are all well.[34]

Translation: German transcription and English translation provided by Ann Sherwin:

2 gulden per mattress for the basting, i.e. just for his work, then 70 kreuzer per lb. for the horsehair and the fabric. He says a good mattress takes 20 lbs. horsehair. It's supposed to be better if you have the mattress made in three parts. I also asked him about feather ticks. But they are so expensive that we will probably forgo those. A pair, including labor and material, would come to 32 gulden. For that, he says, you would need at most 14 lb. horsehair in the mattress that goes with it, so you would save 12 lb. horsehair for two mattresses, i.e. 8 gulden and 40 kreuzer, but it is still expensive. – I think horsehair must cost at least 1 gulden per lb. in Vienna, so we save 30 kreuzer per lb., plus freight, packing costs, and the risk of everything being torn or stolen during shipment. Besides, a worker craftsman like this who does the work locally is much better, because he already knows that he'll have to correct slipshod work. – So I am strongly in favor of having everything of that sort made down here. – Just don't let your parents spend any money on

APPENDIX

feathers, for they are already here, and we can get more. To top it all off, you can also stuff a few live geese into the padding, for I find them repulsive; they do a lot of damage on the Puszta

Address: No envelope

Unpublished. Text: M.S., Pf. Coll., CL'ANA 0421, Box 3, bundle f, number 160

1 At the top of the first page, there is the number 1 written in red ink and underlined twice.
2 German for "hessian".
3 Claire.
4 Romanian word for "barn".
5 German for "the courage to admit it".
6 German for "courage".
7 Wilhelm meant "faire bonne mine à mauvais jeu," French for "to put a good face on the matter".
8 "à tout prix," French for "at all costs".
9 German for "to be in agreement".
10 At the top of this new page, there is the number 2 written in red ink and underlined twice.
11 German for "official visit".
12 Wilhelm referred to the game "skat," a card game for three or more players. However, there is a two-player version of the game which is called "Skat mit Strohmann," German for "Skat with a dummy/placeman". Wilhelm misspelled "Strohmann".
13 German for "beef".
14 German for "renowned" or "celebrated".
15 German for "varied".
16 Unidentified. Possibly the diminutive form of Julia.
17 Wilhelm misspelled "Steigreif," German for "impromptu, improvised".
18 The number 3 is underlined and written in red ink to mark the next set of bifold pages.
19 German: "but that would be much too good to be true" (transcription and translation by Ann Sherwin).
20 German: "Ottilie and Alma are sufficient entirely unto themselves alone" (transcription and translation by Ann Sherwin).
21 German: "the slightest sign of favor from their father means more than anything to them" (transcription and translation by Ann Sherwin).
22 Probably "papa", German for "father".
23 German for "guest beds".
24 German for "inner dimensions" and "straw ticks".
25 German for "feather ticks".
26 German: "what a marvelous, dear, darling sweetheart I have" (transcription and translation by Ann Sherwin).
27 German: "How I look forward to the photograph and the journal! If you have a photograph to spare, please send it to Aunt Claire. Rely on me for this only if it would seem strange for you to send it outright the first time. – My aunt is very interested in things like that, and I promised her in my letter today to see that she gets a photograph of you" (transcription and translation by Ann Sherwin).
28 German for "best wishes".
29 German for "farmers' market".
30 German for "senior lieutenant".

APPENDIX

31 Transcription and translation follow the letter.
32 German: "I can't take time to answer your dear letter received today in this one" (transcription and translation by Ann Sherwin).
33 German for "boring".
34 Wilhelm cross-wrote this final sentence on the last page of the letter. German: "Again I have no time to read the letter through [illeg.] Rudolfs including both the enemies are all well" (transcription and translation by Ann Sherwin). Wilhelm could have been referring to Rudolf's children in a comical manner.

APPENDIX

4 • Wilhelm Gaulis Clairmont to Ottilia von Pichler [later Clairmont]

Offsenitza March 14th 1866.

My dearest Tilly. So you are ill again you noughty child, but I was so glad to receive news of your improved health towards the end of your letter. However I dare not scold you this time for I really believe you are not to blame and moreover there is no knowing what Mater Alma in her anger might not do – I thank you dearest Titsy for the nice good letter you managed to write me notwithstanding. also Alma's letter was a great consolation to me – How curious am I what news I shall have by tomorrow's post! It is quite alarming that you are now all getting ill; I hope poor Alma & your Ma will soon recover – ! My life since my last has been very uniform – All day I am at the pusta – and in the evening I was writing out all the contracts for the different artisans ; mason carpenter etz – etz. This is a tedious labour which requires much care – so as not to forget anything – Today we have sown the last oats; also in the garden & everything is completed only a few more vines are to be set and there I expect to get from Versetz[1] (I could get them neither at Csakova nor Temesvár) on the whole their would be now a little more peace on the Hodaja if it were not for the building which also takes a great deal of time –

I wonder whether poor Pauline was with you on Tuesday last. I thought of you very much – she is dreadfully angehängt[2] at Baden I was much rejoiced at the receipt of your little note that you liked the new houseplan and also that my letters to Alma & your Ma pleased you – Pardon me that I have hitherto not sent you the 3 photographs – they are at Csakova & I cannot send them from here – also the little flour I brought for you from the wood I forgot in my pocket book and could not therefore put it into my last letter but I shall now put it into Claire's letter so that it may not be forgotten –

Thursday afternoon – I have not yet received your dear letter – I shall not get it till evening when I get to Csakova – Rudi & I are going to Temesvár tomorrow morning to buy timber for building, we do not return till Sunday night so you must not expect a long letter on Tuesday for I shall have no time to write Saturday & Sunday at Temesvár. – I am very glad you liked Cl.'s letter so well – I also think it is a very nice warmhearted letter – Today is again a kind of "Epoche tag"[3] it is the 15th again half a month over since I began my letter with hey diddle diddle in the celebration of the 1st of May – Now we may say we have got over the half of [illeg.] our separation, and of course by far the worse half for the pang of separation is now not as acute as at first and the prospect of its speedy termination makes it more easily bearable – Oh my dearest sweetest Tilly how eagerly do I look forward to the time when I shall have you again in my arms – you are right we must meet quite alone for I shall have many kisses [illeg.]

I am glad to perceive from your last that you are reconciled to the new house plan; it is a good pity it can not turn out so nice looking as the last was but I fancy it will turn out fully as convenient. and it will be so nice not to have to go to that infamous Swabian village – And apart of the filth and nuisance of a village; think how dreary it would have been for you immediately after our marriage to sit at home all day quite alone – and I not come home even at dinner time. you would actually even in the summermonths have seen me only at candle light, so you will see me every minute for though I have to do on the fields still, much work is also going on at the homestead and I have to pass through it every minute – Oh I can assure you I am delighted with this arrangement – I dreamed of you my dearest Titsy today; but what I cannot <u>write</u> but I sill tell you some day – Tits if you are ill while I am in Vienna & will not let me come into your room I shall be very vexed –

friday morning. Last night I got your letter but I was too tired ~~still~~ to answer it still yesterday evening as I had slept little the previous night. I am glad dearest Titsy that you are up again, but I should almost have preferred if they had kept you in bed for a fortnight longer till the rough weather was over. for today it snows so you will as a matter of course go out again and then you will be unwell again for another fortnight but I am thankful at least it is only an influenza and nothing more serious – I would now conjure you to take care of yourself, but I think my letter will be too late, by the time it arrives we shall have the Befriedigung[4] to hear of your being in bed again – and then you will be at least safe you noughty child – I was so much delighted at the letter I got from you yesterday it was very nice of you to write to me even from bed; you are my dear sweet girl that will have to suffer quite martyrdom from her tyranical husband – I must inform you at once dearest Tillchen that you must hardly expect any letter at all for next Tuesday as I shall have no time to write. but I shall then send you the long promised photographs which I am afraid to add to this letter as I fancy it would be beyond weight. Emily calls me to breakfast now; then we head for Temesvár it is an awful day wind & snow. Ganz ein für mein Titschen zu schaffen.[5] Say to Alma I thank her for her letter which I have no time to answer any more. tell her I am the most unhappy man on her account. Now I have done so much for our future garden but I could not get strawberry plants from any where! what will she do when she wants to vent her rage at my tyranny? Now goodbye sweetest [illeg.] it was a <u>great consolation</u> to me to perceive from your last that you do not misconstrue the present shortness of my letters – the press of business will be over in a week or fortnight then I shall write more again.

yours affect –
Willy.

Address: No envelope

Unpublished. Text: M.S., Pf. Coll., CL'ANA 0421, Box 1, bundle a, number 64

---

1 Misspelling for Versecz (Hungarian) or Werschetz (German). The town is in Serbia today (Vršac), about 76 kilometers south of Timișoara.
2 German for "attached".
3 German for "epoch day".
4 German for "satisfaction".
5 German: " A perfect one for my Titschen to get things done" (transcription and translation by Ann Sherwin).

5 • Wilhelm Gaulis Clairmont to Ottilia von Pichler [later Clairmont]

Temesvár March 17<u>th</u> morning 1866

My dearest Tilly. We that is Rudi and I started yesterday morning for this blessed place – after dinner we went out to the fair to buy building timber, but we did not succeed in getting all we wanted as the road was so very bad and the Wallachians[1] could not bring the timber – in the evening we went to the theatre and so the Störenfried by Benedix[2] it was however so cold in the theatre that we cut away after the second act – we took our refuge to the bier[3] house opposite where we found Inspector Meyer and the Rittmeister who also came in for the fair – after supping we walked home – This morning I seize the first opportunity to write to you still before breakfast as I know I shall not have any time afterwards –
I am very curious to hear all about Paulines visit to you and how you found her and how you got on with her – very likely she will also write me – Your mamma's letter enclosed in your last pleased me very much only I am doubtful whether I can and should accept her invitation now made to me in a formal manner for the first time, as I am afraid it will put you all (I do not include you in this) to much inconvenience – if it were for a shorter time I could more readily agree to it, but for several weeks I have the greatest scruple. I think I must reflect on this subject before I can answer your mamma – But do you know I am afraid Tilly my stay in Vienna will have to be abbreviated by a good deal on account of my presence being so essential here at the building – and if we are to be married so much sooner than we first expected we can afford to give up a little of our time now – this leads me to what you relate of your conversation with your papa – the house will be sufficiently dry and in summer it does dry so fast, so that if it were not quite dry on the 1<u>st</u> July it would be so in a week or two – the objection about Moritz[4] I do not think tenable he is not a lad of such very susceptible feelings to take your marriage so much to heart as to be disturbed in his studies on that account; and as far as the äußerliche Zerstreuung[5] connected with our marriage it will only last <u>one day</u> & I take for granted your parents will not think of any festivities, so that that will make no difference for Moritz either for if he has not been diligent throughout the year, what little he crams just before the examinations will be of no avail to him – I am not however so selfish as not to be perfectly willing to wait still a week or two for the possession of my treasure provided Moritz's interest <u>really</u> required it – I look upon every day [illeg.] that our separation is protracted as a lost day; but apart from this, if our marriage is not celebrated at the period when I can manage to get away from the farm conveniently we shall have great loss as, for if I go away as your papa desires in August, the people will not only not work during that time, but what is worse they will <u>steal</u> half the wheat as they have done every year hitherto you know I like Rudi very much, but he is utterly untrust worthy in this respect. it would be most ridiculous to suppose that he would attend to anything even in my absence he is afraid of driving in the dark, he always leaves an hour before sunset for home – then the people are sure that he

APPENDIX

will not return any more and so they have the whole evening before them to steal and rob at their pleasure – Do not tell this to any one but höchstens[6] to your papa in private because I do not want it to come round to Rudi who would be offended at it so you see we should [illeg.] a make a very great sacrifice and I dont think that Moritz would gain anything in return.

Saturday [illeg.] evening. I have been to the fair all day today with a view of buying some suitable horses, but I could not find any so I must try again tomorrow – I am very tired and cannot write much – I have not read Emily's letter and I wish you would tell me what was the passage which you say made you so proud and happy I have not had any further conversation with Rudolphs about the winter – we only settled this much that if it is a bad year we should for the winter mangiren[7] together at their house – if now we should take a small lodging in Csakova for the winter for ourselves – I should much prefer the latter – they proposed to give us Rudi's present bedroom for a bedroom or the servants room neither would be very inviting – Do give Alma my best love tell her I thank her very much for her Secretair Brief[8] although I fancied it was a little drier than her usual ones, but this is because she has her giddiness again – Goodbye dearest Tilly. I add the 3 photographs because this letter is so very short – I am not sure whether I shall still have time to add something tomorrow or not

yours affection
Willy.

Address: No envelope

Unpublished. Text: M.S., Pf. Coll., CL'ANA 0421, Box 1, bundle a, number 13

---

1 The term "Wallachia" refers to the region in Romania south of the Carpathian Mountains. Romania's capital, Bucharest, is located in Wallachia, which is divided by the Olt River into Muntenia (eastern Wallachia) and Oltenia (western Wallachia). Bucharest is located in Muntenia.
2 *Der Störenfried*, a comedy by Roderich Benedix (1811–1873). Misspelling for "saw".
3 German for "beer".
4 Ottilia's brother, Moritz von Pichler. See CL'ANA 0275.
5 German for "external amusement".
6 German for "at most".
7 Germanization of the French word, "manger" (to eat).
8 German for "secretarial letter".

6 • Wilhelm Gaulis Clairmont to Ottilia von Pichler [later Clairmont]

Lippa[1] March 24th 1866.

My dearest Tilly. I am afraid you will have but a very short letter this time, for I have had two most fatiguing days yesterday and today and it is now already 9 oclock and tomorrow I have to rise again at 4 oclock I left yesterday at 5 oclock in the morning we did not reach this till 9 oclock because I say <u>we</u> because there were 4 carts for carting timber with me – Lippa is as compared with the Banat a most beautiful place – the Maros[2] a fine and rapid river comes out from a narrow valley between most pittoresc mountains on which there is [illeg.] a most interesting well preserved ruin of an old ~~ca~~ [illeg.]schloss[3]– vis a vis there is a monastery called Radna[4] a much frequented Wahlfahrtsplatz[5]– its quite a Rhine on a small scale – I was so much engaged all day with selecting and bargaining for timber and then loading it that I had no time to devote to amusement but while we were busy on the riverside I used to throw a glance at the monastery and the castle from time to time – I determined however that as soon as all the treading work is done we – that is <u>you</u> and <u>I</u> shall make an escapade to this place and then we shall stop here for a few days and enjoy everything at our leisure – Wont that be jolly my dearest Titsy?

I have read through your letter just now again – I find nothing in particular to answer in it excepting what you say about Alma. the rest I have answered already in my last. I am on this score more confident than you – your fear about her will allay itself – in proportion as your household becomes smaller Alma will be better able to manage it and your M.[6] will be less irritable – Alma will also marry sooner or later and then your romantic Liebschaft[7] for each other will be at an end – for if you are sufficiently stronghearted to have <u>two</u> loves at the same time – she will not be so I should give my consent as far as I have any to give most unwillingly to Alma's becoming married because I am very selfish – for I like her very much & I should delight in having a sister like her but as soon as she gets married she is lost to us – However if it must be and both your happiness requires it, why of course it could not be helped, ~~and~~ only be prepared beforehand that when Alma is once married you will drop down from the complicated dignities of lover, husband uncle etc. to the simple Rang[8] of a sister I asked Emily the width of their sheets but she did not seem to know and I purposely refrained from pressing her further because their beds are all so wretchedly short that my legs from the knees downwards have always to dangl in the air and I should therefore be sorry if you took their dimensions as a pattern for ours – It is just so as if a taylor made me a coat to Rudi's measure – I am afraid I shall not get my Sundays letter tomorrow for the road is bad and I do not think I shall get further than Temesvar tomorrow – I shall post this letter <u>here</u> tomorrow, for fear of our reaching Temesvár too late for posttime or not at all; for if anything about the carts were to break which is likely enough as the timber is very heavy, there is half a days delay at once – A most interesting feature here are the Wallachians[9] – there was Wochenmarkt[10] and it was quite a pretty animated scene – they were[11] a much finer or rather better looking costume than our Wallachians– they also do their hair differently – they another excellent quality; they go in service as house & children maids which ours as you know do not – and the[12] make very capital servants – I hope you understood my commission about the Lodenstoff[13] I want it badly as the cloak is so much torn I am ~~afraid~~ ashamed to wear it and its too warm now for the fur – Goodbye now dearest Tilly – Excuse me for not writing any more but I must be off to bed. Give my love to Alma Moritz & your parents – I also think that the details of the July plan had better be settled when I am in Vienna

Believe me my dearest best girl
yours most sincerely
Willy

Address: 24. Brief den ~~27~~8. März 66[14]/ Fräulein Ottilie Pichler/ Landstrasse / Beatrixgasse N⁰ 19. Wien
Front postmark: LIPPA im[15] BANAT/ $^{25}/_3$
Rear postmark: 9–11 Fr./ WIEN/ 23 [illeg.]; TEMESVÁR/ [illeg.]/3

Unpublished. Text: M.S., Pf. Coll., CL'ANA 0122

---

1 Known in German and Hungarian as Lippa, the town of Lipova is located in Arad county, 59 kilometers north-east of Timişoara.
2 The Mureş River (Maros, in Hungarian) flows directly through Arad County. Lipova is situated on the Mureş.
3 Although the beginning part of the word is illegible, the legible section ("schloss") refers to a castle. Soimos Fortress was built in the thirteenth century in Lipova, Arad County. The castle was uninhabited from 1788 but was protected from demolition ("Cetate Soimos". Web. 24 June 2015. http://www.cetatesoimos.ro/).
4 The Monastery of Saint Maria Radna is located in Arad County (Habenicht, Herbert. "Restoration of Maria Radna Basilica". *Banat Villages*. Web. 24 October 2015. http://www.dvhh.org/banat_villages/Arad/maria_radna/resortation.htm). Engelmann identifies "Maria-Radna" as a "Marian pilgrimage site" (p. 10).
5 Wilhelm misspelled "Wallfahrtsplatz," German for "place of pilgrimage".
6 Mama.
7 German for "love affair".
8 German for "rank".
9 See CL'ANA 0421, Box 1, bundle a, number 13.
10 German for "weekly market".
11 Wilhelm meant to write "wear".
12 Wilhelm misspelled "they".
13 German for "loden," a type of waterproof woolen fabric.
14 German for "24th letter from 28 March 66".
15 German for "in".

APPENDIX

7 • Wilhelm Gaulis Clairmont to Ottilia von Pichler [later Clairmont]

Monday March 26th 1866.
Offsenitze.

My dearest Tilly. Here I am again in my splendid house and glad am I to get back to it although it is neither a cheerful nor a splendid house. I got back so late in the evening that I shall not have time to write you much for it is now already 10 oclock at night. and I must send the letter to Banlock[1] at daylight tomorrow – I passed through Csakova today but I stopped very short time I got your Sundays letter only today – I forgot it at Csakova today together with my other letters but as I read it over twice once aloud to Emily and once to myself I have no doubt I shall be able to answer it pretty well from memory – But first I must tell you about my journey home from Lippa; it was very tedious for we had to go at a slow footpace all the way and every minute there was a stop when (Good gracious me what have I done! I commenced this sheet the wrong way!!)[2]

I[3] hope you will get through your Übertritts[4] business without any discomfort to yourself – at any rate dont mind what any of them tell you but go your own way according to your own conviction – Of course not only my father but also I am a Brittish subject and therefore quite independent of the laws in Austria referring to Religious matters – I shall quite simply go to the clergyman of our Embassy[5] – if he only be not absent from Vienna just then – for then will be the height of London season – Dearest Tilly, there was something in your letter you must answer me truly. I have formed a suspicion against you – you must answer me truly whither I am right or not – I suspect you of having refused Conrads'[6] party on my account, but because I made those jokes about Otto and teased your little mamma for having allowed you to go "in das feindliche Lager"[7] his[8] trial trip and such a good long one it was – but he behaved most splendidly

I would not sell the horse for double what I gave for him – he is immensely strong very eager and tolerably fast and makes a tolerable figure – I bought this horse not for the farm but for myself to either drive the gig with or ride on – for until you come I have enough with one horse – and it saves an extra coachman and feed – the carts which I left behind yesterday at the Hodaja have now also arrived – so the first 4 loads of timber are now at the Hodaja for our new house. the carting of soil for ramming the walls was commenced with last week and is progressing favorably but for the continued rain – a delay with which you will believe me we put up most willingly If it were not for the Easter hollidays the walls would be up in a fortnight from this time – and of course once the walls are up the roof must be finished immediately to prevent the walls being whetted – a[9] rope came undone, or we came to a hill when the wheels had to be locked. On Sunday evening after dark we got to a charda[10] about two hours from Temesvar– as it would have been dangerous to drive with such a heavy load in the night I left the carts behind to stop there for the night, and I went on my way by myself to Temesvar on my Taliga[11] – it rained now and then but still there was enough of moonlight to enable me to find my way besides I have travelled so much at night in Australia that I am accustomed to it and like it better than travelling at day because one meets no carts and need not always ausweichen[12] – also the horses go much better because they are anxious to get to their stable – This morning I had business in Temesvár than I reached Csakova & Offsen.[13] without further adventure – My new horse behaved uncommonly well – this was

If[14] I were but sure that my suspicion is correct I would dich sehr auslachen[15] and look upon it as a new proof that you are so very apt alles für baare Münze zu nehmen[16] – I can assure dearest Tilly that I wish you to go to Conrads or at least not to avoid Otto – it would put either you or myself in a false light, for if he observes that you avoid him he must necessarily think either that he has still some influence on you and that you dread this, or that I dread his rivalry and that you avoid him for my sake – either I hope is utterly false – I can only assure you dearest Tilly that I have not the faintest notion of being jealous of him – and if I were I should be much too proud either to show it myself or to allow you to show it for it would be very humiliating to me to have to dread a rival – I have too good an opinion of you and of my own worth to do so –

Now I was out in the stable and saw the poor horses fed and watered; the poor dears are tired after this trip – I am so glad you are now quite well I hope Alma is so too – I hear nothing more of the naughty girl I think she must be sulky – Pauline writes me she got such a nice letter from you she really loves you very much – Now she sent me such a lot of things 12 pr. new socks 5 nightshirts. Now she wants me to send her 6 more dayshirts to renew – she is so ambitious that my linen should not be in such a very pitiable state when you come to take charge of it – while she was here it was in capital order –

Now Goodbye dearest Tilly give my love to Alma and your parents and believe me dearest Titsy yours most

affecty
Willy

If there is anything more in your letter which I have forgotten to answer I shall do it in my next – I[17] hope you will send me the Loden[18] soon you do not say whether you received the pictures – my cloak looks disgraceful – did you get my letter from Lippa?

Address: Fraulein [illeg.]tilia Pichler/ 19 Beatrixgasse/Landstrasse Wien
Front postmark: CSAKOVA/$^{27}/_3$
Rear postmark: 9–11F[illeg.]/WIEN/[illeg.]; ZSEBELY[19] [illeg.]/$^{27}/_3$

Unpublished. Text: M.S., Pf. Coll., CL'ANA 0118

---

1 Banloc, Romania, is a commune consisting of four villages, Banloc, Ofsenița, Partoș and Soca (http://enciclopediaromaniei.ro). Banloc is seven kilometers south of Ofsenița.

APPENDIX

2 Wilhelm wrote his letter without regard for pagination. He began page one on what was labeled page four.
3 The following section should be read as page four.
4 German for "conversion".
5 As was the custom, the wedding certificate listed the marrying couple's religion. Wilhelm was noted as belonging to "Evang. Anglicanischer Confession" (Protestant, Anglican Confession) while Ottilia's religion was recorded as "Evangelisch Augsb. Confession" (Protestant, Augsburg Confession). See CL'ANA 0408, unpublished manuscript, Pforzheimer, Collection. See also the photograph in this collection of the wedding certificate. Wilhelm also continued to maintain his British citizenship. In January 1881, some six years after the birth of their son, Paul, Wilhelm registered the birth with the British Consulate in Vienna. The acting consul signed the record of "BIRTHS within the District of the British Consulate at Vienna" (CL'ANA 0408, unpublished document, Pforzheimer Collection).
6 Unidentified.
7 German for "into the enemy's camp". Wilhelm, of course, meant this as a joke.
8 As Wilhelm wrote his letter without regard for accurate pagination, this page should have been page three of the letter.
9 Had Wilhelm followed accurate pagination, this section would start the second page.
10 Wilhelm misspelled the Hungarian word "csárda" (a tavern).
11 Hungarian for "tumbrel," a cart used on a farm.
12 German for "swerve" or "sidestep".
13 Wilhelm misspelled the abbreviation for Ofsenița.
14 Had Wilhelm followed accurate pagination, this section would start the fifth page.
15 German for "greatly laugh at you".
16 German for "to take everything at face value".
17 Wilhelm cross-wrote the final sentence.
18 See note 13, CL'ANA 0122.
19 Zsebely is located in Timiș County.

APPENDIX

8 • Wilhelm Gaulis Clairmont to Ottilia von Pichler [later Clairmont]

Offsenitza April 6th 1866

My dearest Tilly.
I am afraid you will have got your last letter one day behind hand that is instead of Sunday or Monday – for an accident happened to the messenger whom I sent with the letter to Banlok in consequence of which I am afraid he reached the post too late for today's mail. Today I was all day at the pusta; poor Rudi has been unwell all this time with a sore mouth I have not seen him for a week; the crops do not look as well as they might considering the favorable weather and this depresses me very much and causes [illeg.] me to give myself up to all sorts of melancholy thoughts which I would communicate to you; but I do not want to give you care and anxiety unnecessarily, for I hope they proceed only from a transient mood of despondency and not from as rational conviction that our prospects are so bad – You know that one often feels that difficulty in tracing back one's feelings to their main springs – But as I have now told you so much I had better tell you all, for fear of this uncertainty being a source of greater uneasiness to you than a knowledge of the thoughts which afflict me. It is no other thought than this my dearest Tilly which makes me so miserable whether I am <u>justified</u> in taking you away from a happy and comfortable home where you are so well beloved by all, and where you have spent your whole life, to this bleak and dreary pusta, where you must share with me not only the perils and discomfort of my arduous vocation, but also the frightful uncertainty of the Banat with reference to pecuniary success – I wrote to you only in yesterday's letter quite in fact that I anticipated nothing "Schrecklichies[1] from our marriage – but the reproaches with which I should have to load myself if it turned out wrong, that would be something terrible indeed – ob ich es mit meinem Gewissen verein baren kann, dich zu vermögen deine gesicherte Stellung zuhause gegen die ganz unsichern welche ich dir nun biethen kann zu vertauschen[2] this is what agitates me; you must understand my Tilly that this is a mere question of reasoning and not of feeling. I take for granted that you are ready to make a sacrifice for me; every girl that is in love does so if required – but that does not lessen my responsibility in accepting your sacrifice which I dare not do unless I see a very strong probability of my being able to requit your sacrifice – However be consoled my Tilly with this that meine Anschauungen[3] <u>just now</u> are not to be implicitly relied on – ich selbst tröste mich hiermit[4] I am subject to such fits of melancholy especially in spring and summer when I have much to do and much mental anxiety to go through – this will be over by the time I come to Vienna and then it will also be decided whether the crops will recover or whether they are bad – so we had better not worry ourselves with premature uneasiness – Julchen's[5] photograph I looked at again & it pleases me very much – if she is only half as wise and natural as she looks on it I shall like her very much – although she is such a dangerous rival of mine – of course I [illeg.] shall be most happy to figure with you on one photograph although it will be very much to my disadvantage – Why do you say you are <u>sorry</u> to confess I was right in my interpretation of your

frequent looks at the barraks? and why was I already then a tyrant? I did nothing tyrannical then did I? that I looked through the secrets of your heart is true but that was not tyrannical was it? and do you know that these unsuccessful attempts to hide your feelings from me made you most fascinating and charming in my eyes because they were a proof of the purity and genuineness of your feelings. – If I only felt as confident in all other respects as in this that I am capable of making you happy I should indeed be the most contented creature on earth – in this one respect I have thank Heavens no misgivings at all. – Your questions about Franz[6] I can not answer because I have no idea what the awful things consist in "welche er mit diesem Subjecte von einer woman thut und treibt"[7] I have no idea what she is like, whether she is ladylike or vulgar, but I suppose the least possible thing she and Franz could have done to merit your strong contempt is to have gone together on the Kohlmarkt during the corso[8] to pick peoples' pockets – Why Rudi & I laughed was not for anything I either approve or disapprove of in Frazen's conduct; for I have no idea of what he had done; but on account of the propensity all, even the best of women have to imitate the Pharisees[9] of old and pounce down upon those unfortunates of their own sex who commit the slightest faux pas in matters of the heart; why are we men so much more tolerant in this respect than you women ? if a woman for any reason whatever cannot love her husband, it is but natural that she will in due course find someone else whom she can and will love. I dont say it is right but still it is an error springing from the good and natural disposition of the female heart and should be tolerated more readily than other vices such as slander, mischiefmaking intriguing against which no one dreams of raising his voice – I quite admit that matrimony is an institution, the sanctity of which must for many reasons be kept inviolate, but on the other hand the feelings of the female breast are all powerful and cannot be either bound up or let loose by the mutterings of a ranting old priest – a woman loads a heap of misery on herself when she allows her feelings to put her in collusion with all the laws and prejudices of humanity, therefore one ought to content oneself with the reflexion that her imprudence will curtail troubles enough to her in due course, and that every individual is not called upon to throw stones at her. – Now my Tits I have told you ein Langes u Breites[10] on this most interesting subject; but you must please remember that I meant this only in general – of this special case I am utterly ignorant of the details. – I am afraid that you will find out that you have a shockingly noughty husband and that you will have to reform him a great deal before he comes up to your standard of moral excellence –

You do not say how Hermans[11] copies of your photograph turned out I am very curious to see some of his productions I fancy it must be comparatively easy to copy from a photograph.

Saturday afternoon – We have now continued fine weather, only there is this eternal southerly breeze which dries up everything and makes everything uncomfortable even to human beings down below the ground has yet sufficient moisture but above it is as arid and hard as a rock in consequence of the hot winds – I am afraid the pusta soil is <u>very</u> much inferior to what the Bobdaer[12] soil was – there we were sure of a crop if there was but rain. but here even with rain it seems doubtful – Last year I had a very fair crop of wheat at Bobda although the mice destroyed one third I still attained an average of 10 Mtz[13] pr. [illeg.] and that wheat of the very best quality while Rudi had no crop at all last year and would have had to buy even the seed wheat had I not joined him in partnership – how ever we shall have patience yet & see what the future brings –

Sunday afternoon. Just now I rec^d your letter dearest Tits. and I kiss you many times for it although the account of your mother's repeated attacks make me sad on your account for I do not see why you should be made to suffer so much if she chooses to be violent – I am afraid I shall not manifest similar Engelsgüte[14] as your papa if she should zum besten geben[15] similar scenes in my house: – be assured if your papa had kept such excess of passion under a firm cheque and held the reins with a tight hand (I mean not now but in former times) she would never have dared to go so far – this is why I view all superreligious people with most particular suspicion, for in proportion as they sing psalms and talk much and highly about "our Lord" they fancy to have sufficiently proved their goodness and by way of indemnification indulge in an unrestrained yielding up to all their evil passions – where as we others who talk less pompously of god and religion have the more time to bestow on our selfimprovement – I am afraid it must have gone far indeed if even your papa could console you with the idea that for you it would not last long any more – !

I have not time now to answer your letter in full, for Bernhard is here (without Judith) and I cannot absent myself for so long a time – Bernhard bought Emily a lot of things from home among others a very nice stylish looking jacket – Goodbye my sweet dear girl, you exact very much indeed when you say I must not flirt with any of your charming Freundinnen[16]

Yours most affectionately
Willy.

Address: No envelope

Unpublished. Text: M.S., Pf. Coll., CL'ANA 0421, Box 1, bundle a, number 1

---

1 German for "terrible". Wilhelm omitted the closing quotation marks.
2 German: "whether I can reconcile it with my conscience to ask you to exchange your secured position at home for the totally unsecured one that I am able to offer you now" (transcription and translation by Ann Sherwin).
3 German for "my opinions".
4 German for : I console myself with this".
5 See CL'ANA 0421, Box 3, bundle f, number 160.
6 Unidentified.
7 German: "that he does with this female character" (transcription and translation by Ann Sherwin).
8 German: "Kohlmarkt during the corso" (transcription and translation by Ann Sherwin). Kohlmarkt is a street in Vienna. "Corso" is Italian for "path".

APPENDIX

9 Jewish scholars (515 BCE-70CE) who "interpreted the Law according to its spirit" as opposed to the Sadducees (the high priests) (The Editors of Encyclopaedia Britannica. "Pharisee" *Encyclopaedia Britannica Online*. Encyclopaedia Britannica Inc., n.d. Web. 3 November 2015. http://www.britannica.com/topic/Pharisee).
10 German: for "a whole lot".
11 Unidentified.
12 See CL'ANA 0254.
13 Abbreviation for "Metzen," a dry measure, particularly for grain. See CL'ANA 0286.
14 German for "angelic kindness".
15 German combined with English for "if she should stage similar scenes".
16 German for "girlfriends".

APPENDIX

9 • Wilhelm Gaulis Clairmont to Ottilia von Pichler [later Clairmont]

Offsenitza April 8th 1866.

My own dear Tilly. After I had posted my letter to you today we spent an hour with Bernhard who then left; immediately afterwards the Rothweils[1] came, about half an hour afterwards I mounted my new charger & I left for home; I did not stop over night at Csakova as this is the Eastersunday of the Wallachians and it is better I should pay a visit to the Hodaja this night, as the greater part of our men will think it necessary to get drunk in honour of the day. I had a beautiful evening for my ride & here I am now after having taken tea as it to answer your letter which gave me great pleasure and made me most desirous of heartily kissing once again my dear, excellent, patient and loving child – I must return to the subject which moved me most in your letter and which I also attended to already in the letter I posed this afternoon – I dont want to say anything harsh against your mother but I really do not perceive where is the use of religion unless it teaches us to conquer our evil passions and to be just and good towards our fellow creatures – although you in your angelic goodness utter not a complaint against your mother still I can see that the provocation under which you suffered must have been <u>monstrous</u> or else your father would not have offered you the to him most humiliating consolation that at last <u>your</u> trials would soon be at an end – I say humiliating to him for it is at once a confession that you were annoyed and that he had not the power to see justice done to his <u>own</u> child in his <u>own</u> house – this my dear speaks volumes – this shall be otherwise when you are my wife for I am not afraid of the devil himself althoug he come in shape of a woman – It was very selfish of me to think so dearest Tilly but I am bound to admit it to you that for myself I drew some consolation from this sad business with reference to the grief and doubts which I communicated to you in my last as to whether I am justified in inducing you to share my uncertain lot; for if they make you lead such an unhappy life at home (and I always suspect from regard for your mother you do not communicate to me one tenth part) I need have less hesitation in taking you from your home for whatever other trials we may have to undergo you will never meet with anything else from me but the deepest and most unchangeable love. – It was a source of the greatest pleasure to me my Tilly that you could assure me you came through all this trouble with a clear conscience and that throughout this affair you have resisted the temptation of yielding to your temper – this is a great triumph indeed on which I congratulate you most sincerely and for which I love you even more. you know my Tilly I too may sometimes be irritated by opposition you will make it worse, but with a kind indulgent word you will <u>instantly</u> break my bad temper – and therefore I rejoice that you have accomplished this selfconquest. I thought much of you this forenoon as I feared that my Friday's letter was not posted in time and that you did not get it today. this would make me very sad for I know it would give you a disappointment – As I am such a very dutyful devoted and you do not wish it I shall give up the "silly intention" of coming to Vienna unexpectedly although I would not consider it silly at all – but on the contrary very jolly indeed – ; your generous intentions towards me (that I may not flirt with any of your lovely friends but only with old aunts etz) is really zum

Gänsehaut bekommen – nur mit dem Unterschiede daß ich dieselbe bekomme und nicht du. es ist doch nur billig daß ich mich für meine lange Enthaltsamkeit hier entschädige – nun habe ich seit 29 oder 28ten Jänner mit keinem weiblichen Wesen als Emilie gesprochen! Das ist ja zum Hunde und Katzen bekommen![2]
With reference to my mother I give you my advice the more readily as I know her so well – I am quite sure you will do better for the present not to write to her anymore – for her answer was not such as to court a further reply and having done for all that was necessary for the present so wirst du ihr durch eine ruhige würdevolle Haltung mehr imponieren als durch ein zu ängstliches Streben nach ihren guten Meinung – sie ist kalt und menschenfeindlich etwa andrer seits sehr gerecht und einsichtsvoll – laß sie jetzt ganz in Ruhe – wenn sie sich nach einigen Jahren überzeugt haben wird, daß du mir wirklich das bist, was ich jetzt schon überzeugt bin, daß du mir sein wirst, so wird sie dir von selbst entgegen kommen. aber liebes Mädchen rede nicht mit andern über sie, denn sie verstehen sie nicht.[3] – Today I got the cloak from the taylor, although one perceives the patch still it matters nothing and looks very well – the old cloak looks quite spruce again – I also admired Emily's Jopperl[4] very much – it is very smartlooking the stuff very nice and the cut elegant, but the kalpak[5] in my opinion does not become her well – she looks jewish in it but dont betray this – That you are not unjust towards me regarding the shortness of my letters I gladly and thankfully acknowledge, you see this is an instance of a new virtue which I did not know before you possessed – With reference to business I have only to observe that no enamelled iron ware is made at Reschitza and Orawitza[6] but it is brought to Temesvár from Bohemia and will therefore be much the same price whether you buy it here or in Vienna – allowing of course for the difference of the freight – but I do not think you will want much ironware as I have I believe enough for our small Sparrherd[7] – there are 6 or 7 pots with lids of different sizes then 2 genzig [illeg.] töpfe then 2 or 3 Bratpfannen[8] I never heard any complaint that there was not enough of this kind of material. of matrasses we of course do not want any more than those for our beds, for the sparebeds I have more than enough already – where would be the use of buying more – about the covering of the beds I have no particular liking at all whatever pleases you will please me; the blankets I shall get washed and then talk to Emily about [illeg.] fitting them up but dont dream dearest of cutting the blankets shorter – for they would be too short for me; it is my permanent curse whenever I sleep away from home to have either my feet or my shoulders uncovered – dont think of it – the remarks about your have not convinced me a bit – only the other day I made a Hohngelächter [illegible] Hölle über eine [illeg.] die grau gewesen wäre, aber nicht war – und zwar mit Bezug auf Louis R.[9] – is it not naughty of me – Goodnight sweetest

Tilly yours affect
Willy.

Love to Alma

Monday night – today I had a most fatiguing day I was at the pusta from half past five in the morning for we began the weeding of the wheat which is a very tedious operation and will keep me engaged for a full fortnight from morning till night

APPENDIX

you must therefore prepare for even shorter letters – another important business we [illeg.] today is the walking round all the wheatfields and deciding which are good enough to remain & which must be ploughed up – in all there are about 150 acres which must be ploughed and sown again with something else (including that which has been ploughed up already –) I am however happy today that the better wheat is now since two days taking a decided turn for the better and much will improve yet – Bernhard also told me that much of his wheat is very bad – so you envied him in vain – With the house there is bad news again – the men who undertook the contract bolted and so now we must look out for fresh people – If but the weeding of the wheat and the planting the [illeg.] is done then the rest is comparatively easy if it were not for the house building I would then escape easily – Now Goodnight dearest Tits give my love to Alma and believe me

dearest Titsy
yours most affectionately
Willy

I wanted to read your last letter to Emily but had no time she is getting an awful Widerspruchsgeist[10] – I said to her yesterday : If Tilly turns out but half as contradictory as you I shall have a fine life of it –

Address: No envelope

Unpublished. Text: M.S., Pf. Coll., CL'ANA 0421, Box 1, bundle a, number 2

---

1 Unidentified.
2 German: "enough to give one goose bumps – but with the difference that I get them and not you. It is only fitting that I compensate myself for my long time of abstinence here – for I haven't spoken with a single female person but Emilie since the 29th or 28th of January! It's enough to drive you mad!" (transcription and translation by Ann Sherwin).
3 German: "you will impress her more with a calm, dignified posture than by trying too anxiously to win her approval – she is cold and misanthropic but on the other hand very fair and insightful – leave her entirely alone for now – if after a few years she becomes convinced that you actually are to me what I am already convinced that you will be to me, then she will approach you on her own. But dear girl, do not talk with others about her, for they don't understand her" (transcription and translation by Ann Sherwin).
4 German for "jacket".
5 A type of hat.
6 Reschitza is German for Reşiţa, a city in Romania today. It is located 100 kilometers south-east of Timişoara. Orawitza is German for Oraviţa, a town in Romania today. It is located some 53 kilometers south-west of Reşiţa and 107 kilometers south-east of Timişoara. Engelmann records that "Reschitza, Orawitza, and Steierdorf-Anina first grew as industrial and mining centers after 1718 and owed their emergence to the metalworkers, miners and foresters, who came there" (*The Banat Germans*, p. 33).
7 German for "economical kitchen stove". The word is usually spelled "Sparherd".
8 German for "then 2 entirely [illeg.] pots, then 2 or 3 frying pans".
9 German: "derisive laughter [illeg.] – hell over a [illeg.] that would have been gray but was not – and with reference to Louis R". (transcription and translation by Ann Sherwin). Louis R. is unidentified.
10 German for "contrariness".

GENEALOGICAL TABLE

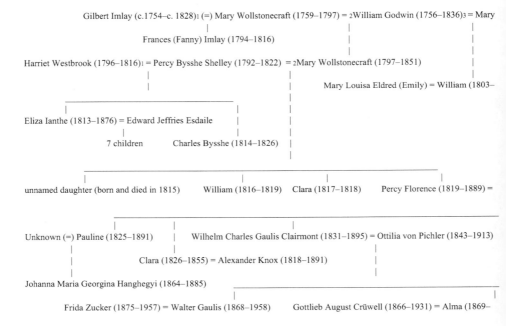

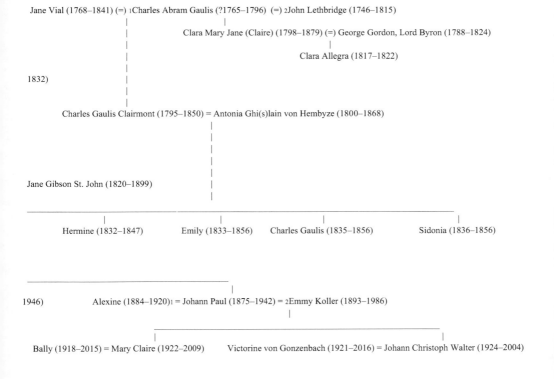

INDEX

Note; Page numbers in bold type refer to images
Page numbers followed by 'n' refer to the numbered notes
Volume numbers are in Roman bold type

Aberle, G. **II** 1, 5, 58n1
Abhandlung **I** 83, 84n12, 85
Accounts and Papers (1875) **II** 204n4
Adams, Major **II** 87n8, 148
Adelaide, Australia **II** 253
Adventures of a Younger Son (Trelawny) **II** 239n3
Agency of the First Privileged Austrian Danube Steamboat Company **II** 30
Agram **II** 131, 139, 140n5&6, 169, 172, 198n1
Ajaccio **II** 261, 262n1,3&7, 263
Albrecht, Archduke **I** 201, 202n6, 209, 210n4, 281n2
All Souls Day **I** 223
Alloway Bank, **I** 147, **II** 218, 220n12&13, 253–4
Allworth family **II** 219, 220n22
Alservorstadt **I** 232, 233n1, 302n6
Altenburg **I** *xx*, *xxiii*, 93, 94n4, 102n1, 103n4, 113n13, 114, 116, 117, 119, 121, 128, 130, 134, 251n2, 285, 288n5, **II** 12n7, 15n2, 63n3, 64, 75n1
Ancona **II** 156, 159n9
Andoe, Captain **I** 20, 22n2, 26, 31, 32, 33, 43, 44, 60, 62, 70, 75, 82, 85, 86n6, 87, 90, 204
Andrews, J. **II** 31n11
Anglo Aust BK (Anglo-Austrian Bank) **II** 80, 80n12
Anglo-International Bank **II** 80n12
anti-Protestant riots (Barletta, 1866) **II** 91n1
anti-Semitism **I** 12n10, 348n7

Antibes **II** 260, 260n10
Appleton's European Guide Book (1886) **II** 122n3
Apponyi, Count T. **II** 241, 242n6
Arenstein (Arnstein) **II** 121, 122n2, 201
Arlt, F.C. von **II** 136–8, 137n2
Armidale **I** 148, 149, 151, 182n1&3, 183n6, 194, 195n7, 217
Armstrong, Mrs **I** 155, 158n24
Arno River **II** 12n11, 20n9, 208
Artaria, Mrs **I** 226, 226n2, 233
Atherstane **I** 187
Auckland **II** 42, 44n4
Australia **I** 145, 147, 161, 175, 201, 240, **II** 1, 7n1, 8, 41, 124, 219, 243, 278, 291; Adelaide **II** 253; Armidale **I** 148, 149, 151, 182n1&3, 183n6, 194, 195n7, 217; Bathurst **I** *xxi*, 146, 150n1, 151,153, 154–5, 156, 157n21, 161, 162n5, 166, 168n1, 186n7, 195n7, 199n14, 219n6, 243n2, **II** 220n11, 253, 255n4; Bombala (New South Wales) **I** 237, 238n12, 256. 259, 262, 268, 296, 309, 310n1; Brisbane **I** 150n1, **II** 253; Darling River **II** 253, 254n9; gold **I** 156n17, 157n21; history of **I** 169n5; immigrants **I** 176n3; Merimbula (New South Wales) **I** 151, 253n2, 257n5, 310n1, 327, 332; Murrumbidgee **I** 149, 155n4, 237n1; Murrumbidgee River **I** 155n3, 162n4, 176n4, 186n5, 235n9, 238n12&13, 240, 260n1, 264–5, 274, 350, 351n5, 354, 355–6; New South Wales **I** 238, 238n12, 310, 350, 351n5; Pambula

(Panbula) (New South Wales) **I** 238n9, 257n6&9; pastoralism **I** 169; population **I** 307n1; Sydney **I** 51, 145–6, 148, 149, 153, 155, 156n9, 158n24, 181, 182, 183n4,5&6, 195n7, 197, 218, 229, 232, 234, 236, 237, 255, 258, 267, 309, 352, 354, 355, 356, 359, **II** 86, 253, 254, 267n7; *Sydney Morning Herald* **I** *xxii*, 145, 149, 155n1, 156n9, 158n24, 186n5, 235n7, 253n3, 259n3, 352n1, **II** 87n6&7, 201; Tantangara (New South Wales) **I** 350, 351n5; Tumut **I** 354, 354n2

Austria **I** 50, 63n8, 114, 123, 294, **II** 1, 7n1, 11, 32, 59, 86, 108–10, 157, 180–2, 290; acre **II** 25–6; Agency of the First Privileged Austrian Danube Steamboat Company **II** 30; Alservorstadt (Vienna) **I** 232, 233, 302n6; Bad Gastein **I** 5, 8n6, 10, 12n6, 15, 16, 22, **II** 42, 44n8, 46–8; Baden bei Wien **I** *xxii*, *xxiii*, 196, 197, 198n1, 199n13, 201, 202n9, 203, 204, 205n7, 206, 207, 209, 213, 214, 216, 218, 221, 223, 225, 226, 231, 232, 244, 246, 250, 252, 254, 260, 262, 264, 265, 267, 272, 276, 278, 280, 282, 284, 285, 289, 291, 294, 297, 299, 301, 304, 306, 312, 315, 319, 320, 321, 323, 326, 328, 329, 335, 337, 339, 344, 345, 346n2, 347, 357, **II** 13–14, 21–3, 29, 30, 38, 77–81, 92–3, 123–6, 138–9, 199, 243; cabinet **I** 89; coronation of Franz Joseph **I** **II** 100; educational system **I** 84n9; Emperor Franz Joseph I **II** 100, 101n2; Empress Elisabeth **II** 77, 78n2, 101n2; government **II** 29; Grätz (Graz) **I** 6, 7, 9n9, **II** 132; Habsburg rulers **II** 1; Innsbruck **II** 78n4, 112n3, 166n7; land purchase **I** 324; Linz **II** 175; Melk **I** 66, 68n5; migration **I** 51; Südbahn **II** 131n6, 174; Tyrol **I** 274, 275n2, 276, 280, **II** 111, 112n3; Vienna **I** 6, 8n6, 10, 17–19, 19n7, 19n11, 24n2, 28, 32, 39, 44, 46, 47, 56, 78, 82, 84n3, 85, 107, 116, 117, 121, 127, 189, 207, 225, 232, 233, 297, 302n6, **II** 2–3, 4, 26–30, 63n1, 76–7, 90n5, 117–18, 121–6, 197–9, 217–18, 289–90, 292n5, 294, 297–8; Weidling **I** 6, 8n1&3, 10–11, 18, 19, 21, 43, 75, 116; Wieden **I** 112n1

Austrian Central Bank **II** 175n3

Austrian Embassy **II** 173, 178
Austrian National Bank **II** 175n4, 196n2
Austro-Hungarian Dual Monarchy **II** 2, 101n2
Austro-Hungarian Empire **II** 3, 9n4, 16n12, 18n3, 252n4
Austro-Prussian War (Seven Weeks' War, 1866) **II** 93n4
Austro-Turkish War (1716–18) **II** 1; Treaty of Passarovitz **II** 1

Baas, J.H. **II** 61n8, 139n1
Bad Gastein **I** 5, 8n6, 10, 12n6, 15, 16, 22, **II** 42, 44n8, 46–8
Baden bei Wien **I** *xxii*, *xxiii*, 196, 197, 198n1, 199n13, 201, 202n9, 203, 204, 205n7, 206, 207, 209, 213, 214, 216, 218, 221, 223, 225, 226, 231, 232, 244, 246, 250, 252, 254, 260, 262, 264, 265, 267, 272, 276, 278, 280, 282, 284, 285, 289, 291, 294, 297, 299, 301, 304, 306, 312, 315, 319, 320, 321, 323, 326, 328, 329, 335, 337, 339, 344, 345, 346n2, 347, 357, **II** 13–14, 21–3, 29, 30, 38, 77–81, 92–3, 123–6, 138–9, 199, 243
Balaton, Lake (Plattensee) **II** 12n6, 15n3, 26, 28n3&4, 154n6
Bally, Hans Jörg **I** *xxiv*, **II** 4
Bally-Clairmont, Mary Claire **I** *xi*, *xxiv*, *xxix*, 73n1, **II** 4, 33n1, 63n1, **75**, 113n1, 127n18, 133n6, 143n3, 221n1
Banat, **I** *xii*, *xxi*, *xxiii*, 79n3, **II** 1–3, 11, 144, 154n4, 155, 167, 170, 181, 277, 288, 293
Bank of England **II** 21, 80n12
banks **I** 278; Anglo Aust BK (Anglo-Austrian Bank) **II** 80, 80n12; Austrian Central Bank **II** 175n3; Austrian National Bank **II** 175n4, 196n2
Banloc **II** 84n3, 290, 291n1, 293
Bariss, A. **II 67–8**, 96n1, 115n2
Bastia **II** 261
Batavia **I** 152, 167, 169n11
Baths of Lucca **II** 141, 142n2, 143n6, 235n4
Bathurst **I** *xxi*, 146, 150n1, 151, 153, 154–5, 156, 157n21, 161, 162n5, 166, 168n1, 186n7, 195n7, 199n14, 219n6, 243n2, **II** 220n11, 253, 255n4
Battiste **II** 214
Bauplatz: **I** 306, 308n5, 324, 337, 338n1, 340, 341n6

INDEX

Beary, A.C. (see Berry, A.C.)
Beauclerk family **II** 21n2
Beauclerk, Aubrey **II** 22n2
Beauclerk, Emily **II** 21n2, 23
Beauclerk, Georgiana **II** 22n2
Becker, Colonel **II** 45, 57, 59–60, 77, 81, 84, 98n4
Beleci **II** 152, 154n4, 167, 168–172, 174
Belgium: Ostende **I** 20, 22n1, 77, 78n1, 262
Bellosquardo **II** 234
Belvedere **I** 190n5&6; Schwarzenberg Gardens **I** 189, 190n5
Benedict Brothers **I** 95, 96n2
Benedix, Roderich **II** 286
Berlin **I** 82, 83n2, 85, 86n1, 262, **II** 3–4, 25, 113n1
Bermondsey, **I** 58, 63n4
Berry, Alexander **I** 51, 54n6, 108n2, 145
Berry, Elizabeth Wollstonecraft **I** 54n6
Beste, Miss Julia V. **I** 40, 42n15, 70, 71n3, 78, 101, 107, 117, 128, 129
Biedermann, Mr **I** 17, 19n2
Big White Lie: Chinese Australians in White Australia (Fitzgerald) **I** 151, 158n23
Billroth, Theodor **II** 4
Binder, Baron **I** 291, 292n1
Bird, Mrs **I** 26
Birra **II** 79–80
Bismarck, Otto von **II** 93n4
Black, John **I** 29, 30n6, 53n3
Blair, Mr **I** 154, 156n9
Bligh, Richard **I** 255, 257n6&9, 258, 296, 309, 310, 321, 327, 331–2, 342
Bobda, **I** *xxiii*, **II** 3, 27–9, 27n1, 30n4, 34–41, 50–1, 55–60, 63–4, 83n1, 84, 294, 295
Boehm, Dr (Böhm) **I** 5, 8n3, 10, 12n4, 33–4n3, 54n9, 85
Bologne (Bologna) **I** 159, **II** 120–1
Bombala **I** 237, 238n12, 256. 259, 262, 268, 296, 309, 310n1
Bombelles, Count Charles **II** 150, 151n2
Borgo alla Collina **II** 17, 18n2
Bottare, Dr **II** 228
Boulogne **I** 237
Bowler, Adelaide Agnes Henrietta (later Suttor) **I** *xxi*, 4n13, 150n4, 358n2, **II** 218, 219n1&11, 220n14, 254n2
Brace, Charles Loring **II** 154n6
Brenner Pass **II** 165, 166n8
Brenner Railway **II** 166n7

Bright, Richard **II** 12n6
Brighton **I** 16n9, 20, 32, 34n5, 36, 37, 38n16, 39, 40, 52, 54n11, 89, 93, 95, 117, 128, 160n7
Brindisi **II** 157, 158n24
Brini **II** 243, 243n6
Brisbane **I** 183n6, **II** 253
British Consulate, Vienna **II** 233n3, 292n5
Brookes, Mr **I** 312
Browne, Dr John Collis **II** 208, 209n4
Brucedale **I** *xxi, xxvii*, 4n11, 146, 147, 150n1, 155n3, 156n7&8, 157n18, 162n5, 166, 168n1, 178, 186, 217, 218, 219n6, **II** 44n3, 219n11, 220n14, 253
Buchanan, Benjamin **II** 253, 254n6&8
Buchanan, Mary **II** 254n7
Bucharest **II** 287n1
Budinsky, August **I** 75, 76n8, 125, 283n3, 324, 345, 346, 347, 352
Burke's Peerage **I** 71n4
Byron, Lord George Gordon **I** *xvii*, 3n2, 11n3, 41n7, 146, **II** 4, 127n5, 209n3, 226n2, 238–9

Calabria **I** 23n11
Canada **II** 3
Cangoura **II** 218, 220n13, 254n4
Cannes **II** 257, 258n8, 260, 260n10
Cape Horn **I** 205n2, 237n5
Carl, Mr **II** 45
Carlin, James **II** 231
Carlstadt **II** 139, 140n7
Carpathian Mountains **II** 287n1
Castelnovo (Castle Park) **II** 259, 260n5
Castries, Duke **II** 232, 233n4
Candelo **I** 255, 257n5, 351n4
Celle **I** 78, 79n7&8
Chalkin, Christopher **I** 34n5, 160n7
Chambers, Sir James **I** 189, 190n3
Chapman, Miss **II** 42
Charles IV **II** 1; *Karolinische Ansiedlung* (Caroline colonization) (1718–37) **II** 1
Chartism **I** 61, 64n20
Château Třeboň **II** 201n3
chicken panado **I** 189, 190n8
chlorodyne **II** 208, 209n4
chloroform **I** 59, 63n8; dentistry **I** 59
cholera **I** *xv*, 34n3, 62, 65n27, 204, 205n5
Crystal Palace **I** 101, 103n6
Cini, Bartolomeo **I** *xx*, 25n7, 113n16, 120n4, 132n2, 298n4, 351n10, **II** 135n4, 145n7, 206n3

Cini, Ellen **II** 148
Cini, Mrs **II** 148
Clairmont, Alexine **II** 4, 5n5, 249n5, 250n5
Clairmont, Antonia (née Ghilain von Hembyze) **I**, *xvii, xviii, xix, xxii, xxiii*, 3n2, 29, 105–6, 136, 159–60, 192, 207, 216, 262, 315, **II 65**, 119n1
Clairmont, Charles (Charley) Gaulis Jr **I** *xvii*, 2, 3n2, 4n16, 10, 11n1, 12n7, 15, 17, 22, 23n16, 25n2, 33, 37, 38n14, 40, 44, 46, 47, 60, 66, 76, 80, 82, 92, 93, 98n5, 105, 111, 112n7&11, 114–5, 117, 119, 121, 123, 126, 129, 133, 134, 135, 136, 138, **144**, 159, 160n4, 161, 163n9, 164, 165n1, 172n5, 173n1&2, 178, 179, 181, 184, 187, 188, 189, 190n4, 191, 192, 198, 200n16, 201, 208, 210, 211, 212n2, 214, 215n2, 216, 217n3, 218, 219, 223n3, 225n4, 227, 228n1, 231, 261n3, 278, 279n4, 284, 314n4, 339
Clairmont, Charles Gaulis **I** *xv, xvii, xviii, xix, xxiv*, 3n2, 5, 6, 7, 14, 15, 66, 75, 92, 93n1, 98n6, 105, 111, 125, **140**, 147
Clairmont, Christoph **I** *xi, xiii, xix, xxiv, xxx*, 115n6, **II** 3–4, 210n1, 221n1
Clairmont, Claire **I** *xii, xv, xvi, xvii, xix–xxiv*, 28–9, 30n1, 36, 137, **II** 2–4, 33n1, 63n1, **65–6**, 133n6, 281, 282n27
Clairmont, Clara (later Knox) **I** *xii, xviii, xxix*, 24, 24–5n2, 29, 36, 43, 49, 58, 97, 135–6, 160n1, 171, 172n7, **II** 251, 252n10
Clairmont, Emily **I** *xvii*, 2, 3n2, 4n15, 15, 66, 73n3, 93, 123, 132n2, 162, 165n1&8, 178–80, 180n4, 187, 188n2, 199n8,15&16, 210n7, 215n2, 223n3, 225n4, 228n1, 233n3&6, 279n6, 314n4
Clairmont family tomb **II 74**
Clairmont, Hermine **I** xvii, 3n2, 4n15, 16n7, 52, 54n10, 223
Clairmont, Johann Paul **I** 300n1, **II** 4, 63n1, **73**, 250n5, 251
Clairmont, Pauline **I** *xx–xxiii*, 2, 17, 18, 39, 72, 80, 97, 98n5, 111, 113n16, 127, 135–6, 145, 146, 156n6,7&10, 211, 225, 264, 272, 304, 344, 345, **II** 2–4, 23–6, 29–31, 34, 43, 46–55, 58–9, **70–1**, 83–5, 91–5, 105–8, 111, 148, 186; Australia **I** 145, 240; Bathurst **I** 154–5; Berlin **I** 85; departure from Australia **I** 147; description of **I** 4n13;

health **I** 240, 350; Hungary **I** 315; letters **I** 145–6; loss of father **I** 147–8; money **I** 161; property **I** 125; relations with Willie **I** 147
Clairmont, Sidonia **I** *xvii*, 3n2, 7, 8, 9n14, 15, 18, 21, 22, 43–45, 47, 66, 73n3, 80, 106n8, 111, 114, 123, 126, 135, 136, 159, 160, 162, 164, 165n1, 171, 172n5, 177, 184, 192, 199n15&16, 210n7, 214, 216, 223, 225n4, 226, 228n1, 231, 232, 250, 256, 257n8
Clairmont-von Gonzenbach, Victorine **I** *xxiv*, **II** 4
Clairmont, Walter **I** *xxii, xxiv*, 3–4, 33n1, 63, **73**, 112n8, 113n1, 199n16, 261, 300n1
Clairmont, Wilhelm Gaulis **I**, *xx–xxiv*, 14, 24, 24n2, 33n3, 43, 44, 63n4, 102n1, 111, 131, 143, 145, 161, 201, 210, 271, 309, **II** 1–3, **66–70**; *Sands and Kenny's Diary 1861* **I** *xxii*, 279n3
Clarence and Richmond Examiner, The **II** 115n5
clippers **I** 239, 239n2
coasting steamers **I** 349n1
Coblenz **I** 335, 336n1, 335, 337, **II** 145n5
Codeina (Codeine) **II** 236
Coles, Dr **II** 152
Cologne **II** 248n7
Como, Lake **II** 165
Conant, Charles **I** 63n13, 102n2, 293n4, 295n1
Cook's Tourist's Handbook for Southern Italy **II** 158n9
Corrompai, Mr **II** 249
Corsica **II** 261, 262n1, 264n7
Corte **II** 261, 262n4
Coulson, Walter **I** 50, 51, 53n3, 145
Court of Chancery **I** 92, 125, 329
Court Journal, The **II** 77, 78n7, 101, 170
Covent Garden **I** 12n11, 136n3, 229
Cox, William **II** 255n14
Creighton, Charles **I** 103n14
Croatia **I** *xxiii*, 208n4, **II** 9n4, 14, 17, 20n4, 59, 132, 155, 180; Agram (Zagreb) **II** 131, 139, 140n5, 169, 172, 198n1; Essegg **II** 17–19; Fiume (Rijeka) **II** 8, 9n4, 19, 85; Miljana **I** 287n2, 292, 293n3, 294; Oroslavje **II** 14–15; Petrijanitz (Nova Ves Petrijanečka) **II** 150; Slavonia **II** 17, 18n3, 129, 131n6; Varaždin **II** 129, 134, 151n4

306

INDEX

Crockford's Clerical Dictionary for 1868 **II** 145n5
Croydon **II** 11–13, 13n1
Crüwell-Clairmont, Alma **I** *xxiv*, 68n5, 73n3, 199n16, 300n1, **II** 3–4, 63, **73**, 92, 113n1, 138–9, 222n1, 273n13, 278–81, 284–5, 299
Crüwell, Gottlieb **I** 199n16, **II** 4
Csakova (Ciacova) **II** 3, 62, 63n3, 81, 99, 103–6, 109, 117, 149, 278
Cseney **II** 36, 39n4, 41–2
Cuba, Australia **I** 149, 150n11, 212n3, 217n7, 219n6, 235n9, 236, 237n1&8, 239, 241, 243, 247, 255, 264, 265, 343, 350, 351, 354, 355, 356, 359, 360, 361
Curran, Amelia **I** *xxxiii*, **137**, **II** 113n1
Czartoryski, Prince **II** 175
Czech Republic **II** 201n3; Olmütz (Olomouc) **I** 17, 18, 18n1, 20, 22, 112n11, **II** 251; Troppau (Opava) **II** 9; Zdislavice **II** 251

Davis, Richard **I** 64n16
Daningers **II** 77
Danube River **II** 1, 26, 29, 175n11
Darling River **II** 253, 254n9
Deák, István **II** 104n6
Debrecin (Debrecen) **II** 146, 147n2
Demidoff, Prince Anatole **II** 266, 266–7n6
dentistry **I** 59, 63n6&9; chloroform **I** 59, 63n8
Der grosse Schwabenzug (Great Swabian Migration) **II** 1
Dini, Countess (see Gozzadini, Countess Maria Teresa di Serrego Alighieri)
Ditta (Deta) **II** 112n8, 180
Dominkusch (Dominkus), Dr **II** 152, 153n1, 171, 184, 189, 192, 199, 200n2
Dowden, Edward **II** 127n5
Drathshmid family **I** 199n8, 224n5, 232, 278
Drathshmid, Frederic **I** 180n4, 199n8, 232, 233, 233n3&6
Drathshmid, Mary **II** 234, 243n7
Drathshmid, Sophie **I** 197
Drau River (Drava) **II** 153n1, 192,
Dresden **I** 20, 22n9, 182n1, 262 **II** 131n6
Drucker, Peter **II** 198n2
Drysedale, Mrs **I** 252, 253n3
Dubsky, Emanual **II** 251
Dunbar (ship) **II** 86, 87n6
Duncan Dunbar (ship) **II** 86, 87n6

Dunn, Miss **II** 148
Durie, Alistair **I** 33n3

East Prussia **II** 4
East Sheen **I** 164, 165n3, 173, 173n2
Ecclesiastical Gazette, The **II** 145n5
Economist, The **II** 250n6
Edict of Toleration **I** 12n10, 348n5
Edmondson, George **I** *xxxiii*, 38n8, 39, 61, 64n18&19, 68n6, 69n12, 72, 112n2, **141**
Eiselsberg, Anton von **II** 4
Elba, Island of **I** 347, 348n2, **II** 265, 266n1
Elements of Agricultural Chemistry (Davy) **I** 53, 54n14
Elisabeth, Empress of Austria (1837–98) **II** 77, 78n6, 101n2
Engelmann, Nikolaus **II** 1, 289n4
England **I** 37, 50, 55, 59, 74, 101, 159, **II** 32, 86, 95, 108, 133, 157, 169, 203, 210, 251; Bank of **II** 21; Brighton **I** 16n9, 20, 32, 34n5, 36, 37, 38n16, 39, 40, 52, 54n11, 89, 93, 95, 117, 128, 160n7; East Sheen 165n3, **I** 164, 173, 173n2; Epsom **I** 278, 279n1; Gravesend **I** 33, 34n11; Hampshire **I** *xx*, 37, 38n8, 39, 62, 63n1, 102, 104n17; London **II** 7n1, 11, 25, 81–2, 108, 174, 185, 212, 290; Malling **I** 24, 24n1, 28, 31, 39, 77, 79n6, 257n11; National Archives **II** 145n5; Queenwood College (Hampshire) **I** 40, 41n8&9, 42n10&12, 58, 60–1, 68, 68n25, 139; Ramsgate **I** *xvi*, 34n5, 160, 160n7, 164, 165n9, 312, 175; Salisbury Cathedral **I** 65n29; Salisbury **I** 62
Epsom **I** 278, 279n1
Erste Schritte zur Erlernung der englischen Sprache, für Kinder von sechs bis zehn Jahren (Clairmont) **I** *xviii*, *xxv*, 23n16
erste Schwabenzug migration **II** 1
Eskeles, Baron Denis von **I** 3n2, 286, 288n7
Essegg **II** 17–8
Esterházy family **I** *xxiii*, 3n2, 302n6, **II** 12n9
Esterházy, Prince Nicholas **I** 302n6, **II** 11, 203
Euclid **I** 55, 57n2
Europe in 1848: Revolution and Reform (Tenorth) **I** 19n6
Exposition Universelle (World Fair): (1867) **II** 101n3; (1889) **II** 263, 264n9
eyes: inflammation of **I** 175

307

INDEX

Falcon, Charles **I** 124n3
Falcon, Mr and Miss **I** 123, 124, 124n3, 271n4
Falcon, Sophie **I** 124, 124n3
Falicon **II** 259
Fallenböck, Mrs **II** 45
Farina, Margherita Cini **II** 206n3, 135n4, 207n9
Farmer's Library, Animal Economy (Youatt and Martin) **I** 90, 91n8
Festetics, Count Alexander **II** 14
Festetics family **II** 15n3, 28n4
First Austrian Danube Steam-Navigation Company (Andrews and Pritchard) **II** 30, 31n11
FitzRoy, Sir Charles Augustus **I** 156n13
Fiume (Rijeka) **II** 8, 9n4, 19, 20n4, 85, 129, 139, 140n5, 146, 147n2, 150, 168
Flannery, Michael **II** 127n11
Florence **II** 19–21, 30–4, 52n4, 53–5, 109–11, 120–3, 138, 196, 202n5, 230, 263–5, 277; Palazzo Piti (museum) **II** 123, 127n6; Piazza Saint Trinità **II** 210
Foggia **II** 156, 157, 158n9
Fónagy, Zoltán **II** 48n5
Fortnightly Review, The **II** 248n5
Fót **II** 218, 219n9
France **II** 133n4; Ajaccio (Corsica) **II** 261; Antibes **II** 260, 260n10; Bastia (Corsica) **II** 261; Cannes **II** 257, 260; Corsica **II** 261; Corte (Corsica) **II** 261; Marseilles **I** 256, 331, 333, **II** 260; Napoléon III **II** 151n3; Nice **II** 259; Paris **II** 13, 100, 101n3, 257, 261–3; Villefranche **II** 259
Frankfort **I** 77
Franz Gotthilf Söhne **II** 82
Franz Joseph I, Emperor of Austria **II** 101n2; coronation **II** 100
Franzensbad **I** 280, 281n3
French, Charlotte Bennet **II** 135n2, 191n2
Fries, Count **II** 217, 219

Galatz **II** 30, 31n11
Galicia **I** 9n16, 207, 281n2
Galleria Demidoff **II** 266, 266n6
Garnett, Richard **II** 127n5
Garnier, Charles **II** 260n6
Gates-Coon, Rebecca **II** 18n4
Gatteschi, Ferdinando **I** 172n3&4, 338n3
Gautier, Mr **II** 228n6, 231
Genoa **II** 126, 165, 266

Geological Society, Vienna **I** 116, 117
Gerding, Dr **I** 78, 79n7&8
Germany **II** 3, 114, 228–30; Berlin **I** 82, 83n2, 85, 86n1, 262, **II** 3–4, 25, 113n1; Celle **I** 78, 79n7&8; Coblenz **I** 225, 336n1, 337, **II** 145n5; Cologne **II** 248n7; Dresden **I** 20, **II** 131n6; Hannover **I** 34n9; Heidelberg **I** 77, 78n2; Heilbron **I** 77, 78n1; Hohenheim **I** 43, 44, 46, 53n1, 55, 58, 59, 60, 70, 78n3, 95, 125, 149; Meclenburgh **II** 27; Nazi regime **II** 3
Gilad (Ghilad) **II** 82, 83n2&6, 112n8
Gladstaner, Mr **II** 253
Godwin, Emily **I** 4n10
Godwin, Mary Jane (née Vial) **I** *xvi*, *xxi*, *xxii*, *xxiv*n4, 3–4n6, 54n7, 112n8&10, 280, **II** 113n1, 223n1
Godwin, William **I** *xi*, *xiv*, *xv*, xvi, *xxiv*n2, 3n2, 4n6, 54n12, 108n2&3, 112n10, 298n4, **II** 225; *Memoirs of the Author of a Vindication of the Rights of Woman* **I** *xiv*
Godwin, William Jr **I** 4n10
Gordon, Thomas **II** 238n3
Goring, Ida **II** 22n2
Görlich, Ernst Joseph **I** xvii, xix, 4n7
Görz **II** 129, 131, 131n9, 144, 145
Gozzadini, Countess Maria Teresa di Serrego Alighieri (la Nina) **II** 206, 206n8
Graefe, C.F. von **II** 138
Gravesend **I** 33, 34n11
Graz **I** 6, 7, 9n9&10, 292n1 **II** 132, 143n3
Greaves, Bernard **II** 220n11
Green, George **I** 237n4
Gregorios Ypsilanti of Greece, Prince **II** 232, 233n4
Grossbetschkerek (Zrenjanin) **II** 2, 16n11&12, 19, 25, 27n1
Gyertyámos (Cărpiniş) **II** 27, 29, 30n4, 34, 41, 81, 83n1

Habercorn, Fraulein **II** 217
Habsburg **II** 1–2, 9n3; Austrian rulers **II** 1
Haggard & Hale (London Broker) **II** 49, 50n6
Haggard, Colonel **II** 263, 264n3
Hall, James **I** 90
Hammond, Marianna **I** 24, 25n7, 167, **II** 42, 49–50
Hampshire **I** *xx*, 37, 38n8, 39, 62, 63n1, 102, 104n17; Stockbridge **I** 58, 62

INDEX

Handbook to the Mediterranean: Its Cities, Coasts and Islands (Murray) **II** 264n3
Handbook for Travellers in Europe and the East (Harper) **I** 34n10
Handbook for Travellers in Southern Germany, A (Murray) **II** 83n5, 131n3, 140n6, 145n2, 153n3, 170n8
Handbook for Travellers in Southern Italy (Coghlan) **II** 161n3
Handels-und Gewerbe-Addressenbuch (Trade and Industry Address Book) **II** 83n4
Hanghegyi, Georgina **I** *xvii, xx, xxii*, 113n16, 261n3, 292n2, 298n4, 344n2, **II** 248n3&15
Hannover (Hanover) **I** 33, 34n9, 40, 78
Harmony Hall **I** 38n8
Harter, Jim **II** 131n6
Hauer, Emily (née von Pichler) **I** *xxiii*, **II** 94, 99n1, 142, 221, 269–71, 274–9, 285–8, 298–9
Hauer, Francis von **II** 83n3
Hauer, Rudolf von **I** xxiii, 102n1, **II** 64, 75n1, 81, 85–8, 180, 269–70, 274–9, 284–8, 295
Hauser, Bernhard von **II** **67–8**, 96n1, 272, 276
Haynau, Julius Jacob Freiherr von **I** 89, 90n3&7
Hearder, Harry **II** 54n3
Heidelberg **I** 78n2; mountains **I** 77
Heilbronn, Germany **I** 77, 78n1
Hein, Baroness **II** 218
Heine, Heinrich **II** 234, 235n10
Hembyze, Georg Ghilain von **I** 62, 65n34, 188, 188n7, 262, 263n4, 345, 346n5, **II** 97, 97n2, 106, 107n3
Her Majesty's Theatre, London **I** 12n3&11, 136n3, 181, 229, 316n3, **II** 105
Hickson, Edna **II** 255n14
Hildegarde **I** 209, 210n4
History of Banking in All the Leading Nations, The (Wirth) **II** 175n4, 196n2
History of Bathurst (Barker) **I**
History of cold bathing (Floyer) **I** 33n3
History of a Six Weeks' Tour (Mary and Percy Shelley) **I** *xvi*
Hitchfeld, Dr **I** 189
Hitschmann, Hugo Hippolyt **I** 102n1&4, 103n13, 251n2, 288n5, **II** 12n7. 15n2, 48n3, 75n1

Hofmann, August Wilhelm von **I** 56, 57, 57n9, 58
Hofmannsthal, Hugo von **II** 4
Hofwyl **I** 61, 64n19
Hohenheim School **I** *xx*, 43, 44, 45, 46, 47, 48n1&7, 52, 53n2, 55, 58, 59, 60, 61, 70, 77, 78n3, 89, 94n5, 95, 95n1, 110, 113n13, 125, **142**, 149, 241n2, 253n2; cost of **I** 43, 44, 53n1; expenses **I** 125; prospectus **I** 53n1
Holtfrerich, Carl-Ludwig **I** 57n7
Honyez, Mr **II** 169
Horneth, Baron **II** 156
Hostiz **II** 246
Hotel Ape **II** 265, 266n2
Hôtel de Rome **II** 157, 158n17
Hôtel de l'Europe **II** 261, 262n7
Hotel Schneiderff **II** 12n11
Hudson, John Corrie **I** 110, 112n10
Humanitäts Classen **I** 17
Hungarian fever **I** 101, 103n14
Hungary **I** 100, 131, 205n3, 207, 315, **II** 1–3, 11–14, 15n3, 24, 59, 77, 81, 118, 132–6, 146, 180; colonies **I** 87; Debrecin (Debrecen) **II** 146; estates **I** 201; Fót **II** 219n9; Lake Balaton **II** 26, 28n3&4; Landschütz **I** 244, 245n2, 251n4, 321; Lower **II** 12n6; Pest (Budapest) **II** 14, 26, 34, 59, 79–81; *puszta* **II** 42, 79, 103, 269, 274, 282; Rakičan (Rakicsán) **I** 292n2, 297, 313, 317, **II** 232n2
Hunt, Dina Williams **I** 284n1, **II** 9n2, 25n8
Hunt, James Henry (Leigh) **I** 12n3, 41n7, 167, 170n13&15
Hunt, Marianne **I** 167, 170n13
Huscher, Herbert **I** *xviii, xxii, xxvi*, 16n7, 19n4, 72n3, 88n5, 99n11, **II** 30n2, 119n1, 126n4, 140n8, 151n3, 161n5
Hussard, Baron **II** 59
hydrotherapy **I**.

illness **I** 1, 5, 7, 15, 21, 39, 62, 74, 129, 131, 187, 189, 213, 216, 232, 250, 297, **II** 238–40, 244; gastric complaint **II** 141; health **I** 21, 39, 74; Hungarian fever **I** 101, 103n14; rheumatism **I** 175n2, 321, **II** 186; scrofula **I** 257n8; typhus fever **II** 159, 166n10
Illustrated London News **I** 41n8, 64n18&19, 68n3
Illyria **II** 8, 9n3

INDEX

Illyrian Provinces **II** 9n3
Imlay, Frances (Fanny) **I** *xiii, xiv, xv, xvii*, 23n16
Imlay, Gilbert **I** *xiii, xiv*
Innsbruck **II** 78n4, 112n3, 166n7
International Exhibition (1862) **II** 25, 25n6, 115n4, 131n7
Ireland **II** 104n2, 181n8
Irving, Washington **I** 101, 103n7
Isekutz, Mr **II** 58
isinglass **I** 223, 224n7, 225, 226
Italy **I** 274, **II** 17, 51, 109, 114, 125, 139, 148, 171–3; anti-Protestant riots (Barletta, 1866) **II** 91n1; Arno River **II** 20n9; Bologna **I** 159, **II** 120–1; Brindisi **II** 157, 158n24; Calabria **I** 23n11; Florence **II** 19–21, 30–4, 52n4, 53–5, 109–11, 120–3, 138, 157, 196, 202n5, 210, 230, 263–5, 277; Foggia **II** 156; Genoa **II** 126, 165, 266; Lake Como **II** 165; Livorno **II** 13, 227, 260n1, 263–5; Meridional Railways **II** 250n6; Milan **II** 165, 165n4&5; Naples **II** 156–7, 162, 265; Piombino **II** 265; Pisa **II** 88–9, 244; Pisa society (1821) **II** 244; Rome **II** 52n4, 160, 230; San Marcello **II** 148; San Miniato **II** 234; San Spirito **II** 157; Starza **II** 157; Trieste **II** 29–30, 133, 139, 144; Turin **II** 53, 126, 165n3; Tuscany **II** 141, 143n6, 235n4; Udine **II** 131n2, 144; Venice **I** *xvii*, 9n19, 18, 187, 286, 297, 301, 302, 303n8, 307, 313, 315, 316n4, 317, 337, 349, **II** 38, 126, 144, 156, 163, 190; Verona **II** 162
Italy Handbook for Travellers (Baedeker) **II** 158, 164n4, 257n1, 262n7

J. Henry Schröder & Company **I** 184, 184n3
James, Henry **II** 229n7; *The Aspern Papers* **I** *xx, xxvi*
Jameson, Anna **II** 204n7
Jarrant, Mr **I** 131
Java **I** 167
Jersey, Isle of **I** 328, 328n2
Jews **I** 8n3, 10, 12n10, 347, 348n5&7, **II** 27, 134, 203–5
Johann, Archduke **II** 131n6
Johnson, James **II** 87n6
Johnston, William **I** 84n9
Jones, Colonel **I** 54n7
Jones, Mrs **II** 139, 140n8, 160, 165
Joseph II **II** 1; *Josephinische Ansiedlung* (1782–7) **II** 1

Kameruka **I** 150n14, 151n16, 352, 354, 355
Kangaroo Hills **I** 150n8, 182n1, 218, 219n6, 309; purchase of **I** 183n4; sale of **I** 24n4
Kanisa (Nagykanizsa) **II** 14
Karlovy Vary **I** 8n5, 263n3
Karlsbad **I** 262, 263n3
Karolinische Ansiedlung (Caroline colonization) (1718–37) **II** 1
Károlyi, Count István **II** 219n9
Károlyi, Countess **II** 232, 232n2
Karos River **II** 1
Kelly, Gary **I** *xiii*
Kensington **I** 55, 57n1&9
Kent, Duchess of **I** 81n2, 203, 209
Kiandra **I** 350, 351n5
Kilkenny Railway Company **II** 102, 104n2
Kilkenny Railway shares **II** 108
Kindleberger, Charles **I** 102n2
Kinsky, Count **II** 217, 219n5
Klagenfurth am Wörthersee **II** 142, 145
Klein, Alfred **II** 203
Kleyle, Karl von **I** 281n2, 283n3, 304, 305
Knox, Alexander **I** *xii, xviii*, 24, 24–5n2, 30n9, 32–3, 39, 40, 49, 51, 58, 72, 87, 88n1, 172n3, 207, **II** 13, 235
Knox, Clara (see Clairmont, Clara)
Kohlmarkt **II** 294
Koll, Countess **II** 203
Koller, Emmy **II** 4, 250n5
Korzo, Mrs **II** 270
Kossuth, Lajos **I** 121, 121n1, 207
Kraus, Mr and Mrs **I** 114, 119, 123
Kumar, Dr Albin **II** 77, 78n6

Lambert, Eduard Labbat de **I** 98, 99n11
Landesmann, Dr Max **II** 77, 78n2, 102
Landschütz **I** 244, 245n2, 250, 251n4, 321
laudanum **II** 234
Lawrence, Dr William **I** 52, 54n11
Laybach (Ljubljana) **II** 3, 8
Leghorn (Livorno) **II** 13, 227, 260n1, 263–5
Lemberg **I** 278
Levy, John **II** 104n2
Lewisham **I** 71n6
Liechtenstein, Prince and Princess **I** 18, 19n8, 302n6, 308n9
Lind, Johanna Maria (Jenny) **I** 11, 12n11, 136n3
Linz **II** 175

INDEX

Lippa (Lipova), **II** 2, 288, 290–1; Soimos Fortress **II** 289n3
Livorno **II** 13, 227, 263–5
Ljubljanica River **II** 10n8
London **I** 20, 27, 28, 32, 49, 51, 56, 58, 70, 95, 101, **II** 7n1, 11, 25, 81–2, 108, 174, 185, 212, 290; Bermondsey **I** 58; Crystal Palace **I** 101; Covent Garden **I** 229; Hagg & Hale **II** 49; Her Majesty's Theatre **II** 105; lodging **I** 77; R. and F. Tooth and Mort **II** 12n10; Richmond **I** 26, 122n4; Royal College of Chemistry **I** 55, 57n9
London Medical Directory **I** 54
Long, Mr and Mrs **I** 279n1, **II** 13
Lower Hungary **II** 12n6
Lower Styrian Beekeeping Society **II** 200n2
Lucam, Baron Wilhelm von (Luccam) **II** 173, 175n4, 196n2
Luccam, Miss **II** 237
Luccam, Mr **II** 237
Lumley, Benjamin **I** 12n11, 40, 42n13, 44, 136n3, 308n4, 316n3
Lynch, Mrs **I** 167
Lyoleand, Blanche **II** 159
Lysice Castle **II** 252n6

Macdonald, Flora Clementine Isabella **I** 80, 81n4
Madeira **II** 78n6, 265
Mahoney, William **II** 12n6
Maier, Mr **I** 197, 199n6, 201, 202n3, 218, 232, 278, 286, 305
Malling **I** 24, 24n1, 28, 31, 39, 77, 79n6, 257n11
Maneroo Telegraph **II** 220n22
Manning, Edye **I** 356, 359n1
Manning, James **I** 149, 151n16, 241n2, 255, 256, 256n4, 257n6,9&12, 259n3, 260, 262, 264, 265, 267, 342n1
Manning, John Edye **I** 156n7, 241n2, 359n1, **II** 254n6, 255n12
Manning, Mrs **I** 258
Māori **II** 44n4, 44n12
Marburg (Maribor) **II** 2, 153n3, 154n3, 173, 178, 185–6
Marburger Zeitung (Marburger Times) **II** 153n1, 154n3, 198n1
Maremma **II** 265
Maria Anna of Bavaria, Princess **I** 81n5
Maria Karoline Schwarzenberg, Princess **II** 78n2

Maria Theresa, Empress **II** 1, 58n1, 241, 242n6; *Maria Theresianische Ansiedlung* (1744–72) **II** 1
Marie Louise, Empress **II** 242n6
Marienbad Waters, **I** 16n4, 202n9
Marien Hospital, Weikersdorf **II** 78n2
Maros (Mureş River) **II** 288
Marseilles **I** 256, 331, 333, **II** 260
Masch, Anton **I** 103n13
Maurocordatus, Prince George **II** 232, 233n4
Maximilian, Archduke Ferdinand (later Maximilian I, Emperor of Mexico) **I** 18n1, 19n4, **II** 151n3
Mayence **I** 77, 78n1
Mayne, Lottie **II** 218
Meclenburgh **II** 27
Melk **I** 22n6, 66, 68n5
Mensdorff-Pouilly, Count Alexander von **I** 81n3, 107, 201–2, 203, 204, 206, 206n2, 208n7, 210n1&2, 216
Meridional Railways **II** 250n6
Merimbula **I** 151, 253n2, 257n5, 310n1, 327, 332
métallique **I** 57n7, 329, 330n1, 335
Metamorphosis (Ovid) **I** 34n6
Mexico **II** 151n3; Emperor Maximilian I **I** 18n1, 19n4 **II** 151n3
Meyer, Inspector **II** 277, 286
Michaelmas **I** 135, 136n2, 207
Michelozzo (Michelozzi) di Bartolommeo **II** 211n4, 235n6
migration **II** 1, 174; Austria **I** 51; *erste Schwabenzug* **II** 1
Miklauz, Dr **II** 214–15
Milan **II** 165, 165n4&5
Miljana **I** 287n2, 292, 293n3, 294
Minden **I** 262, 263n3
Mirkovetz **II** 134, 139, 150, 155, 168–9, 174
Mitchell, Mr **I** 194n5, 215n3, **II** 210–12, 212, 255n16
Monastery of Saint Maria Radna, Arad County **II** 288
Monte Carlo **II** 259
Montenuovo, Princess Mary **II** 241, 242n6
Moravia, **I** 111, 112n11, 114, 117, 164, 173n1, 184, 187, 201, 207, 347, 348n5, **II** 252n3, 252n4
Moravia, Revolution (1848) **II** 252n4
Moreau, Mrs **I** 2, 4n12, 10
Morris, Augustus **I** 148, 155n4, 176n4, 182n1, 356, 356n2

311

INDEX

Mort & Co **II** 253
Mort, Eliza S. **II** 87n7
Mort, Maria **II** 87n7
Mort, Mrs **II** 86
Mort, Thomas Sutcliffe **II** 11, 12n10, 253
Moulson, Miss May **II** 123, 126n4, 131–6, 139, 148, 155
Mount Cashell, Lady Margaret **I** 25n7, 113n16
Mount Grosvenor **II** 253, 254n10
Mowle, Mary Braidwood **I** 151, 241n2, 257n9
Mudgee **II** 254
Mülleitner, Dr Franz **II** 77, 117, 118, 124
Müller (Miller), Miss **II** 123, 125, 127n5, 131–6, 139, 148, 205
Murray, John **II** 83n5, 131n3, 140n6, 145n2, 153n3, 170n8, 264n3
Murrumbidgee **I** 149, 155n4, 237n1
Murrumbidgee River **I** 155n3, 162n4, 176n4, 186n5, 235n9, 238n12&13, 240, 260n1, 264–5, 274, 350, 351n5, 354, 355–6
Murska, Ilma di **II** 259, 260n7

Nabresina **II** 121, 122n3
Nadler, Mr **II** 62, 208
Naples **II** 156–7, 162, 265
Napoléon III of France **II** 151n3
Nation, The **II** 206n8
National Archives of England **II** 145n5
National Education: system **I** 163n7
Naudino **II** 60
Nazi regime **II** 3
New England **I** 149, 150n8, 168n3, 181, 182n1&3, 183n6, 185, 241, 241n4
New England Advertiser **II** 115n5
New South Wales, Australia: Bombala **I** 238, 238n12; Merimbula **I** 310; Tantangara **I** 350, 351n5
New York Times **II** 260n8
New York, USA **II** 159
New Zealand **II** 42–3, 44n4; Auckland **II** 42, 44n4; Māori **II** 44n4, 44n12; North Island **II** 44n4; South Island **II** 44n4; Waikato War (1863–4) **II** 44n12; Wellington **II** 44n4
Nice **II** 259; *L'observatoire de Nice* **II** 260n6
Nikolaifhof **I** *xxiv*, 310n3, **II** 2–3, 174–9, 204n2
No Place for a Nervous Lady (Frost) **I** 151, 158n21, 162n2, 205n6, 235n9

Norton, J. **II** 220n14
Nowotny, Mr and Mrs **I** 299, 300n4, 301, 306–7, 308n6, 335, 339, 340n2, 345, 346n4

Odenburg (Sopron) **II** 12n6, 14, 15n4
Ofseniţa **II** 84n1, 269–70, 272n4, 291n1
Olmütz **I** 17, 18, 18n1, 19n11, 20, 22n5, 112n11, **II** 251
opera box **I** 12n3, 42n13, 101, 167, 194, 194n5, 199n12, 215n3, 217n2, 228, 317, 342 **II** 105, 115
opera house **I** 10, 11, 126, 216, 229, 306; bankruptcy **I** 136
ophthalmia **I** 186n5
Oracle of Delphi **I** 327, 327n2
Oraviţa **II** 298
Oroslavje **II** 14–15, 15n1, 126, 131n2, 198n1
Ostende **I** 20, 22n1, 78n1, 262
Ottoman Empire **II** 1
Our Grandchildren Won't Believe It (Wright) **I** 145, 151, 183n4, 186n1

Pabst, Heinrich Wilhelm von **I** 95n1, 100, 102n4, 111, 114, **142**
Paikert, G.C. **II** 1–2, 48n5, 50n3
Palazzo Ferro Fini **I** 302, 303n7&8
Palazzo Pitti **II** 123, 127n6
Palffy, Prince **II** 249n3, 256, 257n5
Palmerston, Lord Henry John Temple **I** 108, 109n10&11
Pambula (Panbula) **I** 238n9, 253n2, 255, 257n6&9, 310
Paoli, Betti **II** 218
Paparoni, Mrs **II** 32, 33n5
Párdány **II** 57, 58n2
Paris **II** 13, 100, 101n3, 257, 261–3
Parker, W.S. **II** 102, 104n2
Paxton, Joseph **I** 103n6
Payerbach **II** 249
Peacock, Thomas Love **I** 11n3, **II** 247, 248n19
Peep into the Past: Brighton in the Olden Times (Bishop) **I** 54n11
Pergen, Count Johann Anton von **I** 113n14
Pergen, Countess **I** 111, 123
Pest (Budapest) **II** 14, 26, 34, 59, 79–81
Petrijanitz (Nova Ves Petrijanečka) **II** 150, 168, 174
Peyton, Captain John **II** 13
Pharisees **II** 294

312

INDEX

Phillip, Governor Arthur **I** 230n3
Piazza Saint Trinità **II** 210
Pichler, Alma von **II** 62, 143n3
Pichler, Caroline von **II** 128n18
Pichler, Emily von (see Hauer, Emily)
Pichler, Fanny von **II** 156, 158n2
Pichler, Johann Franz Hofrath von **I** *xxiii*, **II** 63n1, 241n4
Pichler, Moritz von **II** 63n1, 92–3, 128–9n18, 143n3, 286–7, 287n4
Pichler, Ottilia von (later Clairmont) **I** *x*, *xxiii*, 199n16, 268n1, **II** 2, 63n1, **67–9**, **72**, **74**, 89, 92
Picture of Vienna **I** 2n1, 4n7, 8n1, 11n2, 19n8, 22n4, 71n1, 93n1, 109n7, 112n1, 118n7, 302n6
Piombino **II** 265
Piper, Captain John **II** 220n12
Pisa **I** *xx*, 41n7, 113n16, 187, **II** 88–9, 244
Plunkett, John Hubert **II** 180, 181n8
Pokrajinski arhiv Maribor (Regional Archives in Maribor) **II** 153n1
Polytechnic school, Vienna **I** 19n7, 82, 84n3
Porto Ferraio **II** 260n1, 265
Postl (Postle), Dr **II** 187
Pragerhof (Pragersko) **II** 26
Prague **I** 262, 278, 279n2, **II** 131n6
Pressburgh **II** 12n6
Pringle, Colonel **I** 23n18, 35n14, 51, 212, **II** 114, 115n5, 116n5
Pringle, Mrs **I** 23n18, 33, 35n14, 212
Pringle, Violet **I** 128, 237, 267, **II** 11–13
Pringle family **I** 101, 107, 128, 129, 167, 186, 228, 237, **II** 11–13
Pritchard, Joseph **II** 31n11
Prokesch, Baroness **I** 82, 85
Prokesch-Osten, Baron Anton von **I** 83n2
Prussia **II** 180, 181n4, 220n16, 230; East **II** 4; University of Königsberg **II** 4
Pulsky, Miss **II** 134
Pulsky, Mr and Mrs **II** 100, 127n4
Punch **II** 53, 54n4
Pusey, Edward Bouverie **I** 127, 128n5
Pusey, Philip **I** 127, 128n4

Quaker **I** 67–8
Queenwood College, Hampshire **I** *xx*, 16n2, 38n8, 40, 41n8&9, 42n10&12, 58, 60–1, 64n16,19&24,25, 68n3&6, 126, **139**

R. and F. Tooth and Mort (London-based company) **II** 12n10
Radetz, Joseph Radetzky von **II** 8, 9n7
Raities, Mr **II** 189
Rakičan (Rakicsán), **I** 261n3, 292n2, 297, 313, 317, **II** 232n2
Ramsbottom, Ada **I** 33, 35n15, 101, 103n12, 245n4, 267, **II** 43, 90n1
Ramsbottom, Captain **I** 70, **II** 44n13
Ramsbottom, Mr and Mrs **I** 35n15, 168
Ramsgate **I** *xvi*, 34n5, 160, 160n7, 164, 165n9, 175, 312
Raponi, Danilo **II** 91n1
Ravac (Rawack), Leopold **I** 352, 352n1, 354, 356, 359, 360
Réaumur scale **I** 165n6
Recollections of the Last Days of Shelley and Byron (Trelawny) **I** 41n7, **II** 238n3
Reichenau **II** 249
Reisner, Baron **II** 53, 101
Reports of the Commissioners of the United States to the International Exhibition Held at Vienna, 1873 **II** 233n4
Reports on the Vienna University Exhibition of 1873 **II** 201n3
Resa, Countess **II** 217
Reschitza (Reşiţa) **II** 298, 299n6
Ribarz **II** 82
Richmond **I** 26, 122n4
Ridpath, John **II** 137n2
Rismondo, Mr **II** 219
Rismondo, Mrs Marie **II** 136, 214–15
Ritchie, Neville **II** 44n12
Ritter, Ellen **II** 4
Rittmeister, Mrs **II** 270
Rittmeister family **II** 271, 274
Robert le Diable (Meyerbeer) **I** 12n11
Robinson, Charles **I** 51, 54n4&6, 145
Rogendorf, Count Robert von **II** 25n2
Rogendorf, József von **II** 16n11, 25n2
Rogendorf (Roggendorf) **II** 21, 24–6
Rohitsch (Rogatec) **II** 129, 131n3, 169, 170n8
Rolle family **I** 38n8
Romania **II** 1–3, 27n1; Banloc **II** 290, 293; Bobda **I** *xxiii*, **II** 3, 27–9, 27n1, 30n4, 34–41, 50–1, 55–60, 63–4, 83n1, 84, 294, 295; Bucharest **II** 287n1; Carpathian Mountains **II** 287n1; Cseney **II** 39n4, 41–2; Galatz (Galaţi) **II** 30, 31n11; Gilad (Ghilad)

INDEX

II 82; Gyertyamos (Cărpiniş) II 29, 34, 41, 81; Lippa (Lipova) II 2, 289n3; Maros (Mureş River) II 288; Ofseniţa II 269–70; Orawitza (Oraviţa) II 298; Párdány II 57, 58n2; Reschitza (Reşiţa) II 298; Temesvár (Timişoara) II 2–3, 41, 81–2, 284, 288, 291, 298; Tschakowa (Ciakova) II 2
Rome I 41n7, 338n3, II 52n4, 160, 230
Rossetti, William Michael II 238n1
Rothstein, William II 127n11
Royal College of Chemistry, London I 57n9
Royal Imperial Agricultural Association, Graz II 200n2
Roznau (Rosenua) I 189
Russell, Lord John I 108, 109n10&11

Saint André de la Roche II 259
St Clair, William I *xv*, *xvii*
Sakula, Alex II 78n6
Salisbury I 62; Cathedral I 65n29
Salzburg II 4
San Marcello II 148
San Miniato II 234
San Spirito II 157
Saxony II 254
Schauer, Gustave II 219
Schauer, Ida I 202, 202n10, 204
Schauer, Mrs I 202, 204, 205n7, 208, 213, 262, 335
Schenetton, Countess II 36, 59
Schmidt's Jahrbücher II 78n6
Schneider, Henry II 32, 33n2
Schneider, John II 33n2
Schönborn, Countess Ernestine von I 98, 99n13, 100
Schottenhof II 236
Schrötter, Anton Konrad Friedrich von I 40, 42n18&20, 53, 57
Schuretton, Rudolf II 181
Schwartze, Charles Eric Rudolph II 253
Schwartze, Mary Buchanan II 253
Schwarzenberg family I *xxiii*, II 201n3
Schwarzenberg Gardens I 189, 190n5
Schwarzenberg, Prince Adolf Joseph Johann II 201, 201–2n3, 203, 204n7
Schwarzenberg, Princess Lori (Eleonore von Liechtenstein) II 203, 204n7
Scotland I 33n3, 165n1, 173, 184n2, 190n4, 198, 199n10, 239n2
Scott, Sir Walter I 101, 103n8, 108, 109n6

Scribe, Franz II 192
Scribe, Maria II 192
scrofula I 257n8
Scully, Richard II 54n4
Serbia II 1, 16n12, 58n2; Versecz II 284; Zrenjanin II 16n12
Sermage, Count Richard von I 285, 286, 288n5, II 14–17, 15n2, 151n5, 155n2, 169, 180
Sermage family II 172
Sermon of Christianity (Godwin) II 225
Seymour, Miranda I 54n12, II 21n2
Shelley, Lady Jane I 24, 24n2, 25n3, 32, 33, 33n1, 36, 108n2
Shelley, Mary Wollstonecroft (née Godwin) I *xi*, *xii*, *xv*, *xvi*, *xvii*, *xviii*, *xix*, *xxiv*, 3n2&6, 4n10,11,12&13, 8, 8n5, 9n14, 11–12n3, 16, 22n2, 23n18, 24n2, 25n3, 39, 40, 51, 53n3, 54n5,6&12, 76, 88n1, 94n6, 97, 98n5, 99n7, 103n7, 107, 108n2&3, 109n4, 110, 111, 113n16, 124n3, 136, 145, 160n2, 170n13&15, 172n3, 257n8, 287n1, 338n3, II 4, 21n2, 22n2, 133n4, 248n19
Shelley, Percy Bysshe I *xii*, *xvi*, *xvii*, 3n3, 8n5, 11n3, 112n5, 113n16, 170n13&15, 314n2, II 109n4, 238, 239n4
Shelley, Sir Percy Florence I *xxii*, 4n6, 108n3, 109n4, 110, 112n5, 131, 172n4, II 225
Silsbee, Edward Augustus I 298n4, II 228, 229n7
Sina (or Sinas), Baron Simon von II 232, 233n4
Sketch-book of Geoffrey Crayon (Irving) I 101, 103n7
Slavonia II 17, 18n3, 129, 131n6
Slavs II 2
Slovenia II 9n5; Laybach (Ljubljana) II 3, 8; Ljubljanica River II 10n8; Marburg (Maribor) II 2, 153n3, 154n3, 173, 178, 185–6; Pragerhof (Pragersko) II 26; Rakičan (Rakicsán) I 261n3, 292n2, 297, 313, 317, II 232n2; Rohitsch (Rogatec) II 129, 131n3, 169, 170n8
Smallbones, Mr I 302, 302n6, II 11, 203
Smetov, Countess II 26
Smith, Horace II 45n5
Smith, I.F. II 45
Soimos Fortress, Lipova II 289n3
Sophie, Archduchess I 18n1, 81n5, 99n13, II 151n3

314

INDEX

South Australian Advertiser **II** 48n5
Stametz and Company **I** 184, 184n1
Stanley, Edward Smith, Earl of Derby **I** 108, 109n12
Starza **II** 157
Steigerwald, Jacob **II** 1–2
Stein, Baroness Marianne von **II** 218
Steinbrück **II** 139, 140n6
Stockbridge **I** 58, 62
Stocking, Marion Kingston **I** *xi, xii, xix, xx, xxii,* 3n2&6, 4n10, 16n7, 38n8, 42n18, 54n7, 57n8, 112n3, 113n16, 348n4, **II** 3, 21n2, 30n2, 113n1, 128n18, 229n7
Strimasko, Tetty **I** 219, 220n8, 225, 231, 232, 233n1, 244, 252, 260, 272, 278, 279n3
Stuttgart **I** 47, 48n1, 60, 77, 78, 78n3, 95, 96n2, 253n2
Styria **I** *xxii,* 6, 9n10, 285, 287n2&3, 291, 292, **II** 153n3, 178–80, 267n7
Südbahn **II** 131n6, 174
Sudbrook Park **I** 122n4
Sunstein, Emily **I** 25n7, 103n7, 113n16, 172n3, 338n3, **II** 21n1, 248n19
Sussex Lennox, Lady Mary Margaret **I** 338n3, **II** 32, 38–43, 111, 187
Suttor, Caroline Elizabeth **I** 356n5, 359n1, **II** 253
Suttor, Charlotte **I** 146, 155, 155n3, 156n6&7, 157n19&21, 167, 169n7&11, 265, 309, 333
Suttor, Emily **II** 218
Suttor family **I** *xxi,* 146, 221, 225
Suttor, George **I** 146, 150n1, 162n7, 168n1, **II** 219n11
Suttor, Herbert **II** 219n11
Suttor, John George **II** 219, 220n22
Suttor, Maria **II** 254
Suttor, Thomas Charles **II** 254n10
Suttor, William Henry **I** 146, 150n3, **II** 218, 220n13
Suttor, William Henry Jr (Willie) **I** *xxi,* 4n13, 9n19, 146, 147, 148, 358n2, **II** 218, 219n11, 220n14, 254n1&4, 255n17; *Australian Stories Retold; and, Sketches of County Life* **I** *xxi–xxii*
Swabian Germans **II** 2
Switzerland **I** *xv, xxiv,* 61, 64n19, 77, 232, **II** 4, 271; Zurich **II** 4
Sydney **I** 51, 145–6, 148, 149, 153, 155, 156n9, 158n24, 181, 182, 183n4,5&6, 195n7, 197, 218, 229, 232, 234, 236, 237, 255, 258, 267, 309, 352, 354, 355, 356, 359, **II** 86, 253, 254, 267n7
Sydney Morning Herald **I** *xxii,* 145, 149, 155n1, 156n9, 158n24, 186n5, 235n7, 253n3, 259n3, 352n1, **II** 87n6&7, 201
Székely, Josef **II** 72

Tantangara **I** 350, 351n5, 354
Taylor, Emma **II** 71, 135n4, 228n3, 238, 244
Taylor, Mr **I** 51
Teatro alla Scala (opera house) **II** 165, 166n6
Technische Universität Wien **I** 19n7, 42n18, 84n3
Temesvár (Timişoara) **II** 2–3, 41, 81–2, 284, 288, 291, 298
Tennyson, Lord Alfred **I** *xxii,* 154, 156n10&11
Theresianum **I** *xviii, xxv*n6, 18n1, 73n3, 85, 92, 93–4n1, 98, 112n1
Thornton, George **II** 87n7
Times, The **I** 121, 122n1, **II** 49
Tokay wine **I** 191, 191n1
Tomalin, Claire **I** 25n7, 113n16, **II** 145n7
Tooth, Edwin **I** 149, 241n2, 253n2, 342n1, 351n2, **II** 12n4&10
Tooth, Frederick **I** 256n4, **II** 12n4, 27
Tooth, Robert **I** 149, 151n16, 241n2, 253n2 342n1, 350, 351n2,3&4, 354, **II** 12n4, 12n10, 27
Travels From Vienna Through Lower Hungary (Bright) **II** 12n6
Treaty of Passarovitz (1718) **II** 1
Treaty of Versailles (1919) **II** 58n2
Trelawny, Edward John **I**, *xx,* 39, 41n7, 94n1, **II** 126n4, 226, 238, 239n3&4, 244–5
Trieste **II** 29–30, 133, 139, 144
Troppau (Opava) **II** 9
Tschakowa (Ciakova) **II** 2
Tucker, Mrs **II** 144, 189
Tucker, Reverend Samuel **II** 144, 145n5
Tucker, Willie **II** 189, 189n2, 213n4
Tullius, Nick **II** 1
Tumut **I** 354, 354n2
Turin **II** 53, 126, 165n3
Turk, Mr **I** 105
Turley, Edward Astbury **I** 54n13
Tuscany, Baths of Lucca **II** 141, 143n6, 235n4
Tusokret (Tuzokrét) **II** 111, 112n8, 136, 144, 149

INDEX

Twofold Bay Pastoral Association **I** 149, 150, 150n14, 151n15, 176n3, 219n6, 234, 238n9, 241n2, 253n2, 256n4, 342n1, 350, 351n2, 356n5
typhus fever **II** 159, 166n10
Tyrol **I** 207, 274, 275n2, 276, 280, 282, **II** 111, 112n3

Udine **II** 131n2, 144
Uffizi Gallery **II** 160, 167n6
United States of America **II** 3; New York **II** 159
University of Königsberg, Prussia **II** 4
University of Vienna **II** 4

Varaždin **II** 129, 134, 151n4
Velden **II** 144, 145n2
Venice **I** *xvii*, 9n19, 18, 187, 286, 297, 301, 302, 303n8, 307, 313, 315, 316n4, 317, 337, 349 **II** 38, 126, 144, 156, 163, 190; carnival **I** 308n3
Verona **II** 162
Versecz **II** 284
Verzeichniss (Hitschmann) **I** 102n1, 102–3n4, 103n13, 251n2, 288n5
Vesuvius, Mount **II** 157
Vienna **I** 17–20, 24n2, 28, 32, 39, 44, 46, 47, 56, 78, 85, 127, **II** 2–3, 26–30, 63n1, 76–7, 90n5, 117–18, 121–6, 197–9, 217–18, 289–90, 297–8; Alservorstadt **I** 232, 233, 302n6; British Consulate **II** 292n5; conflict **I** 19n11; Geological Society **I** 116, 117; Landstrasse **I** 207, 225; Polytechnic school **I** 19n7, 82; property **I** 297; riding schools **I** 107; Technische Universität Wien **I** *xxiv*, 19n7, 84n3; University of **II** 4
Villefranche **II** 259
Vindication of the Rights of Woman (Wollstonecraft) **I** xiii, *xiv*
Vöslau **II** 219n7
Vrišer, Sergej **II** 153n3

Waikato War (1863–4) **II** 44n12
Waldensians **II** 91n1
Walker, Mr **II** 153n1, 173, 179
Walsh, G.P. **II** 255n16
Walter, Mrs **I** 87
Waterford & Kilkenny Railway **II** 102, 104n2

Waterford & Limerick Railway **II** 104n2
Waterford & Tramore Railway Line **II** 104n2
Waterloo vessel **I** 234, 235n7, 236, 239, 240, 253n3
Weidling **I** 6, 8n1&3, 10–11, 14–16, 17, 18, 19n11, 21, 43, 75, 116, 117, 124, 133, 164, 167, 178, 188n1, 202, 278, 297, 306; farm **I** 7; house **I** 8n1; house repairs **I** 116; sale of **I** 123, 159; valley of **I** 161
Wiener Neustadt **II** 208
Wellington **II** 44n4
Werner, Mrs **II** 180, 194–5, 206, 235
Wieden **I** 112n1
Wildner, Dr Franz **II** 77, 78n4
Williams, John **I** *xvi*
Wimpffen, Countess **I** 18
Wimpffen, Franz von **I** 19n11
Windischgrätz, Prince Alfred **I** 19n11, **II** 8, 9n3
Wirth, Max **II** 175n4, 196n2
Wladika, Michael **II** 4
Wollstonecraft, Mary (later Godwin) **I** *xi*, *xiii–xvi*, *xxiv*, 4n6, 23n16, 54n6, 108n2&3, 113n16
Wongwibinda (Wright) **I** 145, 182n1, 183n4, 186n2, 194n4
World War I (1914–18) **II** 3
World War II (1939–45) **II** 3, 58n2, 222n1
Wrbna, Rudolf **II** 217, 219n5
Wright, Denny **II** 43
Wright, Mr **I** 198, 199n11 **II** 43
Württemberg **I** 52, 60, 62, 77, 78, 87, **II** 131n3

Yugoslavia **II** 3, 18n3

Zagreb **II** 140n5
Zdislavice **II** 251, 252n2
Zeepaard **I** 145, 155n1
Zimmermann, Mr **I** 201
Zöpf (Zoepf), Franz **I** 250, 251n2, 304, 305n3, **II** 17, 123, 174, 279
Zrenjanin **II** 2, 16n12
Zschokke (Zchokke), Johann Heinrich **I** 20, 22n7
Zucker, Frida **I** 199n16, **II** 113n1
Zurich **II** 4